Dr Octavia Cerchez

Multilateral Conferences and Diplomatic Negotiations

in the present globalized context

Interdisciplinary Centre for Economics and Law

Geneva, 2016

Samurai Publishing

Acknowledgments

First I want to thank to all those who made possible my successful participation in multilateral fora, colleagues and friends who made me proud in representing my country as negotiator and chairman.

Special thanks go to the United Nations Institute for Training and Research for providing courses on performing effectively in multilateral conferences and diplomacy, and Ambassador Walker Ronald who lead the main lectures.

In the same specter, I wish to thank to all scholars and practitioners whose inputs in the field contributed to the current rich and useful literature.

I also wish to thank to my family for their constant support and patience while the book was written, as well as for the insights and suggestions provided by my husband.

Last but not least, I want to recognize the efforts of Mr. Xavier Beaud, in carrying for the publication and distribution of this book.

CONTENTS

Foreword

Multilateral conferences and diplomatic negotiations have a crucial role in the creation and advancement of sustainable international relations. The overall objective of diplomatic negotiations is to find ways to reach agreement, while multilateral conferences provide the fora for the negotiation process.

This book pleads for efficient multilateral conferences and successful diplomatic negotiations, arguing that both are feasible due to throughout knowledge and adequate application of internationally-established rules, mechanisms, methods and instruments.

Based on an integrated approach, the book intends to be a practical and detailed reference for those engaged in international relations, involved in international conferences, and negotiating at multilateral level. It is also a useful resource for all those interested in the current global world affairs and increasing their awareness of the multilateral negotiation and its implications for domestic constituencies.

The book is structured in eight chapters, offering a detailed and comprehensive synopsis of the exciting and constantly evolving world of diplomatic negotiations and multilateral conferences, with particular emphasis on the United Nations (UN), the World Trade Organizations (WTO) and the European Union (EU).

The book begins by exploring the roles, importance, substance, forms and characteristics of multilateral conferences from the perspectives of international relations' theories, in ancient and modern era. It proceeds with a throughout analysis of the elements, functions and purposes of multilateral conferences, underlining their significance in the very diverse and complex diplomacy of today.

Then it offers a comprehensive practical insights into the documentation elaborated, the processes attended and the procedures shaped by the participants in multilateral conferences and negotiations, and highlights their dynamics and constructiveness. The following chapter synthetizes verbal, written and specific diplomatic communication tools and methods of reaching agreements characteristic to the UN, the WTO and the EU.

Diplomatic negotiation is further revealed with emphasis on its diverse aspects, parties and positions, power and tension, cooperation and competition, stressing the negotiation's role in solving disputes and furthering understanding between states.

Discovering diplomatic negotiations continues with detailed suggestions regarding negotiations strategies, tactics and techniques and approaches to the interactive process whereby parties must grapple with competing concerns in seeking a mutual acceptable agreement.

Then it emphasis the exciting and demanding role of leaders and chairmen in multilateral negotiations, the relevance, the costs and benefits of such prestigious positions and the serious challenges encountered in the UN, the WTO and the EU.

Lastly it tackles the dynamics and future of diplomatic negotiations in multilateral conferences in a globalizing world.

The book builds on personal expertise and experience acquired as negotiator and chairman in the UN, the WTO and the EU context. Through theoretical and practical content, explanation and analysis, rich bibliographies consulted and the numerous references cited, this book aspires to be a worthy contribution to the core literature. It is intended for both specialized and non-specialized audiences.

Chapter 1 – Role and importance of multilateral conferences in global affairs

1.1 Historical background

Civilized human existence is practically impossible without peace, trade and social relations among nation states. These depend on representation of states and adjustment of contracts through international relations. Over the centuries, international relations developed through diplomacy[1] and negotiation,[2] initially bilateral and later in the framework of multilateral conferences.

Diplomacy is a significant form of interaction between sovereign entities since antiquity.

From old times, objectives like wars, constructions, expenses of leaders were discussed by people in various ways. The Greeks, free-born citizens were gathering to hear civic announcements, muster for military campaigns or discuss politics in *agora* (the word agora being applied to an assembly of people), while the Romans were meeting in *forums* for politics, cattle trade, vegetable trade or shows.[3] These meetings did not have a diplomatic role for lack of coherent external policies.

---

[1] Greeks used the word *diplōma* for the official folded document conferring a privilege (often a permit to travel) on the bearer, word that applied later to all solemn documents issued by chancelleries, especially those containing agreements between sovereigns and which is at the origin of the today's word diplomacy. Diplomacy is the established method of influencing the decisions and behavior of foreign governments and peoples through dialogue, negotiation, and other measures short of war or violence. Diplomacy is the art and practice of conducting negotiations between representatives of states. It usually refers to international diplomacy, the conduct of international relations through the intercession of professional diplomats with regard to issues of peace-making, trade, war, economics, culture, environment, and human rights (see Encyclopedia Britannica).

[2] According to Walker, negotiation is a joint effort to reach agreement; it can include, but is not confined to, haggling (see Walker Ronald A., Multilateral Conferences: Purposeful International Negotiation. London: Palgrave Macmillan, 2004).

[3] The Greeks, free-born citizens could gather to hear civic announcements, muster for military campaigns or discuss politics in the *agora*, the word *agora* being applied to an assembly of people and by extend marks the gathering place. Nearly every city of ancient Greece had an agora – meaning meeting place – by about 600 BC, when the classical period of Greek civilization began to flourish. The Romans, when they had to learn or to solve something, were coming out, as Greeks in the *agora*, to meet in *forums* or those on the sea, were running on deck vessels (*per foros cursent*, according to Cicero) or those on land, were going to city markets, for politics

Modern day diplomacy originated in ancient Greece. Theoretically, Greek literature (notably Homer's Iliad and Odyssey) is the earliest evidence of Greek diplomacy. Practically the Greek city-states were sending envoys to convey messages and make oral arguments on behalf of their own cities to justify their positions. Rulers used this method to promote their interests making the process even more popular. In the antiquity, Greeks used the word *diplōma* (origin of the today's word *diplomacy*) for the folded document conferred a privilege on the bearer, while the word *convention* was mentioned by Romans with the meaning of a pact, a meeting or an agreement.[4]

The Greeks developed archives, diplomatic vocabulary, principles of international conduct that anticipated international law and many other elements of modern diplomacy. Truces, neutrality, commercial conventions, conferences, treaties, and alliances were common. In one 25-year period of the 4th century BC, for example, there were eight Greco-Persian congresses, where even the smallest states had the right to be heard. Rome inherited what the Greeks devised and adapted it to the task of imperial administration. The Romans refined the role of emissaries to include trained observation and interpretation of conditions and opinions in the host country and negotiation in pursuit of the empire's interests. When the Western Empire disintegrated in the 5th century AD, most of its diplomatic traditions disappeared but the eastern half of the Roman Empire continued for nearly 1'000 years as the Byzantine Empire. **Byzantium produced the first professional diplomats** and from the 12th century their role as gatherers of information about the conditions in their host states became increasingly vital to the survival of the Byzantine state, timely intelligence from Byzantine diplomats enabling the emperors to play foreign nations off against each other.

In Renaissance Italy, the city-states not only used special representatives, but also established more or less permanent diplomatic posts in each other's cities. During this time, diplomacy was representing the interest of the sovereign abroad through direct and fair representation though its standards were low and ill defined. The ambassador was simply a representation of head of state in a foreign nation. Frequent disputes even wars and duels arose from the lack of well-defined

---

(*Forum Aurelianum, Forum Pacis, Forum Apii*) for cattle trade (forum boarium), for vegetable trade (forum piscatorium) or for shows (*constituitur in foro Laodiceae spectaculum*, according to Cicero). Also, the Romans considered *fora* the honeycomb cells (Virgil) or the board were the dice were thrown (*forus aleatorius*, according to Suetonius).

[4] Năstase Dan, Drept diplomatic și consular, Editura Fundației România de Mâine, Bucuresti, 2006, p. 28.

rules of procedure on questions of precedence and immunity. With the increase of antagonism, diplomacy slowly but surely became more complex. Thus, it became more regulated, which was beneficial for effective negotiation.

The **Peace of Westphalia** changed the meaning of sovereignty. It was concluded in 1648 through a series of bilateral negotiations in the cities of Münster and Osnabrück, and declared for the first time that all countries were legally equal. Westphalia is widely seen as **the mother of all diplomatic conferences** and the beginning of the era of procedural frameworks, because it helped to create more effective negotiation processes as an alternative to warfare.[5] In 1648 after the Treaty of Westphalia diplomacy became a primary form of international discourse and has been evolving since into its classical state centric form of the 20th century.

Negotiation is as old as human history. From ancient clay tablets, there is evidence that negotiating and exchanging treaties occurred in the Middle East some 5,000 years ago. In those early times, political and diplomatic negotiations were bilateral meetings between absolute rulers or the councils of city-states, which occasionally negotiated directly, but usually sent their envoys to bargain with the other party.

Earliest known information about negotiation comes from the Middle East, the Mediterranean, China, and India. About 2850 BC, treaties between Mesopotamian city-states are recorded.[6] In Egypt, the earliest known diplomatic records are the Amarna letters - a diplomatic correspondence from the 14th century BC between the pharaohs of the 18th dynasty of Egypt and the Amurru rulers of Canaan. **Egypt** created also **the oldest known international peace treaties** of which full texts survive in stone tablet fragment, treaty signed between the pharaoh of Egypt Ramses II and ruler of the Hittite Empire following the Battle of Kadesh circa 1274 BC during the era of the 19th dynasty of Egypt.[7] There is significant evidence, mainly in the Bible, of Assyrian diplomacy from the 7th century BC, of the relations of Jewish tribes with each other and other peoples. Ancient India, with its kingdoms and dynasties, also had a long tradition of diplomacy. This tradition was systematized and described by Kautilya in the

---

[5] Meerts Paul (quoting Holsti), Challenges to Diplomatic Negotiation, PIN Policy Brief, The Hague: Clingendael Institute, 2015, p. 2.

[6] Thereafter, Akkadian (Babylonian) became the first diplomatic language, serving as the international tongue of the Middle East until it was replaced by Aramaic (see Encyclopaedia Britannica).

[7] Encyclopedia Britannica, Diplomacy, 2016 (available at britannica.com).

Arthashastra[8] - a complete work on the art of kingship and one of the oldest books in secular Sanskrit literature. In **China**, the 6th century BC military strategist Sun Tzu is considered one of the earliest realists in international relations theory. Author of "The Art of War", he outlines theories of battle, advocates diplomacy and the cultivation of relationships with other nations as essential to the health of a state.[9] He lived in a time in which a great deal of diplomacy in establishing allies, bartering land, and signing peace treaties was necessary as each rival state was starting to pay less attention to the traditional respects of tutelage to the Zhou Dynasty (circa 1050–256 BC).

In Europe, the tradition that ultimately inspired the birth of modern negotiation in post-Renaissance Europe and led to the present world system of international relations began in ancient Greece, as we cited. On some occasions, the Greek city-states sent envoys to each other to negotiate specific issues, such as war and peace or commercial relations. The Greek city-states struggled with the tension between efficient negotiation that rests on confidential discussions and the openness and transparency demanded by the citizens of a democracy or a republic. **The first diplomatic conference** as such was the Sparta Conference of 432 BC held to debate whether or not to declare war on Athens.[10] In 220 BC, the Achaean League entered into war against the Aetolian League.[11] The young king Philip V of Macedon sided with the Achaeans and called for a Panhellenic conference in Corinth, where the Aetolian aggression was condemned.

Since antiquity, the main objectives of pursuing diplomatic activity were international peace and security which had be dealt mainly in international fora to meet the need for international solidarity and cooperation among states. The idea of settlement of disputes between states in the context of international meetings existed for centuries, before the development of modern diplomacy. **Ecumenical Councils**, meetings of bishops, whose series began at Nicaea in 325 AD, took

---

[8] Arthashastra is a complete work on the art of kingship, with long chapters on taxation and on the raising and maintenance of armies, incorporating also a theory of diplomacy, of how in a situation of mutually contesting kingdoms, the wise king builds alliances and tries to checkmate his adversaries (see Encyclopaedia Britannica).

[9] McNeilly Mark R., Sun Tzu and the Art of Modern Warfare, Oxford University Press, 2001, p. 5.

[10] Cooper Andrew F., Heine Jorge, and Thakur Ramesh, Introduction: The Challenges of 21st-Century Diplomacy, The Oxford Handbook of Modern Diplomacy, 2013, p. 3.

[11] The Achaean League, also known as the Aegean League, was a Hellenistic-era confederation of Greek city states on the northern and central Peloponnese. The Aetolian League was a confederation of tribal communities and cities in ancient Greece centred on Aetolia in central Greece (see Encyclopaedia Britannica).

doctrinal decisions, gave regulations in the field of ecclesiastical discipline, had impact on social movements, ideological cultural and proximal regions of Europe and the European area, including interstate relations. In 1623, seeking solutions to maintain peace, a Parisian writer, Emer Cross, in his pamphlet "Le nouveau Cynée", referring to the absurdity of war, recommended the establishment, by princes, of a permanent assembly of ambassadors in Venice, whose mission would be to settle without passion the conflicts between the represented countries.[12]

In 1648, in Osnabrück and Münster in Westphalia, at the end of the 30-years war, peace treaties were concluded at an interstate congress. **The modern European diplomacy was inaugurated** as follows: the confirmation of the dominant idea of Peace of Augsburg which perceived that **religious borders must coincide with national borders** (*cuius regio, eius religio*); the Holy Roman Empire was shattered into hundreds of entities; the king of France became king in his own kingdom; Switzerland independence from the German Empire was recognized; Spain recognized the independence of the Netherlands, giving up parts of Flanders, Brabant, Limburg and the Asian colonies; Bohemia and Moravia became Habsburg possessions. The end of Papal hegemony and the collapse of the unity of the Christian world triggered the willingness to resort to international relations, particularly towards solving problems in relations with the "pagans". Treaties, which recognized the particular status of Christians in Ottoman territories and their non-obligation to Koranic laws, were concluded.

Although the peace treaties of Westphalia are widely seen as the mother of all diplomatic conferences, **the rise to the first modern international fora** was driven by the vital need for maintaining balance in international relations.

Two hundred years after the Peace of Westphalia, the **Congress of Vienna** (1814–1815) became **the first true multi-party negotiation**, although not fully universal, as the number of real negotiating parties was kept at five: Russia, Austria, Prussia, Great Britain and France. Excluded, however, were the other interested countries and parties. They were consulted, but the five did not allow them to be part of the decision-making process. On 20th November 1815, Russia, Austria, Prussia and Great Britain concluded a permanent alliance – A Holy Alliance (which, in 1818, was joined by France), expressed by high-level conferences called Congress (Troppau - 1920, Verona - 1823).

---

[12] Năstase Dan, Drept diplomatic şi consular, Editura Fundaţiei România de Mâine, Bucuresti, 2006, p. 112.

The organization has emerged as "Monarchical Union" and acted as "Directorate of Europe". It was replaced by "Concert of Europe", which also meant a forum of discussion, a series of conferences of powerful states.

In 1899, the United State of America launched the Pan-American Conference, which generated an Office in 1910, the Pan American Union, the predecessor of the current Organization of American States (OAS). In response to their needs for technical collaboration forums, states started the coordination of some areas of activity through regular conferences and permanent offices: International Commission of the Danube (1856), International Telegraph Union (1865) and the Universal Postal Union (1874). Afterward, specialized agencies like these proliferated. The peace conferences held in the Hague (1899 and 1907) - see chapter 2.1, which resulted in conventions aimed at codifying the laws of war and encouraging disarmament, were harbingers of the future.

It is noteworthy mentioning the **Berlin Conference of 1884-1885** which marked the climax of the European competition for territory in Africa, a process commonly known as the "Scramble for Africa".[13] During the conference, major European powers negotiated, formalized and mapped claims to territory in Africa. To enslave the African nations effectively, profound agreements were necessary and the European leaders agreed to allow free trade among the colonies and established a framework for negotiating future European claims in Africa. Neither the Berlin Conference itself nor the framework for future negotiations provided any say for the African peoples over the partitioning of their homelands.[14]

The **Paris Peace Conference of 1919** - concluded by the Treaty of Versailles that ended the First World War - became a major event in the history of diplomacy. As with the Vienna Conference, representatives of hundreds of sovereignties presented their credentials in Paris, but only five were included in the inner circle: the United States of America, France, Great Britain, Italy and Japan. Moreover, the negotiation was *de facto* trilateral, as Japan did not really participate and Italy's role was comparatively weak.[15]

---

[13] "Scramble for Africa" is the phrase often used to describe the European partition and conquest of Africa in the late nineteenth century. The Berlin Conference did not initiate European colonization of Africa, but it did legitimate and formalize the process. In addition, it sparked new interest in Africa. Following the close of the conference, European powers expanded their claims in Africa such that by 1900, European states had claimed nearly 90 percent of African territory (see Encyclopedia of Africa).

[14] Heath Elizabeth, Encyclopedia of Africa, Edited by Henry Louis Gates, Jr. and Kwame Anthony Appiah, Oxford University Press, 2010.

The League of Nations (1919-1946) could be regarded as the first full-fledged multilateral negotiation process. It did some good work in resolving territorial questions after the First World War, but did not live up to expectations in the security field. The League of Nations was an experience rich step that set the stage for the process of proliferation of institutionalizing international fora that followed. After the First World War the process was intensified by the urgency to maintain peace with guarantees founded on clear principles and legal mechanisms.

Only with the San Francisco Conference in 1945, which created the United Nations, a reasonably **effective multilateral diplomatic conference came into existence**. United Nations, the one which brought peace after the Second World War, have exploited the League of Nations' experience especially in terms of association of sovereign states in an organization with a universal vocation. Currently preoccupied with world peace and security, it also identifies and addresses global issues such as human rights, environmental protection, health issues, etc.

The Cold War was held within two international fora the Atlantic Pact and the Warsaw Pact, enfolded around the two superpowers, United States of America (USA) and the Union of Soviet Socialist Republics (USSR). During this confrontation, it became apparent that regional fora could be a useful tool in building a system of collective security. The peaceful coexistence, needed under the conditions where the opposite fora, operating as military-political blocs, were negatively influencing the positive processes for which the UN were intended, was profiled due to diplomatic international fora, which was carried out initially, by the Conference on Security and Cooperation in Europe, and subsequently by the Organization for Security and Co-operation in Europe (OSCE).

In the economic and trade field, during and immediately after the Second World War, the USA, the United Kingdom, and other allied nations engaged in a series of negotiations to establish the rules for the postwar international economy. The result was the creation of the International Monetary Fund (IMF) and the World Bank (WB) at the July 1944 Bretton Woods Conference and the signing of the General Agreement on Tariffs and Trade (GATT)[16] at an international

---

[15] Meerts Paul, Challenges to Diplomatic Negotiation, PIN Policy Brief, The Hague: Clingendael Institute, 2015, p. 2.

[16] After World War II, the United Kingdom and the United States of America submitted proposals to the Economic and Social Council (ECOSOC) of the UN regarding the establishment of an

conference in Geneva in October 1947. The GATT completed 8 rounds of multilateral trade negotiations (MTNs). The Uruguay Round (the 8th round) concluded with the signing of the Final Act on April 15, 1994, in Marrakesh, and produced the WTO Agreement and its annexes.

Currently, the diplomacy and negotiations are displayed in various international fora: coalitions, political and military alliances, international conferences, international organizations, association of states with special profile (European Union, International Organization of the Francophonie – L'Organisation Internationale de la Francophonie (OIF), the Commonwealth, etc.).[17] Thus, the diplomatic activity takes place to a considerable extent, through multilateral meetings and conferences established by states, which through their participation in international fora act as subjects of international law.[18]

Nowadays, the participation in international meetings is considered a criterion for assessing the significance of the role played by the states. The State is the principal actor on the international stage, being, for example, a Permanent Member of the Security Council, and taking part in the "Group of Eight" (G8)[19]

---

international trade body that was to be named the International Trade Organization (ITO). ECOSOC convened a conference, the United Nations Conference on Trade and Employment in 1946 to consider the UK and US proposals. A Preparatory Committee drafted the ITO Charter and it was approved in 1948 at the conference in Havana, Cuba. The Charter is often referred to as the Havana Charter or the ITO Charter. The first round of trade negotiations took place while the Preparatory Committee was still working on drafting the Charter because the participants were anxious to begin the process of trade liberalization as soon as possible. Their results were incorporated into the General Agreement, which was signed in 1947.Since the original signatory nations expected the Agreement to become part of the more permanent ITO Charter, the text of the GATT contains very little "institutional" structure. This lack of detail within the agreement has created increasing difficulties as the GATT membership and roles governing trade between so many of the world's nations have grown. The GATT has functioned as an international organization for many years even though it has never been formalized as such. ECOSOC established an Interim Commission for the ITO that is referred to as ICITO. Unfortunately, when it came time for the members to ratify the ITO Charter, the Congress of the United States refused and the ITO never became a reality. The GATT survived, but remained intact only due to the Protocol of Provisional Application of the General Agreement on Tariffs and Trade which was concluded in 1947 and which entered into force in 1948. The GATT completed 8 rounds of multilateral trade negotiations (MTNs). The Uruguay Round (the 8th round) concluded with the signing of the Final Act on April 15, 1994, in Marrakesh, and produced the WTO Agreement and its annexes (see Georgetown Law Library, From GATT to the WTO and Beyond, Research Guide, 2016).

[17] Anghel I. M., Răspunderea în dreptul internațional, Editura Lumina Lex, București, 1998, p.75.

[18] International law governs relations between States and their dealings with each other. It provides a basis for peace and stability throughout the world and for the protection and well-being of peoples everywhere (see ABC of Diplomacy, Swiss Federal Department of Foreign Affairs (FDFA), Swiss Confederation, 2008).

meetings. The growth of the post-war multilateral diplomacy denoted the periodic involvement of states into the formulation of better international agreements. The new order is by far different from the old atmosphere, as the governments increasingly represent the will of the people through diplomacy and more aspects are subjects to diplomatic negotiations. Today's world and its future is grounded in the different potentials of the different nations for peaceful and better cooperation for building stronger international relations among states through organizations, diplomacy and negotiations.

As we can see, throughout history, the international relations and "conference regime" have gone a long way, a fact that underlines their objective character. They demonstrated huge potential to improve and flexibility to adapt to very different concrete considerations and steps in the world development.

1.2 Concept of multilateral conference

We acknowledged that the international relations and cooperation origins can be traced a long way back through congresses and conferences. In researches on international relations and diplomacy, some authors refer to **multilateralism** or multilateral diplomacy as the collective, cooperative action by states - when necessary, in concert with non-state actors - to deal with common challenges and problems when these are best managed collectively at the international level.[20] In other words, it is the negotiation and discussion which allow these collective and cooperative actions between states and non-states, consequently the multilateral conferences.

There are many different kinds of conferences and no fully uniform denomination. Some conferences are called "assembly", "council", or "committee" or even "meeting", and many other terms are used as well. Sometimes, the meetings organized range from large international conferences to small workshops and expert group meetings. There are also many different types of "conferences-within-conferences", such as the meetings of geographical or political groups which are not part of the formal structure of the conference

---

[19] The Group of Eight (G8) refers to the group of eight highly industrialized nations - France, Germany, Italy, the United Kingdom, Japan, the United States, Canada, and Russia - that hold an annual meeting to foster consensus on global issues like economic growth and crisis management, global security, energy, and terrorism.

[20] Cockburn Andrew Mark (quoting Newman), The Unique Challenges Presented by Multilateral Diplomacy, May 10, 2012, p.1. (available at SSRN: ssrn.com or dx.doi.org).

within which they take place, and arguably each of the several chambers of a large conference (i.e. the plenary and the various committees) can themselves be seen of as conferences in that they have their own agendas, presiding officers, etc.[21] Some of the most noteworthy conferences in the United Nations System are the recurring sessions of the UN General Assembly (UNGA) and the Economic and Social Council (ECOSOC), as well as the meetings of the Security Council, in addition to the ministerial meeting of the United Nations Conference on Trade and Development (UNCTAD). Outside the UN System the most significant ones are the ministerial meetings of the World Trade Organization (WTO),[22] the G8 Summit, the Council of Ministers of the European Union, the BRICS[23] Summit, the Assembly of the African Union and other regional organizations, etc.

Multilateral conferences have increasingly become a highly visible and important dimension of diplomacy. Numerous processes and procedures have evolved over time for handling diplomatic issues and disputes, seeking diplomatic resolution of problems. Thus, resolutions were sought through the convening of international conferences. In such cases, there are fewer ground rules, and fewer formal applications of international law. However, participants are expected to guide themselves through principles of international fairness, logic, and protocol. While various gatherings have been convened for centuries, with the 1815 Congress of Vienna representing a landmark event in modern history, the number and regularity of multilateral conferences have risen considerably over the past 70 years. This rise has resulted largely from the creation of the United Nations and has evolved in parallel with the establishment and growth of many regional and global international organizations, as well as the many issues and concerns which require a collective, regional or global response.[24]

---

[21] Walker Ronald A., Multilateral Conferences: Purposeful International Negotiation. London: Palgrave Macmillan, 2004, p.129-130.

[22] The WTO does not belong to the UN system and have no formal agreement with the UN. Instead, their relationship is governed by exchanges of letters. The WTO has no reporting obligations towards any of the principal organs of the UN, but provides ad-hoc contribution to the work of the GA and ECOSOC.

[23] BRICS is the acronym for an association of five major emerging national economies: Brazil, Russia, India, China and South Africa. The BRICS members are all leading developing or newly industrialized country countries, but they are distinguished by their large, sometimes fast-growing economies and significant influence on regional affairs.

[24] Walker R.A., Manual for UN Delegates - Conference Process, Procedure and Negotiation, UN Publication, 2011, p.12.

Multilateral conference as a mode of international negotiation has been established about 300 years ago, yet it established its organizational format only in the last 100 years.

While Peace of Westphalia concluded in 1648 is seen by some authors as the mother of all diplomatic conferences (see chapter 1.1), others[25] regard the invention of the multilateral conference plus the follow-up conference in 1815, the closing year of the Congress of Vienna, as the **foundation of multilateral diplomacy**. The practice that followed this invention provided the groundwork for today's globalized world. The invention involves governments of states convening a multilateral conference (of three or more states), setting an agenda and discussing the problems raised. At the conference they will consider causes and possible solutions and finally take decisions that are guidelines for solving the problems on the agenda. What matters after this common decision-making process is the implementation by the participating states. In order to gain insights into their national implementation activities, the participating states will convene a follow-up conference, which will use national reports to assess whether states have acted according to the common guiding principles. If all states have implemented the decisions correctly, nothing remains to be done. If this is not, or insufficiently, the case, and that is a more common occurrence, it makes sense to discuss the new situation. This discussion usually leads to new, or adapted, decisions in favor of further implementation. The carrying out of those new decisions may be discussed at another follow-up conference. The process thus reproduces itself and evolves into an ongoing cycle. During a large part of the nineteenth century, convening multilateral conferences was an *ad hoc* matter. But the continuation and further development of common problems and solutions caused a process of institutionalization of multilateral conferences and their follow-up conferences, with regularity and continuity as its main characteristics.

Thus, the **multilateral conferences** are the mechanism of implementation the multilateral diplomacy which is an instrument for long-term commitments, and represents a long-term and complex activity. Multilateral diplomacy is conducted and managed through different methods and ways than those for the bilateral one, which is considered a traditional one, and always involves two states in its activities. Bilateral diplomacy is momentary and as a rule brings quick results and guarantees the interests of the two participant states. It could also be

---

[25] Reinalda Bob, Routledge History of International Organizations From 1815 to the present day, by Routledge 2 Park Square, Milton Park, Abingdon, Oxon OX14 4RN, 2009, p. 10.

discriminatory as the substance and output are likely to be driven by the relative power between the two parties and, by extension, by the interests of the stronger party[26], the powerful state tries to get the best deal according to its interests with other states on an individual and *ad hoc* basis.

In the era of globalization when the emphasis is put more on interdependence and peaceful development, there are global problems, which crucially need the united efforts of all international actors in order to solve them. In these conditions multilateral conferences are one of the appropriate instruments for dealing with the processes of solving these global problems and of assuring global governance. The current system of international relations can be mostly characterized by a multilateral model, which is composed of various groups of specific elements. One such specific element is international actors who are significant participants in multilateral conferences. Consequently, the **multilateral conferences** are meetings of representatives of several (typically three or more, at times nearly 200) states (and in practice their national governments) and, possibly, between them and other actors such as representatives of intergovernmental and nongovernmental organizations.[27]

The invention of the multilateral conference plus follow-up conference in 1815 was a process set in motion by nation-states, which within less than a century led to institutionalization and acceptance of multilateral conferences in international relations. However, the question of importance of multilateral conferences in international relations, in particular compared with nation-states, has been a topic of debates, voiced through various theories and approaches.

1.3 Theories regarding multilateral conferences

In the same time with de development of international relations, many theories have emerged, each treating distinctively the issues related to multilateral conferences. Analyzing the beginning and evolution of international relation theories and based on the significance attributed to multilateral conferences, we distinguished two main schools: realism and liberal institutionalism.

---

[26] Wright T., Bilateral and Multilateral Diplomacy in Normal Times and in Crises, in P Kerr & G Wiseman (eds.), Diplomacy in a Globalizing World: Theories & Practices, Oxford University Press, New York, 2013, p. 175-191.

[27] Walker R.A., Multilateral Conferences: Purposeful International Negotiation. London: Palgrave Macmillan, 2004, p. xix.

The **realist** school in international relations theory regards nation-states as the main players and multilateral conferences as barely relevant. The nation-state is the major international actor, trying to survive in a hostile environment by forming and using power. Ideas about sovereignty and self-help assume a separation between domestic and foreign politics, of which the latter is crucial to survival. In the early 1970s international relations theory widened its scope, when so-called transnationalism included actors other than states as well, among them transnational corporations and interest groups.[28] It questioned the assumption of the states being the only or primary actors in world politics and concluded that research should not focus on organizations, but on broader, more informal forms of cooperation and fora, such as multilateral conferences. It was not until the 1990s that an awareness of their importance began to grow. This was related to their steering role in the process of globalization that was taking place, their contributions to solving military conflicts and civil wars around the end of the Cold War and the increased support of both nation-states and non-sate actors.

Liberal[29] **institutionalism** starts from the idea that democratic institutions can control the power drive of human beings and states. Democratic states, international organizations, multilateral conferences and common rules may contribute to peace and security. Domestic and foreign politics are intertwined when states recognize common interests. Institutionalism relies on microeconomic theory and game theory to reach a radically different conclusion: that co-operation between nations is possible.[30] Institutionalist school reached the conclusion that reciprocity and reputation play a significant role in strengthening international obligations.

The sociologically-oriented **social-constructivist** school developed a new research program on multilateral conferences, which took into account the ideas of citizens focused on change as well as the bureaucratic workings and authority of international fora. A focus on the social context in which international relations occur leads Constructivists to emphasize issues of identity and belief.[31] The

---

[28] Reinalda Bob, Routledge History of International Organizations From 1815 to the present day, by Routledge 2 Park Square, Milton Park, Abingdon, Oxon OX14 4RN, 2009, p. 6.

[29] One of the most prominent developments within liberal theory has been the phenomenon known as the democratic peace. First imagined by Immanuel Kant, the democratic peace describes the absence of war between liberal states, defined as mature liberal democracies.

[30] Slaughter Anne-Marie, International Relations, Principal Theories, Wolfrum, R. (Ed.) Max Planck Encyclopaedia of Public International Law, Oxford University Press, 2011, p.2. (available at princeton.edu).

[31] for this reason Constructivist theories are sometimes called ideational.

perception of friends and enemies, in-groups and out-groups, fairness and justice all become key determinant of a state's behavior. Constructivism is also attentive to the role of social norms in world politics. Constructivist approach regard the social world, including international relations, as a human construction, construction that is a dynamic process, in which ideas are being developed and knowledge and understandings are being shared. **Constructivists have also noted the role of multilateral conferences as actors in their own right**. While Institutionalist theories, for example, see institutions largely as the passive tools of states, Constructivism notes that international bureaucracies may seek to pursue their own interests (for example: free trade or human rights protection) even against the wishes of the states that created them.[32]

Within international relations theory, **four stages with regard to multilateral conference** may be differentiated:

- Throughout the first stage of classical realism, multilateral conferences are agents controlled by the great powers, without contributions of their own to international relations;

- During the second stage, multilateral conferences are interesting fora because the outcome of the political games that are being played within the conferences may add to their autonomous contributions and policies;

- In the course of the third stage, multilateral conferences can help states to solve collective action problems by considering a long-term perspective rather than taking into account short-term interests. However, although it was proved that long-lasting cooperation between states is possible and that multilateral conferences act as intervening variables, attention was barely drawn to the organizational or bureaucratic aspects of this cooperation;

- During the fourth stage of constructivism, attention is paid to what is happening within the multilateral conference (for instance, in socialization and informal processes) and to the roles conferences play on the basis of their rational-legal authority.

Whereas some theories of international relations are prized while others are contested, we observe that each rests on certain assumptions and epistemologies, is constrained within certain specified conditions, and pursues its own analytic goal. While various theories may lead to more or less convincing conclusions

---

[32] Barnett Michael and Finnemore Martha, Rules for the World: International Organizations in Global Politics, Cornell University Press Ithaca 2004, p. 57.

about multilateral conferences, none is definitively appropriate in analyzing the roles and aims of those international fora. We note that each possesses some tools that can be useful to examine and analyze rich, multi-causal phenomena and the characteristics of multilateral conferences.

1.4 Characteristics and forms of multilateral conferences

Multilateral conference has its antecedents in the Eastern Mediterranean in the 4th century BC, when the Greek city-states and Persia convened eight international political congresses and established a mutually guaranteed territorial status quo along with agreed rules of conduct for regulating international affairs.[33] Universal membership and international legitimacy give today's United Nations an unmatched convening and mobilizing power that has been used to organize a large number of global conferences on a diverse range of topics from women to human rights, from population to social development, and from economic development to environmental conservation. Generally, these conferences have been important for articulating new international norms, expanding international law, creating new structures, setting agendas and promoting linkages among the UN, the specialized agencies, NGOs, and governments.[34] In addition, the multilateral character of WTO and its uniqueness as the only international organization dealing with the global rules of trade between nations, makes its ministerial conferences and other multilateral events a flagship towards the debates to ensure that trade flows are as smoothly, predictably and freely as possible. Any large global conference is accompanied by extensive diplomatic activity, sometimes stretching over several years, as countries try to ascertain who the like-minded and therefore likely coalition partners are, to harmonize strategies to advance their own and defeat competing interests and efforts, to mobilize stakeholders' support or to unsharpened detractors dissent.[35]

1. Thus, the **emergence** of the multilateral conferences is one of their characteristics. The invention of the multilateral conference plus follow-up conference in 1815 was a process set in motion by nation-states, which within less than a century would lead to

---

[33] Watson Adam, Diplomacy: The Dialogue between States, London: Methuen, 1982, p.87.

[34] Mingst Karen A. and Karns Margaret P., The United Nations in the Twenty-first Century, 3rd ed., Boulder: Westview, 2006, p. 42.

[35] Cooper Andrew F., Heine Jorge, and Thakur Ramesh, Introduction: The Challenges of 21st-Century Diplomacy, The Oxford Handbook of Modern Diplomacy, 2013, p. 20.

institutionalization and acceptance of multilateral conferences in international relations. The strongest and leading state initiated this new practice. Although this vision corresponds with the realist school, the hegemon does not seek maximum promotion of its interests, as realists suppose, but from a longer-term perspective is satisfied with optimal promotion. Their strategies resulted, respectively, in the Concert of Europe, the League of Nations and the UN (see chapter 1.1). This creates the leeway in which multilateral conferences emerged.

2. Apart from the emergence of the multilateral conferences, another characteristic is their **continuity** and **regularity**. Their very existence may be endangered by exogenous shocks, the First World War being one. However, most of the multilateral conferences created over the decades survived external shocks (petrol crisis, Cold War, economic turmoil, Ebola crisis, environmental issues etc.), showing that the multilateral conferences may adapt and even learn. Adaptation, in the sense of adding new activities and dropping old ones (similar to layering), refers to incremental change with an emphasis on altering means of actions without worrying about their coherence with existing goals. However, the behavior of multilateral conferences changes if actors question implicit theories underlying programs and examine their original values. This learning, which does not occur very often, is associated with a form of managed organizational change. The stimuli that lead to learning mostly come from the external environment in which the multilateral conference is placed and in which something went wrong, in the sense that multilateral conference persisted in making decisions that produced outcomes not desired by the participants. Clusters of bureaucratic entities within governments discuss these developments, with the aim not of dismantling the multilateral conference, but of finding solutions for the problems allowing the continuity of the particular international fora. Two exceptions are worthy of mention: the European Coal and Steel Community (ECSC) which entered into force on 23 July 1952, with a validity period limited to 50 years, thus it expired on 23 July 2002 and the so-called "Brexit" meaning the withdrawal of the United Kingdom from the EU following the UK referendum on EU membership that took place on 23rd June 2016.

3. As in many cases, a conference is **both an instruction-receiver and an instruction-giver**,[36] this being another characteristic of multilateral conferences. The ECOSOC frequently receives request from the UN

---

[36] Kaufmann J., Conference Diplomacy: An Introductory Analysis, 2nd revised edition, Martinus Nijhoff Publishers, UNITAR, 1988, p. 55.

General Assembly (UNGA) and itself transmits its own requests to regional commissions or the so called functional commissions, all of which come under its supervision. A regional commission such as the Economic Commission for Europe (UNECE) has to approve the work programs of a series of sub-committees working under its aegis, just as its own work program must be approved by the ECOSOC. In many international organizations, for instance WHO, ILO, WB, IMF, IEA, it is fairly normal procedure for the plenary conferences to refer to the executive body proposals that are either too controversial or too complicated to be dealt with by the conference.

4.   Another characteristic of the multilateral conferences is given by the ongoing international political process that follows agenda setting at multilateral conferences that can be presented as an **input-output model**.[37] This starts with governments of states revealing their political wishes about one or more common problems, these being inputs for a multilateral conference. Via an output process in the "black box" of the conference or organization, the various wishes and related solutions are geared to one another, usually through the wording of international standards that should be guiding what is to be undertaken at the (sub)national level in order to solve the problems. The output phase ends with a decision, in the form of a multilateral agreement containing the agreed-upon standards and decision-making procedures for what is to be done. In their turn, these international outputs serve as inputs for the states concerned. What follows parallels the ratification[38] process of international treaties, by taking the international decisions to the national parliaments which may agree and ratify. If they do so, the states are supposed to adapt national legislation and regulations and to change existing practices in accordance with the international standards. The national reports about implementation activities and results, which the states must regularly send to the Conference Secretariat (see chapter 2.4), can be regarded as inputs in the "feedback loop" for the follow-up conference which will assess these reports and, if required, take further decisions. This input-output cycle shows how

---

[37] Reinalda Bob, Routledge History of International Organizations From 1815 to the present day, by Routledge 2 Park Square, Milton Park, Abingdon, Oxon OX14 4RN, 2009, p. 15.

[38] Initials, signature and ratification. In the negotiation of an international treaty, *the negotiators initial* the bottom of every page of the agreement as authentication. **The signature** of the plenipotentiaries (country representatives with full negotiating powers) is affixed at the end of a treaty. The signing ceremony marks the end of the treaty negotiations and obliges the signatory States to act in good faith in accordance with a treaty. Unless the treaty provides otherwise, the signature does not yet make the State a party to the treaty. **Ratification** is the act which commits the State to respect the treaty at the international level.

international (global or regional) politics are intertwined with domestic politics.

5. In this interplay between international and domestic politics, governments are more or less simultaneously negotiating the same issues at two levels: nationally within their own political systems and internationally within the multilateral conference to which they are a party. This combination is described as another characteristic of multilateral conferences, as **two-level games**. Governments therefore are exposed to tensions resulting from both the debates and power relations within their national political system, and those within the international arrangement. This combination offers governments opportunities to use arguments from one system in the other. They may use arguments from domestic politics internationally in order to influence the outcome of international agreements, or, the other way round, use international policies or intentions as arguments in domestic politics. The international agreements or conventions would not be successful if they are not able to produce positive direct results for the participant countries at the national level. The negotiators at the international level need to solve economic problems less clear as the needs of their domestic constituencies,[39] which could have an impact both at the national and international level.

6. As states are not the only actors in international relation process, multilateral conferences are also characterized by the **external or internal position attributed to non-state actors**. Big economic-actors such as transnational corporations (TNCs) or sectoral interest groups may lobby, promotional pressure groups, non-governmental organizations (NGOs) or social movements may advocate their views, independent experts or "think tank" may bring forward new ideas and solutions for specific problems during the output phase. Private actors can engage in the multilateral conferences from an external position, by influencing public opinion or lobbying governments and conference's functionaries, but they may also acquire an internal position, such as consultative status at a multilateral conference. In that case they have gained access to the institution, access that substantially enhances their opportunities to influence debates, because they are able to deliver contributions as regards content and they may politically mingle with other actors. Furthermore, they are often able to report about national attitudes towards implementation.

---

[39] Putnam Robert, Diplomacy and domestic Politics: The logic of two-level games, International Organization, Vol. 42, No. 3, The MIT Press, Summer, 1988, pp. 433- 434.

7. Multilateral conferences **are contributor to solving common problems and attaining specific goals in international relations**.[40] They help nation-states to adapt to changing environments and to overcome problems related to these changes. We consider that the creation of multilateral conferences had three motives: the promotion of trade, peace and human dignity. In accordance with these motives, the multilateral conferences have helped states: to adapt to the dynamics of technological developments and the international economy (trade motives); to create, maintain or improve political structures at global and regional levels that promote security (peace motives); to strengthen the states' national socio-economic basis by promoting social welfare and human rights (humanitarian motives); [41] and to diffuse general interests against special ones thanks to the public agendas, and disseminate important technical information that can be implemented and adapted according to the nations' needs (inclusiveness motives). Often a combination of these motives is found. It is assumed that a lively trade combined with respect for human rights will enhance the chances of peaceful relations between states way more than each motive on its own.

Multilateral conferences taking place annually (over 2000 a year) have so many **forms**, and at so many different levels, that it is difficult to measure all of them.[42] However, even a minor endeavor at counting them shows that since the creation of the UN and the Bretton Woods Institutions (BWI) in 1945, the number of multilateral meetings have exploded, especially in the last two decades.

Any attempt to classify all the multilateral meetings will also face serious difficulties. However, if one[43] looks for conceptual basis to capture most of them, these will have the form of universal, functional/specialized, regional and *ad hoc*.

Universal conferences: The creation of the UN and the Bretton Wood Institutions led to the development of the industry of universal gatherings and conferences which tried to get all of humanity represented. These universal gatherings have grown from the regular annual meetings of UN General Assembly (UNGA), the International Monetary Fund (IMF), and World Bank to

---

[40] Reinalda Bob, Routledge History of International Organizations From 1815 to the present day, by Routledge 2 Park Square, Milton Park, Abingdon, Oxon OX14 4RN, 2009, p. 15.

[41] Jacobson H.K., Networks of interdependence. International organizations and the global political system. New York, Alfred A. Knopf, 1979, p. 64.

[42] Walker R.A, Manual for UN Delegates - Conference Process, Procedure and Negotiation, UN Publication, 2011, p.12.

[43] Mahbubani Kishore, Multilateral Diplomacy, The Oxford Handbook of Modern Diplomacy, Edited by Andrew F. Cooper, Jorge Heine, and Ramesh Thakur, 2013, pp. 252-253.

the current inclusion of all kinds of global conferences, from the UN Conference on the Law of the Sea (UNCLOS) to conferences on population, women, and the global environment.

The WTO Ministerial Conference, the biennial highest decision-making gathering of the multilateral trade system is considered universal (see chapter 2.1, on Ministerial Conferences).

Functional/specialized conferences: The UN family has also created a variety of specialized agencies with their own intergovernmental annual conferences and governing councils that provide direction and guidance on the basis of decisions reached through multilateral diplomacy. While some of these meetings have been derailed by political differences, which hamper their ability to provide good global leadership and governance in their respective fields, their track record shows that whenever a common danger is faced, the global community has been able to come together. This is especially true of the reaction to pandemics that do not respect national borders. Hence, it is useful to observe how multilateral diplomacy works well in specialized organizations like WHO to understand how humanity can gather and work together in universal/multilateral conferences.

Similarly, under WTO aegis specialized conferences are organized, conferences that debate and provide guidance on issues related to international trade or implementation of WTO Agreements.

Regional conferences: Multilateral diplomacy is growing very rapidly at the regional level. The most successful example of regional cooperation is provided by the European Union (EU). While most praise the economic achievements of the EU, its most striking achievement is not just that there are no wars, but that there is also no prospect of war between any two EU Member States. This is the gold standard of regional cooperation that all other regions should try to emulate. Another example is the second most successful regional organization, namely the Association of Southeast Asian Nations (ASEAN). The success of multilateral diplomacy in Asia has profound implications for the global order as we moved into a new era of world history marked by the end of Western domination and the return of Asia on world's stage.[44] Another example is the African Union (AU) which is a continental union consisting of 54 countries in

---

[44] From the year 1 to 1820, China and India consistently provided the world's largest economies and by 2050, when it is assumed they will return to their natural places in the global hierarchy of nations, the center of gravity of world history might shift to Asia (see op.cit. 43).

Africa whose aim is to achieve greater unity and solidarity between African countries and people. For the moment, the cooperation in these regions does not come close to that within EU.

Ad hoc conferences: The success of multilateral diplomacy is also demonstrated by the creation of various ad hoc diplomatic gatherings. The most famous and most powerful ad hoc group today is the Group of Twenty (G20).[45] It saved the world from an economic meltdown in early 2009. Unlike established universal and regional groupings, like the UN or EU, the G20 has no headquarters or even rules of procedure.[46] It is still truly ad hoc. But despite this, its ability to deliver results also shows the value of multilateral diplomacy. The success of a club is shown when outsiders clamor to get in and no insiders want to leave it. This is certainly true of the G20. Other ad hoc forms of multilateral diplomacy have also emerged, with varying degrees of legitimacy and success. The initiatives against landmines and cluster bombs, despite initial opposition from established powers like the USA, Russia, and China, found significant international momentum and were subsequently legitimized when both were endorsed by UNGA. A less successful example of ad hoc multilateral diplomacy is provided by the Proliferation Security Initiative (PSI) launched by the USA. Its goal is to stop trafficking of weapons of mass destruction (WMD), their delivery systems, and related materials to and from states and non-state actors of proliferation concern. Even though it has over 100[47] States supporting it, it is still opposed by several countries which disputes its legality, and has therefore not yet been endorsed by the UN System.[48]

The practice of multilateral diplomacy through multilateral conferences for many decades and in many different forums, universal, regional and ad-hoc, developed the sense of community for people and state which come together and interact frequently, which, over time, increased the role and value of these

---

[45] The Group of Twenty (G20) Finance Ministers and Central Bank Governors was established in 1999 to bring together industrialized and developing economies to discuss key issues in the global economy. The G20 is made up of the finance ministers and central bank governors of 19 countries: Argentina, Australia, Brazil, Canada, China, France, Germany, India, Indonesia, Italy, Japan, Mexico, Russia, Saudi Arabia, South Africa, South Korea, Turkey, the United Kingdom, the United States of America. The remaining seat is held by the European Union, which is represented by the rotating Council Presidency and the European Central Bank.

[46] Rules of procedures: A set of rules adopted by a conference or its parent body to govern how the conference is to be run.

[47] 103 States support PSI, out of 193 UN Members

[48] UN System: The UN itself, together with all its main organs, subsidiary bodies, programs and specialized agencies.

international fora. This in turn reduces the prospects for conflict and enhances the prospects for cooperation, providing clear and powerful proof of the significance and importance of multilateral conferences in international relations.

Chapter 2 – Multilateral conferences – significant dimension of diplomacy

As we mentioned, multilateral conferences may involve several nations acting together as in the UN and WTO or may involve regional or military alliances, pacts, or groupings such as NATO. As these multilateral conferences were not imposed on states but were created and accepted by them in order to increase their ability to seek their own interests through the coordination of their policies, much of these international institutions lack tools of enforcement while instead work as frameworks that constrain opportunistic behavior and points for coordination by facilitating exchange of information about the actual behavior of states with reference to the standards to which they have consented.[49]

2.1 Classification of multilateral conferences

Nevertheless, the great multitude and diversity of conferences enables the distinction of at least **eleven categories**: Summit Conferences, Ministerial Conferences, Expert Meetings, Management Conferences, Conferences of the Parties (COPs), Donor Conferences, Committees and Working Groups, Heads of Delegations (HODs), Negotiating Conferences and Diplomatic Conferences.

Summit[50] Conferences. The Summits are conferences of Heads of States or Governments or political leaders and the highest representative of an international organization, a key element of any summit being executive participation, diplomacy at the highest possible level.[51] Also, the setting of the

---

[49] Keohane, Robert O., Joseph S. Nye, and Stanley Hoffmann, The End of the Cold War in Europe. Introduction. After the Cold War / International Institutions and State Strategies in Europe, 1989-1991. Cambridge, MA: Harvard UP, 1993, p. 20.

[50] According to Melissen, The word "summit" did not have any political or diplomatic meaning until Winston Churchill introduced it into international parlance. It was in 1950, four years after he employed the "Iron Curtain" metaphor to refer to the frontier between capitalism and communism in Europe, that Britain's Prime Minister started calling meetings between the leaders of the great powers "summit meetings".

[51] In the media many other meetings of some international importance are nowadays labelled as summits including gatherings of WTO Finance Ministers or global meetings of transnational pressure groups. Foreign Ministers' meetings, however important, are not summits, even though they may be essential for the preparation of summits, as was the case with the meeting of EU Foreign Ministers that cleared the way for the 1997 summit where the Amsterdam Treaty was agreed. (see Melissen Jan, Summit Diplomacy Coming of Age, Discussion Papers in Diplomacy,

agenda is a highly political process and the specific subjects of summits can vary greatly. Summits come in many shapes and sizes, and serial ones seem particularly well suited for purposes of negotiation. Many summits take place outside the UN System, such as the meetings of the European Council,[52] the annual Assembly of the African Union, the Asia-Europe Meeting, the Arab League Summit, the Islamic Summit Conference, the annual Ibero-American Summit, the Commonwealth Heads of Government Meeting, and the G20 or G8 Summits. In America, top-level meetings have flourished as a result of the creation of groupings like the "Group of three" (G3),[53] the Southern Common Market (MERCOSUR),[54] the Caribbean Community (CARICOM),[55] the North American Free Trade Agreement (NAFTA)[56] and the Community of Latin American and Caribbean States (CELAC).[57] The Organization of American States

---

Netherlands Institute of International Relations Clingendael, Editor: Spencer Mawby, University of Nottingham, 1999).

[52] The European Council consists of the heads of state or government of the EU's Member States, together with its President and the European Commission President. It defines the EU's general political direction and priorities.

[53] The Group of three (G3) was made of Colombia, Mexico and Venezuela. The G3 was a free trade agreement between Colombia, Mexico, and Venezuela that came into effect on January 1, 1995, which created an extended market of 149 million consumers. Venezuela left the bloc in November 2006.

[54] Mercosur or Mercosul (in Spanish: Mercado Común del Sur and in Portuguese: Mercado Comum do Sul) is a sub-regional bloc originated in 1988, when Argentina and Brazil signed the Argentina-Brazil Integration and Economics Cooperation Program (PICE). Mercosur was established in 1991 and later amended and updated in 1994. Currently, its full members are Argentina, Brazil, Paraguay, Uruguay and Venezuela. Its associate countries are Bolivia, Chile, Peru, Colombia, Ecuador and Suriname. Observer countries are New Zealand and Mexico. Its purpose is to promote free trade and the fluid movement of goods, people, and currency. It is now a full customs union and a trading bloc.

[55] Established in 1973, the Caribbean Community (CARICOM) is an organization of fifteen Caribbean nations and dependencies. CARICOM's main purposes are to promote economic integration and cooperation among its members, to ensure that the benefits of integration are equitably shared, and to coordinate foreign policy.

[56] The North American Free Trade Agreement (NAFTA) is an agreement signed by Canada, Mexico, and the United States of America, creating a trilateral trade bloc in North America. The agreement came into force on January 1, 1994.

[57] The Community of Latin American and Caribbean States (CELAC) is a regional bloc of Latin American and Caribbean states thought out on February 23, 2010, at the Rio Group–Caribbean Community Unity Summit and created on December 3, 2011, in Caracas, Venezuela, with the signature of The Declaration of Caracas. It consists of 33 sovereign countries in the Americas representing roughly 600 million people. Due to the focus of the organization on Latin American and Caribbean countries, other countries and territories in the Americas, Canada and the United States of America, as well as the territories of France, the Netherlands, Denmark and the United Kingdom in the Americas are not included. CELAC is an example of a decade-long push for deeper integration within Latin America.

(OAS) meets currently more frequently at the highest level than previously. In addition to these, the UN has also provided the framework for a number of noteworthy summit conferences, such as: the World Summits on the Information Society (WSIS), the World Summit on Sustainable Development (WSSD), the UN Conference on Environment and Development ("Earth Summit"), the UN Millennium Summit and the UN Sustainable Development Summit. Although it is difficult to measure the success of summitry, this form of dialogue has distinct diplomatic functions such as: flexibility - for leaders without international experience, it has educational value as it alerts them to the importance of international issues and provides them with an opportunity to become familiarized with their peers, while the experienced politicians may employ the summit to get personal impression of counterparts, sound them out or use the occasion of the meeting to "fly a kite"; ideal for private consultations, bypassing multiple bureaucratic layers; and suppleness to take place at any stage of international negotiations.[58]

Ministerial Conferences. The Ministerial Conference is the top decision making body of the WTO. There have been ten conferences from 1996 to 2015, usually every two years. It brings together all members of the WTO, all of which are countries or customs unions. The Ministerial Conference can take decisions on all matters under any of the multilateral trade agreements by adopting authoritative interpretations of the WTO agreements, granting waivers, adopting amendments, decisions on accession, appointing Director-General and adopting staff regulations. Also, the highest decision-making body of United Nations Conference on Trade and Development (UNCTAD) is the quadrennial (Ministerial) Conference, at which Members make assessments of current trade and development issues, discuss policy options and formulate global policy responses. The conference also sets the organization's mandate and work priorities. In addition ministerial conferences are held in the framework of different international organizations (WHO, UNEP, IATA, etc.) or regional organizations. The participation is at the high level and the setting of the agenda is a highly political process but the subject of the conferences do not necessary vary as these conferences deal with the specific issues to which the participant ministers are assigned to.

---

[58] Melissen Jan, Summit Diplomacy Coming of Age, Discussion Papers in Diplomacy, Netherlands Institute of International Relations Clingendael, Editor: Spencer Mawby, University of Nottingham, 1999, p. 3.

Expert Meetings. At the other end, in the sense of having a much lower public profile and are far less solemn, are meetings at which the participants are individuals selected for their scientific or technical expertise on the subject matter of the conference. Because of this, they are not called upon to represent the political preferences of their governments and such meetings usually do not attempt to make decisions which engage governments, although they may decide to recommend a technical measure or standard to another conference which is capable of making such decisions. Many of the UN specialized agencies and other organizations and programs organize expert meetings regularly to further their work programs and activities. In addition to expert meetings convened under UN bodies, regional organizations also hold similar events.[59] An example in the European Union context is the Commission Expert Group on Banking, Payments and Insurance which is a consultative entity, composed of experts appointed by the EU Member States, in order to provide advice and expertise in the preparation of draft delegated acts[60] in the area of banking, payments and insurance to the Commission and its services. In the African Union context, an example is the African Union Customs Experts whose mandate is to develop a Trade Facilitation Strategy for Africa. The Expert Meeting of the Employment and Skills Strategies in Southeast Asia which focuses on building effective strategies to reduce skills mismatches while fostering quality job creation and growth is an example in the Asian region.

Management Conferences. Most UN specialized agencies and programs have governing bodies, which are conferences of representatives of UN Members, charged with overseeing the work of the agency or the operation of the program,

---

[59] Walker R.A., Multilateral Conferences: Purposeful International Negotiation. London: Palgrave Macmillan, 2004, p. 90.

[60] Delegated acts: Article 290 of the TFEU allows the EU legislator (generally, the European Parliament and the Council) to delegate to the Commission the power to adopt non-legislative acts of general application that supplement or amend certain non-essential elements of a legislative act. For example, delegated acts may add new (non-essential) rules or involve a subsequent amendment to certain aspects of a legislative act. The legislator can thus concentrate on policy direction and objectives without entering into overly detailed and often highly technical debates. The delegation of power to adopt delegated acts is nevertheless subject to strict limits. Indeed, only the European Commission can be empowered to adopt delegated acts. Furthermore, the essential elements of an area may not be subject to a delegation of power. In addition, the objectives, content, scope and duration of the delegation of power must be defined in the legislative acts. Lastly, the legislator must explicitly set in the legislative act the conditions under which this delegation may be exercised. In this respect, the Parliament and the Council may provide for the right to revoke the delegation or to express objections to the delegated act. This procedure is widely used in many areas, for example: internal market, agriculture, environment, consumer protection, transport, and the area of freedom, security and justice.

giving policy directions and making managerial decisions, notably the adoption of the budget and appointment of the Chief Executive Officer (CEO). Most of the specialized agencies have two such bodies: a general assembly and a smaller executive committee, elected by and from the membership, which meets more frequently and oversees the agency or program more closely[61] (see Table no.1).

Table no.1- Examples of Governing Bodies in the UN System

UN Agency or Program	Governing Bodies	
	General Assembly	Executive Committee
Food and Agriculture Organization (FAO)	Conference of Member Nations	Council
International Labour Organization (ILO)	International Labour Conference	Executive Council
International Monetary Fund (IMF)	Board of Governors	Executive Board
United Nations Environment Programme (UNEP)	Governing Council	Committee of Permanent Representatives
United Nations High Commission for Refugees (UNHCR)	Executive Committee	
United Nations Framework Convention for Climate Change (UNFCCC)	Conference of the Parties	
UN International Children's Emergency Fund (UNICEF)	Executive Board	
UN Conference on Trade and Development (UNCTAD)	Trade and Development Board	
United Nations Education, Science and Culture Organization (UNESCO)	General Conference	Executive Board
World Health Organization (WHO)	World Health Assembly	Executive Board
World Meteorological Organization (WMO)	World Meteorological Council	Executive Council
World Bank	Board of Governors	

Source: Adapted from UNITAR, Performing Effectively in Multilateral Conferences and Diplomacy - Welcome to the World of Multilateral Conferences, 2006, p.8.

Outside the UN System, most of the organizations have one such body, with the notable exception of the European Union and the African Union, and

---

[61] United Nations Institute for Training and Research (UNITAR), Performing Effectively in Multilateral Conferences and Diplomacy - Welcome to the World of Multilateral Conferences, 2006, p.8.

despite various denomination they smoothly administer the activity of the organization (see Table no. 2).

Table no.2 - Examples of Governing Bodies outside the UN System

Organization	Governing Body	Executive body
African Union (AU)	Assembly of the AU	Executive council
Association of Southeast Asian Nations (ASEAN)	Standing Committee	
European Union	European Council	European Commission
North Atlantic Treaty Organisation (NATO)	Standing Committee	
Organisation for Economic Co-operation and Development (OECD)	OECD Council	
World Trade Organization (WTO)	General Council	

Source: Author's research

General Assemblies (or **General Conferences**). These are meetings which are usually held annually or every two years of the whole membership of an organization. Their function includes policy and managerial decision-making for the organization concerned but they are also occasions for representatives of the Members to exchange information and discuss all issues the organization addresses.[62] For example, in the UN System: the UN General Assembly and the World Health Assembly (WHA); and outside the UN System: the International Conference of the Red Cross and Red Crescent, the Council of the International Organization for Migration (IOM), the General Conference of the International Atomic Energy Agency (IAEA).

Special examples are the WTO General Council which is the WTO's highest-level decision-making body in Geneva, meeting regularly to carry out the functions of the WTO. It has representatives (usually ambassadors or equivalent) from all Members and has the authority to act on behalf of the ministerial conference which only meets about every two years; and the Council of the EU which represents the Member States' governments. Also known informally as the

---

[62] Walker Ronald A., Multilateral Conferences: Purposeful International Negotiation. London: Palgrave Macmillan, 2004, pp. 90-91.

EU Council, it is where national ministers from each EU country meet to adopt laws and coordinate policies.

Conferences of the Parties or **Meetings of the Parties** (COPs or MOPs).[63] These are regular meetings of representatives of the parties to a particular treaty to review the administration and implementation of the treaty, give policy guidance and managerial decisions for the relevant secretariat (if there is one), exchange information and discuss issues pertinent to the subject matter of the treaty, sometimes including negotiations on amendments to the treaty. Their function is very similar to that of management conferences, general assemblies and even negotiating conferences. For example: the annual COPs to the UN Framework Convention on Climate Change (UNFCCC), the supreme governing body of the Convention; the COPs of the Convention on International Trade of Endangered Species of Wild Flora and Fauna (CITES), and the review conferences of the Nuclear Non-Proliferation Treaty (NPT). As mentioned, the terms used to describe conferences vary widely and sometimes there is an overlap. The COPs of many environmental treaties are, for example, assembly, managerial and negotiating type conferences.

Donor Conferences. This term is sometimes applied to conferences of representatives of governments and international organizations which provide assistance, notably emergency relief, for a particular recipient or in response to a specific need. A subset of donor conferences are pledging conferences at which, as the name suggests, representatives of donors announce what contribution they will make to a specific assistance or relief programme. For example the WTO-led Aid for Trade Initiative that encourages developing country governments and donors to recognize the role that trade can play in development. In particular, the initiative seeks to mobilize resources to address the trade-related constraints identified by developing and least-developed countries. Organized biannually, the Global Review of Aid for Trade Conferences are an opportunity to survey what has been achieved since the launch of the Aid for Trade Initiative at the Sixth WTO Ministerial Conference in Hong Kong in 2005.[64]

Committees and **Working Groups.** These are conferences usually composed of all or a part of the participants in large conference. The words "committee" or "working group" also imply that they have been given a specific

---

[63] Walker R.A., Manual for UN Delegates - Conference Process, Procedure and Negotiation, UN Publication, 2011, p.32.

[64] See wto.org.

task to perform having some of the same connotations as the term taskforce.[65] The relationship between a committee and the conference which created it (known as the parent conference or parent body) vary from quite distant to very close. Thus, for example, the former Committee on Disarmament, (and likewise its predecessor, the Eighteen Nation Disarmament Committee) was created by the UN General Assembly (UNGA) which also determined its general mandate and initial composition. Thereafter, however, the Committee pursued a fully independent course, before being replaced in 1979, by the Conference on Disarmament. Another example of committees that can be independent from their parent conference are the preparatory committees (PrepComs) sometimes called to prepare for a large conference (e.g. summit) or the creation of a new organization.[66] In many cases, the conference ceases to exist once it finishes its work. Typically, committees are said to be subsidiary to their parent conference. They are given detailed tasks by the parent conference and report to it regularly, sometimes making recommendations. Examples of this kind of committee include the Subsidiary Body for Implementation (SBI) and the Subsidiary Body for Scientific and Technical Advice (SBSTA) of the UNFCCC, and the many functional commissions[67] which report to ECOSOC. More closely connected to their parent bodies are the committees of large conferences focusing on one aspect of the work of the parent body (e.g. the Second Committee of the UN General Assembly, which makes recommendations to the General Assembly on its agenda items relating to economic issues). In WTO we find examples of committees that are linked to their parents conference, General Council having the following subsidiary bodies which oversee committees in different areas: Council for Trade in Goods,[68] Council for Trade-Related Aspects of Intellectual Property Rights (TRIPs),[69] Council for Trade in Services[70] and the Trade Negotiations Committee (TNC).[71]

---

[65] Taskforce is a unit specially organized for a task, by Governments, international organizations, etc.

[66] For example, a Preparatory Committee (PrepCom) drafted the International Trade Organization (ITO) Charter and it was approved in 1948 at the conference in Havana, Cuba. The first round of trade negotiations took place while the Preparatory Committee was still working on drafting the Charter because the participants were anxious to begin the process of trade liberalization as soon as possible. Their results were incorporated into the General Agreement on Tariff and Trade (GATT), which was signed in 1947.

[67] A commission tends to be a committee with a permanent secretariat, although we underline that formal classification in such matters is by no means uniform or consistent.

[68] There are 11 committees under the jurisdiction of the Goods Council each with a specific task. All members of the WTO participate in the committees.

[69] It deals with Information on intellectual property in the WTO, news and official records of the

The term **working group** is reserved for small conferences dedicated to a very specific issue or task, often within a short time frame. Working groups and/or sub-committees are often subsidiaries of committees. Sometimes, a working group may be established as an *ad hoc* group of experts working to achieve specified goals. The groups are domain-specific and focus on a specific subject area.[72]

Heads of Delegations (HODs). These are informal meetings that are one step away from the formal meetings, but HODs meetings still include the full membership. In the WTO we find the particularity of the "Green Room" meetings which is a phrase taken from the informal name of the Director-General's conference room. It is used to refer to meetings of 20-40 delegations, usually at the level of heads of delegations.

Negotiating Conferences. Also called intergovernmental negotiating committees (INCs) they have the mandate to draft and agree on a text (e.g. treaty, declaration, plan of implementation, etc.). This term is often *contrasted with deliberative bodies*, which refers to conferences which can discuss issues and make recommendations, but have not been assigned (and have no authority) to negotiate a text intended to impose legally-binding commitments. Negotiating conferences, however, are not empowered to go beyond agreeing on a text. Thus, they cannot take additional steps and commit governments to adhere to the treaty or otherwise adopt the text. That is the role of another type of conference called Diplomatic Conference.

Diplomatic Conferences. The traditional method for the negotiation of treaties has been through the holding of a diplomatic conference of plenipotentiaries[73] specifically convened for that purpose. This technique

---

activities of the TRIPS Council, and details of the WTO's work with other international organizations in the field.

[70] The Council for Trade in Services operates under the guidance of the General Council and is responsible for overseeing the functioning of the General Agreement on Trade in Services (GATS). It is open to all WTO members, and can create subsidiary bodies as required.

[71] The Trade Negotiations Committee (TNC) is the committee that deals with the current trade talks round. The chair is WTO's director-general. As of June 2012 the committee was tasked with the Doha Development Round.

[72] Walker R.A., Multilateral Conferences: Purposeful International Negotiation. London: Palgrave Macmillan, 2004, p. 92.

[73] Plenipotentiary is a person, especially a diplomat fully authorized to represent a government as a prerogative (e.g., ambassador). The Plenipotentiary is invested with the full power of independent action on behalf of their government, typically in a foreign country.

precedes the UN, with prominent examples including the Hague Conferences of 1899 and 1907 (see chapter 1.1). In the contemporary practice of treaty-making many multilateral treaties are negotiated and adopted by the organs of international organizations such as the UN, partly for reasons of practicality and cost-effectiveness. Nonetheless, diplomatic conferences continue to be held, from time to time, in order to negotiate and adopt multilateral treaties of particular significance to the international community.[74] Diplomatic Conferences are meeting of plenipotentiaries, that is to say representative who carry "full powers"[75] to represent their governments by signing the text of a treaty. A diplomatic conference may be convened once a negotiating conference has completed its task. The task of a diplomatic conference is to finally approve the text and declare it open for signature.

In addition to these types of conferences, regular meetings of the UN, its agencies, WTO, EU and regional organizations provide forums for parliamentary diplomacy, oratory, propaganda, and negotiation. International bureaucracies negotiate with each other and with individual states. This is particularly true of the UN and the EU, the latter has assumed some attributes of sovereignty.

The numbers and types of conferences taking place in both standing bodies and in ad hoc arrangements can easily give rise to a **system of conferences**[76] (and negotiations). Although each conference has a specific purpose, several conferences often deal with different aspects or stages of the same broad or narrow topic, and texts produced by one conference are later taken up in one or more other conferences. In various thematic areas, such as trade, human rights, environment and sustainable development, this conference system is quite extensive with meetings and their outcomes complexly linked. In many cases, linkages across conferences are mutually reinforcing, each conference helping the others to achieve their objectives. This is the case in the area of sustainable development or women's rights, where dozen conferences are organized yearly to deal with these topics in a variety of ways. Similarly, there are situations when

---

[74] See legal.un.org.

[75] "Full Powers" is a term in international law and is the authority of a person to sign a treaty or convention on behalf of a sovereign state. Persons other than the head of state, head of government or foreign minister of the state must produce "Full Powers" in order to sign a treaty in the name of his/her government. Such a person is called a plenipotentiary. It is defined in articles 2 and 7 of the Vienna Convention on the Law of Treaties.

[76] United Nations Institute for Training and Research (UNITAR), Performing Effectively in Multilateral Conferences and Diplomacy - Welcome to the World of Multilateral Conferences, 2006, p.8.

global conferences require the organization of regional conferences (or vice versa) to give practical effect to the implementation of a conference outcome.

There are many conferences that appear to run against each other in terms of mandates, objectives and approaches as there are many conferences, as well as their outcomes, that are mutually reinforced. This is the case when an issue is considered from one perspective and subsequently re-examined from another. For example, the negotiations in the Working Group on Access to Genetic Resources and Benefit-sharing, established as a follow-up negotiating conference of the Convention on Biological Diversity (CBD) and convened under the auspices of UNEP, is linked to the outcomes of previous negotiations, such as the WTO Agreement on Trade-related Aspects of Intellectual Property Rights (TRIPS), the FAO International Treaty on Plant and Genetic Resources for Food and Agriculture (IT PGRFA)[77] and the World Intellectual Property Organization (WIPO) Patent Cooperation Treaty. Similarly, in the discussions on access to medicine[78] nine relevant UN and international organizations[79] are involved.

2.2 Functions of multilateral conferences

While the above categorization of conferences is not exhaustive, it is sufficient to enable identification of some multilateral conferences' functions,[80] which can be common to all conferences or specific to some.

---

[77] IT PGRFA is popularly known as the International Seed Treaty.

[78] The 32nd session of the UN Human Rights Council (13 June - 1 July 2016) adopted a resolution on access to medicines proposed by a number of developing countries. This marks yet another UN forum in which developing countries seek to raise the issue of access to medicines, particularly with regard to high prices. The resolution calls in particular for "Members and the international community to increase investment, building on existing mechanisms and through partnership, to improve health systems in developing countries and countries with economies in transition with the aim of providing sufficient health workers, infrastructures, management systems and supplies to achieve the Sustainable Development Goals by 2030".

[79] World Health Organisation (WHO), World Intellectual Property Organization (WIPO), World Trade Organization (WTO), United Nations Industrial Development Organisation (UNIDO), United Nations Conference on Trade and Development (UNCTAD), United Nations Children's Fund (UNICEF), the Office of the UN High Commissioner for Human Rights (OHCHR), the UN Special Rapporteur on the Right to Health, Joint United Nations Programme on HIV/AIDS Secretariat (UNAIDS) and United Nations Development Programme (UNDP).

[80] Walker R.A., Multilateral Conferences: Purposeful International Negotiation. London: Palgrave Macmillan, 2004, p. 95.

The common functions of all conferences are: platform for exchanging information, venues for organized discussion and opportunities for governments to demonstrate their commitment to a specific issue.

All conferences are **platforms for exchanging information**, as they are uniquely efficient mechanisms that function through a wide range of formal and informal processes. This flow of information is so valuable to governments that it justifies the cost of participation in many conferences, regardless of the conference does or is supposed to do.

All conferences are **venues for organized discussion** of issues of concern to governments, which enable them to learn from each other's experience, to learn of each other's intentions and to help each other analyse and cope with many of the challenges they face.

Most conferences offers **opportunities for governments to demonstrate their commitment** to particular objectives or courses of action, their solidarity with others, the strength of their emotion and so on. Due to their effectiveness as a mean of disseminating information, most conferences serve governments as a communication tool with domestic and foreign audiences.

The functions specific to only some conferences are: platforms for making decisions, setting aspirational goals for humanity, key elements in international regimes (frameworks of rules), norms and rules creation and/or standard setting, mean to negotiate international treaties that improve the state of the world.

Thus, conferences are **platforms for making decisions** by states' representatives. The conferences provide the opportunity of expressing concerns of multiple participants and finding ways of integrating, reconciling or seeking solutions for these concerns to the extend where a widely acceptable outcome is identified and adopted. A conference decision, therefore, is the pooling of knowledge, concerns and authority of all the participants. For example, the Asia-Europe Meeting (ASEM) organizes a biennial Asia-Europe Finance Ministers' Meeting (ASEM FiNMM) in order to discuss on macroeconomic developments, financial stability and increased connectivity. The African Union organizes a Conference of Ministers of Health (CAMH) every two years, which provides an opportunity for African Health Ministers and partners to share experiences and best practices on how to improve the health situation in Africa.

Another related function of multilateral conferences is to **set aspirational goals for humanity**.[81] Hence, the UN Millennium Summit of 2000 set the

Millennium Development Goals (MDGs) for 2015 and further on the 2015 UN Sustainable Development Summit set the Sustainable Development Goals (SDGs) for 2030, SDGs being officially known as "Transforming our world: the 2030 Agenda for Sustainable Development". As MDGs, many SDGs will not be met but they have nonetheless inspired actions on several fronts to improve the living conditions of the very poor on the Planet. Without universal organizations like the UN, such agreements would be more difficult.

Many conferences are also **key elements in the international regimes (frameworks of rules)**[82] established by the governments to manage the problems they face. Thus, for example, there is a nuclear non-proliferation regime, which consists of many elements, including firmly established norms, mutual expectations and ways of handling issues in this area of policy. Other important components of the regime are a number of international treaties (most notably, the Nuclear Non-Proliferation Treaty (NPT) and the five nuclear weapon free zone treaties (NWFZ)), the International Atomic Energy Agency (IAEA) safeguards regime and many policies and programmes of national governments. Similarly there are clusters of conferences dealing with the control of narcotic drugs, climate change, international maritime affairs, health, trade and almost every other broad or narrow topic of interest to governments - in each case constituting elements of entire regimes for addressing these issues.

A related function is that multilateral conference is **the mean to negotiate international treaties that improve the state of the world**.[83] Two significant examples: the Nuclear Non-Proliferation Treaty (NPT), adopted on 1 July 1968, in force since 5 March 1970, and renewed indefinitely on 11 May 1995, which prohibits the development or transfer of nuclear weapons or related technologies by and to non-weapon holding states; and the UN Convention on the Law of the Sea (UNCLOS) that has created a common set of rules for the use of the world's oceans, which represent 70%of the Earth's surface.

One function to which conferences are particularly suited is that of **norms and rules creation** and/or **standard setting**,[84] in at least three ways:

---

[81] Mahbubani Kishore, Multilateral Diplomacy, The Oxford Handbook of Modern Diplomacy, Edited by Andrew F. Cooper, Jorge Heine, and Ramesh Thakur, 2013, p. 249.

[82] United Nations Institute for Training and Research (UNITAR), Performing Effectively in Multilateral Conferences and Diplomacy - Welcome to the World of Multilateral Conferences, 2006, p.17.

[83] Mahbubani Kishore, Multilateral Diplomacy, The Oxford Handbook of Modern Diplomacy, Edited by Andrew F. Cooper, Jorge Heine, and Ramesh Thakur, 2013, p. 249.

- the most formal is by *negotiating treaties*. In addition to their force in international law, treaties also represent a political commitment, a solemn promise made by a government, on behalf of the State it represents, to the other parties to the agreement and to all people everywhere, including the citizens of the State which contracts the treaty obligations;

- by codifying standards in texts which do not have the legal status of treaties. For example, the International Atomic Energy Agency issues "information circulars" (many other UN agencies as well as WTO issue similar documents) which specify technical standards or best practice. These do not have the force of law because governments have not made formal commitments to enforce them, but they do respond to a widespread need for international standards in many fields;

- by helping to establish standards by repeated exhortation. If conferences repeatedly applaud and encourage a particular course of action or pattern of behaviour, and denounce infractions, the majority of the world's governments are in effect making a statement as to what is correct and permissible: in other words, they are expressing, reinforcing and sometimes creating standards.

The multiple functions of multilateral conferences make it important to understand how they work.

2.3 Purposes of multilateral conferences

In the classic formulation, the overriding goal of international relations was the promotion, pursuit, and defence of the national interest. Did the establishment and development of multilateral conferences change those goals?

As conferences can serve multiple functions, the purpose(s) of a conference need to be clearly provided in the mandate.

The mandate of the conference is a statement of what the conference is supposed to do and is often contained in a decision, resolution or statute. The purpose of each conference will have been decided before governments are invited to send representatives.[85] Very often in the UN System, the WTO, the EU

---

[84] United Nations Institute for Training and Research (UNITAR), Performing Effectively in Multilateral Conferences and Diplomacy - Welcome to the World of Multilateral Conferences, 2006, p.16.

[85] Walker R.A., Manual for UN Delegates - Conference Process, Procedure and Negotiation, UN Publication, 2011, pp. 31-33.

and various regional organizations the decision to hold a conference for a particular purpose is taken by a prior conference. For example:

- The statutes of specialized agencies (which were drawn up by international conferences) provide for regular meetings of their governing bodies and indicate, explicitly or inferentially, what the conferences should do. As a result, the secretariat of each organization sends out invitations for each session of organization's general assembly or executive committee.

- The UN General Assembly (UNGA) has frequently decided, by adopting a resolution, that a conference should be called for a particular purpose (e.g. to review the Law of the Sea or to negotiate a Convention on Climate Change). Similarly, invitations are sent stating the conference's purpose.

- The Agreement establishing WTO provides through various councils and committees the decisions on modalities and frequency of meetings; topmost is the ministerial conference which has to meet at least once every two years. On each occasion, invitations are sent to Members stating the mandate of the conference.

- In the case of the EU, the Council of the EU, among other things, provides the mandate to the European Commission to negotiate on behalf of the EU agreements between the EU and non-EU countries and international organisations.[86] This mandate is carried out in various meetings, councils, committees, etc. for each an invitation to participants (EU representatives or no-EU countries representatives) is send out.

The mandate of the conference[87] can be:

- fully explicit (e.g. to conclude an Agreement on global climate[88]), or

- clearly inferred (e.g. an invitation to attend the WTO Ministerial Conference or the World Health Assembly (WHA) does not need to spell out the

---

[86] The Council of the EU plays an important role in the negotiation and conclusion of agreements between the EU and non-EU countries or international organisations. It is involved at all stages of the procedure; from providing the mandate for negotiations to the European Commission, to signing the agreement on behalf of the EU and adopting the final decision implementing it into EU law.

[87] United Nations Institute for Training and Research (UNITAR), Performing Effectively in Multilateral Conferences and Diplomacy - Welcome to the World of Multilateral Conferences, 2006, p.20.

[88] See the Paris Agreement (L'Accord de Paris) - an agreement within the framework of the United Nations Framework Convention on Climate Change (UNFCCC) dealing with greenhouse gases emissions mitigation, adaptation and finance starting in the year 2020. An agreement on the language of the treaty was negotiated by representatives of 195 countries at the 21st Conference of the Parties of the UNFCCC in Paris and adopted by consensus on 12 December 2015.

inference that the conference is expected to perform the functions assigned by the statute of the WTO or WHO, respectively).

The mandate of the conference[89] is both:

* permissive (i.e. they say what the conference can do) and

* limiting (a conference convened to negotiate a Convention on Tobacco Control or to perform the function the statute of the UNCTAD assigns to the UNCTAD Ministerial Conference has no standing to address other topics such telecommunication networks standards; likewise a conference called to discuss an issue cannot draft a treaty).

For example, in one of the decisions of the UNFCCC's first COPs, in 1995, the Parties agreed to further discuss on commitments for industrialized countries. This decision known as the Berlin Mandate, paved the way for the adoption of the Kyoto Protocol in 1997. Similarly, the creation of WTO is built on previous mandates and rounds of negotiation. The bulk of the WTO's current work comes from the 1986-1994 negotiations called the Uruguay Round and earlier negotiations under the General Agreement on Tariffs and Trade (GATT). The Marrakesh Agreement, manifested by the Marrakesh Declaration, was an agreement signed in Marrakesh, Morocco in 15 April 1994, marking the conclusion of the 8 years-long Uruguay Round and establishing the WTO.

The works of the conference end once the duration is completed or once the objectives are reached. It is noteworthy that the prolongation of the duration of a conference does not mean institutionalisation,[90] as the fulfilment of the mandate coincides with the completion of the work's conference.[91] The successful and in-time outcome of the conference also depend on the commitment of the participating States towards the conference objectives as well as the national objectives.

Accurately, the **national purposes**[92] need to be promoted and some governments might be more committed than others to the purpose set out in the

---

[89] United Nations Institute for Training and Research (UNITAR), Performing Effectively in Multilateral Conferences and Diplomacy - Welcome to the World of Multilateral Conferences, 2006, pp. 20-21.

[90] Institutionalisation means transformation of the conference into a different kind of international fora, such as international organization, alliance, etc. (see op.cit.).

[91] Năstase Dan (quoting Chebeleu), Drept diplomatic și consular, Editura Fundației România de Mâine, Bucuresti, 2006, p. 118.

[92] Walker R.A., Manual for UN Delegates - Conference Process, Procedure and Negotiation, UN Publication, 2011, p.14.

mandate, while other governments have different preoccupations and might see the conference as an opportunity to pursue other objectives as well. Even states pursue multiple goals and interests, not just one interest - the national one. For example:[93]

- Many governments send representatives to major UN conferences as a matter of routine, without immediate or particular prior objective. It is a matter of general policy and of meeting expectations, both international and domestic;

- All governments are interested in knowing the outcome of most conferences in the UN System, in case they may have consequences for them;

- They also wish to be present to have an opportunity to head off or mitigate any development at the conference which is undesirable to them;

- Similarly, they see such conferences as opportunities to advance a wide range of objectives, including the "promotion" of their own policies and achievements;

- One very common purpose pursued by governments is to use the conference as an occasion to exchange with other governments, often on matters beyond the mandate of the conference.

However, at every conference, several governments have interests focused in at least a couple of aspects of the conference's work. Sometimes this derives from idealism or ideology (belief in respecting and upholding human rights or promoting free trade, for example). More often, though, it comes from a belief that government's national objectives can be served by identifying purposes common with other governments and ways, acceptable to them, of advancing these mutual purposes. If this is achieved, it is a way of harnessing the energy and resources of other government to the service of one's own government's objectives. It enables governments to achieve objectives that would be more costly or even unachievable by national efforts alone.[94]

Nevertheless, decision-makers need to see **beyond the national interest** and to take into account the competition, tension, and even outright conflict between the various clusters of values, goals, and interests being pursued by the

---

[93] United Nations Institute for Training and Research (UNITAR), Performing Effectively in Multilateral Conferences and Diplomacy - Welcome to the World of Multilateral Conferences, 2006, pp.22-23.

[94] Thus, for example, concerted international action against malaria or bird flu on a global scale is widely supported for idealistic reasons.

diverse actors. The decision-makers have to strike a balance among the different interests and actors, between domestic demands and international imperatives, between principle and pragmatism, between idealistic values and material interests, between what is the expedient and what is the right thing to do, between the national constituency and the international community, and between the immediate, medium, and long terms.[95]

It is noteworthy the **purposes of individual delegates**,[96] which might alter (but not necessarily) the outcome of the conference. Governments (and sometimes other entities such as intergovernmental and non-governmental organizations) are represented at international conferences by delegates. These are individuals who have their own purposes. In most cases, it is primarily to properly do their jobs, as they see them, which includes acting on any instructions they have from their government and in accordance with its known objectives. But as human beings, before the conference they have differing degrees of knowledge and enthusiasm related to different issues. Often, if they know an issue well, they have more developed ideas than their government. They may also have other concerns which are more personal than national: such as developing their knowledge and professional experience, being seen to perform well and achieving a sense of personal accomplishment, pursuing bilateral exchanges at the conference rather than following whatever the conference itself is doing, etc. Others may be distracted by personal, family or national difficulties. A few sometimes allow themselves to be carried away by personal or national vanity, or by their combative spirit or other emotions. Such individual purposes are very similar to the notion of private interests that negotiators have.

There are four distinct typologies/orientations of personal motivation formed by an individual's standing across two dimensions: degree of personal interest and degree of interest in outcome of the conference: the individualistic, the altruistic, the cooperative, and the competitive. A person exhibiting an individualistic orientation is motivated by an exclusive concern for his or her own outcomes. One who is altruistic displays an orientation characterized by exclusive concern for the well-being (outcomes) of other parties. A person with a cooperative motivational style is orientated towards concern for the well-being

---

[95] Cooper Andrew F., Heine Jorge, and Thakur Ramesh, Introduction: The Challenges of 21st-Century Diplomacy, The Oxford Handbook of Modern Diplomacy, 2013, p. 21.

[96] United Nations Institute for Training and Research (UNITAR), Performing Effectively in Multilateral Conferences and Diplomacy - Welcome to the World of Multilateral Conferences, 2006, p.26.

(outcomes) of both parties. While the competitively-oriented individual is one who is driven by a desire to out-do his or her opponent.[97]

The interaction between these three categories of purposes causes much of the complexity of multilateral conferences. For optimal outcomes in terms of a conference's mandate, it is useful that governments and delegates have common views, approaches and positions. But the co-existence of different purposes or agendas is not all negative. Most national purposes of governments and personal purposes of individual delegates are neither reprehensible nor illegitimate. On the contrary, governments and countries derive many benefits from conferences other than those which flow directly from their mandates. Moreover, it often happens that individual delegates are more closely informed about the details of issues than their governments and more dedicated to achieving technically sound outcomes. This can produce superior results in the real world.

Successful conference managers (chairmen, supported by all constructively motivated delegations), lead the conference (see chapter 7) to accommodate the national and personal agendas of governments and delegates to the extent that this is not inimical to fulfilling the mandate. In contrast, it must be frustrating when individual purposes are damaging for the collective ones.

With the widely spread idea that the outcome of multilateral conferences is largely determined by the relative power of the countries represented, we need to tackle the aspect of **power in conferences**. *Balance of power* [98] is regarded as stable to the extent that it satisfies three conditions: an alliance structure in which the distribution of benefits reflects the distribution of power among its members; a substantial ideological agreement among the principal powers on what the conference is intended to achieve or protect; and a commonly accepted procedure for managing the conference. It is also true that the relative power of governments (or other actors) does not evaporate when their representatives enter a conference room, and that representatives of governments with extensive resources, knowledge and influence have unquestionable advantages. A powerful country is often able to use extraneous consideration than a less powerful one, to get its objectives accomplished.[99] But such factors do not automatically translate into an

---

[97] Alfredson Tanya and Cungu Azeta, Negotiation Theory and Practice. A Review of the Literature, FAO Policy Learning Program, EASYPol Module 179, 2008, p.14.

[98] Reinalda Bob, Routledge History of International Organizations From 1815 to the present day, by Routledge 2 Park Square, Milton Park, Abingdon, Oxon OX14 4RN, 2009, p. 20.

[99] Walker R.A., Multilateral Conferences: Purposeful International Negotiation. London: Palgrave Macmillan, 2004, p. 25.

ability to determine the outcome of conferences. The history of international conferences is full of examples of representatives of relatively small and less wealthy countries playing a very important role. Two noteworthy examples is the influential role that Malta played in launching the Third United Nations Conference on the Law of the Sea (UNCLOS) and the role that the Cairns Group[100] played in the Uruguay Round of trade negotiations.

The general rule is that the **leading delegations** are those which contribute most to determining the outcome of the conference. Many factors can come into such a leadership role but the most obvious one is not the power but the ability of the country to develop proposals which attract widespread support because they meet the objectives of many delegations. There is also power, in a conference, in the willingness to **consult widely** and take account of the views of other delegations and in the ability to operate within the rules of procedure and more generally to understand the sometimes unseen conference process.[101]

The use of the described combination of conditions aims at solving problems raised during the multilateral conference and making it work smoothly and successfully. Before analysing the various aspects of the conference's work (see chapter 3), we present the essential elements common to all multilateral conferences and quite fundamental to understanding how conferences work.

2.4 Elements of multilateral conferences

We noted that the world of multilateral conferences has become more diverse and complex in terms of its tasks and those involved in it. We acknowledged that the conference's institutions currently have to work with a growing community of "stakeholders" and that multilateral conference is a key feature of the today's international relations. In this regards, a multilateral conference needs to be fluid and evolving, while the basic elements that provided

---

[100] The Cairns Group is a unique coalition of 19 developed and developing agricultural exporting countries with a commitment to achieving free trade in agriculture. Members of the Cairns Group are: Argentina, Australia, Brazil, Canada, Chile, Colombia, Costa Rica, Guatemala, Indonesia, Malaysia, New Zealand, Pakistan, Paraguay, Peru, the Philippines, South Africa, Thailand, Uruguay and Viet Nam. Hungary (now part of the European Union) and Fiji were founding members of the Cairns Group, but have since withdrawn. Bolivia's status as a Cairns Group Member is under review.

[101] United Nations Institute for Training and Research (UNITAR), Performing Effectively in Multilateral Conferences and Diplomacy - Welcome to the World of Multilateral Conferences, 2006, p.28.

the framework for past conferences will remain as familiar landmarks of multilateral conference's diplomatic interaction. Accordingly, the eleven elements common to all multilateral conferences are:

1. Mandate. We underlined that every conference needs a mandate, defining what it is supposed to do (see chapter 2.3). Decidedly, this is one of the essential determinants of what the conference will actually do. We need to emphasize that the mandate is determined before the conference begins and cannot be changed by the conference.

2. Delegates. We noted that a multilateral conference is a meeting of representatives of states, and sometimes other actors[102] are involved. These representatives are called delegates because authority has been delegated to them to speak on behalf of their government or organization. There is a distinction between **observers** and **full members**. Strictly speaking, in many UN conferences there is only one delegate per participating State who leads a delegation. In general usage, however, all members of delegations are referred to as delegates. The word delegate is also loosely applied to people whose formal title is observer or who are members of a delegation and led by an observer (informally known as an observer delegation). These are representatives of entities which are not entitled to full participation in the conference but nonetheless are allowed to attend at least part of the time. For example: at a COPs meeting to a treaty, non-parties are not full members but may wish to follow the proceedings; the Executive Committee of WHO consists of representatives of 32 Members elected by the WHA, still, other Members may also wish to follow its work; at conferences in which only states participate, international organizations and/or NGOs may also wish to be present. Many conferences have arrangements to accommodate non-members by providing for observer status. The *degree of access* allowed to observer delegations – if indeed any are allowed to attend - varies considerably from conference to conference. In any case, the observer delegations have not accepted the mandate of the conference and in no case can they participate in decision-making.[103] It is noteworthy that when the WTO was

---

[102] The other actors - entities which are sometimes invited to send delegates to multilateral conferences are international organizations, the EU and non-governmental organizations (NGOs). A donor's meeting might, for example, include representatives of UN agencies such as the United Nations Development Programme (UNDP) and the World Food Programme (WFP), besides the representatives of donor governments. NGOs focused on Human Rights are represented at meetings of the Human Rights Council as observers. Other NGOs are full members of some conferences, notably conferences of the International Labour Organization (ILO) where Worker and Employer Delegations, (representing national NGOs) sit alongside government delegations.

created in 1995, WTO Members established a legal basis for consultation and cooperation with NGOs. NGOs can register to take part in Ministerial Conferences and during a Ministerial Conference NGOs are briefed regularly about the progress of discussions between WTO members. Outside the Ministerial Conference framework, the NGOs representatives accredited to the WTO receive regular briefings on WTO issues.

Another category of participants that are present at some conferences, are neither full member delegates nor observers. These are called **"interested parties"**, "experts", "partners" even in most conferences they have no official designation. For example: the representatives of the secretariat of an international organization at a meeting of the governing body of that organization; an expert invited to contribute to discussions. Any such participants are present by invitation and, like observers, excluded from some meetings and from all decision-making. They are only allowed to participate in other conference activities to the degree determined by the conference. Conferences admit the delegations representatives of observers or "interested parties" or "experts" or "partners" (if the conference's rules of procedure allow) which do not wish to participate in debates and negotiations but are interested in the discussions and outcome of the conference.[104]

Credentials are an important aspect of a multilateral conference as all delegates need to establish their entitlement to be present in the conference room. This involves satisfying two criteria: that they represent the State or other entity which they claim to represent; and that that entity is entitled to send a representative to the conference.

The word credentials (originally, "letters of credence") was initially applied to the document identifying an ambassador and introducing him or her to the host authorities. For an international conference, credentials take the form of a *letter of appointment* - usually issued by an appropriate representative of the Government or international organization. These Credentials have to be original letters. In case of major conferences, government delegates need credentials from their Head of State, Head of Government or Foreign Affairs Minister. Heads of State, Heads of

---

[103] United Nations Institute for Training and Research (UNITAR), Performing Effectively in Multilateral Conferences and Diplomacy - Welcome to the World of Multilateral Conferences, 2006, pp.29-31.

[104] Năstase Dan, Drept diplomatic şi consular, Editura Fundaţiei România de Mâine, Bucuresti, 2006, p.123.

Government and Foreign Affairs Ministers do not need credentials to identify them. For less formal conferences or conferences of lower status, a letter from the head of the Permanent Mission suffices.[105] The Credentials for international organizations delegates need to be signed by the Head of the international organizations. Similarly, non-State delegations need documents from the organization they represent to establishing their status. In the case of NGOs this is called an *accreditation form*.

It is usual for the Conference Secretariat to check the credentials and entitlement of observers and at less formal conferences for other delegates as well. Many of the big conferences have a *Credentials Committee* composed of full member delegates to perform this task. In most cases, this checking is only a formality and often no fuss will be made if credentials arrive late. Technically, a delegation which does not have credentials in good order is not entitled to participate in the conference and in particular it cannot take part in decision-making by the conference - and these rules could be enforced at any time. *We underline that failure to submit credentials or to submit them properly can result in exclusion from decision-making.* Many conferences also establish time limits before the opening of the conference for the submission of credentials. Delegations might send the Credentials by fax initially, with the obligation to present the originals before the conference begins, the latest at the first day of the conference. We underline that credentials need to be submitted in their original; faxes and copies are not accepted.

Any delegate can at any time oppose the credentials of another delegation, for various reasons:[106] opposition to the regime in charge of that country, popular resentment at home against that country or its government, belief that to question the existence of that country is in own government interests, elimination for tactical reasons as the delegation in question cannot vote (if its credential are found not in order) or block consensus (this is very rarely done as the delegation might retaliate in future conferences). A frivolous or quarrelsome opposition could be costly to the delegation raising it, as a majority of delegations would see this as inappropriate and unfavourable to their objectives. However, there are some situations in which a challenge is unavoidable as in the situation when two governments or two delegations claim to represent the same State, or when there

---

[105] Walker R.A., Manual for UN Delegates - Conference Process, Procedure and Negotiation, UN Publication, 2011, p.57.

[106] Op.cit., p. 59.

are grounds for questioning a state's right to participate in the conference (for example: following the dismantlement of the Socialist Federal Republic of Yugoslavia (SFRY) and the demise of that State, several UN Members objected to the Federal Republic of Yugoslavia's claim that as successor State, it automatically inherited the SFRY membership).[107]

The most important observation about delegates (and other participants) is that they are the people who actually perform the conference. Everything that happens during the conference depends on their personal characteristics and individual abilities and weaknesses. The delegates are principal "performers" and have personal responsibility for the course and outcome of the conference.

3. Bureau (Steering Committee). It is composed of the Presiding officer (Conference Chairman) plus the vice-presidents (vice-chairmen) and sometimes a Rapporteur[108] and the presidents of main committees. It sometimes meets as a steering committee.[109] Every conference needs to be managed, which means it needs a manager (known as President or Chairman) or management team. Usually in the UN System and the WTO context, this team is elected by the conference, however in some circumstances it is appointed (mainly for some working groups, expert groups, contact groups, host country representative, etc.). We noted that each national (or other) delegation has its own objectives and concerns. To be successful a conference needs not only a management team but also an effective leader in the person of a Chairman who serves the collective purpose of the conference, as opposed to the concerns of any particular government or organization.

A **conference Chairman** (which is also called President) leads the negotiations (or debates) and combines the roles of conference manager and that of the "delegate for the conference as a whole" (see chapter 7).[110] Although the Chairman has authority on the formal proceedings of the conference and exercise leadership, he or she can only act with the consent of the conference, as the

---

[107] United Nations Institute for Training and Research (UNITAR), Performing Effectively in Multilateral Conferences and Diplomacy - Welcome to the World of Multilateral Conferences, 2006, p.32.

[108] According to Walker, Rapporteur is a person charged with responsibility for the preparation of a report (see Walker Ronald A., Multilateral Conferences: Purposeful International Negotiation. London: Palgrave Macmillan, 2004).

[109] Walker R.A., Multilateral Conferences: Purposeful International Negotiation. London: Palgrave Macmillan, 2004, p. xvi.

[110] Năstase Dan, Drept diplomatic şi consular, Editura Fundaţiei România de Mâine, Bucureşti, 2006, p.124.

authority belongs to the conference (not to the Chairman) and it unfolds based on the principle of equal sovereignty.[111] In larger conferences, the Chairman is assisted by a number of **vice-chairmen** and a **Rapporteur**. The role of vice-chairman is largely honorific, but they substitute for the chairman if the latter has to be out of the conference room during a meeting. The Rapporteur is in charge of the conference report. As this is a more "hands-on" role, it is sometimes allocated to a lower ranking officer than are the offices of chairman and vice-chairmen.

This team of conference officers is often referred to as the **Bureau of the conference**.[112] The vice chairmen and rapporteur are elected by the conference and from among the delegates (see chapter 3.1.7). Chairmen come to their position by election, by rotation or by prior arrangement. However, (as a general rule) a Chairman does not concurrently act as representative of one of the Members or organizations. If he or she is a delegate (as it is often the case), once becoming Chairman he or she ceases to act as a delegate and another delegation member takes over to speak and vote for the delegation.

4. Secretariat. Every conference has one other *conference officer*: the secretary, who heads the *Conference Secretariat*. The secretary and Secretariat staff are not elected, they are international civil servants[113] (often members of the secretariat of an international organization or an ad hoc body mandated to service a conference, sometimes it consists of a team specially recruited from a variety of sources for a particular conference). As such, they do not represent any state or party participating in the conference. **The formal role of the Conference Secretariat** is to *provide administrative support to the conference*. Similar to the procedural roles of the presiding officers, the functions of a conference secretariat are often indicated in the statute of the organization, in a treaty and/or in a conference's rules of procedure. For example, secretariats receive and distribute papers for the conference; some of them write *verbatim*[114] or summary records of

---

[111] Op.cit., p.124.

[112] Walker R.A., Manual for UN Delegates - Conference Process, Procedure and Negotiation, UN Publication, 2011, pp.60-62.

[113] International civil servants are individuals who are in the exclusive long term employment of an international organisation and who have international status. In principle, they enjoy the same privileges and immunities as diplomats. Their status is defined in the statutes of the international organisation which employs them and is also regulated by the Headquarters agreement that this international organisation has concluded with the State that hosts its headquarters. International civil servants are not allowed to receive instructions from their countries of origin (see ABC of Diplomacy, Swiss Federal Department of Foreign Affairs (FDFA), Swiss Confederation, 2008).

[114] *Verbatim*: Word-for-word, in full. How a statement is to be reproduced in the official records or conference report (Latin). *Verbatim records* (only at some major conferences) - Verbatim (i.e.

what is said in the conference; others provide translation and interpretation services, etc. They may also write papers to the attention of the conference or its chairman (e.g. a compilation of proposals or a draft report). **The informal role of the Conference Secretariat** is much wider. The Secretariat staff is knowledgeable of precedents and procedures and as such it is well placed to advise the Chairman and delegations. More generally, it has a very important role in disseminating information to delegations. Although it is supposed to be impartial, in practice it is often committed to the mandate of the conference and, consequently, allies of the chairman and all delegations that do not want the conference to fail. In both its formal and informal roles, the Secretariat can be very helpful to delegations.[115]

The Secretariat's task is very demanding, always subject to deadlines and often under financial pressures and working in difficult conditions. Just as conferences can fail if it is poorly managed, or if delegates behave unconstructively, the work of a conference will be severely impeded if the Secretariat's performance is inadequate. Conversely, a smoothly and professionally functioning secretariat can play a big role in the success of a conference. It is noteworthy that delegates not only make full use of the Secretariat's assistance but they also provide help to the Secretariat if they can.

5. Host Country. Host Country proposes a venue (city, town, other site) on its territory where the conditions for organizing a conference are met. Generally, the venue of the conference (site of conference's work) is inviolable and the authorities of the Host Country cannot act there without the approval of the conference - those nominated by the participants to represent the conference. Also, the Host Country needs to give assurance and take the necessary measures that the conference's work unfolds in security and the delegates are protected.[116] Many conferences hosted by countries, including large *ad hoc* conferences (for example: World Summit on Sustainable Development - WSSD, World Summit on Information Society - WSIS) and regularly scheduled conferences (for example: WTO biannual Ministerial Conference, annual World Innovation

---

full) records of all statements made in a conference. It is prepared by the conference secretariat (see A Glossary of Terms for UN Delegates, UNITAR, 2005).

[115] United Nations Institute for Training and Research (UNITAR), Performing Effectively in Multilateral Conferences and Diplomacy - Welcome to the World of Multilateral Conferences, 2006, pp.34-35.

[116] Năstase Dan, Drept diplomatic şi consular, Editura Fundaţiei România de Mâine, Bucuresti, 2006, p.124.

Summit for Education - WISE, annual COPs) require a Host Country secretariat to assume important on-site preparatory arrangements in close coordination with the (international) Secretariat. These tasks include identifying and securing a suitable conference venue, ensuring that there is sufficient accommodation given the expected number of delegates, arranging venues for parallel events,[117] etc. Apart from the considerable amount of income that can be generated locally, governments often want to host an international conference for reasons of visibility, reputation and prestige, or due to their support and commitments to the conference's collective purpose.[118] Beyond supporting the conference through on-site operations and logistics, some host countries organize pre-conference events that address important issues related to the substance and process of the conference.

6. Conference Structure. Conferences generally have a *hierarchical structure*, with the Plenary[119] of the conference always at the top. Most conferences create a subsidiary body, that is to say a *conference-within-the-conference* with a mandate assigned to it by the main conference, to perform a specified task and to report back. These subsidiary bodies are often called **committees** or sub-committees (whose mandate might be, for example, to draft a text for consideration by the parent conference), which, in turn, sometimes establish **working groups** to continue discussion and negotiation on more detailed elements of a document. Usually, such subsidiary bodies are smaller than their parent conference.[120] If they are **open-ended meetings** any delegation can participate but some choose not to; if their membership is **restricted** the selection is usually by election. For example: the many **functional commissions** of ECOSOC, such as the Commission on Narcotic Drugs and the Commission on

---

[117] According to Walker, Parallel events are events organized by someone other than the organizers of an international conference to run concurrently with the conference. Parallel events are often organized by NGOs and sometimes by a government or international organization (see Walker Ronald A., Multilateral Conferences: Purposeful International Negotiation. London: Palgrave Macmillan, 2004).

[118] Walker R.A., Multilateral Conferences: Purposeful International Negotiation. London: Palgrave Macmillan, 2004, p. 99.

[119] According to Walker, Plenary is the whole conference meeting as such, as opposed to its committees or other offshoots (see Walker Ronald A., Multilateral Conferences: Purposeful International Negotiation. London: Palgrave Macmillan, 2004).

[120] According to Walker, Parent conference is the conference that creates committees or other subsidiary bodies that are dependent on the conference which created them (see Walker Ronald A., Multilateral Conferences: Purposeful International Negotiation. London: Palgrave Macmillan, 2004).

Sustainable Development, are subsidiary bodies of ECOSOC, with a **restricted membership**, elected by ECOSOC from among its Members.

Large conferences, notably in the **UN System**, often have a pre-determined structure. Besides the full conference, known as the **Plenary**, there are a number of **open-ended main committees** amongst which the work programme of the conference is distributed. The questions are discussed and the suggested decisions are debated "in committees", "in commissions", "in expert groups", whichever seems appropriate.

Sometimes there is a **Committee of the whole**, which is effectively a single main committee; there can also be a **Credentials Committee**[121] (usually of restricted membership). Sometimes there is also a **Steering Committee,**[122] to help the Chairman manage some aspects of the organization of the conference's work. But the committees and other subsidiary bodies do not take decisions on behalf of the parent conference. They report to and can make recommendations to the plenary. The Plenary considers these reports and recommendations and takes all the decisions (which usually follow the committee's recommendations but can depart from them).[123] The relationship and division of work between the plenary and its subsidiaries, shows that subsidiary bodies tend to do more detailed work, hold more negotiation and be less formal and less open to the public than their parent conferences. This is least pronounced in the case of large, important, long established subsidiaries, such as the Main Committees of the UN General Assembly (UNGA) and the functional commissions of ECOSOC (which are very formal and public), but it remains valid for their subsidiary bodies.

In the **WTO context**, the Ministerial Conference provides a Plenary session, which offers an opportunity for Ministers to make prepared statements in accordance with the list of speakers opened for inscription before the conference. The list of speakers is taken up, starting with the hosts and chairmen of previous WTO Ministerial Conferences in chronological order, in keeping with established

---

[121] According to Walker, Credential Committee is the Committee whose function is to verify the validity of credentials. (see Walker Ronald A., Multilateral Conferences: Purposeful International Negotiation. London: Palgrave Macmillan, 2004).

[122] According to Walker, Steering Committee is a committee composed of a relatively small number of the members of a conference, charged with organising its work (see Walker Ronald A., Multilateral Conferences: Purposeful International Negotiation. London: Palgrave Macmillan, 2004).

[123] United Nations Institute for Training and Research (UNITAR), Performing Effectively in Multilateral Conferences and Diplomacy - Welcome to the World of Multilateral Conferences, 2006, p.39.

practice. In parallel to the Plenary session, informal sessions for Ministers might be organized.

All multilateral conferences, large or small, end with a **Closing Session,** where the participants take stock of the results of the conference.

7. Venues. Conference venues include, first and foremost, the conference rooms. Although they come in different shapes and sizes, they have several points in common. There are rows of desks or tables, with each desk or section of table identified by a **nameplate** or **placard** for each delegation. With each nameplate, there are a number of seats, with up to three rows in some conferences behind the desk or table and, in large rooms, a microphone. All the desks face a raised **podium** at which there are seats, nameplates and microphones for the Chairman, secretary and Rapporteur. A variation on this arrangement is used in conferences where the chairmanship rotates monthly (for example: in the Security Council the table is a broken circle, in the Conference on Disarmament the table is a hollow square) or every six month (for example in the EU, where the table is a square or circle depending on the meeting settings: in the European Commission or Council of the EU).

The seating is arranged in alphabetical order. This order can be the main **working language** of the conference, of the States and organizations represented, starting with either A or a letter chosen at random. For example, at the UN General Assembly in New York, Members are seated according to the alphabetical order in English. In Geneva, at the Council for Human Rights for example, this order is according to the alphabetical order in French.

These arrangements show the importance of diplomatic protocol[124] in multilateral conferences. At the 1818 Congress of Aix-la-Chapelle it was agreed that states would sign treaties in alphabetical order. Currently, many international organizations use this principle for seating representatives, rather than working out precedence as one still does with ambassadors accredited to states. While alphabetization is popular, there are several forms in use. The UN seats delegations alphabetically by the state's name in English, with the first letter of the alphabet being determined annually by lot. NATO's Permanent Representatives are seated alphabetically. The Council of Europe uses a mixed system, with the Committee of Ministers being arranged by their date of taking

---

[124] According to Walker, Diplomatic protocol is the universally applicable rules governing the interaction of representatives of sovereign states (see Walker Ronald A., Multilateral Conferences: Purposeful International Negotiation. London: Palgrave Macmillan, 2004).

office, the Assembly by age, and at official meetings of the Council by alphabetical order in French. Alphabetization can raise issues of language politics, and the EU Council resolved this issue by seating states in alphabetical order following the state's own language, following the sequence of the rotation Presidency of the Council of the European Union, according to Lisbon Treaty,[125] while the EU Commissioners sit by date of appointment. The Organization of American States (OAS) draws countries by lot each time it meets.[126]

In the conference room, the seating at the front is reserved for the delegations of full members of the conference. Following these, or down the sides of the room are seated, again in alphabetical order, delegations representing observer States, then observer delegations of international organizations and finally observer NGOs. Sometimes there is also separate seating for media representatives and for the public. In large conference rooms there is also provision for various categories of secretariat staff: record writers, interpreters, documentation service, etc.

In addition to these large conference rooms (which are used for plenary and the main committees) there is a need for several smaller conference rooms (the smallest often have desks arranged in a hollow square, no nameplates and no microphones or interpretation) and extensive lobbies or wide corridors. Delegates use these rooms for appropriate purposes (see chapter 3).

8. Rules of Procedure. As a conference needs a leader to manage the conference's works, it also needs rules for smooth unfolding. The major particularity of the multilateral conference is the importance of the rules of procedure (see chapter 3). When, as in the case of the UN, 193 delegations or as in the case of the WTO, 164 delegations have to communicate with each other at the same time, there must be some rather clear and strict rules to maintain orderly interactions. Thus, the rules of procedure have been called *the highway code of the multilateral conference.*[127] They are a set of rules, which describe in detail how the conference should operate. One of the main functions of the Chairman is

---

[125] Treaty of Lisbon amending the Treaty on European Union and the Treaty establishing the European Community (2007/C 306/01). The Treaty of Lisbon was signed by the EU Member States on 13.12.2007, and entered into force on 01.12.2009.

[126] Goldstein Erik, Developments in protocol, Modern Diplomacy. Edited by J. Kurbalija, 1998. (available at diplomacy.edu).

[127] Chrisspeels Erik, Procedures of Multilateral Conference Diplomacy, in M.A. Boisard and E.M. Chossudovsky, Multilateral Diplomacy: The United Nations System at Geneva, A Working Guide. The Hague: Kluwer Law International, 1998, p.119.

to apply the rules and when necessary enforce them. Each conference has its own rules of procedure, which it has adopted or received from a main body (for example, ECOSOC has adopted a set of rules of procedure which apply to all of its subsidiary bodies).

9. Sovereignty. One of the defining characteristics of multilateral conferences is that they are composed of representatives of sovereign states[128] and sometimes various organizations. According to international law, the state has the right to exist, the right of independence and the right of equality.[129] The last two has the most consequences in terms of multilateral conference, like:

- The representatives of sovereign States are entitled to be treated with respect and they are entitled to strictly equal treatment. For example, in a typical formal conference room, each delegation has the same desk space and the same number of seats reserved for it, whether its national population is 100,000 or over 1,000 million. Likewise, whether its state is a military power or if it comes to a vote, each delegation has one vote, which is equal to that of any other delegation. (Still there are conferences were weighted voting is applied, like in the European Union or the Bretton Woods Institutions - World Bank, IMF, where not every Member has the same number of votes. The principle is the same in the other development banks for Asia, Africa and America). If interventions must be limited due to time constraints, the same duration is applied to all.

- No-one can tell sovereign states (represented in conferences by their delegates) what to do. They only do what they consent to do. A Chairman never directs representatives of sovereign states, he or she asks or invites them to do certain things or suggests a course of action. The conference mandate and rules of procedure apply to delegates and limit their freedom of action, but only because the states and organizations they represent have accepted them - either by participating in their adoption or by accepting an invitation to participate in a conference that is subject to them.

- Authority belongs to the conference, "every conference is sovereign". It can take whatever decisions it chooses, alter its own rules of procedure, but it cannot issue directions to any other conference.

---

[128] According to Article 1 of Montevideo Convention on Rights and Duties of States, enacted on 26.12.1933 and entered into force on 26.12.1934, the state as a person of international law should possess the following qualifications: a) permanent population; b) defined territory; c) government; and d) capacity to enter into relations with the other states.

[129] Marshall Brown Philip, The Theory of the Independence and Equality of States, The American Journal of International Law Vol. 9, No. 2/ April 1915, pp. 305-335, Published by: American Society of International Law DOI: 10.2307/2187161, p. 305. (available at jstor.org).

- No conference can issue directions to any sovereign state. But conversely, all decisions or statements by multilateral conferences are very authoritative: they carry the weight and authority of all the participating states (even if any abstained or voted against, since they are parties to the agreement, that voting is a way whereby the conference can make collective decisions). A statement or decision by a conference is a statement or decision by all the states represented (or all those entitled to be represented) in that conference. A government can legitimately say that its own views are different, but it cannot change the fact that the statement represents the collective view of the conference. In the case of conference decisions, governments are more tightly bound (even if they put forward - where possible - a legally valid explicit disclaimer at the time the decision is made). Any government which does not conform to such decisions acts contrary to what it solemnly told all other governments (and people, including its own electorate) it would do. As it had made this commitment on behalf of its state, to later renege is to bring the state into contempt. In addition, depending on the specifics of each case, it might act illegally.[130]

10. Results of conferences: Agreement or disagreement (no agreement). We noted that conferences do a lot of things, including demonstrating shared commitments or emotions and providing venues for the exchange of information and the dissemination of the views and policies of governments. However, in terms of concrete results by the conference itself, it can only do one thing: it can adopt sets of words (i.e. making these words become words of the conference). These sets of words can be exhortations, declarations, treaties, technical standards, reports of many kinds, etc. but they are all adopted in the same manner: **by consent**. It flows from the sovereignty of the represented states that the conference can only act by agreement. It can only act with the consent of all or, in those cases where the relevant rules of procedure permit decisions by a vote, only in accordance with rules which all have previously accepted.[131]

This is the foundation of any conference. Since conferences can only act by agreement (by adopting words), the only way each delegate can hope to achieve his or her objectives is by securing the agreement of the conference. Sometimes, multilateral conferences are unproductive for advancing objectives which are

---

[130] United Nations Institute for Training and Research (UNITAR), Performing Effectively in Multilateral Conferences and Diplomacy - Welcome to the World of Multilateral Conferences, 2006, pp. 41-43.

[131] States accept rules by becoming parties to treaties or by accepting invitations to participate in conferences/meetings subject to those rules.

contrary to the objectives or principles of most governments, but they can be very effective for advancing widely shared objectives and principles. Moreover, the best way to achieve one's own objectives is to reflect them in proposals which will be attractive to most others because they serve their objectives. Still, since the states are sovereigns, they remain able to refrain from complying even after giving their word or a verbal commitment. Thus, the best way of achieving one's own real-world objectives is to incorporate them in proposals which other governments will willingly implement because they serve their objectives. Also, the art of compromise (a concession in secondary matters) could be useful in achieving one's own real-world objectives, taking into account that if there is no political will even the best representative of a sovereign state cannot do much. Achieving one's own real-world objectives is by getting the conference to agree to a proposal which advances those goals, anything impeding agreement hampering the achievement of those objectives. Equally, if the conference is moving towards agreement on a proposal contrary to one's own real-world objectives, anything which impedes agreement discourages that proposal. If the proposal is one on which the conference was approaching agreement, it means it is seen by most delegations helpful to their objectives. The delegations will be resentful of any attempt to sabotage agreement and will work against the perpetrator. Impeding agreement or attempting to do so is not only selfish, it can be costly. Undoubtedly multilateral diplomacy drastically limits the egoistical aspirations of the States.[132]

11. Conference dynamics. A multilateral conference is a meeting of sovereign States (and at times organizations) but the meeting takes place between representatives (i.e. the delegates, including observers): in the last resort, a conference is a room full of people. Of course, these are a special kind of people. They often carry instructions from the authority which sent them and are always accountable for their actions. They have responsibilities (the most prominent being to do the best they can for the entity they represent). They have each their own distinctive perspective (largely determined by the entity they represent). They have differing personalities, degrees of motivation, value systems and capabilities etc. and, finally, they are all human beings, with all the characteristics that entails, including such simple things as wishing to be treated with respect and satiating basic needs. Therefore, what happens in a conference room, including the decisions taken, depends on the behaviour of these people and thus on everything influencing their behaviour. This is why conference managers - and

---

[132] Petrovsky Vladimir, Diplomacy as an instrument of good governance, Modern Diplomacy, Edited by J. Kurbalija, 1998. (available at diplomacy.edu).

everyone concerned for the conference's outcome - see the merit of ensuring that delegates are not subject to conditions which predispose them to disagreement (such as: excessive stress of any kind, irritation on any grounds, etc.) and of promoting everything that contributes to a sense of harmony and predilection to seek to accommodate each other's concerns.

The conference dynamics comprise its collective mood, which can be constructive or to the contrary unfavourable to agreement. The ability to handle this attitude is one of the high level conference diplomatic skills. However, the delegates should be alert to the evolving conference mood, not surrender to it without consciously choosing to do so and notice attempts to control it for reprehensible purposes. Ideally, the delegates participate in overcoming any harmful influence and join in promoting an atmosphere conducive to positive outcome and agreements for their own country and entire humanity.

Chapter 3 – Process of multilateral conferences

All the characteristics and functions of multilateral conferences are highlighted during the conference's process, the course of action that makes a conference work.

3.1 Phases of multilateral conferences

There is a wide spectrum of complexity and formality between, on one hand, a small meeting of short duration, attended by officers of relatively lower ranks and not called upon to make crucial decisions (like an expert meeting) and, on the other hand, a large conference such as the UN General Assembly (UNGA), WTO Ministerial Conference or the COP21[133] which was attended by more than 40,000 delegates from 195 countries, many of them led at very senior, often ministerial, levels, and called upon to make a number of decisions that are politically contentious.

We analyse big conferences, in scale and complexity, like UNGA, COPs or WTO Ministerial Conference, which are large meetings with a heavy and politically sensitive work load and lasting several weeks (in the case of UNGA) or days (in the case of WTO Ministerial Conference). The smaller and less politically charged conferences are the less formal and less complicated. Nevertheless, what happens at less elaborate conferences can be seen as a "minimalist" version of the larger ones. Hence, the phases of a multilateral conference are specific to all, big or small, with the same applicable principles, but with different manifestation in a more or less elaborate manner.

There is, however, no rigid template to which all conferences must conform. To the contrary, for practical, institutional, historical and/or other reasons, each conference has its own peculiarities, especially concerning the nomenclature. Broad principles generally applicable and widely recurring patterns are relevant for all multilateral conferences, those being adapted and flexible depending of the particularities of each conference.[134]

---

[133] In December 2015, COP21, also known as the 2015 Paris Climate Conference, for the first time in over 20 years of United Nations negotiations, achieved a legally binding and universal agreement on climate, with the aim of keeping global warming below 2°C.

[134] United Nations Institute for Training and Research (UNITAR), Performing Effectively in Multilateral Conferences and Diplomacy - The Formal and Informal Process of Conferences,

3.1.1 Pre-conference preparations

A regular character of a conference is achieved either by the statute prescribing or itself determining a regular periodicity. If periodicity is not provided by the establishment agreement or another international instrument, it is essential to have the agreement of the Members/Participating States on the date of reconvening a meeting.[135]

It is noteworthy that once the periodicity of certain conferences is firmly established, it is extremely difficult to modify the frequency of its meetings; many delegates who return each year will resent such a modification. Hence, it is important that the planning of meetings' organization begins with few gatherings rather than with a relatively large number. It is always easier to add a few meetings than to renounce to some of them when they have become an established routine.[136] Thus, and as we noted in chapter 2, some conferences are held on a **regular basis**, the most famous examples being the UN General Assembly (UNGA) which gathers in New York each September and runs through into the first half of the following year; and the WTO Ministerial Conference which takes place every two years in diverse locations and whose attributes are carried on by the WTO General Council in between the two sessions of the Ministerial Conference. Other organizations, like FAO or UNESCO, have their plenary conference every two years. Other examples of conferences taking place at regular intervals are some Conferences or Meetings of the Parties to a treaty (COPs/MOPs) and the annual pledging conferences organized by UNHCR to support its assistance to refugees. Similarly, there are the annually held BRICS Summits or the annually held Arab League Summits. At European level, meetings of the European Council usually take place four times a year in Brussels. Meetings traditionally last for two days, sometimes even longer when contentious issues are on the agenda. On the other hand, there are so called "*ad hoc* conferences*", the oldest form of multilateral diplomacy and utilized for casual, temporary and specific matters, conferences that are specially convened to address an issue that is thought not to be adequately addressed by the permanent (regular) conferences: they are either "one offs" or the first in a new series of

---

2006, p. 7.

[135] Kaufmann J., Conference Diplomacy: An Introductory Analysis, 2nd revised edition, Martinus Nijhoff Publishers, UNITAR, 1988, p. 49.

[136] The date on which a meeting starts is sometimes fixed by tradition like the UNGA which normally begins the third Tuesday in September or the ILO Conference which starts the first Wednesday in June.

conferences. Occasionally, general conferences (see chapter 2.1) decides that a negotiating conference should be called to draw up a draft treaty on a particular topic.[137] Sometimes, other conferences arise as a result of the initiative of one or more governments or international organizations.[138]

Long before conferences convene, the governments and organizations most interested in the issues the conference addresses start exchanging ideas about what the conference should do precisely, how it should be organized, etc. Five of the most important topics in such **preliminary exchanges** are as follows:

- **The place of the conference. The Host Country and the venue**. The place of the conference is where the conference is held. Most conferences are held under the auspices of an international organization, being relatively easy to maintain a certain routine. Like the UN General Assembly (UNGA) and the main organs of the specialize agencies, many conferences have a regularly established frequency and venue; but for other conferences, especially new conferences, the venue needs to be chosen. This is partly a matter of practicality, such as where adequate conference facilities are available at the requested period or which country invites the conference to one of its cities and provides funding. Certain organizations have adopted a pattern of periodically convening elsewhere but the headquarters. The annual session of the Governors of the International Bank for Reconstruction and Development (the World Bank) and the International Monetary Fund (IMF) meets every other year away from Washington DC, the headquarters site. Similarly, the WTO Ministerial Conference is very often held away from Geneva, WTO's headquarters. A special case is represented by the European Union, as the rotating Presidency of the Council of the EU, among other tasks, organises various formal and informal meetings in Brussels and in the country which holds the rotating presidency.[139] A meeting away from headquarters, unless prepared with special care, may create some confusion, as the normal conference procedure somehow is not immediately functional in the new environment. This danger is overcome by combined action of the Host Country and the Secretariat, as a result of which delegates are aware, before or immediately after the arrival, of various practical details and any special procedures. Even with fully

---

[137] The intergovernmental negotiating committees to elaborate the climate and biodiversity conventions were established by resolutions of the General Assembly, as was the Third United Nations Conference on the Law of the Sea (UNCLOS).

[138] The conference which led to the Mine Ban Treaty was called at the initiative of Canada after the Convention on Certain Conventional Weapons (CCW) review process resulted in an agreement that some considered inadequate to respond to the global landmine crisis.

[139] The Presidency of the Council of the EU rotates among Member States every 6 months.

adequate services and facilities on the Secretariat and Host Country's part, some uncertainness resulting from the unfamiliarity of the conference site may persist and unfavourably affect the smooth unfolding of the conference. Occasionally, the place of the conference is chosen for other considerations such as: political reasons [140] or conferences intentionally held in specific place directly related to the subject.[141] In a wider sense, it is useful that certain periodically held conferences are from time to time convened in an environment where the delegates can observe some of the problems they are dealing with. Thus, UN Conference on Trade and Development (UNCTAD), which deals with problems of developing countries, held in developing countries twelve out of its fourteen Conferences[142] organized till date, and two at its headquarters in Geneva.

- **The Presiding officer (Chairman)**. Some chairmen are elected by the conference over which they will preside (see chapter 2.4). Choosing an individual who has the right personal qualities and who is widely acceptable from a political point of view can be decisive for the success of the conference. Consequently, there is often very wide consultation before a conference to reach a prior agreement as to who is the most appropriate Chairman (see chapter 7).

- **The agenda**. It consists of subjects to be discussed during the conference. The conference decides on its work programme or agenda, but initially it must have a *provisional agenda* prepared well before it meets and which participants have had time to consider. The provisional agenda is usually prepared by the Secretariat (in close consultation with the proposed chairman) and typically consists of a number of regular or otherwise obvious items, plus items referred by other conferences and/or (in many cases) items proposed by individual Members. Frequently, some items

---

[140] For example, it was considered appropriate that the follow-up 1972 UN Conference on the Human Environment (Stockholm Conference) - UN Conference on the environment and development (UNCED) to be held in a developing country exposed to the twin challenges of economic development and environmental sustainability. Both considerations are sometimes answered when an appropriate government, which is in a position to do so, offers one of its cities as the conference venue, as, in this case, the Brazilian government did for the 1992 Earth Summit which was held in Rio de Janeiro.

[141] For example, a WMO/UNESCO Symposium on Hydrological Forecast met in 1967 in Surfers' Paradise, Queensland, Australia.

[142] The first UNCTAD conference took place in Geneva in 1964, the second in New Delhi in 1968, the third in Santiago in 1972, fourth in Nairobi in 1976, the fifth in Manila in 1979, the sixth in Belgrade in 1983, the seventh in Geneva in 1987, the eighth in Cartagena in 1992, the ninth at Johannesburg (South Africa) in 1996, the tenth in Bangkok (Thailand) in 2000, the eleventh in São Paulo (Brazil) in 2004, the twelfth in Accra in 2008, the thirteenth in Doha (Qatar) in 2012 and the fourteenth in Nairobi (Kenya) in 2016.

proposed for inclusion require discussions among interested governments and/or organizations prior to the conference.

- **The length.** The time factor plays an essential role in multilateral conferences, even though it is not possible to establish an automatic and generally valid causal relation between the length of the conference and its degree of success or failure. A conference with a fairly heavy agenda lasting for one week makes, immediately after opening, a careful allocation of the various items over the available conference days. A one week conference is in fact a five or at most six days conference. There is bound to be irritation when at the end of the fourth day it becomes clear that the conference is hopelessly short of time. A conference scheduled to last a fairly long period, three or four weeks, suffers from a phenomenon called "conference myopia": attention is focused on the immediate following day, the weeks beyond appear far off and plenty of time seems to be available to deal with the agenda. Suddenly the last week arrives, time is running out and tempers get correspondingly short. Delegates must make careful use of the time available to prepare for the moment of truth, the last days of the conference when the principal decisions must be taken.[143] Each conference must have an optimal duration, which is the length of time needed to get the conference objective accomplished. It may not be optimal to crowd as many sessions as possible into each conference day to shorten the total duration of the conference. Given enough time for informal consultation and negotiations among delegations and for individual delegation to consult with their capitals will often be time gained, not wasted.

Apart from the place (the host country and venue), the Presiding officer, the agenda and the length of the conference, another important element of pre-conference preparations is the drafting and distribution of pre-session conference documents (notifications, background papers, annotated provisional agenda, etc.) which delegates need before or at the conference. These papers are usually prepared by the Conference Secretariat, but sometimes a government or governments also prepare and circulate papers to the participants or, if the applicable rules permit, ask the secretariat to distribute them. Occasionally, the background papers also include texts (reports, for example) adopted by earlier conferences. Other documents are sometimes distributed at conferences (see chapter 3.1.2).

---

[143] Kaufmann J., Conference Diplomacy: An Introductory Analysis, 2nd revised edition, Martinus Nijhoff Publishers, UNITAR, 1988, p. 52.

The political preparations for the conference is also very elaborate and have strong influence on the course and outcome of the conference. Thus, for example, many of the governments having an interest in the substantive matters to be addressed by a conference hold extensive discussions in advance, clarifying the issues, arguing for one or other outcome, lobbying each other for support, etc. Occasionally, some governments may have already engaged in preliminary negotiation on the issues or formed coalitions and plans, in view of advancing their positions and/or proposals. For major conferences, and especially conferences which address a relatively new topic on the international agenda, there are often preliminary meetings of various groups seeking to develop a common approach. There can also be information and exploratory meetings designed to help governments understand the issues the conference addresses and get a preliminary idea of each other's views. Sometimes, such events are organized at the Secretariat's initiative, the Host Country (usually a strong supporter of the conference mandate), other governments, international organizations and even non-governmental organizations (NGOs).[144] For example, in preparation for the fourteenth UNCTAD Conference - UNCTAD XIV (held in Nairobi, Kenya between 17-22 July 2016) the Members had two preparatory hearings with civil society and the private sector, hearings that provided participating organizations the opportunity to contribute to the preparatory process for UNCTAD XIV, to comment on the pre-conference negotiating text, and to discuss with Members issues relevant to the theme and sub-themes of UNCTAD XIV.

3.1.2 Conference documents

We noted that a number of pre-session conference documents are prepared and distributed to delegations before the conference begins. Most pre-session documents (see Table no.3), at least for the larger conferences, can be downloaded and printed from the Conference Secretariat's website. As the conferences vary so much, the number and nature of these pre-session documents range from no more than a **provisional agenda** and **provisional list of participants** to a long list of documents, including notifications, background papers, working papers, non-papers, relevant decisions of previous conferences, and reports from subsidiary bodies.

---

[144] United Nations Institute for Training and Research (UNITAR), Performing Effectively in Multilateral Conferences and Diplomacy - The Formal and Informal Process of Conferences, 2006, p. 10.

Table no. 3 – Examples of pre-session documents

Document name	When it usually appears	Produced by	Circulated by
Notifications	Usually several months before the conference	Secretariat, Members	Secretariat
Provisional agenda	Usually several weeks before the conference	Secretariat (in consultation with Chairman)	Secretariat
Provisional list of participants	Usually a week or two before the conference	Secretariat	Secretariat
Background papers	Distributed on a rolling basis, beginning usually several weeks before the conference	Secretariat, Members, intergovernmental organizations	Secretariat
Relevant decisions of previous conferences	Distributed on a rolling basis, beginning normally several weeks before the conference	Secretariat	Secretariat
Non-papers	Distributed on a rolling basis, beginning usually several weeks before the conference	Delegations, Chairman and, exceptionally, Secretariat	Secretariat or Members
Reports	Several weeks before the conference	Secretariat, subsidiary bodies, other conferences, intergovernmental organizations	Secretariat
Communications from Members	Distributed on a rolling basis, beginning normally several weeks before the conference	Members	Secretariat, Members

Source: Walker Roland A., Manual for UN Delegates - Conference Process, Procedure and Negotiation, UN Publication, 2011, p.64.

At the opening session and during the conference, the secretariat distributes a number of in-session documents (see Table no.4), usually in pigeon holes where delegations can retrieve them during the day. Occasionally, documents are also distributed by the secretariat to each delegation at their desk. In addition, at large conferences (as at the headquarters of the organization), there is a central documents desk (known as **document distribution centre**) where additional copies can be obtained. It is absolutely vital that at least one member of each delegation knows how, when and where the distribution of documents takes place. Among the various conference documents, two are essential for all delegates who wish to participate in the conference's work. One of these is the **schedule of meetings** and other events which is distributed soon after the start of the conference. In addition, at very large conferences, there is a **journal** or **daily programme** issued early each morning, which includes the scheduled meetings of the conference and sometimes a number of special announcements from the secretariat. The other essential document is the **list of participants**. A provisional version is often issued as a pre-session document and a final version is provided a few days after the start of the conference when all delegates have registered. This is an extremely important "tool-of-trade" for delegates as it identifies the people with whom they will have to interact.[145]

---

[145] Walker R.A., Multilateral Conferences: Purposeful International Negotiation. London: Palgrave Macmillan, 2004, p. 132.

Table no. 4 – Examples of in-session documents

Document name	When it usually appears	Produced by	Circulated by
Agenda (definitive)	Very early in the session	Plenary	Secretariat
List of participants (definitive)	2 or 3 days after the start of the conference	Secretariat	Secretariat
Organization of work, schedule of meetings	2 or 3 days after the start of the conference	Chairman, with Secretariat and sometimes a Steering Committee	Secretariat
Daily Journal	Daily	Secretariat	Secretariat
Text of general debate statements	As soon as the speaker starts to deliver it	Delegations	The relevant delegation, sometimes the Secretariat also
Non-papers	Any time before and during a conference, but normally not in the concluding stages	Delegation(s), working group or contact group, chairman and/or bureau	Delegation(s) or Secretariat
Draft proposals (draft resolutions or draft decisions)	Typically, after debate in committee has made some progress	Delegations	Before tabling, the sponsor(s). After tabling, the Secretariat
Amendments to proposals (draft decisions and resolutions)	Any time after the formal proposals have been tabled and discussed	Delegations	Before they are tabled, the sponsor(s). After they are tabled, the Secretariat
Conference room papers (CRPs)	Any time during a conference	Delegation(s), working group, Chairman, bureau or Secretariat	Secretariat
Chairman's compilation, synthesis of proposals, or Chairman's text	After negotiations have been going for a long time	Chairman, sometimes aided by the Secretariat, Friends of the Chair or facilitator	Secretariat
Committee reports	In the final phase	Committee	Secretariat
Draft final document or conference report	Towards the end of the session	Rapporteur or Secretariat	Secretariat

Source: Walker Roland A., Manual for UN Delegates - Conference Process, Procedure and Negotiation, UN Publication, 2011, p. 64.

There are two documents requiring additional explanation:

- A **non-paper**[146] is a text circulated by a delegation, the chairman or (in some conferences) the bureau. It is unofficial and its tentative nature is emphasized. Non-papers are drafted as an aid to understanding or an exploration of a possible initiative or way forward. Non-papers are not formal proposals, but they quite frequently provide the basis for a formal proposal.[147]

- A **conference room paper** (CRP), as its name suggests, is used only in-session and usually does not exist anymore when the conference is over. CRPs serve multiple purposes: as a draft text or draft decision proposed by a delegation or group of delegations; as a report used by the chairman to inform the conference about the status of negotiations or to report on the work of a subsidiary body; as a mean to transmit a Chairman's text to the conference. Contrary to a non-paper, CRPs are officially numbered (for example: CRP1, CRP2). Due to limited time (and sometimes resources) to translate into all of conference's working languages, these documents are often issued only in their original language (usually English).

The UN document numbering system

All official documents of the conference are numbered by the Secretariat in accordance with a standard system (subject to very minor variations) which indicates the text's nature and status, as well as the body for which it was prepared. It is very important that delegates understand the system and be able to recognize the exact status and category of any document. The only papers in circulation at the conference that will not have such a number are those produced and distributed by delegations (e.g. general debate texts) or observers (NGOs). Formally, these are not conference documents. At some large conferences, as the many conferences on environment or sustainable development, in addition to the official documents, there is a daily newspaper, produced by an NGO, which reports on the work of the conference.[148]

---

[146] Non-paper: a text whose lack of formal status is emphasized (see A Glossary of Terms for UN Delegates, UNITAR, 2005).

[147] Walker R.A., Multilateral Conferences: Purposeful International Negotiation. London: Palgrave Macmillan, 2004, p. 204.

[148] Gazarian Jean, UN documentation and document symbols, UNITAR, 2006.

The WTO document numbering system

In general, the document symbol numbers for the WTO use common standard abbreviations: INF for Information note, LET for Letter, M for Minutes, N for Notification, R for Report, SPEC for Special Series, SR for Meeting Summary, W for Working Paper. The WTO applies series of symbols to its basic documentation. The basic scheme is twofold. The first element of the symbol describes a "common legal framework". Within the legal framework, a second element describes a "series" concept. For example, for World Trade Organization Bodies: General Council (WT/GC/), Balance of Payments (WT/BOP/), Dispute Settlement (WT/DS/); for Trade in Goods: Council (G/C), Anti-Dumping (G/ADP/), Safeguards (G/SG/); for Trade in Services: Council (S/C/), Trade in Financial Services (S/FIN/); Intellectual Property: Council (IP/C/), Notifications (IP/N/).[149]

If the documents are circulated during the Ministerial Conference, they are preceded by the symbol "WT/MIN", symbol used also for ministerial declarations or decisions.

3.1.3 Delegate registration

One or two days before the conference is opened the delegates arrive at the venue or, if they are permanently posted there, they turn attention to the conference. The first formality a delegate must perform is to register. This means that they present themselves at the conference venue, with their credentials and passport, so that the Secretariat can check the identity and issue a pass or badge giving the participant access to the conference building. Normally, this formality is performed on the first day of the conference, but it is more efficient to be done earlier. For small informal meetings, such as expert meetings, registration formalities are typically reduced to the delegates completing a short form they find on their desks in the conference room on the opening day.

3.1.4 Opening of the conference and election of the Chairman

The opening of a conference is largely ceremonial and includes the election of the Chairman, unless the Chairman is pre-determined by a system of rotation (for example, as in the Security Council or in the Council of the EU). Although in

---

[149] Eckman C., Documentation and publication of the GATT and WTO-GATT Digital Library, StanfordEdu, 1981, p. 98.

most large conferences the first session is opened by the outgoing Chairman from the previous session or by some other appropriate individual (sometimes the conference secretary or the President of a preparatory committee), the first item on the agenda is always the Chairman's election. In order to avoid any time waste or contention over the choice of Chairman, there is usually prior agreement as to who is elected and thus only one candidate whose election is unanimous.

There is a natural and courteous instinct on the part of delegates to congratulate the Chairman on his or her election as soon as that takes place or whenever the delegates first take the floor,[150] however if they all do, a lot of time would be wasted to the detriment of all participants. Efficient chairmen therefore request delegates to refrain from congratulating them and some rules of procedure strictly limit the number of speakers who may do so. Moreover, in some cultures, such effusions are far from agreeable and some people find them irritating. If some delegates think it is essential to say something polite to the chairman, a sincere statement of looking forward to working constructively with him or her will, in most cases, be appropriate and welcome.[151]

3.1.5 Adoption of the rules of procedure

Following the formal opening and the election of the conference president or chairman, one of the first organizational matters before the conference is the adoption of its rules of procedure. No such action is needed if the conference already has rules of procedure (inherited from previous sessions of the same body, for example) - see chapter 3.2.1.

3.1.6 Adoption of the agenda

The next phase of the conference is to adopt its agenda[152] (i.e. the list of items it will address, the program for a session on an established body). As noted, drafting this document is not a task that is left until the conference starts: a provisional or draft agenda (and often an annotated provisional agenda) is prepared by the secretariat (in consultation and/or agreement with the designated

---

[150] Speaking to the conference, through the Chairman, after being invited by the Chairman to do so.

[151] United Nations Institute for Training and Research (UNITAR), Performing Effectively in Multilateral Conferences and Diplomacy - The Formal and Informal Process of Conferences, 2006, p. 18-19.

[152] Chrisspeels Erik, Procedures of Multilateral Conference Diplomacy, in M.A. Boisard and E.M. Chossudovsky, Multilateral Diplomacy: The United Nations System at Geneva, A Working Guide. The Hague: Kluwer Law International, 1998, p. 122.

chairman) and distributed to delegates some weeks beforehand. If any contentious points existed, most of the differences would have been solved well before the conference opens over thoroughly discussions among interested governments and organizations. However, it occasionally happens that one or another delegate (perhaps one whose government did not participate in the pre-conference consultations or was unable to persuade the others of its preferred position) proposes some change to the provisional agenda. Such questions are usually solved promptly as constructive proposals generally receive instant approval, whereas all delegates understand that to persist in a widely opposed view on the agenda is futile and thus either pointless or deliberate trouble-making, to the detriment of all delegations seriously interested in the conference's work. Once any such issue is settled, the conference adopts the agenda - the conference makes the agenda its own and it is no longer provisional.

3.1.7 Election of the Bureau

The next task of the conference is the election of officers other than the President/Chairman, meaning to give itself the requisite number of vice-chairmen and a Rapporteur. In the interests of expediency and of avoiding controversy, there is usually prior agreement based on consultations as to whom to elect. The Rapporteur needs to be competent, and is usually chosen on merit. However, the positions of vice-chairmen are far less demanding and individual qualifications less important. Consequently, the choice here is likely to be dominated by political factors and specifically the desire and, in the case of some conferences, the requirement of its main body, mandate or rules of procedure, for **geographical balance**. This term refers to the agreed distribution of such elective positions (as well as to membership in some committees or commissions) among the electoral groups.[153] The number and composition of these groups[154] varies greatly from one UN body to another, although most organizations have an African, a Latin American and Caribbean and an Eastern European group.

---

[153] Electoral groups: the groups into which delegations are divided for electoral purposes and for other purposes where geographical equity or representation is wanted (for example,. the distribution of bureau positions in a large conference). The UNGA and each of the specialized agencies have different electoral groups. In general, electoral groups do not caucus on political issues, although a small number of regional groups (notably the African Group and GRULAC) are both electoral and caucus groups (see A Glossary of Terms for UN Delegates, UNITAR, 2005).

[154] Regional Groups of the UN General Assembly: African States (53 States), Asian States (53 States), Eastern European States (23 States), Latin American and Caribbean States (33 States), Western European and Other States (29).

Electoral groups should not be confused with caucus groups [155] (see chapter 3.3.3), although two of the electoral groups (African, and Latin America and the Caribbean) usually also function as a caucus group, as does sometimes the Asia Group.[156] The elective posts are distributed among the regional groups in accordance with a fixed-cycle of rotation. [157] The candidates are nominated by a representative or by regional spokesman, and their nomination is seconded by another representative or regional spokesman.[158]

In the case of WTO, the chairperson of the Ministerial Conference is a high level representative of the Host Country – usually the Minister in charge with trade (for example the Indonesia's Trade for the 9th Ministerial Conference which took place in Bali - 2013, the Kenyan Cabinet Secretary for Foreign Affairs and Trade for the 10th Ministerial Conference which took place in Nairobi - 2015) and the vice-chairs are elected as to keep balance between developed and developing WTO Members. The Officers of the WTO Ministerial Conferences are elected by the General Council before the Ministerial Conference, by consensus[159] of WTO Members.

3.1.8 Organization of work and other administrative issues

Once the agenda is adopted and the bureau elected, the next phase is to decide on the organization of work. Some items are dealt with by the plenary: for example, receiving a report from another body and deciding when and where future meetings of the conference take place. Many agenda items, however, need

---

[155] Caucus group: A group of delegations which meets in the margins of international conferences and outside them, in some cases, to discuss issues relevant to the conference(s) and, in some cases, seek to develop common positions (see A Glossary of Terms for UN Delegates, UNITAR, 2005).

[156] United Nations Institute for Training and Research (UNITAR), Performing Effectively in Multilateral Conferences and Diplomacy - The Formal and Informal Process of Conferences, 2006, p. 20.

[157] For example, UNCTAD's Trade and Development Board has a formal cycle of rotation of groups for the purpose of electing its President and Rapporteur.

[158] Chrisspeels Erik, Procedures of Multilateral Conference Diplomacy, in M.A. Boisard and E.M. Chossudovsky, Multilateral Diplomacy: The United Nations System at Geneva, A Working Guide. The Hague: Kluwer Law International, 1998, p. 124.

[159] Agreement on a given question. The consensus principle applies to decisions taken in the framework of multilateral conferences and international organisations. Consensus is often mistaken for unanimity. The two differ in that consensus is the acceptance of a decision without a vote. If no State expressly declares opposition then a consensus is said to have been reached. This permits one or more States to make reservations without officially blocking consensus. In a formal vote, a State with reservations would be forced to vote against the proposal in question, thus preventing the adoption of the decision.

to be discussed and negotiated in committee before the plenary takes any decisions. Consequently, the agenda is divided between the main committees and, at some conferences, a Committee of the whole, which is, in effect, the Plenary meeting as a committee to facilitate the negotiation of a text.

This organization of work is the allocation of agenda items in a logical manner to assist delegations.[160] The allocation of work includes also an allocation of time to address each agenda item. In particular, each committee reports to its parent body in time for that body (ultimately, the Plenary) to consider the report and take any decisions recommended by the committee report.

The proposed allocation of agenda items and time between the different slots of the conference is submitted by the chairman to the conference for its approval in a document sometimes called the schedule of meetings. In drawing up this proposal (as in many other matters), the Chairman does not act alone. Even for the smallest and most simple conference he/she consults the secretariat, who might prepare a draft allocation for consideration by the Chairman. In the case that the proposed allocation contains aspects that are not obvious or routine, the Chairman consults a number of delegations before making his or her proposal. In large and official conferences, there is often a Steering Committee to assist the Chairman in developing the proposed allocation of work and timetable. In the most formal cases, this Steering Committee is sometimes called the General Committee and composed of the bureau of the plenary plus the chairmen of the main committees. This extensive involvement of other delegations in the preparation of the Chairman's proposal is needed to ensure the proposal takes into account all concerns and consequently is accepted without debate.[161]

This organization of work is similar in WTO Ministerial Conference, providing a Plenary session and, in parallel, informal sessions for Ministers might be organized (see chapter 2.4).

---

[160] For example, at the UNGA, economic issues are allocated to the Second Committee and legal issues to the Sixth. This enables delegations to assign their economic experts to cover the Second Committee and their legal experts to the Sixth.

[161] United Nations Institute for Training and Research (UNITAR), Performing Effectively in Multilateral Conferences and Diplomacy - The Formal and Informal Process of Conferences, 2006, pp. 22-23.

3.1.9 General debate

At almost every conference and in each committee's consideration of each agenda item, the delegations want to open discussions by making some general remarks in which they explain their understanding of the issue and their general ideas as to what needs to be done by the conference. They may also, at the outset, want to give advance notice of any proposals they intend to put forth and of their other intentions. At formal conferences, this stage of the discussions is called the **general debate**. Delegations wishing to speak in the general debate are invited to put their name on a <u>list of speakers</u> kept by the chairman (or for him by the Secretariat). As most delegations are likely to wish to participate, the chairman usually has to limit the length of time allocated for each delegate's intervention in the general debate, thus each delegate has the same allocation of time.

At major conferences, general debate statements are usually prepared in advance - often before the conference assembles and often at headquarters. Hence, the delegations do not really respond to each other and therefor this exchange is not what it is usually understood by "debate".[162] In working groups or other "small" meetings in the UN System and other regional organizations, especially in the EU, real debates take place, and sometimes they are very lively and long. This is also the case for WTO Rounds of trade negotiation and in the financial/monetary sphere were debates become more complicated due to the interaction between existing or new bodies with the formal organs, the Board of Governors, the Boards of Executive Directors and the Executive Heads of the World Bank and the IMF.[163]

3.1.10 Committee work

Similarly, each committee starts by electing its bureau and establishing its own work programme and timetable. Like the Plenary, each committee has the option of establishing one or more subsidiary bodies (called subcommittees, working groups, etc.) to work on particular issues. In due course, each of these subsidiary bodies have to report to its parent committee in time for that committee to consider the report and take such action as it deems appropriate, such as, perhaps, incorporating it into the committee's own report to the Plenary.

---

[162] Walker R.A., Multilateral Conferences: Purposeful International Negotiation. London: Palgrave Macmillan, 2004, p. 140.

[163] Kaufmann J., Conference Diplomacy: An Introductory Analysis, 2nd revised edition, Martinus Nijhoff Publishers, UNITAR, 1988, p. 55.

Committee work usually involves more detailed examination of agenda items and often discussions on possible course of action, including recommendations to the plenary. Thus, these discussions are real "debate" as delegates respond to their counterparts, negotiate and try to persuade each other to an agreed text.

In terms of time and attitude, at most large conferences, committee work lasts longer than the Plenary and the attitude is different between the two. Working methods in committee is less formal and mostly unrecorded. In fact, the rules of procedure, while formally adopted and applicable to committees, are sometimes relaxed and applied with less rigour. The Plenary is more solemn and ceremonial and focuses on "the big picture" and decision-making.[164] Its Presiding officer and other participants attempt to maintain harmony and common purpose awareness, which is less evident in the sometimes heated detailed committees' discussions.

Each committee, concluding its deliberations and within the time allocated by the Plenary, takes decisions as it agrees upon. A committee being a subsidiary body of the Plenary, the only decisions it takes are those relating to its own work ordering and those to recommend texts or actions to the plenary. No committee decides on behalf of its main body.

3.1.11 Reports and decisions

The agenda items which are referred to committees by the Plenary, reoccur to the plenary with the committees' reports. The plenary considers these reports, which can result in further discussions on the issues and the committees' work. Eventually, the plenary either takes note of each committee report and/or act on its recommendations. It is also possible, but not very common, that the Plenary does not accept a committee's recommendation(s) and/or decides differently than its recommendation(s). In most cases, the Plenary takes also several administrative decisions, and in particular decides on the date (and if it is not fixed, the location) of its next meeting. It establishes also committees or working groups to perform certain tasks before the next meeting and report to it when it reconvenes. The plenary adopts also the report on the conference's work, sometimes known as a Final Act (final document), which records the

---

[164] Decision-making is usually defined as a process or sequence of activities involving stages of problem recognition, search for information, definition of alternatives and the selection of an actor of one from two or more alternatives consistent with the ranked preferences (see Political Science Notes/2013 - available at politicalsciencenotes.com).

accomplishments of the conference. This Final Act[165] is a formal summary of the proceedings of a conference and it contains information on the background to the conference, the participating states and organizations. The officers, the committees, the main documents, the resolutions and international agreements adopted, if any, by the conference.

3.1.12 Conference closure and follow-up

When all the committees' reports have been received and considered by plenary, and plenary has taken all the decisions it wants to take (or is able to agree upon), the conference has finished its work and can close.

Before declaring the conference closed, Chairman usually makes **concluding remarks** in which he or she briefly reviews the work of the conference and thanks the Host Country or organization, the various office holders, and of course the Secretariat (see chapter 7). The Chairman always attempts to transmit a message as positive as possible of the conference's work, underlying the achievements and the possibilities opened for the future by the conference.[166]

Once the Chairman declares the conference closed, the delegates disperse but their work in relation to the conference is not finished. They still have to report to their colleagues and government (see chapter 3.4.9).[167] Similarly, the work of the Conference Secretariat is not finished as many decisions taken by the conference have to be finalized due to, for example, last minute changes or too long texts as the Final Act. The Secretariat's task immediately after the conference concludes is to print final versions of all texts and translate them into all the working languages of the conference. These final documents (see Table no. 5) are distributed to the participating governments, often via their relevant permanent missions.[168] Almost all Secretariats post such documents on their websites.

---

[165] Chrisspeels E., Procedures of Multilateral Conference Diplomacy, in M.A. Boisard and E.M. Chossudovsky, Multilateral Diplomacy: The United Nations System at Geneva, A Working Guide. The Hague: Kluwer Law International, 1998, p. 133.

[166] Walker R.A., Manual for UN Delegates - Conference Process, Procedure and Negotiation, UN Publication, 2011, p. 81.

[167] Walker R.A., Multilateral Conferences: Purposeful International Negotiation. London: Palgrave Macmillan, 2004, p. 197.

[168] A diplomatic mission accredited to an international organization. A permanent diplomatic mission is typically known as an Embassy, and the head of the mission is known as an Ambassador, or High Commissioner. All permanent diplomatic missions to the UN and WTO are known as permanent missions, while EU Member States' missions to the EU are known as

Table no. 5 - Examples of post-session documents

Document name	When it usually appears	Produced by	Circulated by
Final Act or Final Document or Resolutions	Immediately (depending on the length and the need for translations, sometimes several days to weeks afterwards)	Conference Plenary	Secretariat
Report of the conference (final version)	Soon after the conference (depending on the length of the conference, sometimes several days to weeks afterwards)	Rapporteur or Secretariat	Secretariat
Verbatim or summary records/report of the conference	Soon after the conference (usually several days afterwards)	Secretariat	Secretariat
Other final documents	Several hours to days afterwards	Conference	Secretariat
Other than English versions / translations of adopted texts	Sometime after the conference	Secretariat	Secretariat

Source: Walker Roland A., Manual for UN Delegates - Conference Process, Procedure and Negotiation, UN Publication, 2011, p. 65; UNITAR, Performing Effectively in Multilateral Conferences and Diplomacy - The Formal and Informal Process of Conferences, 2006, p. 26.

All these phases of multilateral conferences show their role in serving the objectives of the conference. These practices are fairly standard, though multilateral conferences vary greatly in terms of subject covered and profile of participants. Still, the parties have the common interest to agree on a mutually beneficial outcome, including by establishing and applying a framework of agreed principles. Accordingly, the formal along with the informal processes are important elements in the success or failure of a conference.

3.2 Formal procedures

Multilateral conferences vary a lot in formality, but the formal proceedings are important as they are the most constraining and the delegates need to be ready to operate within their confine. In a multilateral conference, the formal procedures

permanent representations and the head of such a mission is typically both a permanent representative and an ambassador. European Union missions abroad are known as EU delegations.

are helpful as they advance the development of the conference's phases and improve the decision-making performance of participants. The purpose of formal procedures is to protect conference and delegates from any problem that might occur. Their goal is to help conference and delegates to avoid difficulties and still let them take advantage of the potential strengths of the debates and conference's results.

3.2.1 Rules of Procedure - Background information

Perhaps, the major peculiarity of the multilateral conferences is the importance of the rules of procedure. We noted that there must be some rather clear and strict rules to maintain orderly interactions in cases like the UN, where 193 delegations have to communicate or the WTO where 164 delegations have to communicate with each other at the same time.

Each conference has **rules of procedure**[169] (RoP) in order to guide the conference and delegates as the successive phases unfold. The rules of procedures are sometimes referred to as "rules of the game" as they specify what must and must not (or may and may not) be done by delegates, the Chairman and other Presiding officers, and the Conference and, sometimes, the Secretariat. As each conference is sovereign it must adopt its own rules of procedure - except that once adopted, they are routinely used for all successive conferences of the same body and that in some cases a conference adopts rules of procedure for its subsidiary bodies.[170] For example, ECOSOC has adopted a standard set of rules for all its functional commissions, as well as WTO for all its councils, committees or working groups.

Once adopted, the rules of procedure are binding on the Conference as a whole, the States being obliged under customary international law to comply with

---

[169] Some bodies and conferences have not adopted rules of procedure, but continue to meet and conduct business. At its first meeting in 1946, the Security Council adopted "Provisional Rules of Procedure" which have been amended 11 times, the last of which was in 1982. The Conferences of the Parties of the Climate Change, Biological Diversity, Desertification and Stockholm (on Persistent Organic Pollutants) Conventions, have been unable to adopt their rules as a result of disagreement among the Parties on the draft voting provisions of the respective bodies. As a result, and to enable the conferences to move on with their respective work programs, the draft rules of procedure of these bodies have been "applied" with the exception of their draft rule(s) on voting.

[170] United Nations Institute for Training and Research (UNITAR), Performing Effectively in Multilateral Conferences and Diplomacy - The Formal and Informal Process of Conferences, 2006, p. 27.

the rules of any conference in which they participate.[171] Although each conference adopts whatever rules it wishes, there is a lot of commonality between the RoP of all conferences. For example, there is a tendency in the UN System to base all the rules on the RoP model of UN General Assembly (UNGA) and the rules within WTO tend to be grounded on the model of RoP of General Council. Despite similarities there are also differences, some rules of subsidiary bodies, such as committees, might be different from the rules of their main bodies. The differences might have an impact as the conference unfolds, notably in relations with the provisions for decision-making.

We conclude with the importance for delegates to read and understand the applicable rules before attending a conference, knowing the RoP might give them a considerable advantage in achieving their objectives.

3.2.2 Rules of procedures - standard elements[172]

Most frequent and important matters usually covered by RoP are the following:

1. Invitations to participate. This covers the question of who is entitled to send delegates to the conference.

2. Credentials of delegates - see chapter 2.4.

3. Conference officers - see chapter 2.4. The rules also provide the powers and responsibilities of the Chairman (see chapter 7).

4. Quorum. This rule requires a certain proportion of the participants to be present in the conference when it debates and when it makes decisions. The quorum rules are among those which vary most significantly from one conference to another (see Table no. 6).

---

[171] Sabel Robbie, Procedure at International Conferences: A Study of the Rules of Procedure of International, Inter-governmental Conferences. Cambridge: Cambridge University Press, 1997, p. 42.

[172] Usual elements of RoP are: Participants, membership and observers; Arrangements of the meetings; Subsidiary bodies and committees; Public or private meetings; Officers and bureau; Rules of order and debate or conduct of business; Voting / decision-making; Secretariat; Languages; Records and reports.

Table no. 6 - Examples of quorum rules

Body or Conference	Open and Debate	To Decide
GA Plenary	1/3 of Members	Majority
GA Committees	1/4 of Members	Majority
ECOSOC	1/3 of Members	Majority
ECOSOC Functional Commissions	Majority	Majority
World Conference Against Racism	1/3 Members	Majority
CITES COP	One-half of Parties registered for meeting	One-half of Parties registered for meeting
WTO	A simple majority of the WTO Members	A simple majority of the WTO Members
European Union	Majority of the EU Member States	Simple Majority, Qualified Majority, Unanimity
ILO	Majority	Majority
WIPO	½ of Members	Majority
IMF	Majority	Majority
International Atomic Energy Agency (IAEA)	Majority	Majority, 2/3 Majority

Source: Adapted from UNITAR, Performing Effectively in Multilateral Conferences and Diplomacy - The Formal and Informal Process of Conferences, 2006, p.29.

A Chairman starting a meeting in the absence of a quorum (with fewer delegations present that the RoP require) is **out of order**.[173] Under some rules, a meeting is also out of order if it proceeds when fewer than that number is present (if there originally was a quorum but a number of delegations have since left the room). Other rules are not entirely clear on this point. In practice, there are many occasions on which chairmen allow a committee or sometimes the Plenary to continue to debate without a quorum (when they believe this will be accepted by delegations). However, it is careless to allow a decision to be made in the absence of the requisite quorum since the validity of that decision is insecure - later, when the quorum is present, delegates could ask for a new vote. Some rules specifically

---

[173] Not (behaving) in accordance with the rules of procedure.

provide this right, but these situations should not occur since the quorum rule is established by RoP and thus, binding for conference and delegates, alike.[174]

5. Statements by delegates. Rules oblige delegates to address their interventions (remarks) to the Chairman and they may not speak unless given the floor (permission to speak) by the Chairman. In most large conference rooms, each delegation has a microphone, which is turned on when the Chairman gives the floor to the delegate (see chapter 4.2 on intervening in multilateral conferences). RoP provide limits, or allow the Chairman to propose limits to, the number of times and the length of time for which each delegation may speak. The purpose is to give every delegation an equal opportunity to express itself while also enabling the conference to complete its work on time. According to RoP, the Chairman keeps a list of speakers and he/she has to give the floor to delegates in the order in which they signify their desire to speak. There are also some exceptions to this rule.[175]

6. Right of reply. Apart from ensuring that each delegation has an equal opportunity to speak, RoP typically provide that a delegate has a right to reply to statements made by other delegates, notably during the general debate. This right is usually limited as to the number of times a delegate may use it and for how long he/she can speak. Traditionally (often not specified in the RoP), this right is exercised only at the end of the day or the conclusion of the general debate. Some rules specify the circumstances in which this right can be invoked.[176]

7. **Languages**. The rules of all UN bodies specify a limited number of **official languages**. For the UN General Assembly (UNGA) and most other bodies in the UN System, these languages are Arabic, Chinese, English, French, Spanish and Russian. For large conferences, the rules require all official documents to be issued in all official languages and, at least in the Plenary, all interventions to be simultaneously interpreted into each of these languages. However, many smaller bodies, driven by the idea of savings and efficiency, limit themselves to two or three **working languages** (e.g. English, French and sometimes Spanish) and most of the debate, especially in informal meetings takes place in English. For the WTO, the official language and working language are

[174] Năstase Dan, Drept diplomatic şi consular, Editura Fundaţiei România de Mâine, Bucuresti, 2006, p. 125.

[175] Chrisspeels E., Procedures of Multilateral Conference Diplomacy, in M.A. Boisard and E.M. Chossudovsky, Multilateral Diplomacy: The United Nations System at Geneva, A Working Guide. The Hague: Kluwer Law International, 1998, p. 128.

[176] Op.cit., p.128

English, French and Spanish and the official documents are issued in all these three languages, with the exception of small meetings where the working language is English and sometimes French. The European Union currently has 24 official languages, with English and French as main working languages.

8. Submission of proposals.[177] Many conferences adopt texts, often in the form of resolutions (see chapter 4.3.3 on resolutions). In this context, adoption is a decision by the conference to make the text its own. The proposals in question are therefore **draft decisions** or **draft resolutions** submitted to the conference for its consideration and, if it agrees, adoption, sometimes with amendments to the original proposal.

Usually, the RoP provide that texts proposed for adoption by the conference to be submitted in writing (and, in many cases, in each of the official languages) to the Secretariat at least 24 hours before they are debated,[178] with specifications about who may submit such proposals. The delegation which proposes a text is known as its **sponsor**. When several delegations jointly sponsor a text, they are **co-sponsors**. When a proposal has several co-sponsors, the one who takes the initiative and/or introduces the text to the conference is referred to as the **lead sponsor**.[179] At the appropriate time, the sponsor or lead sponsor will make a statement to the conference (or committee) explaining the proposal and commending it to the conference. This is called **tabling a proposal** or draft resolution or introducing it to the conference. Thereafter the text is debated by the conference (or committee). During the discussion of a proposed text, the co-sponsors may agree to amend it, which may lead them to issue a revised version of the proposal. Most rules also provide a procedure whereby other delegations can formally propose amendments and require the conference to take a decision on the proposed amendment. (They would not do this unless the sponsors refuse to amend the proposal accordingly.)

We note that, although it is not explicit in the rules, there is no need for written proposals for all the decisions which the conferences adopt if the text is

---

[177] United Nations Institute for Training and Research (UNITAR), Performing Effectively in Multilateral Conferences and Diplomacy - The Formal and Informal Process of Conferences, 2006, pp. 32-33.

[178] This rule is not always enforced, especially at committee stage, but, if invoked, it is usually respected.

[179] Unusually, the RoP of the former Commission on Human Rights allowed observer delegations to cosponsor draft resolutions and a similar procedure exists in the new Human Rights Council established in 2006.

long, complicated and/or potentially controversial. Verbal decisions - decisions that are proposed orally by delegates or the Chairman - are also common and have the same validity as decisions based on written proposals.

9. Procedural motions. Conference customs and rules allow for a range of procedural motions.[180] These are formal proposals by delegations relating to a few procedural issues, which (in most cases) are specified in the rules. For example: "to suspend the meeting (for a specified period)", "to adjourn the meeting (to a specified future time)", "to adjourn the debate (on an agenda item, to a specified other time or date)" and "closure of the debate (on an item)". The RoP normally place tight limits on debate of such motions and they are usually resolved by a simple majority vote. Similarly, the RoP provide an order of precedence in case several procedural motions are moved on the same issue.[181] A procedural motion, as provided for in the UN General Assembly rules, is related to the suspension or the adjournment of the meeting. Rule 77[182] of the UNGA lays down the order in which procedural motions have precedence over all other proposals or motions before the meeting (see Table no. 7).

Table no. 7 - Rules on the handling of procedural motions in the UNGA

To adjourn debate on an item	2 speakers for and 2 against
To close debate on item	2 speakers against
To adjourn or suspend meeting	No speakers
The motion is then put to the vote	
Precedence of motions (Rule 77)	
1. Suspend meeting	
2. Adjourn meeting	
3. Close debate on item	
4. Adjourn item	

Source: UNITAR, Performing Effectively in Multilateral Conferences and Diplomacy - The Formal and Informal Process of Conferences, 2006, p. 34.

---

[180] According to Sabel a procedural motion is a request by a delegation for the conference or assembly to decide on an issue of procedure - there is no exhaustive list of what issues constitute issues of procedure (see Sabel Robbie, Procedure at International Conferences. A Study of the Rules of Procedure at the UN and at Inter-governmental Conferences, Second edition, Cambridge: Cambridge University Press, 2006).

[181] Chrisspeels E., Procedures of Multilateral Conference Diplomacy, in M.A. Boisard and E.M. Chossudovsky, Multilateral Diplomacy: The United Nations System at Geneva, A Working Guide. The Hague: Kluwer Law International, 1998, p. 127.

[182] See document A/520/Rev.17 - Rules of procedure of the General Assembly.

A procedural motion as provided for in the WTO rules[183] is related to the adjournment and closure of the debate, specifically in rules 19 and 20 (see Table no. 8).

Table no. 8 - Rules on the handling of procedural motions in the WTO

adjournment of the debate	In addition to the proponent of the motion, one representative may be allowed to speak in favour of, and two representatives against, the motion, after which the motion shall be submitted for decision immediately.
closure of the debate	In addition to the proponent of the motion, not more than one representative may be granted permission to speak in favour of the motion and not more than two representatives may be granted permission to speak against the motion, after which the motion shall be submitted for decision immediately.

Source: WTO Document WT/L/161/25 July 1996

The use of procedural motions is a combative strategy,[184] not normally resorted to as long as delegates still hope for agreement or if they value their ongoing relationship with each other. An even more combative procedural motion that is controversial but allowed in some conferences is called a **no action motion**. If agreed by the conference, instead of deciding whether or not to adopt a proposal (e.g. a draft resolution), the conference decides not to take a decision.

Points of order

Typical rules provide that, during the discussion of any matter, a representative may at any time raise a **point of order**. A delegate raising a point of order is given the floor straightaway even another delegate may be speaking.[185] The most important aspect of a point of order is that it has to be decided immediately by the Chairman in accordance with RoP.

A delegate may **appeal** against the **ruling** of the Chairman. The appeal is immediately put to the vote, and the Chairman's ruling is confirmed unless

---

[183] See document WT/L/161/25 July 1996 - Rules of procedure for sessions of the Ministerial Conference and meetings of the General Council.

[184] Combative (also known as adversial or competitive) strategy is an approach that treats the process as a competition that is to win or lose.

[185] Chrisspeels E., Procedures of Multilateral Conference Diplomacy, in M.A. Boisard and E.M. Chossudovsky, Multilateral Diplomacy: The United Nations System at Geneva, A Working Guide. The Hague: Kluwer Law International, 1998, p. 127.

overturned by a majority of the members present and voting.[186] In other words, the question, on which no debate is allowed, is always: "*that the Chairman's ruling stands*". A point of order, as the name suggests, relates to procedural matters only. A delegate who, in raising a point of order, speaks on the substance of the matter under discussion is "*out of order*" (acting contrary to the RoP).

Points of order are quite common and are delivered in a non-confrontational style. Chairmen have to be alert to unruly delegations attempting to use the point of order procedure to speak on substantive issues, or to waste time or for other illegitimate purposes. Appeals against the Chairman's ruling are highly confrontational and extremely unusual.

10. Methods of taking decisions (see chapter 4.4). Rulings on points of order aside, chairmen do not make decisions on behalf of the conference. They ask the conference whether it is willing to adopt a particular proposed decision or text. As they do so only after the matter has been the subject of full debate and, if necessary, negotiation, this question is usually affirmatively answered by delegates either registering their assent or refraining from raising any objection. In the case of dissent (common in the UNGA, but rare in most conferences), it is solved in accordance with the rules if the conference is unable to decide on that matter.

The rules may provide for **voting** but many conferences never vote and in most bodies there is a general desire to avoid voting (even it is permitted by the rules). Thus, the vast majority of conference decisions are taken with the support or at least acquiescence of all delegations present. When conferences do resort to voting, in most cases, the rules allow delegations that wish to do so to make a statement in explanation of their vote, which enables them to register any views they want to put on the record, either before or after the vote. A complex and controversial question on which rules are not always clear is whether such statements go so far as to register a formal reservation about a decision which has just been adopted, or what effect, if any, such a statement might have.[187]

---

[186] Winslow Anne, Benchmarks for Newcomers, in M.A. Boisard and E.M. Chossudovsky, Multilateral Diplomacy: The United Nations System at Geneva, A Working Guide. The Hague: Kluwer Law International, 1998, p.186.

[187] United Nations Institute for Training and Research (UNITAR), Performing Effectively in Multilateral Conferences and Diplomacy - The Formal and Informal Process of Conferences, 2006, p. 36.

In the WTO context, the RoP provide that the Ministerial Conference shall take decisions in accordance with the decision-making provisions of the WTO Agreement, in particular Article IX entitled "Decision-Making" and when, in accordance with the WTO Agreement, decisions are required to be taken by vote, such votes shall be taken by ballot. Still, the process of decision-making in the WTO is dominated by the practice of consensus.[188]

11. Records. They are produced by conferences and show what the conferences have done. Secretariat Staff (called **précis** or **record writers)** produce **verbatim**, or more usually, **summary records** of all interventions. For large conferences, digital audio and video recording and webcasting are very common nowadays. Delegates may help the record writers by informally providing them with the written text of their interventions or summarizing suggestions but the summary records are the responsibility of the Secretariat alone.

The conferences also produce **reports**, or Final Document, or **Final Act** (see chapter 3.1.11) which incorporates an account of the debate and, most importantly, the text of any decisions the conference took. These reports are documents of the conference and as such (unlike the summary records) engage all delegations. Moreover, they are important in setting the starting point for any future debate or negotiation on the same issues and can serve as *travaux preparatoires*[189] - and as evidentiary documents for interpreting treaties or other texts produced by the conference. Consequently, it is usual for the report to be examined in detail by delegations and it is often the subject of debate and negotiation. This report is drafted, theoretically, by the Rapporteur, but in practice the first draft is usually written by the Secretariat. Still, the Rapporteur is responsible for its content and she/he needs to consult widely to ensure that it is acceptable to all delegations. This may require meetings of a formal or informal **drafting committee** and sometimes (although this is rarely optimal) debate and negotiation in plenary itself.

---

[188] Ehlermann Claus-Dieter, Decision Making in the World Trade Organization: Is the Consensus Practice of the World Trade Organization Adequate for Making, Revising and Implementing Rules on International Trade?, WilmerHale, 2005, p.9.

[189] According to Walker, *travaux preparatoires* represent, agreed record of what was said during the negotiation of a treaty. Can assist in its interpretation (see Walker R.A., Multilateral Conferences: Purposeful International Negotiation. London: Palgrave Macmillan, 2004).

3.3 Informal processes

Though the whole conference seems to be all about formality, this is just one side of multilateral meetings. The informal processes are, at least, equally important as a much greater volume of activity takes place through informal processes.

3.3.1 Informal processes

Informal processes are central component of multilateral conferences, requiring a great volume of activity, being time consuming and sometimes more important than the formal ones, though they are not as transparent and certainly not in the "public eye". Most of the exchanges of information, attempts at mutual persuasion and negotiation take place in the corridors, therefore outside the formal conference process. So-called "corridor work" (outside the conference room) and "huddling" (small groups of negotiators talking informally in the conference room during a break in the formal session) are an essential part of a conference.[190]

This work is not regulated by the rules of procedure and is neither recorded in any report the conference may produce nor mentioned in any conference document. Essentially, it consists of delegates talking to each other as opposed to talking to the conference (or one of its subsidiary bodies) as a whole and through the chairman (see chapter 3.3.4).

The term used to describe these conversations is **consultation**.[191] Strictly speaking "to consult" means to ask them what they think. In diplomacy, one also speaks of "consulting headquarters" which means explaining a situation to them and asking them for advice or instructions. In a multilateral conference, delegates consult each other to exchange information, to learn about each other's perspectives and opinions, to attempt to persuade each other and to negotiate agreements. Any conversation between delegates that relates to the work of the conference is consultation.[192]

---

[190] Meerts Paul, Diplomatic Negotiation, Essence and Evolution. The Hague: Clingendael Institute, 2015, p.56.

[191] Consult (verb), consultations (noun): To talk to another delegation, the secretariat, or home authorities, with the purpose of learning their views (see UNITAR, A Glossary of Terms for UN Delegates, 2005).

[192] Walker R.A., Multilateral Conferences: Purposeful International Negotiation. London: Palgrave Macmillan, 2004, p. 76.

There are differences[193] between the formal and informal work of a conference:

- the formal work is "public" (in the sense that all delegations - and sometimes the general public - can hear or later read what it is said) whereas the exchanges which take place as "consultations" are private (only those present hear what it is said). Some people condemn deals struck in "corridor talk" or in "informals", but the reality is that in everyday life, not only in conferences, the reasoning for individuals' attitudes and decisions are usually private and most conversations in which people develop understanding of issues and reach agreements take place in private. The results of such private conversations are private understandings, as the actual decisions of the conference have to be made in and by the Plenary, meaning in "public", and with the participation of all delegations. Still, there are legitimate wish for transparency and requirements for accountability.[194]

- not only the rules of procedures but also the many unwritten conventions applied to formal conference proceedings (including, for example, the terms in which delegates refer to each other) are not followed in informal work. Nevertheless, informal consultations are official interactions between representatives of sovereign states, who additionally have a considerable stake in efficiency and in preserving - and enhancing - relationships both personal and official. Consequently, they are conducted with courtesy, mutual respect, professionalism, tact and diplomacy.

3.3.2 Formats for consultation

Various places and different formats are used by delegates to consult each other. Many consultations take place in the conference room, while formal work is in progress. Delegations talk in the aisles or while sitting in any available seat. They also talk outside the conference room, in the corridors of the conference hall (hence the term "corridor work"), its lobbies, coffee shops and cafeterias. They can also meet at each other's permanent mission, in restaurants or any other private or public venue. When the conversation involves more than three or four delegations, they often make use of one of the many small conference rooms

---

[193] United Nations Institute for Training and Research (UNITAR), Performing Effectively in Multilateral Conferences and Diplomacy - The Formal and Informal Process of Conferences, 2006, p. 41.

[194] Bernstein Steven and Erin Hannah, The WTO and Institutional (In)Coherence and (Un)Accountability in Global Economic Governance, International Studies Association Conference, Montreal, March 16-19, 2011, p.43.

available at large conference venues.[195] These are sometimes called **"back rooms"**, which seemingly carries a mildly pejorative connotation.

Most of these consultations take place on spontaneous basis but some need prearranging and even a degree of formality. For example:

- **meetings of co-sponsors**: the co-sponsors of a draft resolution might want to meet to discuss proposals to amend their text and tactics for getting it adopted, and they want to do so in private. Consequently, they hold pre-arranged co-sponsors meetings in pre-booked small conference rooms. Such meetings are usually convened by the **lead sponsor** (see chapter 3.2.2) who also act as informal chairman during the meeting to the extent of keeping the discussion orderly and focused and making sure that the meeting outcome is understood and agreed and that it is recorded. This is done without he or she giving up him/her role as national delegate (clear distinction from Chairman of the conference and its subsidiaries);

- **Chairman's consultations**: consultations undertaken by a Chairman or a delegate mandated by the Chairman to act on his or her behalf, often known as a **Friend of the Chair**,[196] Group of friends of the Chair or **Facilitator**, who systematically consult most relevant delegations on a particular issue, often seeking agreement among them. In some cases Chairman calls consultations in the form of a smaller conference room meeting. Similarly, the conference Chairman presides this meeting and although rules of procedure cannot be invoked, their general essence is applied. During many large conferences there are often working lunches attended by key delegations, and sometimes the Chairman as well, operating as an informal Steering Committee or even Negotiating Committee, seeking to develop a common understanding of the conference outcome.

3.3.3 Groups

Probably the most elaborate format for consultations takes place in **caucus groups**,[197] groups which meet to discuss the conference's issues and in many cases, to develop common positions. We underline that for many countries, the

---

[195] Walker R.A., Manual for UN Delegates - Conference Process, Procedure and Negotiation, UN Publication, 2011, p. 45.

[196] Friend of the Chair: A delegate who has been mandated by the presiding officer to undertake a task, usually that of finding consensus on a particular issue or body of issues (see A Glossary of Terms for UN Delegates, UNITAR, 2005).

[197] Caucusing is a parliamentary term for diplomatic negotiation. Effective multilateral caucusing methods vary considerably depending on the respective policies of individual Members or other participants and the forum in which deliberation is taking place.

caucus group - if any - is different from the electoral group (see chapter 3.1.7). Some of these are **ginger groups**,[198] groups of delegations which have a common purpose of prompting new thinking by the conference on a particular issue (for example: the G10[199] active on nuclear non-proliferation, the G20[200] active on agriculture issues in WTO).

On a regional level, the UN recognizes five blocs: African States, Asian States, Eastern European States, Latin American and Caribbean States, and Western European and Other States. Additionally, States operating within trade blocs such as NAFTA, the EU, or ASEAN will often consult and work with one another on many global issues.

There are also many other groups of delegations which meet during a particular conference or which reconvene at a number of related conferences. Some of these focus on exchanging information or otherwise helping each other, without attempting to develop common positions. In the field of disarmament, the Western Group[201] has a varying membership in the Conference on Disarmament (CD) and the treaty bodies of the Biological Weapons Convention (BWC), the Convention on Certain Conventional Weapons (CCW) and the Nuclear Non-Proliferation Treaty (NPT). The particular dynamics of these conferences, added to the fact that some "Western" States are not party to all of the above-mentioned treaties, does not facilitate the adoption of common Western Group positions. Therefore, the main focus of the group remains exchange of information.[202]

Yet, within the Western Group, Members who are also Member States of the European Union (EU) do develop common positions. EU Members States are drawn together by joint interest and common institutions to the 28 Member States. For example, in the Conference of Disarmament or in the Conference on Trade and Development (UNCTAD), the Member State holding the rotating

---

[198] (Informal) A like-minded group of delegations dedicated to promoting a particular idea or philosophy (see A Glossary of Terms for UN Delegates, UNITAR, 2005).

[199] A ginger group which seeks to forge consensus in support of nuclear non-proliferation.

[200] Coalition of developing countries pressing for ambitious reforms of agriculture in developed countries with some flexibility for developing countries (not to be confused with the G20 Group of finance ministers and central bank governors).

[201] Argentina, Australia, Austria, Belgium, Canada, Finland, France, Germany, Hungary, Ireland, Israel, Italy, Japan, Netherlands, New Zealand, Norway, Poland, Republic of Korea, Slovakia, Spain, Sweden, Switzerland, Turkey, United Kingdom, United States of America.

[202] United Nations Institute for Training and Research (UNITAR), Performing Effectively in Multilateral Conferences and Diplomacy - The Formal and Informal Process of Conferences, 2006, p. 46.

presidency of the Council of the EU may make a statement on behalf of the 28 EU Member States, expressing a common position. In the WTO context, the European Commission negotiates on behalf of the European Union as authorised by the Council of the EU and the European Commission - the EU's executive arm - speaks for all EU Member States at almost all WTO meetings.[203]

Another group trying to develop common positions is the Association of South East Asian Nations (ASEAN). And also the African Group, which is an electoral group in the UN General Assembly and in most UN specialized agencies. Moreover, the members of this group also constitute the membership of the African Union.[204] Other groups vary in function of the subject matter of the conference, reflecting similar policy, those being **subject-specific group**s. The most prominent example is the G77,[205] grouping all the developing countries, active in conferences with economic theme. The Non-Aligned Movement,[206] operating in conferences with security theme and having broadly similar membership to the G77, is another example. Some of these subject-specific groups are more narrowly focused – as, for example the Organization of Petroleum Exporting Countries (OPEC). Subject-specific groups which share a

---

[203] Both the European Union (EU) and the 28 EU Member States are WTO Members.

[204] The African Union (AU) is the principal and supreme regional organization in Africa, and successor organization to the former Organization of African Unity (OAU). All members of the African Group are members of the African Union, with the exception of Morocco (see UNITAR, A Glossary of Terms for UN Delegates, 2005).

[205] The Group of 77 (G77) was established on 15 June 1964 by seventy-seven developing countries signatories of the "Joint Declaration of the Seventy-Seven Developing Countries" issued at the end of the first session of the United Nations Conference on Trade and Development (UNCTAD) in Geneva. Beginning with the first "Ministerial Meeting of the Group of 77 in Algiers (Algeria) on 10 – 25 October 1967, which adopted the Charter of Algiers", a permanent institutional structure gradually developed which led to the creation of Chapters of the G77 with Liaison offices in Geneva (UNCTAD), Nairobi (UNEP), Paris (UNESCO), Rome (FAO/IFAD), Vienna (UNIDO), and the Group of 24 (G24) in Washington, DC (IMF and World Bank). Although the members of the G77 have increased to 134 countries, the original name was retained due to its historic significance. The G77 is the largest intergovernmental organization of developing countries in the UN, which provides the means for the countries of the South to articulate and promote their collective economic interests and enhance their joint negotiating capacity on all major international economic issues within UN System, and promote South-South cooperation for development.

[206] The Non-Aligned Movement (NAM) was created and founded during the collapse of the colonial system and the independence struggles of the peoples of Africa, Asia, Latin America and other regions of the world and at the height of the Cold War. During the early days of the Movement, its actions were a key factor in the decolonization process, which led later to the attainment of freedom and independence by many countries and peoples and to the founding of tens of new sovereign states. Throughout its history, the Movement of Non-Aligned Countries has played a fundamental role in the preservation of world peace and security.

similar outlook are often referred to as **like-minded groups**. Some of them are short-lived, but others, as the G77, have become permanent institutions and hold conferences of their own. A subset of issue-specific, like-minded groups are **single issue coalitions**. One of the most formally established of these is the Geneva Group,[207] active in several UN specialized agencies. This is composed of representatives of major contributors to the budget of these organizations and concerned not with policy issues as such but with good financial and budgetary management. The Geneva Group mainly pools information, but at times identifies points on which there is agreement within the group, in which case is it passed on to others, mainly the secretariats of the relevant bodies. It meets before some conferences.

In the WTO, for example in the agriculture negotiations, several groups emerged like: the "G20" - currently comprises 19 developing country members of the WTO, led by Brazil and India, the "G20" has become one of the most important groupings in the WTO negotiation since the Cancun ministerial in 2003; the "G33", known as "friends of special products" is understood to comprise 42 countries; the Cairns Group which comprises the traditionally agriculture exporting countries and has an obvious offensive interest in market access; the "G10" which is made of ten countries with the most defensive interest in agriculture negotiation; African Union/Group, African, Caribbean and Pacific Group (ACP), least-developed countries - also known as the "G90", has 64 WTO Members. Although Members of the group do not share all positions in the negotiations, the most crucial and common concern of the group is the preference erosion, which is related to all three pillars of the agriculture negotiation.

Many such groups meet during the conferences in which they operate, constituting in effect "**conferences-within-the-conference**". They have their own procedure, either formally adopted or informally understood, as well as their own chairman, own convener for meetings or/and other office holders. Each group serves its Members as a source for information and often a forum in which

---

[207] The Geneva Group (GG) has existed since 1964. Permanently co-chaired by the US and UK, the GG consists of sixteen members that possess "like-mindedness" on administrative and financial matters. The current members are: Australia, Belgium, Canada, France, Germany, Japan, Italy, Mexico, Netherlands, Russia, Republic of Korea, Spain, Sweden, Switzerland, Turkey, United Kingdom, and United States of America. The Geneva Group functions at three levels: (1) UN Directors, (2) Mission personnel who focus on governance and management issues or otherwise work directly with the UN and its affiliated agencies and funds and programs and (3) Ambassadors, who meet periodically to take a strategic overview of the progress being made at expert level.

common positions are developed before the conference, on at least some of the issues. Frequently such groups draft joint **group statements** which are delivered by a **group spokesman** (see chapter 4). In some conferences the groups also serve as channels for the receipt and dissemination of information and both consultations with the chairman and negotiation can take place through the group spokesmen.[208]

In the European Union, the **EU Member States** organize themselves into **coalitions**. These coalitions entail the pooling of power and resources by the constituent parties in pursuit of a desired outcome. The coalitions are based around the North-South cleavage (rich–poor, but primarily Germanic versus Latin cultures). There is a "supranationalist-intergovernmentalist" axis; an "Atlanticist" coalition versus a "Continentalist" coalition; there are free-traders versus protectionists; and big versus small countries. Because of the euro crisis, the North-South divide seems to be of importance, and even then its salience is limited: no clear cleavage lines can be discerned in the EU decision-making, except for a moderate North–South division. It should be noted that these coalitions are becoming more fluid over time, thereby enhancing flexibility and instability simultaneously. All of these cleavages are cross-cutting: one country is always part of more than one "structural" alliance, and there are countless numbers of different coalitions on different dossiers.[209]

The States have full liberty to organize among themselves and be part to whatever group or coalition they prefer. There is no rule of international law which forbids the states to form groups or associate themselves. Contrary, this is considered the most efficient way to promote mutual interests and attain common objectives.[210]

3.3.4 Relationship between formal and informal work

All informal consultations[211] and the more organized consultations which take place in caucus groups, meetings of co-sponsors and many other such

---

[208] United Nations Institute for Training and Research (UNITAR), Performing Effectively in Multilateral Conferences and Diplomacy - The Formal and Informal Process of Conferences, 2006, p. 47.

[209] Meerts Paul (quoting also Blavoukos and Pagoulatos, Hosli and Arnold), Diplomatic Negotiation, Essence and Evolution. The Hague: Clingendael Institute, 2015, p. 253.

[210] Năstase Dan, Drept diplomatic şi consular, Editura Fundaţiei România de Mâine, Bucuresti, 2006, p. 126.

[211] Conversations between delegates, in two, three and larger groups, or between the Chairman or

forums, as well as the (formal) meetings of Chairman's contact groups, all take place before, during and after the formal work of the plenary conference and its subsidiary bodies. A caucus is essentially "marginal", as formal session temporarily ends and the plenary conference and its subsidiary bodies breaks down into smaller groups for the purpose of discussing the topic, drafting resolutions, or debating the merits of various resolutions. The formal, substantive debate via the list of speakers is an effective tool for expressing opinions about the topics, but it is not as conducive to formulating agreement about the topic or to drafting resolutions.

Nevertheless, the work in the formal and informal processes is closely connected: they both have the same subject matter and the same ultimate objective: to determine the decisions to be made by the conference. The two usually take place in parallel, but the consultations are so important that sometimes chairmen adjourn formal proceedings to permit delegates to participate in informal consultations. Also at times, a chairman who has undertaken consultations personally may report to the conference on the outcome; alternatively, if the chairman has delegated such consultations to a Facilitator or Friend of the Chair, the latter may report formally to the conference. There are two important distinctions[212] to be applied:

- the way informal work is conducted: without the benefit of the rules of procedure of the conference or the various structures which these provide.

- the informal work is, by definition, not formally part of the conference: all decisions - everything about the conference which is officially recorded and can be referred to (formally) in future conferences - are part of the formal proceedings.

Delegates gain more support by employing both formal proceedings and informal processes pertinent to the topic in discussion through caucusing efforts and implementation of appropriate strategies.

---

his representative and individual delegates or groups of delegates.

[212] United Nations Institute for Training and Research (UNITAR), Performing Effectively in Multilateral Conferences and Diplomacy - The Formal and Informal Process of Conferences, 2006, p. 49.

3.4 Approaches to multilateral conferences

Undoubtedly, approaches to multilateral conferences by delegates are of tremendous importance for its success or failure. These approaches focus on the identification and implementation of the **most effective course of action** available to delegates to help them achieve their objectives. The overview below is based on the best practices. It is important to acknowledge that in "conference arena" most delegates use a combination of approaches trying to employ the best methods and to have the best attitude.

3.4.1 Pre-conference preparations

Without adequate preparations it is extremely difficult to be effective in diplomatic negotiations and consequently, successful in multilateral conferences. Pre-conference preparations include everything that the involved parties (delegates, delegation leader and the officials responsible for sending the delegation) need to do before the conference in order to maximize the performance of the delegation and thus achieve its or their government's objectives. The informational and strategic ground for the conference must be laid down in this period since the increasingly severe time-constraints under which a multilateral conference is required to unfold do not allow for "zero-base" negotiations.[213] Those pre-conference preparations require: knowing the mandate of the conference and the potential conference outcome(s), if any; understanding the history of the conference, the issues or agenda items to be discussed and debated; and the interests and objectives that drive negotiations and conferences forward. In a nutshell, pre-conference preparations means to know what it is all about, what the government's expectations are, and as much as possible about the interests, objectives and intentions of the other participants.

3.4.2 Representation

The most important function of a conference participant is to (successfully) represent the sending government or organization. It also shows the importance of registration, as giving access to the conference room and documents. Registration is the most minimal duty of a delegation, but the impact is tremendous because it

---

[213] Rittberger Volker, International Conference Diplomacy: A Conspectus, in M.A. Boisard and E.M. Chossudovsky, Multilateral Diplomacy: The United Nations System at Geneva, A Working Guide. The Hague: Kluwer Law International, 1998, p. 23.

ensures that the state or organization's participation is reflected in the record of the conference and other conference papers. Delegations deliver statements in general debates and attend receptions given by the Chairman at an early stage of the conference, if they want to have higher profile participation. This is a very adequate behaviour but more need to be done if the delegation has specific objectives to achieve during and after the conference.

3.4.3 Establishing networks and maintaining relationships

If the delegation wishes to do more than register its attendance it has to engage with other delegations, mostly in informal exchanges (see chapter 3.3). For this purpose an essential working document is the <u>list of participants</u> which is prepared by the Secretariat. These are the people with whom delegates interact, and on whose cooperation depends any achievement of the delegation and the conference itself. By studying the list, the participants decide beforehand (even before the conference formally assembles) whom they wish or need to discuss with. In this regards, some elements[214] are fundamental:

- it is elementary courtesy to make early contact with the delegations of all governments and organizations with which their own government has particularly close relations and with individuals with whom the representative have a friendly relationship - perhaps having met them at previous conferences. In addition, the question of how to manoeuvre in multilateral conferences depends in the first instance on the objectives to be attained (subject of the conference), and once the objectives have been defined, the delegations can start mustering support commencing with friends and acquaintances;

- it is elementary prudence to consider which other individuals might be most useful to the delegation and to seek them out, also at an early stage. Some of these include: the secretariat, delegates with whom there are hopes for cooperation (notably including formal and informal leaders of any caucus group(s) in which the delegation expects to join), delegates who are likely to be good sources of information and delegates who are identified as potential trouble (expecting them to oppose the conference outcomes). It is very important for the delegate to know as much as possible and as early as possible about the intentions of any other delegation, since achieving own objectives depends also on meeting others objectives and concerns.

---

[214] United Nations Institute for Training and Research (UNITAR), Performing Effectively in Multilateral Conferences and Diplomacy - The Formal and Informal Process of Conferences, 2006, p. 51.

Apart from the fact that thorough knowledge of all pertinent documentation is indispensable, the delegation must also be ready for the patient, persistent and persuasive efforts required to discuss with and sway all those whose support may be needed.[215] To be effective, the delegates must give full consideration to everybody who can be supportive of the topics under discussions in the conference and helpful in achievement their objectives.

3.4.4 Informal gatherings

Gathering information should be one of the delegation's objectives, if its participation in the conference goes beyond registering its presence. Rightly, in some cases, all the delegation wishes to do is to understand the conference outcome, but many delegates have an interest in gathering information, whether or not this is explicitly called for by their brief (see chapter 5.4) and regardless if the information has anything to do with the subject of the conference. This information could be factual, or relate to the policies of other governments and international organizations or to the relations between them, etc. In any situation, the main challenge for the delegations is to set priorities and to focus on gathering the information of greatest value to their governments/organizations, due to the impressive amount of available information of interest to participants and their governments/organization.

If delegations want to understand what is happening in the conference as it unfolds, this very challenging task requires the devotion of a big share of their resources, even for the largest delegations. Due to the fact that this is a big and complex task, it needs to be carefully managed and planned well in advance. Some of the most valuable sources of information[216] are:

- **The Secretariat**. It produces a number of documents showing what activities are scheduled for each day, where they are held etc. At some large conferences the secretariat produces a daily journal or programme, available early each morning, with the day's activities. Secretariat staff can also be approached directly and questioned, especially on procedural and administrative issues but

---

[215] Winslow Anne, Benchmarks for Newcomers, in M.A. Boisard and E.M. Chossudovsky, Multilateral Diplomacy: The United Nations System at Geneva, A Working Guide. The Hague: Kluwer Law International, 1998, p. 190.

[216] United Nations Institute for Training and Research (UNITAR), Performing Effectively in Multilateral Conferences and Diplomacy - The Formal and Informal Process of Conferences, 2006, p. 53.

they can also help with substantive questions (e.g. by referring to the most useful documents).

- **Group coordinators**. Among other tasks, they have to be well informed and to disseminate information to members of their own group. They are also willing to inform members of other groups who approach them about their group's intentions, attitudes etc.

- **Active delegations**, especially those active in trying to find compromises and solutions to any problems facing the conference (including differences of view).

- **The Chairman**. He or she gives guidance, explaining the state of play in the conference's work, explaining procedural and sometimes substantive issues and his or her ideas about the tasks ahead. He or she may also, at times, convene informal briefing sessions or Chairman's consultations for the purpose of imparting or exchanging information with delegations. Although chairmen are very busy and should not be importuned needlessly, there are suitable opportunities to speak informally with them, often in a group.

3.4.5 Advancing the mandate

Another delegations' involvement is assisting the conference to execute its mandate, meaning to achieve the purpose for which it was convened. Most probably, this is part of government's objectives, since it accepted the invitation to participate in a conference with this mandate. Sometimes, the participants or their governments/organizations have also specific objectives as to the decisions to be taken by the conference, but this goes beyond the broad support and it is likely to depend on the overall outcome of the conference.

In support to the conference in fulfilling its mandate, delegates may **contribute constructively to debate** and **negotiation** and **help to head off or overcome problems** which can threaten the conference outcome. **Supporting** and **assisting the chairman** is the most fundamental approach in this direction. For example, the delegates can cooperate in meeting Chairman's requests, passing him or her useful information and offering, discreetly, useful and pertinent advice.

3.4.6 Evaluating proposals

This is a very important delegates' task as they need to consider whether or not to support a proposal put forward by another delegation. The first rule in this case is to separate the proposal from the proponent ("play the ball, not the man"). **Each proposal should be assessed on its merits**, not rejected because of any general dislike or mistrust of its sponsor. Similarly, it is usually unsound to support a proposal just to show solidarity with or sympathy for its proponent (unless this is the objective of one's own delegation). The only elements to be taken into consideration should be whether the proposal contributes to the delegation's objectives and its impact on the successful outcome of the conference. Sometimes, the reasons for supporting or opposing a proposal may be not only related to substance, but also because it goes too far or not far enough.[217]

Another factor to weigh in **evaluating a proposal** is **to assess where it leads**. For example, most proposals, if adopted, do not result in a complete solution to the problem at hand. But if they constitute an incremental step in the right direction - even a first step towards raising awareness of the problem - it would be counterproductive to reject them just for not doing everything we would like. Conversely, if a proposal tends to undermine valued principles and patterns of behaviour, that is grounds for looking at it very critically, perhaps seeking to amend it or ultimately opposing it.[218]

3.4.7 Defensive methods

Another aim of all delegations is to discourage others in making statements which are contrary to own government's objectives. "Corridor work" and negotiations are useful demarches but sometimes delegations, having failed in these efforts, find themselves in a losing position as the conference advances towards the adoption of a statement or decision that the delegation considers damaging. However, this is a difficult dilemma, as the situation occurs only if there is general support for whatever own delegation opposes and, besides, the conference always supports those seeking agreement as a prerequisite for all delegations achieving their own objectives. Thus, delegations risk resentment from most other delegations if they stand in the way of a potential agreement. It is often wiser **to avoid confrontation** because, in general, very confrontational negotiations do not reach agreement,[219] so the delegations accept, for example,

---

[217] Winslow Anne, Benchmarks for Newcomers, in M.A. Boisard and E.M. Chossudovsky, Multilateral Diplomacy: The United Nations System at Geneva, A Working Guide. The Hague: Kluwer Law International, 1998, p. 191.

[218] United Nations Institute for Training and Research (UNITAR), Performing Effectively in Multilateral Conferences and Diplomacy - The Formal and Informal Process of Conferences, 2006, p. 55.

[219] Meerts Paul, Diplomatic Negotiation, Essence and Evolution. The Hague: Clingendael Institute, 2015, p.292.

relying on their abilities to place different interpretations on the text, and/or registering their dissent or reservations in both oral statements and in the report of the conference. If it is considered necessary to go further, it is often possible **to secure some softening, ambiguity or explicit exemptions** in the text in exchange for desisting from outright opposition. Occasionally, delegations are going even further and either try to hold the conference hostage to its isolated position or, even more extremely, try to derail the conference.[220] Such strategy incurs widespread hostility as it involves setting oneself in opposition to the mandate of the conference (the collective purpose of most other delegations) and to other delegations individual purposes, all of which depending on the conference succeeding. This strategy is very costly in terms of retaliations and long-term relations with other delegations, but delegations promoting it might consider it worthy, especially if it is successful.

3.4.8 Advancing a proposal

For delegations that wish to advance proposals of their own or join others in supporting a proposal, several strategies are more effective than others,[221] such:

- *appealing the proposal to a large majority of delegations and preferably to all*. This has the best prospects of success. To have any chance at all it has to appeal to many delegations and be seen by most other delegations as inoffensive to their objectives. This in turn means that to draft a successful proposal and to successfully market a proposal, it is necessary to consult widely, to understand the concerns and objectives of other delegations and to cater to these, to the extent, of course, that this is compatible with advancing your own objectives.

- *getting the proposal on the table early, preferably before any competing proposals*. This has a considerable advantage. The text that is submitted first often becomes the basis for negotiation or at least the reference point in the thinking of many delegations.

- *"floating"[222] proposals in draft form* to other delegations, giving them forewarning, explaining the purpose, hearing their reactions and taking these

---

[220] Walker R.A., Multilateral Conferences: Purposeful International Negotiation. London: Palgrave Macmillan, 2004, p.154.

[221] United Nations Institute for Training and Research (UNITAR), Performing Effectively in Multilateral Conferences and Diplomacy - The Formal and Informal Process of Conferences, 2006, p. 57.

[222] Walker R.A., Manual for UN Delegates - Conference Process, Procedure and Negotiation, UN Publication, 2011, p.44 (to **float** a proposal means to describe and discuss it and perhaps show a

into account, perhaps in revisions of the text and/or in its presentation. Such process enables the sponsors to refine their proposal into one gaining wider support, often being able to line up support in advance. In addition to fostering a general predisposition to accept the proposal, this is an opportunity to recruit co-sponsors and delegations willing to support the proposal.

Another means to advance a proposal is through the "non-paper" (see chapter 3.1.2) which is widely circulated and thus gains early-tabling advantages but does not have the status of a definitive proposal. It serves mainly as a discussion-shaping paper or can be reissued, probably in modified form, as a formal proposal at a later stage.

3.4.9 Evaluating the conference and reporting

Another fundamental task of delegations is **to report**[223] to headquarters. Once conference ends, the delegate's work is not finished. The conference has to be evaluated, **its achievement(s), if any, and its most probable consequences have to be assessed**. Consequently, the delegations are asked to deliver to their governments a report, which is generally structured in three parts (Introduction, Mandate, Conclusions and Recommendations) that evaluate, analyse and eventually propose conference-related future actions.[224]

A report has to cover all these issues, the most important aspect being the decisions taken by the conference, especially on those issues of interest to the governments. Beyond that, the level of details and the quantity one should report depends on the government's headquarters ability to use and handle documents, as well as on the disposable time for analyse. In some cases, it is important to keep a record at the permanent mission as well, to help delegations to future meetings. In order to report to headquarters, the delegations should do the followings, in order of complexity:

- Collect and send back to headquarters the final document and/or the text of all decisions taken by the conference (as a minimum task). Other conference documents, including texts of statements made by own delegation, statements of other delegations may be added. It is preferable to make a good selection of

---

draft informally in an exploratory manner before deciding whether or not to make it a formal proposal).

[223] Walker R.A., Multilateral Conferences: Purposeful International Negotiation. London: Palgrave Macmillan, 2004, p.197.

[224] Năstase Dan, Drept diplomatic şi consular, Editura Fundaţiei România de Mâine, Bucuresti, 2006, p. 346.

documents whose contents are carefully assessed and ordered, accompanied by a short text drawing attention to points of interest.

- Provide a report of what happened at the conference, especially on matters of main interest to the government and delegations to future conferences (a more complex task). The report is based on what the delegation did and witnessed but often it is also useful to talk to some key sources (the secretariat, conference officers, group coordinators and other delegations) to find out what happened in meetings and informal consultations where own delegation was not present.

- Asses the significance of what took place at the conference (the most complex task). The delegates need to analyse, for example: any concrete progress made towards solution of some particular problems, the way in which the course and outcome of the conference is going to affect debate and negotiation in other conferences, the useful or warning points (if any) for own country's delegations to other conferences, any significant event in dealing with other delegations (the most relevant facts being good cooperation or any frictions with certain delegations, along with explanations of the circumstances).

Evaluating a conference and reporting require a lot of time, reflexion and ability to assess and summarize huge amount of information. Its preparation in advance makes it easier and less time consuming. Apart from these approaches to multilateral conferences which delegates can use to advance their objectives, the participants in multilateral conferences must pay attention to both oral and written means of communication.

Chapter 4 – Communication in multilateral conferences

Multilateral conferences are, certainly, influenced by cultural elements. In a multilateral context, problems of language, etiquette, form, and tradition can present challenging barriers to reaching an agreement. Thus, both oral and written communication are important. As multilateral conferences have specific characteristics, verbal communication (how delegates word their interventions and their exchanges in informal consultations) and written communication (through written means, such as when they draft resolutions and other conference documents), are essential for their success or failure.

4.1 Verbal communication in multilateral conference

Behaviour of people in multilateral conferences is strongly influenced by generally accepted rules, tradition and expectations. This statement is valid also for oral communication during such events.

4.1.1 General considerations

Multilateral conferences often entail dealing with representatives of several different cultures, thus presenting a unique challenge of how to deal with delegates who conduct their affairs in different ways. The following considerations should be taken into account by participants in multilateral conferences: focus, politeness, languages, mechanics of speaking.

1. Focus. The conference's formal proceedings consist of the chairman speaking to the conference and delegates (and occasionally other participants, such as the Secretariat) taking the floor, one at a time, when the Chairman invites them to do so (see chapter 2). **Taking the floor** means speaking to the conference, whereas the Chairman addresses the conference directly, delegates address their remarks to the Chairman. It is called **debate** everything that is said in this manner. Each speaker, when he or she speaks, is said **to intervene** (in the debate) and what they say is called an **intervention**. Most conference rooms - and certainly all the large ones - are equipped with microphones and earphones. The microphone enhances the volume of delegate's voice when they have the floor, following the Chairman invitation to intervene. The ear phones enable delegates to hear the speaker over the background noise of private conversations or to listen to the interpreter who is relaying what the speaker is saying. During their statements, delegates should avoid scaring the microphone with papers or pencils, etc. and should avoid drumming on the table. These extraneous noises make it difficult for the interpreter and other delegates to understand.[225]

When a delegate takes the floor, he or she must **address the Chairman**[226] by his or her correct title as set out in the conference documents (i.e. "President", "Chairperson", "Chairman", "Mr./Madame Chairman", "Mr/Madame Chair"). It is usual and polite to start by thanking the Chairman for giving the floor. Nevertheless, all interventions are heard by the entire conference. If a delegate asks for the floor and the Chairman is not calling him/her (which is not at all common, but might very rarely happen), he or she has to inform the Secretariat or the Head of delegation, neither complain to other delegates nor call out the Chairman.

2. Politeness. Since the delegate is addressing the Chairman, if he or she wishes to speak or refer to another delegate the third person must be used, respecting the tradition of delegates referring to each other in formal debate. We emphasize that the customs and traditions of different conferences are not uniform. The plenary debate of a large conference is conducted in very **formal terms** (e.g. "as the <u>distinguished</u> delegate of Peru stated…"); while a negotiating group of the same conference may use much less formal terms (e.g. "as my <u>colleague</u> from Morocco pointed out…").[227] In **very informal consultations** and at some summits where an intimate atmosphere is deliberately maintained, the use of first names is not uncommon and delegates in many cases address each other directly rather than speak through a chairman/moderator. If in doubt, it is advisable to observe what is practiced in the attended conference, to ask someone who knows and to conform to expectations. Sometimes, it is an offence if the word "distinguished" is omitted in circumstances where it is routine, and even worse, because by withholding "distinguished" the delegate is inferentially disrespecting the State which the other delegate represents. Although this formal way of speaking is used only in formal debate, the spirit of elaborate politeness

---

[225] Draz-Wolstencraft Susan and Garnier Alain, Further Working Suggestions by Interpreters, in M.A. Boisard and E.M. Chossudovsky, Multilateral Diplomacy: The United Nations System at Geneva, A Working Guide. The Hague: Kluwer Law International, 1998, p. 165.

[226] Walker R.A., Manual for UN Delegates - Conference Process, Procedure and Negotiation, UN Publication, 2011, p.86.

[227] United Nations Institute for Training and Research (UNITAR), Performing Effectively in Multilateral Conferences and Diplomacy - Interventions, Documents and Resolutions, 2006, p. 7.

extends to every aspect of conference work, both formal and informal. The expected way of speaking is to sound respectful of both the person and the wishes of all other delegates and especially respectful to the States that they represent.[228] No matter what country a delegate represents, within the multilateral conferences, they are afforded basic diplomatic respect.

3. Languages. The UN System has six **official languages** (Arabic, Chinese, English, French, Russian and Spanish), while WTO has three official languages (English, French and Spanish) and EU has 24 official languages, and for many formal meetings simultaneous interpretation is provided into all of these. This means that any of the official languages can be used on such occasions and all present are able to follow what is said. A number of conferences have fewer official languages (for example: the ECOSOC regional commissions, the working groups within the Council of the EU) and some operate in a restricted number of **working languages**, at least for their less formal sessions. We note that in the UN Security Council there is both simultaneous and consecutive interpretation, but otherwise the latter is not very common.[229]

Although the general standard is high, **simultaneous interpretation** is very difficult. It is not always entirely accurate and sometimes it fails to transmit a significant tone of voice. If delegates listen to interventions in the original voice, they probably get a truer or fuller sense of what the speaker is trying to convey. Similarly, as delegates want to be well understood, if they make a long or important intervention, it is a good idea to give the text well in advance to the interpreters.[230] This facilitates their task and enable them to better interpret the intervention in question. In many committees, negotiating groups and formal consultations, interpretation is not provided, and it is rarely provided in contact groups and informal consultations. Also, as some meetings continue beyond the interpreters' working hours, the conference decides to continue debate without interpretation. In these cases, although all official languages are permissible, English seems to be universally understood and it becomes the working language. In practice, there are variations between these two extremes. Official languages

---

[228] Walker R.A., Manual for UN Delegates - Conference Process, Procedure and Negotiation, UN Publication, 2011, p.88.

[229] Kaufmann Johan, Conference Diplomacy: An Introductory Analysis, 2nd revised edition, Martinus Nijhoff Publishers, UNITAR, 1988, p. 175.

[230] Carter Peers, From the Interpreters' Booth, in M.A. Boisard and E.M.Chossudovsky, Multilateral Diplomacy: The United Nations System at Geneva, A Working Guide. The Hague: Kluwer Law International, 1998, p.162.

other than English are used primarily for the most formal statements and for the most formal and public occasions. As the debate becomes less pretentious and more like real conversation, the proportion of interventions made in English increases. Speakers of Arabic, Chinese and Russian usually admit that their languages are not widely understood by other delegates. Sometimes, speakers of French and Spanish persist longer in their own language as matter of policy, to uphold its status, but they also reach often a point where the instant gains by speaking a language that all present understand seem more important. All official conference documents are translated into conference's working languages and a major effort is made by Secretariats to get written translations in useful time, taking into account that translation is by its very nature more precise than interpretation, for it seeks to convey in another language every nuance of the original text.[231] Nevertheless, in practice all texts are negotiated in English. English is also by far the language most widely used in informal consultations. French, Spanish and Arabic continue to be useful in informal exchanges between delegations that command one of these languages.

UN and WTO interpreters are highly skilled, but many things simply do not translate. This applies to all culture specific references. Slang and colloquialisms are very difficult and sometimes impossible to translate. Unusual words are at risk of not being well translated. Humour, except of the most elementary kind, is not only difficult to translate, but has great difficulty crossing cultural boundaries. Humour becomes easily offensive in translation.[232] The fact that audience is listening either through the interpreters or directly in a language that is not its own has another consequence. It is important to use simple sentence construction and short sentences, as well as to speak slowly with pauses, hence interpreters and delegates who are not fully comfortable with the language are allowed time to catch up.

4. The mechanics of speaking. Speaking in public and **through a microphone** is different from **face to face conversation**. An upright, open shouldered posture is important. Microphones deep voices: if the natural pitch is high, it is worth making an effort to lower it. It is also most effective to convey an

---

[231] Hywel D. Davies, From the Translators' Workshop, in M.A. Boisard and E.M. Chossudovsky, Multilateral Diplomacy: The United Nations System at Geneva, A Working Guide. The Hague: Kluwer Law International, 1998, p. 169.

[232] Carter Peers, From the Interpreters' Booth, in M.A. Boisard and E.M.Chossudovsky, Multilateral Diplomacy: The United Nations System at Geneva, A Working Guide. The Hague: Kluwer Law International, 1998, p.162.

impression of **sincerity**. Any hint of lack of conviction is magnified and seriously weaken (even negate) - the message one is trying to convey. **Clarity** and **being well understood** are prime concerns. Also, delegates need to remember that they speak to human beings and want to engage their attention.[233] Reading a prepared text, unless it is a formal group statement or a general debate statement, is more engaging if the impression of reading is not given. And even when it is obvious that one is reading from a lengthy text, it is important to raise the eyes and (where the seating plan allows) engage the audience from time to time and vary the tone and speed of delivery.[234] In large meetings **gestures** are used to brighten the speech delivery, but only in moderation, and mainly as self-help, because in most situations, few people are looking at the speaker. On the contrary, in small group discussions, appropriate gestures are welcomed and support the communication.

We underline that the delegates should use the style of language and formulas that are traditionally used in the conference they are participating in. Everything in their behaviour and attitude, not only their words but also the tone, speed and pitch of their voice, posture and gestures should reflect respect for the Chairman and fellow delegates.

4.1.2 General debate

Most conferences begin with a **general debate**,[235] which is held in the Plenary. This is not really a debate, in the sense that speakers do not respond to each other, delegates reading out formal statements, prepared in advance and often at headquarters in their capitals. To make a general debate statement a delegate has to inscribe him or herself, or the delegation leader, ("to reserve a place") on the list of speakers kept by the Secretariat for the Chairman, well in advance, sometimes days before the conference begins (see chapter 3.1.9).

4.1.3 Formal debate and negotiation

The word debate is applied to everything that is said in the formal proceedings of the conference, both in the plenary and any of the committees and/or other subsidiary bodies, by the Chairman speaking to the conference or by

---

[233] Walker R.A., Manual for UN Delegates - Conference Process, Procedure and Negotiation, UN Publication, 2011, p.86.

[234] op.cit., p. 88.

[235] Walker R.A., Multilateral Conferences: Purposeful International Negotiation. London: Palgrave Macmillan, 2004, p.140.

delegates when they have the floor. During formal debates, delegates should always pay attention to what other countries are stating in their speeches and should never talk to anyone because it is perceived as rude and disrespectful (no side conversations). On the other hand, one would not want to see people speaking during his or her speeches, so that courtesy should be extended to others. Conversely, delegates might send notes to other countries during formal debates, especially if their policy aligns with something they presented before the conference. It is noteworthy that during formal debates, delegates should avoid using points of order or personal privileges because it is seen as disrespectful to the Chairman and conference.[236]

There are several phases of formal debate: the general debate (see chapters 3.1.9 and 4.1.2), procedural debate, substantive debate and negotiation, with an overlap between the last three.

Procedural debate[237] is the discussions on how the conference organizes its work. **Substantive debate** is the discussion of the policy or technical issues the conference addressees. **Negotiation** is a prolongation of either procedural or, more commonly, substantive debate, to try to reach agreement. The overlap exists because sometimes, what is presented as a procedural question has in fact a substantive purpose, and there is no clear distinction between discussion and negotiation in terms of both procedure and substance. However, delegates often speak about a negotiation phase or a negotiating body, referring to a phase or body in which discussion is narrowly focused on finding agreement on specific words, as opposed to broader ideas. In large conferences, the more detailed substantive debate and negotiation mainly takes place in committees or councils. Sometimes particular issues are sent to working groups, sub-committees or other subsidiary bodies for even more focused and detailed negotiation.[238]

---

[236] James Katie, Marmo Elena, Zona Michael and Bolton Matthew, Model United Nations Program, Diplomatic Language, Conduct and Decorum, Pace University New York City, 2013 (available at pacenycmun.org).

[237] Some conferences distinguish between procedure and substance by allocating work to different subsidiary bodies. For example, at the first plenary session of the PrepCom of the World Summit on the Information Society in 2002, delegates allocated adopting the Summit's rules of procedure to Sub-committee 1, and substantive issues related to the Summit's theme and outcomes were debated in Sub-committee 2.

[238] United Nations Institute for Training and Research (UNITAR), Performing Effectively in Multilateral Conferences and Diplomacy - Interventions, Documents and Resolutions, 2006, pp. 12-13.

The content and style of **statements** in substantive and procedural debate and negotiation are part of the intervening process of multilateral conferences (see chapter 4.2). As debates move forward, there is a **gradation of formality**, opening and closing ceremonies, along with the general debate, being the most solemn and formal occasions. Substantive debate (in plenary and in committees) often starts fairly formally but becomes less formal as it moves closer to negotiation and, particularly, when negotiation continues into the late hours of the evening (or the early hours of the following morning). Procedural debate and textual negotiation are the least formal phases, but even during these discussions the tendency is to start with greater formality and to relax the formality as the discussion proceeds.

4.1.4 Informal exchanges

Informal consultations are all conference-related conversations which take place outside the formal debate (see chapter 3.3). In most cases, delegates speak directly to each other, in the second person. It is very much like everyday conversation, except that it is coloured by the particularly high level of the mutual respect expected between representatives of States. Even though un-moderated caucuses have a more informal style, delegates still work with each other in a diplomatic and respectful manner. For example, the delegates do not avoid other delegates because they have different positions, the delegates do not criticize or defame other delegates even their ideas are not similar, the delegates do not boss around and do not manipulate other delegates to perform further duties than the assigned ones. Everybody makes an effort to exchange ideas and respect the positions of others in order to build consensus.[239]

Informal consultations have also **variable degrees of formality**. In some contact groups, presided over by the conference Chairman or a representative nominated by the Chairman, delegates' behaviour is very much like the one in formal proceedings. Besides, some caucus groups have chairmen (and other officers) and rules of procedure, written or unwritten. Short of these two extremes, some informal consultations have a structured format and a corresponding degree of formality. For example, in consultations within groups of delegates, such as a co-sponsors group, someone takes the responsibility to

---

[239] James Katie, Marmo Elena, Zona Michael and Bolton Matthew, Model United Nations Program, Diplomatic Language, Conduct and Decorum, Pace University New York City, 2013 (available at pacenycmun.org).

convene the meeting and act, to a degree, as moderator. That individual is an informal chairman of the group. There are no written rules of procedure, but there are mutual expectations and practical requirements (e.g. delegates should speak one at a time and not for too long, someone needs to sum up and record whatever is decided, etc.). To summarize, there are minimal unwritten rules of procedure which amount to a very simplified version of the formal ones.[240]

These aspects relate not only to consultations, but also to social exchanges between delegates. They conduct themselves in a way that eases communication between people from different cultures and traditions, who are representatives of sovereign States and parties with whom agreement have to be found if the conference is to succeed. The success of any multilateral conference is dependent on the effectiveness in establishing communication with the other parties, and on conducting the informal consultations in similar manner to the official consultations.

4.2 Intervening in multilateral conferences

All people and all communication situations are unique. Effective intervening in multilateral conferences comes from being able to sense accurately what other delegates are feeling or thinking at any given time and then responding in such a way as to avoid bad feelings or awkwardness, whilst at the same time asserting or reflecting own ideas and feelings back in a subtle and well-meaning manner.

4.2.1 Preparing to intervene

In **formal debate**, one of the advantages is that delegates have time to prepare their remarks, while other delegates take their turn ahead on the list of speakers. As only the Chairman knows how long the list of speakers is, if one delegate says something to which another one thinks he/she should reply, this does not have to be done immediately. Often the delegate delays before seeking the floor and there is further delay until his/her turn to speak. This gives time to delegates to prepare their remarks, a very important aspect during debates as there are some factors and challenges to consider, and the stakes are high:

---

[240] United Nations Institute for Training and Research (UNITAR), Performing Effectively in Multilateral Conferences and Diplomacy - Interventions, Documents and Resolutions, 2006, p. 14-15.

- the delegate is a spokesman for a government and country (or organization), speaking in a forum which is both public and/or exposed to disclosures and an important arena of interaction with other governments;

- the delegates are often engaged in a delicate task: trying to get the representatives of other governments to do what their government wants, so the statements should be calmly and judiciously prepare.

In **introducing a formal proposal**, the delegates prepare the statement before the meeting or while the conference is addressing other agenda items. As we noted, general debate statements are always prepared well in advance. If a delegate is speaking on behalf of a group, often the statement was subject of careful negotiation and discussed with the group before he/she speak. Sometimes, as in the framework of the UN Conference on Trade and Development (UNCTAD), individual countries and spokesmen often take the floor to explain their positions or to pint out their unique interests which, at times, may not be in harmony with the general position of the group as expressed by the spokesmen.[241]

Whether in formal debate or informal exchanges, preparing the interventions is not only about calmly and carefully thinking on the substantive content and wording of the statement, but two other dimensions: **timing** and **consultation**. Just as in face-to-face conversation, the **timing** of a statement in a conference is very important. The same words can have a very different impact, depending on when (and where) they are said. Thus, for example, if a delegate is making a proposal, he/she needs to sense whether the conference is receptive. In this regard he/she asses if: he/she was sufficiently well informed on the issue, the others said what they wanted to say, the others were looking for wording or a procedural suggestion, the others are tired and keen to go home, the others are tired it means they might see the proposal as a welcome quick way out or on the contrary as an unwelcome new complication. Similarly, an apology or concession which might save the day at one time, is useless if made too late. **Consultation** is the "heart and soul" of multilateral conferences. It is often very important to prepare the ground for the intervention by talking to other delegations in advance. If taken by surprise, they might react negatively to what it is said. Sometimes, explaining in advance the purpose of the intervention makes others more

---

[241] Benham Awni, The Group System, in M.A. Boisard and E.M. Chossudovsky, Multilateral Diplomacy: The United Nations System at Geneva, A Working Guide. The Hague: Kluwer Law International, 1998, p. 199.

receptive. At times, consultations are used to encourage other delegates to support the proposal or otherwise intervene helpfully, before or after the intervention.[242]

Considering the purpose of intervention, whether it is really necessary to intervene is also an important part of preparing to speak and some elements[243] need to be taken into consideration:

- *necessity of direct, personal intervention*: if a delegate thinks a comment or proposal is needed, it does not mean that she/he necessarily should be the one doing it. If another delegate says what one wanted to say, there is often no benefit in repeating or supporting what was already said. Sometimes, to be effective a message needs to be conveyed once and rarely gains from being reinforced, even if it is a compelling argument or an insight which changes other delegates' awareness or a notification of opposition to a proposal.

- *Being silent, as the best policy when another delegate says something that others consider provocative.* If this happens, consider carefully what it is gained by allowing to be provoked. Some delegates may deliberately resort to goading others, probably to create a diversion to advance some of their objectives. A delegate gains respect and appreciation from other delegates either passing over a provocative remark, or responding very briefly and in a very measured manner. In opposition, a delegate attracts blame from most other delegates (including the provocative one) for wasting the time and souring the atmosphere by allowing to be drawn into a prolonged or heated exchange.

- political reasons, as sometimes an intervention might be more effective if it is done from another delegation than the interested one. If, for political reasons, a delegation considers it should not intervene, prompting another delegation to speak would do more to advance the specific objectives than own statement.

We underline that a decision not to speak is often the most effective way of advancing the delegation's objectives.[244]

In multilateral conferences, due to the international relations specificity and diplomatic nature of communication, it is very important to understand what is the most appropriate behaviour and in which situation delegations should act. At times the most appropriate action might be withholding the proposal, or introducing a position as a favoured outcome,

---

[242] United Nations Institute for Training and Research (UNITAR), Performing Effectively in Multilateral Conferences and Diplomacy - Interventions, Documents and Resolutions, 2006, p. 17-18.

[243] op.cit., pp. 18-19.

[244] Walker R.A., Manual for UN Delegates - Conference Process, Procedure and Negotiation, UN Publication, 2011, p. 93.

in such a manner that other delegates take credit for it. Sometimes, the best might be a direct attitude, stating exactly what the government wants and how the delegation intends to achieve it. The delegates need to consider carefully every situation and opportunity in order to decide the best course of action. Nevertheless, apart from diplomatic skills, good judgement, practice and experience, the preparation to intervene relies on other elements[245] too, such as:

* *attentive listening*: listening to not just what is said but also how it is said in order to understand, and react appropriately;

* *emotional intelligence*: understanding our own emotions and the emotions of other delegates; it is considered that people with higher emotional intelligence can usually use tact and diplomacy more naturally in communication.

* *showing empathy*: seeing the conference from another delegation's perspective; showing empathy is considered an extension to emotional intelligence;

* *assertiveness*: reasoning for preparing to intervene being able to persuade or influence other delegations to think or behave in a certain way, useful for achieving the desired outcome;

* *affinity*: getting along with other (or same) delegations, enabling better communication and more effective actions toward reaching agreement on a desired result;

* *politeness*: being polite and courteous, respecting of other delegates' points of view and cultural differences is important in international relations and diplomacy;

* *being classy*: reaction in a calm and respectful manner, providing evidence, if requested, for delegation's positions and showing appreciation as necessary.

Prepared delegates are able to manage difficult situations and capable of being effective in multilateral conferences. Although a certain amount may be attributed to luck in isolated instances, successful delegations are based on good preparation and planning, strong communication skills, self-control and confidence, as well as knowledge of the target audience and the precise message to be delivered.

---

[245] Adapted from The Art of Tact and Diplomacy - Prerequisites for Successful Tact and Diplomacy, 2016 (available at skillsyouneed.com).

4.2.2 Targeting interventions

At each stage of a debate, it is important to know who the target audience is and what precisely need to be conveyed (and what is not to be conveyed). Normally, there is more than one audience to think about and in general, all interventions present big challenges for all delegates. On one hand, in interventions made in public or at risk of being disclosed to **domestic audience**, the delegate wants to give the impression of defending national interests and advancing the government's objectives. On the other hand, for an **international audience**, such as multilateral conferences and the wider international audience which might follow the conference, the delegate wants to convey the impression of seeking to advance collective or shared interests, not specifically those of his/her country and certainly not any national objectives that may be inconsistent with other governments' objectives. For domestic audience it is important that government's representatives is seen promoting the national pride and taking a prominent role and speaking about the nation's fine characteristics. For international audience this sounds vain if not arrogant and it harms the pride of other delegations, either of which reduces the chances of gaining any support.

The **domestic audience** is most prominent in the **general debate** (where the media are present and a written text is distributed) and especially when the statement is delivered by a minister, Head of Government or Head of State. Its importance declines as the conference focuses more on detail and the discussions move to subsidiary bodies (from which external observers are excluded) and particularly to informal consultations, which, by their nature, are usually private. Commonly, general debate's statements have a considerable component primarily directed at domestic audiences and perhaps at other audiences outside the conference room (for example: specific foreign governments, particular international organization, potential investors, and potential visitors). It is obvious that these audiences hear of or read the general debate's statements. Nevertheless, these statements are also an opportunity to underpin important aspects for achieving the national objectives at the conference.[246] These relate to using the conference as a means of reinforcing relationships or other broad policy objectives. For example, the states seeking membership to the EU, can use the occasion to demonstrate both the degree to which their policies align with those of the EU and their solidarity with the EU Member States. Similarly, a

---

[246] Walker Ronald A., Manual for UN Delegates - Conference Process, Procedure and Negotiation, UN Publication, 2011, pp. 94-95.

government seeking support in a forthcoming election (for example to the Security Council) can display its qualifications.[247]

The **general debate** is also often used to try **to influence the conference outcome**. Thus, for example, it is an opportunity to provide information about the national concerns and objectives. This is very important to achieving government's objectives as all delegations understand that the most helpful conference outcome is the one that not only advances their objectives but also is widely supported (giving other governments an incentive to support and implement it). This gives a reason to delegations to accommodate others wishes and concerns to the extent this is not incompatible with their own objectives. To summarize, publicizing delegation's concerns and objectives stimulates dynamic delegations to start working in its interest. Also, if a delegation intends to launch or support an initiative at the conference, the general debate statement is an excellent opportunity to improve the prospects for that initiative by hinting it to other delegations and beginning the promotion of its merits.

As the debate moves on and becomes more like a **conversation between the delegates** (conducted via the Chairman), they naturally focus more closely on what they are conveying to each other and **less on external audiences**. Nevertheless, the delegation still has to consider the effect of the intervention on all those who were hearing - meaning that the delegate wishes the intervention to be effective for those who already support him/her, those who have yet to make up their minds and those who are, at least for the present, opposed to the proposal - and the delegate wants to convey different, although necessarily mutually consistent messages to all three factions.[248]

These messages need to be transmitted through effective communication means making one delegation's intervention understood by others and understanding oneself other delegation's thoughts and ideas. Three potential stumbling blocks for effective communication in multilateral conferences are distinguished:[249]

---

[247] United Nations Institute for Training and Research (UNITAR), Performing Effectively in Multilateral Conferences and Diplomacy - Interventions, Documents and Resolutions, 2006, p. 20.

[248] op.cit., p. 21.

[249] Kaufmann Johan, Conference Diplomacy: An Introductory Analysis, 2nd revised edition, Martinus Nijhoff Publishers, UNITAR, 1988, pp. 173-175.

- *linguistic difficulties*: delegates and Secretariat must not run into serious language difficulties in talking to each other (interpretation solves this issue in formal meetings);

- *intellectual short-circuits*: there must be an ability to grasp what other delegations are saying - delegates needs to explain the advantages or disadvantages of specific courses of action. It is necessary that their reasoning is understood and followed by other delegations;

- *conceptual roadblocks*: in different parts of the world different value systems exists: basic standards and norms are not the same, so that a word might have a different significance for different people. In some conferences, the Latin tendency to define everything in considerable detail clashes with Anglo-Saxon pragmatism, with its preference for leaving things vague. To establish communication in the conceptual sense, the delegates have to make sure that their interventions, proposals and defending arguments are presented in such a way that they are "understandable" in the communication sense to those to whom they are addressed.

In multilateral conferences it is undesirable not to properly target the audience because there will be a lack of communication on one of these three scores. Intertwined with these potential obstacles, the **clarity**[250] of the communication is an essential element in conveying the message to target audience. The central concern in the construction of a statement in the course of debate is to make sure that the message is well understood, an aspect even more important than adjusting the message for different audiences. This is partly a question of choice of words (see chapter 4.1.1, on interpretation), but it is also very much a matter of the structuring of the intervention. Nevertheless, some recommendations[251] might be followed:

- explain the goals and scope of the statement, from the very beginning;

- situate the remarks in the debate;

- situate the remarks in the context of the known policy positions of the government or previous statements by the delegation;

- compose the statement as a logical progression from one point to another, particularly if the intervention is lengthy; it is easier to understand and more persuasive;

---

[250] Walker R.A., Manual for UN Delegates - Conference Process, Procedure and Negotiation, UN Publication, 2011, p. 97.

[251] United Nations Institute for Training and Research (UNITAR), Performing Effectively in Multilateral Conferences and Diplomacy - Interventions, Documents and Resolutions, 2006, pp. 24-26.

- speak about only one point at a time; if there is a need to speak about several points, it is often more effective to intervene separately on each; Also, if one have several points to make, it is often more effective to make several short interventions rather than one long statement;[252]

- take every opportunity to frame the remarks as supportive of, or, at the very least, responsive to, what other delegates have already said;

In this regard, other considerations might be reflected upon:

- showing courtesy, support or at least respect[253] and sympathy for other delegations increases the chances of them taking a similar attitude towards own concerns;

- advertising oneself as a possible supporter of their positions, is giving them a reason to try to accommodate their proposal according to own delegation's position;

- presenting own position as one which already has considerable support, strengthen its appeal to other delegations.

Delegations participating in caucus groups that make group statements have a specificity: they frequently feel the necessity to speak to express their national concerns which they consider not being adequately covered in the group statement or to differentiate their national position somewhat from that statement without appearing to break solidarity with their group.

- prepare the statement well in advance. We previously elaborated on this and it demonstrated that few delegates can speak effectively without the benefit of written notes or a fully prepared text. However, interventions are more effective if they do not sound fully rehearsed and delegates need special skill to be able to read from a prepared text and still sound sincere and retain the full attention of the audience;

- be, always, as brief as possible and refrain from intervening at all, if possible. Time "is running" in multilateral conferences and should be always wisely managed. Time management is permanently a central dimension of conference management and time is always the most

---

[252] Walker R.A., Manual for UN Delegates - Conference Process, Procedure and Negotiation, UN Publication, 2011, p. 91.

[253] Delegations should pay attention in never fail to display respect for other delegations and their concerns. This respect is their due, as human beings and as representatives of sovereign States. Beyond this, nothing is achieved if one antagonizes other delegations. Not only they become less responsive to one's concerns, but other delegations as well see this behavior as inimical to their interests, since these are more likely to be advanced as long as a harmonious atmosphere is maintained.

precious commodity.[254] Every portion used by a delegation is at the expense both of other delegations being able to advance their objectives and the conference as a whole being able to successfully complete its work. Often other delegations have said what oneself wanted to say, or that the conference does what oneself wants without intervening. If so, it is usually highly preferable that the delegation remain silent;

- remember that it is not the personal opinion that is illustrated and defended, but the represented country. Be aware of different political perspectives and attain a good knowledge of the allies and the opposition. Knowing their positions helps predicting their arguments during debate and it is very useful in helping to decide in advance where it might be useful to seek cooperation or compromise;

- avoid, always, damaging diplomatic relations[255] with important allies and trading partners. Multilateral conferences are opportunities to build new alliances or further develop the existing ones. If a delegate feels that the message is not convincing enough, he or she might summon international treaties supportive of the cause, might introduce reassuring statistics, etc., keeping all the time in mind the government's objectives.

Targeting interventions involves ensuring that all the pertinent facts[256] of the situation are known in order to clarify oneself position. Knowing the target audience and what precisely need to be (or not) conveyed to the domestic or international audience help delegates avoid further conflict, unnecessarily wasting time during the conference, and achievement of their objectives. Nowadays, multilateral conferences and international organizations, as well as national institutions and governmental authorities are increasing the use of all communicational tools to promote better understanding and sustainable relationships with target audiences.

---

[254] Walker R.A., Manual for UN Delegates - Conference Process, Procedure and Negotiation, UN Publication, 2011, p. 91.

[255] Delegations should never forget that an international conference is not only multilateral, but also a large number of bilateral intergovernmental dealings. If the delegate behaves insensitively, or worse, towards another delegation, there can be repercussions for the relationship between the two governments.

[256] The mentioned elements are only general principles. They do not all apply to every situation and the way delegates should apply them vary from one situation to another. In particular many conferences at some stage (notably the latter stages of negotiation) become much less formal and the policy perspective of each delegation, once it has been expressed, is usually taken as generally known. This allows for much shorter, more direct statements, much more like everyday conversation between people who know each other well. Nevertheless, clarity and displaying respect for each other's position remain categorical imperatives, and brevity is even more valued.

4.3 Written communication in multilateral conferences

Delegates, chairmen and other conference participants exchange view and arguments not only verbally, through informal consultations and formal interventions, but also in the form of written texts.

Some of these are papers expressing the views or other contributions of individual delegations or groups of delegations (see chapter 4.3.1), others are texts which are ultimately **adopted**, or at least proposed for **adoption**, by the conference. When a conference adopts a text it makes that text its own: it becomes a <u>conference text</u>. We underlined that *the only thing that a conference can do is agree (or not agree),* in the case of agreement, its text is expressed in words and recorded in written form. **Resolutions** and **Ministerial Declarations** are the best-known examples of agreement texts (documents) produced by multilateral conferences. But they also produce other kinds of texts, such as final documents, declarations, (draft) treaties, reports of many kinds, programmes of action, information circulars, guidelines, etc. Moreover, there are various different documents circulating prior to conferences, during conferences and after the conferences, by way of background papers, provisional agendas, etc. (see chapter 3.1.2 and 3.1.12), all of which being intended to help delegates and the conference itself.[257]

All these documents have in common the fact that they are drafted as clearly as possible and in a format that corresponds to the needs and expectations of delegates. There are various aspects of drafting related to these different kinds of documents, but some general principles apply to all. In some cases (in the UN System, EU context) long time honoured traditional forms are rigorously followed. A particular attention is paid to drafting resolutions (as a very common conference output in the UN System) and to drafting (Ministerial) declarations (as a very common conference output in the WTO context).

4.3.1 National papers

The texts that a delegate drafts in the name of his/her own delegation for distribution during or in preparation for a conference is either **discussion papers**, intended to clarify the subject under discussion and/or to stimulate thinking and guide the debate in a particular direction, or **specific proposals**.[258] In these cases,

---

[257] United Nations Institute for Training and Research (UNITAR), Performing Effectively in Multilateral Conferences and Diplomacy - Interventions, Documents and Resolutions, 2006, p. 27.

the same general considerations apply as to drafting interventions but to some extent differently[259]:

* *brevity and clarity*, as well as a *careful consideration* of the target audience(s) remain essential;

* *success of a text depends on its favourable perception by a large majority of delegations* (aspect more important than in oral interventions). This means that the delegate has to be able to put him/herself "in the shoes" of other delegations and see how the text is acknowledged: with respect for what they said and for their other, perhaps unexpressed, concerns, as going towards meeting their objectives, as avoiding unnecessarily offending their sensitivities (if the text analyses an issue or describes its history), as presenting arguments that they consider persuasive (if the text asks them to move from their present position), with respect to the forms they are expecting, etc. Delegates have to consult very widely with other delegations and to be familiar with the relevant background documents and precedents in order to be able to write texts that meet these criteria;

* *full acceptance and formal identification of the consent.* This is essential for texts which the delegate intends to submit in the name of several delegations or a whole group - not only the text should be fully acceptable to all in whose name it is put forward but also their consent to be formally identified with the text should have been given. Nothing is more damaging, for example, than for a member of a certain group to take the floor and say: "The statement just made on behalf of Group X does not reflect the views of all its members". It is a formal requirement at many conferences that all co-sponsors of a resolution or formal amendment should literally sign the paper given to the Secretariat. Even for group statements, it is prudent practice to get all participating delegations to initial the text.

The **European Union** is a special case worth mentioning. The point of departure here is that EU Member States, broadly speaking, have three formal representation options at their disposal, due to the three different categories of EU competences:[260] the EU has <u>exclusive competence</u> (only the EU can act), <u>competences are shared between the EU and the Member States</u> (the Member States can act only if the EU has chosen not to), and the <u>EU has competence to</u>

---

[258] Walker R.A., Manual for UN Delegates - Conference Process, Procedure and Negotiation, UN Publication, 2011, p. 107.

[259] United Nations Institute for Training and Research (UNITAR), Performing Effectively in Multilateral Conferences and Diplomacy - Interventions, Documents and Resolutions, 2006, p. 28.

[260] The competences of the European Union are defined in the EU Treaties, articles 2-6 of the Treaty on the functioning of the European Union (TFEU).

support, coordinate or supplement the actions of the Member States (in these areas, the EU may not adopt legally binding acts that require the Member States to harmonise their laws and regulations). Thus, the EU Member States have the possibility to draft national papers in their own names. However, formal EU representation in multilateral conferences and drafting "EU papers" varies a great deal, in particular because the EU applies those three different kinds of legal competence. Hence, asking specifically who engages on behalf of the EU in multilateral conferences, a reference to legal competence is insufficient because even a lack of legal competence does not exclude European Commission officials from being accepted as part of the Council of the EU Presidency[261] delegation at a given international conference.[262] The EU's presence in multilateral conferences can be approximated by three different models:[263]

- *the Unconditional Delegation Model*, model that is rarely applied in the EU's engagement in multilateral diplomacy. When it is applied, EU interventions reflects the consent of all EU Member States, for example when a specific case plays a role in the context of a trade dispute and is therefore handled within the WTO setting;

- *the Supervised Delegation Model*. When this model is used, EU Member States delegate have authority to present papers, speak and negotiate with third parties, yet maintain formal representation, provide guidelines and mandates to their negotiator, closely supervise their negotiator's behaviour, and preserve the right to call back the delegation. There are three prime examples of this model being used:

  * the multilateral trade negotiations within the WTO is formally an issue-area that is characterized by both exclusive competence (goods) and shared competence (services and investment) yet the applied governance model is supervised delegation, implying that EU Member States during negotiations are essentially mute and instead carefully supervise how their agent, the European Commission, behaves on their behalf;

---

[261] The Presidency of the Council of the EU is held for six months by each Member State on a rotating basis. It is the driving force in carrying out the Council's work. In December of each year the two countries that are to hold the Presidency in the following year must jointly present a draft annual program. The incoming Presidency must also draw up the provisional agenda for the meetings scheduled during its term of office.

[262] Jorgensen Knud Erik, The European Union in Multilateral Diplomacy, The Hague Journal of Diplomacy, August 2009, p. 196 (available at researchgate.net).

[263] op.cit., pp. 197,198.

* development policy agreements, which are currently the negotiation of the Economic Partnership Agreements (EPAs),[264] are also negotiated by the European Commission on behalf of the EU;

* the EU team negotiating international climate policy has a very diverse background. The rotating Council Presidency is essentially orchestrating a team consisting of issue-specific lead nations, plus European Commission representatives and national experts.

- *the Coordination Model.* This is the most widely used model - consider, for instance, the EU's presence in international financial institutions. EU Member States have clearly stated their commitment to a strengthened role within the two major international financial institutions (the International Monetary Fund and the World Bank). However, in contrast to trade policy, we witness an example of each Member State for itself, not an example of the EU in multilateral conferences. De facto, the four EU Members of the G7/G8[265] enjoy so much their (limited) privileges, prestige and powers within the two international financial institutions that they fiercely resist any change to supervised delegation.

Whatever papers a delegate drafts in national name or group's name, it is meant to be a contribution to the conference that advances or retards it, pushes it in one direction or diverts it into another and in other ways determines the outcome of the conference. Therefore, the delegates need to consider what they achieve by proposing that specific paper.[266]

4.3.2 Conference texts

However, in multilateral conferences, most of the texts in which elaboration delegates contribute, are not national or group papers or proposals but documents written collectively by the conference.[267] In this context, also, *brevity*

---

[264] Economic Partnership Agreements (EPAs) are trade and development agreements negotiated between the EU and African, Caribbean and Pacific (ACP) partners engaged in regional economic integration processes.

[265] The Group of Seven (G7) is an informal bloc of industrialized democracies - the United States of America, Canada, France, Germany, Italy, Japan, and the United Kingdom - that meets annually to discuss issues such as global economic governance, international security, and energy policy. Formerly known as the Group of Eight (G8), Russia belonged to the forum from 1998 through 2014, but it was suspended after its annexation of Crimea in March of that year.

[266] Walker R.A., Manual for UN Delegates - Conference Process, Procedure and Negotiation, UN Publication, 2011, p. 93.

[267] Examples of collectively drafted conference texts are: Reports of committees, working groups, expert groups, etc.; Action programmes; Codes of conduct; Guidelines; Information circulars; Treaties and declarations; Final documents; and Some resolutions and other decisions.

and respect for the concerns of all delegations are very important, but precedents and expected forms and language become more important than in the national or group texts.

Absolute clarity and accuracy are of the highest importance in the case of texts with a standard setting effect, like **treaties**.[268] Sometimes delegations deliberately attempt to introduce an element of ambiguity with the objective of reducing the constraining nature of the document, but those who value the standard-setting do everything in their power to keep this tendency to a minimum.

In elaborating **conference reports**, the practice is to avoid naming countries for praise or condemnation (unless it is the object of the report), while in writing **reports of discussion** the practice is to prevent exaggerating the role of any delegation or conveying tendentious impressions (only the expressed views are recorded not the (number of) delegations or the specific delegations which supported or opposed particular suggestions). However, there is the tradition of allowing a delegation a fuller account of its position in the conference report, if the delegation in question has refrained from pressing objections that would have prevented consensus. Each type of document has its own language and expected forms.[269] As a rule, drafting conference texts demands for clarity, brevity and logical coherence, and they are characterized by: appropriate vocabulary, specific terminology and thoroughness.[270]

No doubt, drafting conference texts is necessarily a collaborative process. The Secretariat and participating delegations (including the Chairman and the Rapporteur) may suggest words or longer texts but these are included in the final version if the conference agrees.

---

[268] An international treaty is an agreement between States or between one or more States and an international organisation, stipulating international rules in a given area. Together with the customary international law, the international treaty is one of the two fundamental instruments forming the basis of the rights and obligations of States. Such agreements go under various names, all of which confer the same legal status. Such names include: Convention, Agreement, Protocol, Declaration, Charter (e.g. the UN Charter), Covenant, Exchange of Letters, etc. (see ABC of Diplomacy, Swiss Federal Department of Foreign Affairs (FDFA), Swiss Confederation, 2008).

[269] Walker R.A., Manual for UN Delegates - Conference Process, Procedure and Negotiation, UN Publication, 2011, p. 107.

[270] Năstase Dan, Drept diplomatic şi consular, Editura Fundaţiei România de Mâine, Bucuresti, 2006, p.346.

4.3.3 Resolutions

Resolutions are recommendations or decisions by conferences, expressed in a particular format. This format is used widely in the more formal bodies of the UN System, notably the General Assembly (GA),[271] the Security Council, ECOSOC and the policy making organs of many of the specialized agencies. The practices of the UNGA in regard to resolutions are better known but what is valid for UNGA it applies to the other bodies as well, subject to some minor variations or necessary adaptations. Although resolutions are a widely used format, they do not carry any special status, in the sense that, for example, a decision taken by the same body in any other format (e.g. that of a verbal decision), would have exactly the same force as a decision in the form of a resolution.[272]

The essential character of a resolution is that it has a particular structure. It is one sentence, starting with the name of the conference, followed by any number - from zero up - of *preambular paragraphs,* followed in turn by at least one - and usually a higher number - of *operative paragraphs.*

Preambular paragraphs.[273] Each preambular paragraph[274] starts with an adjectival gerund (e.g. "recalling", "wishing", etc.) or adjective (e.g. "conscious", "mindful", etc.). Sometimes, there may be more than one word forming the key element at the beginning of a paragraph (e.g. "recalling also", "noting with satisfaction", etc.). The paragraphs are not numbered. They are referred to as "first preambular paragraph", "second preambular paragraph", etc. and informally referred to as PP1, PP2, etc. Each paragraph ends with a comma. Preambular paragraphs are used to explain the basis for the operative paragraph(s) (e.g. they frequently start by recalling previous decisions or authoritative documents that

---

[271] The number of resolutions passed by the General Assembly each year has climbed to more than 300, and many resolutions are adopted without opposition (see Encyclopedia Britannica, United Nations General Assembly, available at britannica.com).

[272] United Nations Institute for Training and Research (UNITAR), Performing Effectively in Multilateral Conferences and Diplomacy - Interventions, Documents and Resolutions, 2006, p. 30.

[273] Walker Ronald A., Manual for UN Delegates - Conference Process, Procedure and Negotiation, UN Publication, 2011, pp.101-104.

[274] Words commonly used to introduce preambular paragraphs: Acknowledging, Affirming, Appreciating, Approving, Aware, Bearing in mind, Believing, Commending, Concerned, Conscious, Considering, Convinced, Desiring, Emphasizing, Expecting, Expressing, Fully aware, Guided by, Having adopted, Having considered, Having noted, Having reviewed, Mindful, Noting, Noting with approval, Noting with concern, Noting with satisfaction, Observing, Realizing, Recalling, Recognizing, Seeking, Taking into consideration, Underlining, Welcoming (Walker R.A., Manual for UN Delegates - Conference Process, Procedure and Negotiation, UN Publication, 2011).

help justify the operative paragraphs). They are also used to build support for the resolution (e.g. by moderating the force of operative paragraphs or by expressing positions that governments wish to support). Because they often express principles, their tone is elevated, but since they do not express decisions or recommendations, a lack of precision in the wording is tolerable. Generally, preambular paragraphs are less valued by delegates than the operative ones. If the preambular paragraphs begin with references to other documents, it is customary to take two further factors into consideration, both deriving from the existing hierarchy among such texts, reflecting the degree to which they are regarded as authoritative. Such reference-texts are listed in their hierarchical order (e.g. the Charter of the UN takes precedence over all others and the Universal Declaration of Human Rights ranks very close to the top. More recent, narrowly focussed and less widely accepted texts are closer to the bottom). Likewise, while it may be appropriate to "reaffirm" a recent decision, a document of unquestioned authority such as the Charter of the UN or the Universal Declaration of Human Rights is "recalled". References to earlier decisions or resolutions include their reference number and date.

Operative paragraphs.[275] Each operative paragraph[276] starts with a verb in the present active tense (decides, invites, expresses, etc.) and ends with a semicolon (except the last which has a full stop). The paragraphs are numbered. They are referred to as "paragraph 1", "paragraph 2", etc. and informally referred to as OP1, OP2, etc. The operative part is the one that describes the action taken by the conference. Some operative paragraphs express judgements (e.g. "notes with satisfaction", "deplores", etc.). Others authorize or seek prompt action by others ("approves the budget", "requests the Secretary General to....", "Urges all Member States to ...", etc.). Yet others relate to the procedures of the conference ("decides to include in the provisional agenda of its next session...", "adopts the guidelines", etc.).

---

[275] Walker Ronald A., Manual for UN Delegates - Conference Process, Procedure and Negotiation, UN Publication, 2011, pp.104,105.

[276] Words commonly used to introduce operative paragraphs: Accepts, Adopts, Agrees, Appeals, Approves, Authorizes, Calls upon, Commends, Considers, Directs, Decides, Declares, Determines, Emphasizes, Encourages, Endorses, Expresses appreciation, Expresses hope, Further invites, Further proclaims, Further reminds, Further request, Further resolves, Invites, Notes, Proclaims, Reaffirms, Recommends, Reminds, Repeals, Requests, Resolves, Suggests, Supports, Takes note, Urges (see Walker R.A., Manual for UN Delegates - Conference Process, Procedure and Negotiation, UN Publication, 2011).

Recommendations[277] **for drafting** both preambular and operative paragraphs include:

- *For both parts of the resolution, clarity and accuracy are highly desirable*, especially if they specify actions to be taken by governments, international organizations, etc. This does not preclude delegates from deliberately choosing ambiguous wording if this serves their purposes (e.g. to secure consensus on a contentious issue);

- *Responsibility for the drafting rests with the sponsors of the draft resolution.* Sometimes conference secretariats help the "drafters" with informal advice about references and other such technical aspects. They can also edit the text of adopted resolutions to correct spelling mistakes or errors in references to pre-existing texts. But in doing so, they must be careful not to alter the meaning of any decision taken by the conference;

- The wording of operative paragraphs must take account of the relationship between the conference and whichever party the resolution calls upon to act. In conferences the authority belongs to the conference (conference is sovereign) and it unfolds based on the principle of equal sovereignty.[278] Thus, for example, most conferences have no authority to issue directions to sovereign States or to other conferences. Consequently, the "drafters" use words such as "urges Member States to...", "invites (Member States or another conference) to...". Nevertheless, the governing conferences of international organizations do have power to issue directions to their respective secretariat. But courtesy and tradition favour softer formulations (e.g. "requests the Secretary General to...");

- *Assessing exactly how forcefully the conference should express itself.* Knowing how powerfully the conference wants to manifest itself, the drafters use various languages for different level. For example, increased forcefulness is shown in preamble by building up "Noting", "Noting with appreciation" and lastly "Noting with deep satisfaction", while for the operative part is shown by crescendo using "Notes", "Notes with regret", "Notes with deep regret", "Expresses its preoccupation", "Expresses its deep concern", "Deplores", "Strongly deplores" and lastly "Condemns".

One should note that there are very specific rules for drafting resolutions, more details being provided in Annex 1.

---

[277] United Nations Institute for Training and Research (UNITAR), Performing Effectively in Multilateral Conferences and Diplomacy - Interventions, Documents and Resolutions, 2006, pp. 33,34.

[278] Năstase Dan, Drept diplomatic şi consular, Editura Fundaţiei România de Mâine, Bucuresti, 2006, p.124.

These elements are just a few that need to be taken into account by the "drafters" of resolutions. In addition to the content of the resolutions, these details might play an important role in analysing and amending proposed resolutions.

Analysing proposed resolutions[279]

The task of analysing resolutions involves identifying first the topic, then the sponsor(s), and finally the intent. Once these have been established, the resolution can be examined in greater detail for the specific actions proposed. The tone of the resolution should be noted. A mild, conciliatory resolution calls on parties to seek a peaceful settlement to a dispute through negotiations and might not make any reference to a specific solution or outcome. A stronger resolution takes a clear stand by condemning certain actions by a country or countries and calling for specific actions to solve the dispute.

One should keep in mind that some resolutions are intentionally vague, while others are more comprehensive and bring in specific details from many different sources to guide future actions. Both types can be used to gain widespread support. The structure of the conference itself dictates the strength of the resolution; if the conference is only advisory, then the wording of the resolutions uses phrases such as "suggests" and "supports". Language can be stronger depending on the mandate of the conference. If the conference has its own budget and its own Executive Council, then the resolution should be a detailed outline for future conference actions in that topic area.

The precise wording of the resolution must be examined carefully when debating whether to support it in negotiations and how to vote. The references in the preamble should be checked; delegates should know if their state opposed a certain UN resolution or opposes items mentioned in the preamble. If the position of the state is to support the general goal of the resolution, but delegates have reservations about certain wording in sections of the resolution, they should pursue changes in the language to make the resolution acceptable.

Amending proposed resolutions[280]

An amendment is a clarification or a change in a resolution that incorporates additional interests or concerns after the resolution has been formally submitted to a conference. It is necessary to keep in mind that changes can be

---

[279] National Model United Nations, The Process of Debate: Understanding the Conference, NMUN Conference, 2011, p. 16.
[280] Op.cit., p. 17.

incorporated into the resolution, prior to its formal submission, without resorting to the amendment process if all the sponsors agree. This should be done during caucus informal sessions.

There are two types of amendments:

- *Friendly*: A friendly amendment is proposed by any Member and accepted by the original sponsors of the resolution. It is typically used to clarify a point. Upon agreement of all the original sponsors, the change is incorporated into the resolution without a vote of the committee. As all sponsors must concur for an amendment to be friendly, "drafters" of a resolution should carefully consider whom they accept as co-sponsors;

- *Unfriendly*: An unfriendly amendment is a modification that can be proposed by any Member but does not have the support of all of the sponsors. Unfriendly amendments must be formally submitted to the Chairman in writing with a given number of signatures (this number varies by conference and will be provided by the Chairman). A vote is taken on all unfriendly amendments to a resolution immediately after to the vote on the entire resolution. It should be noted that the term "unfriendly" does not mean that such amendments are intended to degrade or contradict the resolution in anyway. It simply means that the amendment has not received the support of all of the resolution's sponsors.

Acceptable amendments may add and/or strike words, phrases, or full clauses of a resolution. The addition of new operative paragraphs is also acceptable. It is noteworthy that only operative clauses can be amended. Preambular paragraphs cannot be changed in any way (except to correct spelling, punctuation, or grammar) following formal submission of the resolution to the membership of the conference. Corrections in spelling, punctuation, or grammar in the operative clauses are made automatically as they are brought to the attention of the conference and do not need to be submitted as official amendments. All amendments, whether friendly or unfriendly, must be presented to the conference and approved prior to the onset of voting procedure. If the time permits, the Chairman have amendments printed out and distributed to the conference before voting procedure. Otherwise, the Chairman reads the amendments to the conference before the vote.

4.3.4 Ministerial Declarations

Ministerial Declarations are official documents that are passed by the Ministerial Conferences (in case of WTO or UNCTAD, for example) or

Committee of Ministers (in case of Council of Europe, for example) aiming to address a particular problem or all aspects discussed in the conference. Ministerial Declarations are considered to be binding for the Members, since they are adopted by consensus based on good faith and strong commitment to common goals. Initially, Ministerial Declarations are submitted to the membership in draft form, under the sponsorship of the participants' delegations. Primarily, Ministerial Declarations address the general concern, as well as particular aspects of a given situation and recommend actions to be taken by the Members of the WTO, Council of Europe, etc. As in the case of resolutions, wording in drafting a Ministerial Declaration influences its acceptance by all delegates. The draft Ministerial Declarations should be clear and concise. The better the substance of a Draft Ministerial Declaration the higher the chances of success in achieving consensus and adopting a final Ministerial Declaration by the conference.

In the WTO setting and **according to the WTO rules**, a Ministerial Declaration is a declaration of the highest decision-making body of the WTO, and embodies a political mandate and further guidance regarding the round of negotiations. The legal basis for Ministerial Declarations is imbedded in Article IV.1 of the WTO Agreement (entitled Structure of the WTO).[281] Article IV.1 of the WTO Agreement sets the general decision-making power of the Ministerial Conference, and provides the Ministerial Conference with "the authority to take decisions on all matters under any of the Multilateral Trade Agreements, if so requested by a Member".

Ministerial Declarations are instruments that reflect a text negotiated among WTO Members. For adoption purposes, the Ministerial Declaration is supposed to be included among the legal texts that the Chair of a Ministerial Conference gavels for adoption purposes.

A Ministerial Declaration can be altered only by another Ministerial Declaration or decision of the General Council[282] conducting the functions of the Ministerial Conference in the intervals between ministerial meetings. In case a

---

[281] Article IV.1 of the WTO Agreement provides that: "There shall be a Ministerial Conference composed of representatives of all the Members, which shall meet at least once every two years. The Ministerial Conference shall carry out the functions of the WTO and take actions necessary to this effect. The Ministerial Conference shall have the authority to take decisions on all matters under any of the Multilateral Trade Agreements, if so requested by a Member, in accordance with the specific requirements for decision-making in this Agreement and in the relevant Multilateral Trade Agreement".

[282] The General Council is granted the authority to conduct the functions of the Ministerial Conference in the intervals between meetings pursuant to Article IV:2 of the WTO Agreement.

Ministerial Conference does not result in a Ministerial Declaration, the previous declarations continue to operate as the basis for the way forward in the negotiations.

In practice, in the WTO, the Director-General appoints facilitators (usually three) to support Members to develop a Ministerial Declaration for the next WTO Ministerial Conference. The facilitators prepare the text at the request of WTO Members, after an intensive period of consultations on the shape, structure and content of a potential Ministerial Declaration. The facilitators use textual proposals made by WTO Members to develop their draft. At the request of WTO Members, they also exclude the most contentious issues from their draft, leaving them to be addressed via a separate process.

For example,[283] in the run up towards the tenth WTO Ministerial Conference in Nairobi, Kenya (December 2015), the discussions of the Ministerial Declaration's content were handled in multiple tracks. The Director General appointed three Ambassadors (Ambassadors of Kenya, Colombia, and Norway) to facilitate the process of gathering inputs from Members. The three facilitators held closed meetings with individual Members and Members representing groupings of countries (in total 58 delegations were consulted, some of which represented groups[284]). On the 29th of October 2015, the facilitators issued a report entitled "Tenth Ministerial Conference - Consultations on Ministerial Declaration",[285] through which they sought to summarize what they heard from delegations. The three Ambassadors, in their capacity as facilitators of the Members' discussions in regard to the tenth Ministerial Conference Declaration presented a "consolidated draft by the facilitators" (RD/WTO/7*, 27 November 2015). The facilitators' draft was organized in three parts: Part I as a preamble and speaking of the WTO's 20th anniversary, its achievements and challenges, Part II including a listing of the decision adopted in Nairobi, and Part III dealing with the way forward in the negotiations. Members have asked to pursue an architecture for the Ministerial Declaration that is similar to the one adopted for the Bali Ministerial Declaration (2013), which was also organized in three such parts.[286]

---

[283] South Center, WTO's MC10: The Nairobi Ministerial Declaration, Analytical Note SC/TDP/AN/MC10/4, December 2015, p.12.

[284] See JOB/TNC/55, 29 October, 2015.

[285] See JOB/TNC/55, 29 October, 2015.

[286] South Center, WTO's MC10: The Nairobi Ministerial Declaration, Analytical Note SC/TDP/AN/MC10/4, December 2015, p.14.

Analogous to drafting UN resolutions, WTO Ministerial Declarations need to have **clarity and accuracy**, especially if certain actions to be taken by the WTO or WTO Members are stated.

It is noteworthy that, due to the specificity of WTO and characteristics of trade negotiation rounds, and in order to avoid ambiguity, more indications and streamlines should be given, such as: "to proceed towards the conclusion of the negotiations" (Cancun Ministerial Statement WT/MIN(03)/20, 23 September 2003); "complete the Doha Work Programme fully and to conclude the negotiations launched at Doha successfully in 2006" (Hong Kong Ministerial Declaration WT/MIN(05)/DEC, 22 December 2005); implication on using: Doha mandate/Doha framework/Doha issues, "addressing" versus "concluding", terms as "explicit consensus".

As mentioned, the WTO Ministerial Declarations[287] are organized in three parts, with the Preamble starting with "We, the Ministers...". Each preambular paragraph starts with verb in the present tense (e.g. "we note", "we reaffirm", "we acknowledge", "we pledge", "we recognize", etc.). Part II continues by making reference to the Decisions and Declarations adopted at the present Ministerial Conference. Part III refers to the way forward in the negotiations. More details on drafting WTO Ministerial Declarations are provided in Annex 2.

Resolutions and Ministerial Declarations are the two most common outputs of multilateral conferences (in the UN System and WTO setting, respectively). Their drafting requires a lot of knowledge and skills as well as a good format and structure, all of which help reaching agreement.

4.4 Reaching agreement

All verbal or written debates aim to attain the conference and the delegate's objectives - to have result, to take decisions, to reach agreement. Reaching agreement is accomplished through different ways (like voting and consensus) and is influenced by organizational and human factors, the role of presiding officers, secretariats and groups, the characteristics and requirements of delegations, permanent missions and conference participants, as well as tactics, instructions, statements and coalition-building. The methods of reaching agreement do not vary a lot, even the interplay of delegations and the Secretariat,

---

[287] See WT/MIN(15)/W/33/19 December 2015.

and the Chairman (whenever he or she assumes an active role) might produce a large number of combinations and permutation between participants' positions.[288]. The situation is similar, with different nuances, in the UN System, the WTO or the EU context. As a rule, all proposals for a decision must be put to the conference then the conference decides.

4.4.1 Reaching agreement in the UN System

The United Nations, from its inception, has served as the primary international arena for governments to come together, discuss common global concerns, and make decisions on collective actions to take in response. Despite the often complex interaction of differing political perspectives, Members work together to reach agreement in the belief that strong collective support can help transform written agreements into effective action.[289]

Decision by the Chairman[290]

In multilateral conferences the Chairman makes a very small number of decisions on behalf of the conference: rulings on points of order. Even then, that decision can be "appealed". The word implies an appeal to a higher authority, with the power to overrule the original decision. The higher authority in this case is the conference itself. This is the only exception to the rule that all proposals for a decision must be put to the conference and the conference then decides. A proposal can be made verbally or in writing by any delegate or by the Chairman then put to the conference by the chairman.

Acclamation[291]

If the vast majority of delegations enthusiastically agree with the proposal and wish to make a demonstration of that enthusiasm, they can signify their assent by applauding. If the clamour sounds like overwhelming, universal support, the chairman will usually declare the decision to have been taken **"by acclamation"**.

---

[288] Kaufmann Johan, Some Practical Aspects of United Nations Decision-Making, in M.A. Boisard and E.M. Chossudovsky, Multilateral Diplomacy: The United Nations System at Geneva, A Working Guide. The Hague: Kluwer Law International, 1998, p.231.

[289] UN Non-Governmental Liaison Service (NGLS) with Gretchen Sidhu, Intergovernmental Negotiations and Decision Making at the United Nations: A Guide, 2nd Updated Edition, United Nations, 2007, p. VII.

[290] Walker R.A., Multilateral Conferences: Purposeful International Negotiation. London: Palgrave Macmillan, 2004, p.159.

[291] Op.cit., p.159.

In practice, decisions by acclamation are unusual and almost exclusively used for the unopposed election of a chairman, or sometimes for the adoption of a final document which generates near universal enthusiasm. Acclamation gives the appearance of unanimity,[292] nevertheless, the most commonly form of making a decision is consensus.

Consensus

Consensus is a procedure whereby a conference takes a decision without a vote. Delegations can agree to adopt a decision without a vote but still have reservations about certain parts of the decision, because consensus does not mean that all delegations agreed on every word or even every paragraph of the decision, as some aspects might not be entirely to their liking. The important point is that there is nothing in the decision that is so disagreeable to any delegation that they feel it must be put to a vote. Consensus is distinct from unanimity. Unanimity can only result from taking a vote while consensus can coexist with differing views, to a degree. It is similar with acclamation in the sense there is no checking to see whether all delegations agreed or not.

Delegations join consensus in a decision, even there are disagreements on certain parts because of: respect for the wishes of the majority, acknowledgement of the futility of opposition in given circumstances, apprehension at the possible consequences of opposing the majority will and/or a calculation that active opposition does more harm to their objectives than the adoption by the conference of that particular decision.

The Chairman/Presiding officer declares consensus in the light of the views expressed by delegations, but like all other decisions by the chairman, is subject to its acceptance by the conference. Some rules of procedure define consensus, many do not.

Thus, consensus is a subtle or nuanced concept. It can reflect unanimity but it can also co-exist with a degree of opposition, the most important question being how much opposition? The traditional definition is that there should not be "a substantial body of opinion" against the proposal – which leaves unanswered the question: "exactly what is a substantial body of opinion?" It also leaves open the

---

[292] Unanimity, unanimously or by unanimity: Said of a conference decision taken with the support of all delegations (established by a show of hands or other form of voting, or by the presiding officer asking: "Are we all agreed?" and no dissent being expressed). It contrasts with consensus, the more common form of decision-making (see UNITAR, A Glossary of Terms for UN Delegates, 2005).

possibility of chairmen in extremis taking decisions "by consensus minus one" (a questionable practice). Several sets of rules of procedure explicitly state that "the Chairman shall not declare consensus if any delegation raises a formal objection", and it seems there is an application of this view on consensus in all conferences. The contrary view is that it is preferable to leave the term undefined and to let chairmen and conferences interpret it as they wish. Thus, there are two sides: those who fear the possible outcome of multilateral conferences and consequently wish to increase their own ability to block decisions which they dislike, versus those with more confidence in the ability of conferences to reach agreement and consequently fear nothing.[293]

Whatever the views, delegates have to check the rules of procedure of each conference in which they participate, to see whether they define consensus and if so how.

There is also the possibility of *blocking consensus*, meaning that if several delegations or any single delegation raises and maintains a categorical formal objection to a proposed decision, then there is no consensus, the conference being prevented from taking a decision. Thus, the will of the vast majority is frustrated and a delegate who has some objections to a proposed decision, may be subject to the odium that goes with blocking consensus. Still, when a delegate does not support a decision, he or she does not necessarily need to block it, as he/she may use other means[294] to uphold their national position, such as:

-    expressing their national position clearly, both formally in the conference and widely in informal consultations. They can also distribute papers which further expresses their position, ensuring that all delegations are informed and those working for consensus will do what they can to accommodate these concerns. This, together with the delegates' own efforts in the negotiation, enable them to report that, however unsatisfactory, the conference outcome was the best achievable (for that delegation's purposes);

-    making sure that their position is clear on the public record. They give a condensed version of their remarks to the record writers. In addition, they ask that a comprehensive statement of their position be incorporated in

[293] Walker R.A., Multilateral Conferences: Purposeful International Negotiation. London: Palgrave Macmillan, 2004, p.160.

[294] United Nations Institute for Training and Research (UNITAR), Performing Effectively in Multilateral Conferences and Diplomacy - Negotiation and Decision-making, 2006, p. 56.

the report of the conference (where its general format allows). Often this is given in exchange for not blocking consensus;

- making a show of their opposition, if it is important for domestic political purposes or if their personal emotions require it, by being absent from the room while the decision is taken.

The delegates should weight the benefits and disadvantage of taking any action at all, <u>before</u> engaging in any of these. In many cases, doing nothing - or the least of a range of possibilities - is the choice most compatible with serving one's national interest. This is because in most cases the mandate of multilateral conferences is supportive of the interests of most delegations and the decisions they reach, while not always to everyone's liking in every respect, are the best the international community is capable of doing at the time. Moreover, in the future there will be other opportunities to attempt to secure decisions more in line with national policy, especially if relationships are not eroded by persistence on getting one's own way to the detriment of everyone else.

Voting

Despite or because of its subtle and flexible meaning, consensus is the preferred mode of decision-making in all conferences and the only one in many. Although consensus is by far the most widespread form of decision-making, the rules of procedure of some conferences provide an alternative to consensus, which can be used when consensus is blocked: **voting**. The vote is extensively used in a few high profile conferences, notably the Security Council and the General Assembly, but across the totality of multilateral conferences, it is relatively uncommon. Even where the rules of procedure allow it, it tends to be a last resort, when efforts to find a text that could be adopted by consensus have failed - or when delegations choose to make a show of their disagreement.

If a conference decides to vote, there are a number of different ways it can do so:

- *show of hands*,[295] which subsequent to the questions "those in favour?" and "those against?" are counted as "affirmative" or "negative" by the secretary. Finally the secretary calls for abstentions and counts those as well;

- *unrecorded votes*, if the secretary does not record how each individual delegation votes. Some conference rooms are equipped with an electronic

---

[295] Show of hands is a way of voting in which delegations are invited to raise a hand (or the delegation nameplate) for "yes", "no" or "abstain". A vote by show of hands is an non-recorded vote (see UNITAR, A Glossary of Terms for UN Delegates, 2005).

system by which, when the chairman announces a vote, each delegation can press one of three buttons on its desk and on a large overhead screen, the corresponding light lights up: green for yes, red for no and yellow for an abstention. For an unrecorded vote it is a matter of counting the number of green, red and yellow lights in turn (the electronic system shows the total);

- *recorded vote*, as the lights line up with the name of the delegation casting the vote, the screen also shows how each delegation voted, and this information is recorded in the conference report. Routinely votes are not recorded (the totals always are) but the result of any particular vote can be recorded if the conference so decides.

Roll-call[296] and other recorded votes

In rooms not equipped with this electronic voting system, the way a recorded vote is obtained is by the *secretary calling on each delegation in alphabetical order* (usually starting with a letter drawn at random). At the end again the secretary communicates the result, e.g. "22 in favour 125 against and 17 abstentions". Then the Chairman announces: "The motion is defeated". This is a very time-consuming process in a large conference and usually only resorted to for dramatic effect or by delegations wishing to waste the time of the conference or to increase tension. The justification for a recorded vote is that it increases the public accountability of each delegation; but in practice, this is not necessary: all diligent delegations and media observers can themselves record how any or each delegation voted in a formally unrecorded vote. However, typical rules of procedure which allow voting also provide that a roll-call (or electronic recorded) vote will be held if any delegation so requests.

There is also the system for *contested elections*. If there are more candidates than there are vacancies, the election is by *secret ballot* [297] and the names of the candidates are listed on the ballot paper. The number of candidates corresponding to the number of vacancies who receive the highest number of votes are elected. In the case of *elections to a single position* (for example, the UN Secretary General or the Executive Director of a specialized agency), the conference (the Security Council in the case of the Secretary General) it often starts by holding a *straw poll*.[298] This is a (an informal) ballot where the results

[296] Roll-call vote is the one in which the delegations are called to vote individually, in alphabetical order. Not to be confused with "recorded vote" (see UNITAR, A Glossary of Terms for UN Delegates, 2005).

[297] Secret ballot/vote is a vote organized to ensure that each individual delegation votes remains secret. Widely used for elections (see UNITAR, A Glossary of Terms for UN Delegates, 2005).

are announced, but not recorded in the official records of the conference. This enables candidates with little support to stand down with minimal embarrassment. Thereafter, a first (formal) ballot is held and the candidate who receives the smallest number of votes is eliminated. A second ballot is then held of the reduced number of candidates. Once again, the least successful candidate is eliminated, and so on until there are only two candidates remain and a last round of voting determines the winner. The field of candidates is also reduced by candidates withdrawing from the contest at any stage. Finally, in case of a stalemate, the only solution is to hold another round of voting. In practice, this is delayed for a round of consultations in the hope of breaking the deadlock.

It is noteworthy that not all delegations participate in every vote, for various reasons: the delegation may have lost its voting rights as a result of its government being in arrears with its contributions to the organization holding the conference; the delegates may choose to be absent from the room during the vote or simply refrain from voting; a delegation may not vote because, quite frequently, it is busy elsewhere (in another committee that is meeting simultaneously). "Not participating" has the same effect as an abstention. Compared to a positive vote, it reduces the number of votes needed to defeat a proposal, but the political message is less negative. It is usual for delegates to be engaged elsewhere and not in the conference room when a vote is taken. In that case, if they wish to place their government's position on the record, they can ask for the floor and make an appropriate statement. Although this does not affect the result of the vote, it may be politically important.[299]

Evaluating a vote

On questions other than elections, if a decision is taken by vote, the outcome is usually determined by whether or not there is a **simple majority** (50% + 1) "of delegations present and voting" in favour. In some bodies, for some purposes - as specified in their rules of procedure - the majority required to adopt a proposal is more than a simple majority. For example, in the UN General Assembly, "important questions" (defined in its rules of procedure) require a two thirds majority. (In the World Bank Board, there is a system of weighted voting,

---

[298] Straw poll (election) means an initial round of voting, the result of which is not recorded (see UNITAR, A Glossary of Terms for UN Delegates, 2005).

[299] United Nations Institute for Training and Research (UNITAR), Performing Effectively in Multilateral Conferences and Diplomacy - Negotiation and Decision-making, 2006, p. 61.

related to the financial contribution each country makes to the WB.) In the Security Council the five Permanent Members have a veto.

It is worth mentioning that when the UN was created in 1945, there were only 51 Members and resolutions were adopted by a vote. Today, in contrast, there are 193 Members and roughly 80% of the UN General Assembly resolutions are adopted by consensus, that is, without taking a vote.[300]

4.4.2 Reaching agreement in the WTO

The WTO continues GATT's tradition of making decisions not by voting but by consensus. Where consensus is not possible the WTO Agreement allows for voting - Decisions of the Ministerial Conference and the General Council shall be taken by a majority of the votes cast and on the basis of "one country one vote". The Agreement Establishing the WTO envisages four specific situations involving voting: interpretation of the multilateral trade agreements; decisions on waivers; decisions to amend most of the provisions of the multilateral agreements (depending on the nature of the provision concerned and binding only for those Members which accept them); and decisions to admit a new Member.

Consensus

The WTO is a Member-driven, consensus-based organization. Consensus is defined in footnote 1 to Article IX of the Agreement Establishing the WTO, which states "The Body concerned shall be deemed to have **decided by consensus** on a matter submitted for its consideration, **if no Member present at the meeting when the decision is taken, formally objects to the proposed decision"**.

Voting if consensus is not reached

Where a decision cannot be reached by consensus, the Agreement Establishing the WTO permits voting. At meetings of the Ministerial Conference and the General Council, each Member of the WTO shall have one vote. Except as otherwise provided, where a decision cannot be reached by consensus, the matter at issue shall be decided by voting.[301] Decisions of the Ministerial Conference and the General Council shall be taken by a majority of votes cast, unless otherwise provided in the Agreement Establishing the WTO or

---

[300] UN4MUN, How Decisions are Made at the UN (available at outreach.un.org).

[301] Article IX of the Agreement Establishing the WTO, concluded at Marrakesh on 15 April 1994.

in the relevant multilateral trade agreement (those WTO Agreements that apply to all WTO Members). Most of the WTO Agreements enter into this category.

Article IX of the Agreement Establishing the WTO envisages voting, whenever a decision cannot be reached by consensus. Voting can be exercised in the following situations:

a. Interpretations. Three fourths majority of WTO Members in the Ministerial Conference or the General Council can adopt an interpretation of the Agreement Establishing the WTO and of the multilateral trade agreements.[302] In the case of an interpretation of a multilateral trade agreement in Annex 1, they shall exercise their authority on the basis of a recommendation by the Council overseeing the functioning of the Agreement;

b. Waivers. In exceptional circumstances, the Ministerial Conference may decide, by three fourths, to waive an obligation imposed on a Member by the Agreement Establishing the WTO or any of the multilateral trade agreements;[303]

c. Amendments. Any Member of the WTO may initiate a proposal to amend the provisions of the Agreement Establishing the WTO or the multilateral trade agreements in Annex 1 by submitting such proposal to the Ministerial Conference, which shall decide by consensus to submit the proposed amendment to the Members for acceptance. If consensus is not reached, the Ministerial Conference shall decide by a two-thirds majority according to the rules set forth in Article X of the Agreement Establishing the WTO. The rules applicable to decisions on amendments vary depending on the provision subject to amendment. Amendment to certain provisions of the WTO Agreements (e.g. Article IX of the Agreement Establishing the WTO, Article I - MFN Principle - and Article II - Schedules of Concessions - of the GATT 1994) shall take effect only upon acceptance by all Members;

d. Accession. Article XII of the Agreement Establishing the WTO provides that decisions on accession of new WTO Members are taken by Ministerial Conference and by a two thirds majority of all WTO Members (in practice however, decisions on accession have been taken by consensus in accordance with WTO practice);

e. Financial Regulations and Annual Budget Estimate. Article VII:3 of the Agreement Establishing the WTO provides that the financial regulations

---

[302] Article IX:2 of the Agreement Establishing the WTO, concluded at Marrakesh on 15 April 1994.
[303] Article IX:3 of the Agreement Establishing the WTO, concluded at Marrakesh on 15 April 1994.

and the annual budget estimate are adopted by a two-thirds majority of the General Council comprising more than half of the Members of the WTO.

We underline that when voting within the WTO, the EU has a number of votes equal to the number of its Member States which are Members of the WTO.

Formal and informal meetings

Since decisions in the WTO are generally made by consensus, without voting, WTO informal consultations play a vital role in bringing the diverse interests of its Members towards reaching an agreement.

Some informal meetings include the full Membership, such as those of the heads of delegations. However difficult issues are more effectively discussed in smaller groups. One practice is for the Chairperson of a negotiating group to attempt to forge a compromise by holding consultations with twos or threes delegations, or in groups of 20 to 30 delegations ensuring that the full spectrum of Members' views and interests are represented. Some "variable geometry"[304] may be needed depending on the issues being discussed.

These smaller meetings have to be handled with sensitivity. The key is to ensure that the process is transparent, keeping everybody informed even if they are not in a particular consultation or meeting, and that they have an opportunity to participate or to provide input (it must be "inclusive").

Some meetings take place in the "Green Room" (the Director-General's conference room at the WTO building), which are convened by a Committee Chairman, as well as by the Director-General and can take place elsewhere, such as at Ministerial Conferences.

In the end, decisions have to be taken by all Members and by consensus. However, informal consultations play a vital role in generating consensus to

---

[304] Variable geometry is a strategy that allows negotiations of one or more particular issues to lead to an agreement that is not binding on all of the parties to the agreement. In practice, it is a strategy found in many-issue many-country negotiations. Variable geometry is an alternative to strategies that require all parties to be bound by all of the terms agreed in a complex many-country many-issue negotiation. Variable geometry may apply to either a regional agreement or a multilateral agreement. The term first appeared in documents and treaties of the EU but it has arisen in other negotiations, particularly in the WTO where it is being discussed as a possible method of breaking through the impasse in the negotiations of the Doha Development Round of the WTO (see Lloyd Peter, The Variable Geometry Approach to International Economic Integration, International Journal of Business and Development Studies, Volume 1, Issue 1, Autumn 2009).

facilitate formal decisions in the Councils and Committees. Formal meetings are the forums for putting the positions of all Members on the record, and ultimately adopting decisions. These formal and informal meetings form the basis of negotiations in the WTO.

4.4.3 Reaching agreement in the European Union

The process of reaching agreement in the European Union is very complex, with the Council of the EU as an essential EU decision-maker. The Council of the EU (referred to as "the Council") is the EU's legislator, together with the European Parliament.[305] The Council of the EU also delegates the implementation of legislative acts to the European Commission. The Council's[306] decisions are generally adopted by a simple majority of its Member States.

Depending on the issue, the Council of the EU takes decisions by:

- simple majority (15 Member States vote in favour);

- qualified majority (55% of Member States, representing at least 65% of the EU population, vote in favour);

- unanimous vote (all vote in favour).

The Council's standard voting method is qualified majority, used for about 80 EU legislation. The Council can vote only if a **majority of its Members States is present**. One Member State of the Council may only act on behalf of one other Member State. The Council can vote on a legislative act **8 weeks after the draft act has been sent to national parliaments for examination**. The national parliaments have to decide whether the draft legislation complies with the *principle of subsidiarity*.[307] Earlier voting is only possible in special urgent cases.

---

[305] In most cases, the Council decides together with the European Parliament through the ordinary legislative procedure, also known as "codecision". Codecision is used for policy areas where the EU has exclusive or shared competence with the member states. In these cases, the Council legislates on the basis of proposals submitted by the European Commission. In a number of very specific areas, the Council takes decisions using special legislative procedures - the consent procedure and the consultation procedure - where the role of the Parliament is limited.

[306] The Council of the European Union, Voting System in the Council of the EU (available at consilium.europa.eu).

[307] The principle of subsidiarity is defined in Article 5 of the Treaty on EU. It aims to ensure that decisions are taken as closely as possible to the citizen and that constant checks are made to verify that action at EU level is justified in light of the possibilities available at national, regional or local level. Specifically, it is the principle whereby the EU does not take action (except in the areas that fall within its exclusive competence), unless it is more effective than action taken at national,

Voting is initiated by the President of the Council. A Member State of the Council or the European Commission may also initiate the voting procedure, provided that a majority of the Council's Member States approve this initiative.

The **results of Council votes are automatically made public** when the Council acts in its capacity as legislator. If a Member State wants to add an explanatory note to the vote, it will also be made public, if a legal act is adopted or on the author's request. Where the Council is not acting as legislator, it is also possible for the results and explanations of votes to be made public by a unanimous Council decision. The Council and European Commission Member States may make statements and request that they be included in the Council minutes. Such statements have no legal effect and are regarded as a political instrument intended to facilitate decision-making.

Inside the Council there is **three-stage procedure for reaching agreement**. More than **150 working parties and committees** help prepare the work of ministers who examine proposals in the different Council configurations. These working parties and committees are comprised of officials from all the member states.

Once a European Commission proposal has been received by the Council, the text is examined **simultaneously by the Council and the European Parliament**. This examination is known as a "reading". There can be up to three readings before the Council and the Parliament agree on or reject a legislative proposal.

The Council may sometimes adopt a political agreement pending first reading position of the Parliament, also known as a **"general approach"**. A general approach agreed in the Council can help to **speed up the legislative procedure** and even facilitate an agreement between the two institutions, as it gives the Parliament an indication of the Council's position prior to their first reading opinion. The Council's final position, however, cannot be adopted until the Parliament has delivered its own first reading opinion.

At each reading the proposal passes through **three levels at the Council**: working party, Permanent Representatives Committee ("Coreper") and Council configuration.

---

regional or local level. It is closely bound up with the principle of proportionality, which requires that any action by the EU should not go beyond what is necessary to achieve the objectives of the Treaties.

This ensures that there is technical scrutiny of the proposal at the working party level, political responsibility at ministers' level, as well as scrutiny by ambassadors in Coreper, thus combining technical expertise with political consideration.

1. **The working party**. The Presidency of the Council, with the assistance of the General Secretariat, identifies and convenes the appropriate working party to handle a proposal. A working party begins with a general examination of the proposal, and then scrutinizes it line-by-line. There is no formal time limit for a working party to complete its work; the duration depends on the nature of the proposal. There is also **no obligation for the working party to present an agreement, but the outcome of their discussions is presented to Coreper**.

2. **Permanent Representatives Committee (Coreper)**. Coreper treatment of the proposal **depends on the level of agreement reached at working party level**. If agreement can be reached without discussion, items appear on Part I of the Coreper agenda. If further discussion is needed within Coreper because agreement has not been reached in the working party on certain aspects of a proposal, items are listed in Part II of the Coreper agenda. In this case, Coreper can: try to negotiate a settlement itself; refer the proposal back to the working party, perhaps with suggestions for a compromise; pass the matter up to the Council. Most proposals feature on the agenda of Coreper several times, as they **try to resolve differences** that the working party has not overcome.

3. **Council configuration**. If Coreper has finalised discussions on a proposal, it becomes an "**A**" **item on the Council agenda**, meaning that agreement is expected without debate. As a rule, around two-thirds of the items on a Council agenda will be for adoption as "A" items. Discussion on these items can nevertheless be re-opened if one or more member states so request. The "**B**" **section of the Council agenda** includes points: left over from previous Council meetings; upon which no agreement was reached in Coreper or at working party level; that are too politically sensitive to be settled at a lower level. As mentioned, the results of Council votes **are automatically made public** when the Council acts in its capacity as legislator. If a Member State wants to add an explanatory note to the vote, this note will also be made public, if a legal act is adopted. In other cases, when explanations of votes are not automatically published, it can be made public on the request of the author.

As the Council is a **single legal entity**, any of its 10 configurations[308] can adopt a Council act that falls under the remit of another configuration.

We conclude by underlying the importance of communication in multilateral conferences, the importance of the way the way delegates and other participants express themselves when they speak, when they draft texts to distribute in the name of their delegation and when they draft texts for adoption by the conference. All these are very important in reaching the objectives of the conferences - having (or not) an agreement. Delegates, representatives of sovereign States, do not ignore these rules, traditions and expectations, as their disregard might lead to a potentially high cost of doing so, including the impact of a failed multilateral conference on the international relations arena.

We emphasized that multilateral conferences can only move forward and can only produce outcomes by agreement (or the a near agreement that is a majority decision). The process through which a conference comes to agreement is negotiation. Thus, negotiation is absolutely central to the workings of multilateral conferences.

---

[308] Actually the ten Council configurations are: General Affairs, Foreign Affairs (including European security and defence policy and development cooperation); Economic and Financial Affairs (including budget); Justice and Home Affairs (including civil protection); Employment, Social Policy, Health and Consumer Affairs; Competitiveness (Internal Market, Industry and Research, including tourism); Transport, Telecommunications and Energy; Agriculture and Fisheries; Environment; Education, Youth and Culture (including audio-visual affairs) [Decision 2009/878].

Chapter 5 – Diplomatic negotiations

In international relations, negotiation is the instrument for settling disputes between states and fostering interstate cooperation, therefore international law provides for the immediate passage to negotiate in case of dispute. Article 33.1 of Chapter VI of the Charter of the United Nations, concerning the "Pacific Settlement of Disputes",[309] negotiation is stated as the first instrument of seven methods to be used in cases of conflict.[310] Therefore, in accordance with international law, negotiation has a diplomatic base and for decades, has been the most important tool of diplomacy. Negotiations characterises every detail and the overall diplomatic activities and international relations.

Negotiation is one of most important means of conducting diplomacy, and in many cases results in the conclusion of treaties and the codification of international law. The primary aim of international treaties is to strike a balance between States' interests. Negotiation is about finding a way to reach agreement. When agreement is reached, a dispute is settled and a joint decision has been made.

5.1 Concept of diplomatic negotiations

Since at least the middle of the third millennium BC, the city-states of the ancient Near East maintained friendly relations - or prepared for war - **using the paraphernalia of diplomacy**. Well organized bureaucracies, based on the palace and consisting of officials trained in scribal schools, exchanged ambassadors and

---

[309] Procedures to achieve the peaceful settlement of a dispute between two or more states can take the following forms: • Negotiation, which is the first and most usual way of resolving disputes. A meeting between the states in question might for example lead to an agreement; • Procedures involving Good offices, where a third state mediates between the parties and ensures the material organization of a meeting (Facilitation and mediation); • Conciliation and resolution procedures, where a third state or a conciliation commission proposes a solution to the parties concerned, which is not binding; • Inquiries which, in principle, serve to establish the facts only; • In the case of an arbitration procedure a panel of individuals designated by the parties has the power to make a final decision, which is binding. The states concerned may also submit the case to the International Court of Justice, whose decisions are binding (International justice) – see ABC of Diplomacy, Swiss Federal Department of Foreign Affairs (FDFA), Swiss Confederation, 2008.

[310] The parties to any dispute, the continuance of which is likely to endanger the maintenance of international peace and security, shall, first of all, seek a solution by negotiation, enquiry, mediation, conciliation, arbitration, judicial settlement, resort to regional agencies or arrangements, or other peaceful means of their own choice (treaties.un.org).

messengers bearing cuneiform tablets written in Old Babylonian. Calling each other "brother", kings "at peace" exchanged gifts, cemented their relationships with dynastic marriages, traded along the major routes, made military alliances, settled boundary disputes, and in general "gratified each other's desires". Their relations were regulated by an elaborate system of law, protocol and finance, and they negotiated numerous treaties.[311]

Diplomatic negotiation is as old as the international system itself. Since the birth of the first sovereign units in China, the Indian subcontinent and the Middle East, the desire to establish official relations has existed. Representatives were sent back and forth to establish international hierarchy and to spy on one another. Yet it was only during the Renaissance that a system was established in which representatives were accredited to another country and stayed there for some time.[312] The travelling ambassador made way for the ambassador-in-residence and, as a result, negotiations developed a more structured character. Only as an exception were ambassadors sent who returned to their sovereign directly after negotiations. The resident ambassador became the first-level negotiator, a role that lessened somewhat during the last century with the development of large international conferences and increased ability to communicate between capitals, made possible by advances in transportation and communication.[313]

More recently, **diplomatic negotiation** was introduced as a method to regulate the international power structure, thereby facilitating successful outcomes. A lot of international organizations came into being after the Second World War, from regional to universal, and from sector-specific to general. These organizations formed a forum for the peaceful solutions of conflicts and joint problems. International organizations differ greatly in their degree of institutionalization, ranging from the refined Conference Secretariat of, for instance, the Group of 77 to the partly sovereign European Commission. The result of this development is a patchwork of multilateral forums, where diplomatic negotiation is the activity driving multilateral conferences - from the beginning to their outcomes and hopefully agreement.

---

[311] Meerts Paul, Diplomatic Negotiation, Essence and Evolution. The Hague: Clingendael Institute, 2015, p. 50.

[312] Berridge G.R., Diplomacy. London: Prentice-Hall, 1995, pp. 32-55.

[313] Meerts Paul, Diplomatic Negotiation, Essence and Evolution. The Hague: Clingendael Institute, 2015, p. 49.

Negotiation can be defined as an interactive process whereby two or more interdependent parties seek to reach an acceptable agreement over an issue or set of issues. Negotiation presumes that parties have both common and conflicting interests. It has been said that without common interest, there is nothing to negotiate for, without conflict, nothing to negotiate about.[314] In many respects, this is the "raison d'être" of negotiation; it is always present, and it creates both major challenges and considerable opportunities for delegates at multilateral conferences. Thus, *negotiations have the following characteristics*:[315] (1) there are two or more parties; who (2) have a conflict of needs and desires; they (3) choose to negotiate because they think it is in their interest to do so; (4) "give and take" is to be expected; (5) they prefer negotiation over open fighting; while (6) successful negotiation involves the management of tangibles and the resolution of intangibles.

Some authors see diplomacy as the best means of preserving peace that a society of sovereign states has to offer, where negotiators seek to produce a formula for agreement on the resolution of a problem, which is then translated into acceptable implementation details, whereby the "principle of justice" is its basic subject. Other authors see diplomacy as a negotiation process in a legitimate context - thus diplomacy in the classic sense [is] the adjustment of differences through negotiations [and it] is possible only in "legitimate" international orders. [Legitimacy] implies the acceptance of the framework of the international order by all major powers, while others consider that diplomacy, the art of finding [...] accommodation, is timeless. But in the recent period [...] a narrower definition may be given of diplomacy as the management of relations among sovereign entities through negotiations conducted by the appropriate agents. It is also added that sovereignty, by its very nature, means the denial of any higher authority. This exemplifies *the main characteristic of diplomatic negotiation*: to harmonize the interests of different states without an overarching framework that is strong enough to direct them to a common agreement.[316] Diplomatic dialogue and negotiation are synonyms, and diplomacy is synonym with negotiation.[317]

---

[314] Iklé Fred Charles, How Nations Negotiate. London: Harper and Row, 1987, p.2.

[315] Lewicki R.J., Saunders D.M. and Barry B., Negotiation: Readings, Exercises, and Cases, New York, NY: McGraw-Hill, 2006, pp.6-8.

[316] Meerts Paul, Diplomatic Negotiation, Essence and Evolution. The Hague: Clingendael Institute, 2015, p.57.

[317] Diaconu Ion, Tratat de drept internaţional public, volumul II, Bucuresti, 2003, p.82.

Diplomatic negotiation processes are vital instruments in international relations between countries and in international organizations. **Diplomatic negotiation** is define as *an exchange of concessions and compensations in a framework of international order accepted by sovereign entities.* Such a peaceful process is successful only if there is enough common ground between the adversaries. Effective diplomatic negotiators will diagnose - and if needed create - this common space.[318] Negotiation processes are critical for reaching agreement in multilateral conferences, being a factor with the potential to shape policy outcomes and to influence which policies are implemented and how. All parties in a negotiation process have the interest to achieve a successful outcome and reach agreement.

5.2 Parties and interests in diplomatic negotiations

Approaches to diplomatic negotiation are manifold. The main components of diplomatic negotiation need to be considered: parties and their positions, the process and power involved, and the tension between bashing and bargaining, between competition and cooperation.

5.2.1 Actors in diplomatic negotiation

We stated that negotiation is an interactive process between or among parties. But who conducts the negotiations? The actors appear at the negotiation table from different positions. Although multilateral negotiations are conducted primarily between **official authorities**, representatives of States or Governments (usually experts from specialized ministries or national diplomats), **other actors**, such as international organizations (for example: the World Bank and International Monetary Fund (IMF) technocrat, the UN peacekeeper, the World Health Organization (WHO) health official, the International Atomic Energy Agency (IAEA) inspector, "Eurocrats" and officials of other regional organizations[319]), non-governmental organizations (NGOs),[320] including

---

[318] Meerts Paul, Diplomatic Negotiation, Essence and Evolution. The Hague: Clingendael Institute, 2015, p. 11.

[319] Cooper Andrew F., Heine Jorge, and Thakur Ramesh, Introduction: The Challenges of 21st-Century Diplomacy, The Oxford Handbook of Modern Diplomacy, 2013, p. 7.

[320] Non-governmental organisations (NGOs) are private-law institutions which carry out their activities independently of State authorities. NGOs can exercise considerable influence on public perceptions of issues and situations and on forming public opinion. They can obtain consultative

businesses and trade unions, and, increasingly, parliaments and local governments, are often involved and contribute to determining outcomes. In fact, at many contemporary intergovernmental negotiations and particularly those taking place in the context of large multilateral conferences on economic, social or environmental issues, the number of representatives from "non-state" sectors often surpasses that of state-delegates.[321]

The proliferation of non-state actors has led to questioning the primacy of the state as the main actor in international relations, but the states continue to be the central authoritative decision units with respect to routine, critical and strategic decisions over the conduct of external policy, international relations and diplomatic negotiations. States and governments assign specific task to dedicated individuals (elected officials and civil servants), consequently diplomatic negotiations are also conducted by individuals. But the negotiators sitting in multilateral conferences are particular kind of individual - **national delegates represent states** (see chapter 2), they have responsibilities towards their states and governments.[322] These delegates act under a higher authority which issues instructions and guidelines and they are accountable for their actions, mainly to the government, but sometimes to wider constituencies. (Similarly, representatives of international organizations and NGOs, when they participate in conferences, have responsibilities, accountabilities, instructions or guidelines).

Most negotiators are expected to interpret their instructions with some degree of **flexibility**. This may range anywhere from very limited to quite extensive, depending on how explicit (or vague) the delegates' instructions are. While such flexibility creates some degree of autonomy, successful negotiation almost always requires regular consultation and even considerable negotiation between the delegates and their government (or sending organization). Delegations may contact headquarters and seek new or additional instructions as negotiations unfold, even headquarters never have the same sense of all factors involved at a particular point in a negotiation as those who are actually

---

status within an international organisation, enter into cooperation agreements, or carry out mandates (e.g. humanitarian or protection missions) - (see ABC of Diplomacy, Swiss Federal Department of Foreign Affairs (FDFA), Swiss Confederation, 2008).

[321] For example, at the 2002 World Summit on Sustainable Development in Johannesburg, for instance, NGO representatives outnumbered State delegates by a margin of more than four to one (see UNITAR, Performing Effectively in Multilateral Conferences and Diplomacy - Negotiation and Decision-making, 2006).

[322] United Nations Institute for Training and Research (UNITAR), Performing Effectively in Multilateral Conferences and Diplomacy - Negotiation and Decision-making, 2006, p. 9.

negotiating. To achieve the best results, there is no substitute to giving maximum freedom of decision to the negotiators.[323]

In addition the best results can be achieved and the state's position can be strengthen with a well-qualified negotiation delegation, in which participants combine good knowledge of dossiers along with good negotiation skills. It is considered that the ideal profile is that of a negotiator who is tough on interest and power and lenient on relationship and exploration. Apart from the interests (see chapter 5.2.2) that the delegates have to consider, it is assumed that one negotiator is more skilled than the other, have a better knowledge of his dossier, he/she is more motivated, better trained and have more credit within his delegation, ministry or government than the other. Human differences will influence the course of the negotiations, not in the sense that they would be the most influencing factor on their own, but at decisive moments they can tip the balance. Thus, the more the other factors that influence the negotiation process are balanced against each other, the greater the margins in which the negotiator's personal characteristics will play a role. Therefore, effective negotiators have to have five attributes:[324]

- flexibility: negotiators have to be flexible on means and firm on goals;

- sensitiveness: negotiators have to be sensitive to various social cues about the other negotiator, although this does not necessarily mean that they have to react to that;

- inventiveness: this attribute is very important as an effective negotiator has to be creative;

- patience: negotiators have to be patient and should not react right away;

- tenacious: negotiators have to be tenacious as persistence is important.

All of these traits are influenced not only by character and experience, but also very much by culture.

The readiness of actors to be involved in the process depends on their interests. Negotiations will only take place when the parties, in one way or another, actually need each other. A relationship should exist between (at least parts of) the parties' interests.

---

[323] Walker R.A., Manual for UN Delegates - Conference Process, Procedure and Negotiation, UN Publication, 2011, p. 117.

[324] Meerts Paul, Diplomatic Negotiation, Essence and Evolution. The Hague: Clingendael Institute, 2015, pp. 23, 35, 40.

5.2.2 Interests of negotiators

Negotiation presupposes a conflict of interest, because without it there is nothing to negotiate about and also proceeds from the assumption of the existence of complementary interests, because without them there is nothing to negotiate for.[325] As long as delegates do not participate in multilateral conferences to disrupt them, negotiators have important common interests, however great the divergence between their objectives is. An international conference can only adopt words or make other decisions by agreement or close approximations to agreement (see chapter 4.4 on the different ways in which conferences reach agreement). Failure by the conference to agree means no outcome - either on any specific point or on the whole conference mandate. This means that every delegation which wants the conference to adopt any particular set of words or to take any other decision, shares with every other delegate who is constructively interested in the conference outcome a common interest in the conference reaching agreement. We emphasize that this **common interest** is quite independent of whether or not the delegates have similar positions on the substantive and procedural questions before the conference. In other words, each delegate has an incentive to produce or support proposals which are attractive to as many delegations as possible - preferably all other delegations (because this gives them an incentive to agree). In short, it is very much in the interest of each delegate to make efforts to achieve as much as possible of the objectives of other delegations (as well as their own objectives) to the extent that this does not do unacceptable damage to own aims. Therefore, successful negotiation in multilateral conference often takes the form of a **joint effort to achieve as much as possible of each other's objectives** - not withstanding any differences or even conflicts of objectives. Conversely, negotiations in which the participants lose sight of this factor are rarely very productive.[326]

This mutual interdependence of the negotiators is the cornerstone of successful strategies in multilateral conferences. How much common interest and objectives (or conflicting interests and objectives) may exist and how it affects a negotiation process will ultimately depend on a number of **factors**, such as the nature of the questions or issues under negotiation, the existence of alternatives that parties may have to a negotiated settlement, the preferences and priorities that

---

[325] Rittberger Volker, International Conference Diplomacy: A Conspectus, in M.A. Boisard and E.M. Chossudovsky, Multilateral Diplomacy: The United Nations System at Geneva, A Working Guide. The Hague: Kluwer Law International, 1998, p. 18.

[326] UN4MUN, Fundamentals of Negotiation (available at outreach.un.org).

delegates assign to agenda items, stages in the negotiation, time, negotiator personality and behaviour, pressure and/or expectations from the government, etc. Obviously, the more common interests and objectives (see chapter 5.2.3) shared by the delegates, the more likely that negotiation takes on cooperative features and results in agreement. In opposition, the more interests and objectives diverge, the more likely conflict overshadows the negotiation process and the more challenging will be to reach agreement.[327]

The dynamics of negotiation unfold in conferences as parties exchange proposals and use a range of tactics and techniques to uphold their interests, needs and concerns, promote their objectives and goals, and seek to narrow gaps in order to forge an agreement. Sometimes, these dynamics reflect a highly competitive environment, while at other times, they reveal a greater degree of cooperation, favouring problem-solving. This latter case is facilitated when negotiators share common goals and interests. As the degree of conflict over issues diminishes, agreement becomes feasible and is hopefully achieved.[328] The negotiation behaviour and strategies that parties adopt also depend on a range of factors and conditions. (see chapter 6).

5.2.3 Issues, interests and objectives of negotiation

Issues, interests and objectives are related and important in negotiation, and they are sometimes the source of confusion. **Issues** in negotiation derive largely from the tangible, concrete and substantive questions on (or underlying) a conference's agenda. They are what negotiators tend to focus on, and they may be quantitative (e.g. price, acceptable levels of pollution or emission reduction targets, commitment periods, schedules for tariff reductions, levels of financial assistance, dates of entry into force of a treaty), qualitative (e.g. definitions, terms, or simply the choice of words or punctuation in drafting agreements) or both. It is important to emphasize, however, that in multilateral conferences, negotiations do not just deal with the substantive issues that are generally reflected in a conference's outcome, but also, and often, the underlying legal, technical and procedural details that guide conference processes. In other words, there are **both substantive and procedural** issues.[329] Another procedural issue in a conference

---

[327] Walker R.A., Manual for UN Delegates - Conference Process, Procedure and Negotiation, UN Publication, 2011, p. 116.

[328] United Nations Institute for Training and Research (UNITAR), Performing Effectively in Multilateral Conferences and Diplomacy - Negotiation and Decision-making, 2006, p. 8.

[329] For example, prior to, during and as a follow-up to the first session of the Conference of the

is deciding on the agenda, or on how the conference will organize its work (e.g. how many committees or working groups, and which questions will be discussed). Stakeholders often view agenda-setting as vital to the essence of the negotiation process. Stakes can even be so high as to induce parties break-off discussions over disagreements related to agenda setting alone. At this stage, skilled negotiators can make a difference in shaping the process and overcoming any communication hurdles that might stand in the way of an agreement.[330]

Interests are the foundation to negotiation, and **objectives** are important drivers of the process. Both interests and objectives underlie the positions that negotiators define on issues. Interests (and objectives) are what negotiators want to satisfy (and meet) and, in the end, they are what negotiators care (or ought to care) about. It is quite common to hear heads of State and government officials pronounce the words "national interest" or what is described even in legal instruments as "overwhelming national interest",[331] in support of or against any policy or action. But *interests can also be much more specific, tangible or substantive*, such as promoting trade, promoting human rights, protecting a species from extinction, eradicating poverty, or improving economic and social well-being. There are situations when interests and objectives may appear to be one and same, if, for example, it is said that the objectives are to eradicate poverty or to ensure that all citizens are provided with access to essential medicines. However, an important difference exists. While interests are for the most part static in that they are not likely to change or change significantly over time, objectives can (and may well) change in the course of a negotiation.[332]

Parties to the UNFCCC in 1995, considerable negotiations were held on the procedures by which the conference would take decisions, voting or by consensus (see Performing Effectively in Multilateral Conferences and Diplomacy, UNITAR, 2006).

[330] Alfredson Tanya and Cungu Azeta, Negotiation Theory and Practice. A Review of the Literature, FAO Policy Learning Program, EASYPol Module 179, 2008, p.4.

[331] Nyerges Janos, How to negotiate, in M.A. Boisard and E.M. Chossudovsky, Multilateral Diplomacy: The United Nations System at Geneva, A Working Guide. The Hague: Kluwer Law International, 1998, p.178.

[332] For example: 1) in the mid-1980s, many countries voiced concern over scientific reports that the stratospheric ozone layer which protects the Earth from harmful ultraviolet radiation was being depleted. (Countries generally share common **interests** in combating greenhouse warming. As we have seen from the global climate negotiations, the **issues** that respond to these interests are multiple: emission reduction targets for developed countries Party to the UNFCCC, greenhouse gases, emissions trading, promoting "clean development" in developing countries, etc. And the **positions** that countries have taken up on these issues vary widely.) The USA was one of the countries that shared this concern: its interest was to protect the ozone layer. The USA government's interim objective was to move other governments gradually towards a consensus on the science and risks of ozone depletion. Months after international negotiations got underway, the

Contrary to *issues which are usually tangible, interests and objectives may also be intangible*, such as wanting to demonstrate international solidarity, wanting a proposal to include certain wording in a draft to prevail for personal satisfaction (and not necessarily to address the substance of an issue under negotiation) or simply just wanting to be treated with respect, dignity or fairly. Intangible interests are normally less visible than tangible ones, but they may be just as present and even at times overshadow negotiation processes. One should keep in mind that negotiators are above all human beings, their personal characteristics always play a role and they often see the world from different points of view.

Just as there are different types of issues in negotiation, there are also **different types of interests (and objectives)**: private (i.e. those of the individual negotiator or those of the governmental authority he or she represents); public (i.e. those reflecting the collective objectives of a government, those of the group on behalf of which a negotiator speaks, or those of the conference as a whole); and those in relation to the substance of the negotiation, the process in which a negotiation unfolds, procedures, relationship or even principles.

Some authors[333] differentiate between "intrinsic" and "instrumental" interests. Interests are said to be intrinsic when negotiators value them for their

---

USA government's objectives evolved to supporting an agreement with far reaching reduction commitments, which was articulated in a carefully prepared opening proposal/position; 2) all countries share interests in eradicating deadly diseases (such as HIV/AIDS, malaria and tuberculosis) and ensuring that medication is available to treat people who suffer. In response to the Doha Declaration on Trade-Related Aspects of Intellectual Property Rights (TRIPS) and Public Health, which was adopted at the Doha Ministerial Conference of the WTO in 2001, all countries also shared a common interest to address these concerns by finding a solution to the problems that developing countries face accessing essential medicines and treatment. But member countries pursued different objectives. Many developing countries pushed to renegotiate parts of the TRIPS Agreement and make amendments to certain articles and the position of some developing countries even went as far as proposing that some articles are deleted from the text. And some developed country members had objectives to ensure that this did not happen, and stressed that what was important was upholding incentives for research and development.

[333] United Nations Institute for Training and Research (UNITAR) (quoting David Lax and James Sebenius), Performing Effectively in Multilateral Conferences and Diplomacy - Negotiation and Decision-making, 2006, p. 8. There are also other types of interests: **Substantive interests** are those which negotiators address up-front. They relate to the focal issues, such as seeking increased economic gains from market access, reducing a threat to security or protecting a species from extinction; **Process-based interests** usually involve a delegate's desire to participate or reaffirm his or her standing in the negotiation process (e.g. wanting to take part in a contact group or to convene that group). They can also have tactical objectives (e.g. to avoid delay, that could impede progress towards agreement, or, conversely, to derail an approaching agreement); **Procedural interests** based on procedure focus on how a decision is made, the order in which questions are addressed, etc.; **Relationship interests** are those that take into account any type of affiliations

very essence, or if a favourable settlement on an issue or set of issues is entirely independent of any subsequent or parallel action or negotiation. Conversely, a negotiator's interests are instrumental if they are viewed as an indirect means to an end, for example, if the aim is to achieve a long-term goal or to meet an objective that is not directly related to the negotiation at hand. In many instances, interests are neither "intrinsic" nor "instrumental", but both, and often difficult to distinguish.

Other authors[334] distinguish between "parallel" and "excluding" interests. A relationship should exist between (parts of) the parties' interests. It is very important for the negotiator to know to what extent the interests of both parties run parallel, or whether they largely exclude each other. For parallel interests, a strategy of cooperation is chosen (integrative negotiating), while the second case sees a more competing approach (competitive negotiation). Negotiations take place in two situations. When interests converge there is reason to cooperate and when they do not converge there is reason to consult. Outside these situations, there is no question of negotiating parties may enter in conflict or stay detached.

We conclude that the readiness of actors to be involved in the negotiation process depends on their interests. Negotiations will only take place when the parties, in one way or another, actually need each other. The better knowing the interests, the better the relationship and the more cooperation each side gets from the other, the more information can be shared comfortably, and the higher the prospects for successful negotiation. To succeed in negotiation it is fundamental to clearly identify the issues and interests at stake, both in the overall negotiation and in each particular phase of the negotiation. Obviously interests are a key component in defining positions, and those interests to which a negotiator attaches highest importance likely determine (or at least largely contribute to determining) a delegate's position on any question.

(geographic, economic, environmental, strategic, cultural, etc.) that negotiators may have with others. A delegate may support a proposal simply because it comes from a member of the same regional group, and not necessarily because the delegate shares "substantive" interests with the proponent of a proposal. Interests based **in principles or visions** can also shape positions. Delegates may support a proposal because the sponsor places emphasis on principles, like, for example: transparency in government, the rule of law or emerging principles like sustainable trade or common but differentiated responsibilities and respective capabilities (see UNITAR, Performing effectively in multilateral conferences and diplomacy, 2006, adapted from David Lax and James Sebenius. The Manager as Negotiator: Bargaining for Cooperation and Competitive Gain. New York: The Free Press, 1986).

[334] Meerts Paul, Diplomatic Negotiation, Essence and Evolution. The Hague: Clingendael Institute, 2015, p. 25.

5.3 Positions and phases of diplomatic negotiations

Diplomatic negotiations are conducted if it is in the interest of the involved parties to solve their problems in a peaceful manner through an agreement. Negotiations have been used since time immemorial as an instrument to reach goals in situations where parties strive towards a common goal, while their interests are not exactly running parallel. Conducting diplomatic negotiations is influenced by the context, cultural element, power asymmetry, the impact of the gap between the needs, and the question of how to bridge it in such a way that closure is possible.

5.3.1 Negotiating positions

Positions represent the stated stances and objectives of the negotiating parties. Parties take positions connected to their needs. These positions are normally more radical than the interests that they have to defend. Depending on the situation, these positions are more or less exaggerated. Negotiators can conceivably define positions on all issues or questions subject to negotiation and debate.

On the many important questions on the agenda, effective negotiators actually define several positions or options, including a solution which would bring him or her maximum satisfaction, a realistic option taking into consideration the interests and priorities of other parties, and a point or outcome below which agreement simply would not be acceptable. This last position is called the **"reservation point"** or **"resistance point"** or **"reservation value"**, meaning that it is the minimally acceptable point beyond which a negotiator would no longer accept agreement (i.e. the "walk away point").[335] In any negotiation, each side has a reservation point, sometimes referred to as a **"bottom line"**. It is a point beyond which a person will not go and instead breaks off negotiations. The reservation points of negotiating parties help to frame the likelihood and possible scope of an agreement.[336] Nevertheless, as soon as there is an overlap of interest an outcome can be expected. Even without the parties having overlapping minimum and maximum reservation points, an outcome could still be constructed, provided that the parties have included more than one issue in

---

[335] United Nations Institute for Training and Research (UNITAR), Performing Effectively in Multilateral Conferences and Diplomacy - Negotiation and Decision-making, 2006, p. 15.

[336] Alfredson Tanya and Cungu Azeta (quoting Raiffa), Negotiation Theory and Practice. A Review of the Literature, FAO Policy Learning Program, EASYPol Module 179, 2008, p.14.

their negotiation process, and that by combining these issues, overlap is created (so-called "package deals").[337]

The overlap range between reservation points constitutes "**zone of possible agreement**" (ZOPA) or the "**zone of agreement**". In a bilateral negotiation, the ZOPA on an issue or question is simply the "space" between the resistance points/reservation values of the two negotiators (i.e. the range of outcomes on which agreement can be theoretically achieved). If the negotiators are successful, they come to an agreement somewhere within this range, and thus both come out better than they would have, had they gone elsewhere. If, on the other hand, the reservation points do not overlap, then no ZOPA exists. An agreement in such cases is highly unlikely and the parties may do better in some other arrangement. When a ZOPA exists, there is a possibility (but not certainty) that the parties may come to a mutually acceptable arrangement. Calculating where the ZOPA lies can be a difficult task given possible gaps in information, uncertainties about true values and the need for estimations. This is, however, a critical step if the negotiator is to have a clear view of the situation.[338] Apparently, the ZOPA is seldom clearly defined and does not remain fixed as a negotiation progresses. Certainly this zone is easier to define when parties are limited to two than when they are 193 States (in the UN) or 164 Members (in the WTO), and when issues are limited in number and quantitative than when they are numerous and qualitative in nature. Although defining a clear zone is often difficult, successful negotiation can be facilitated if negotiators are able to identify at least the rough contours of such a zone:

- knowing, even vaguely, the "walk away" point of the counterpart(s), greatly improves the negotiating leverage. It also helps the delegate make important decisions, such as whether or not to table a proposal at the outset of a negotiation and, if so, how to make it sounds as realistic as possible so the counterparts accept it rather than reject it out of hand.

- knowing the contours of a zone help also negotiators imagine what a "baseline" agreement might look like and thus provides them with the needed information to assist the crafting of a superior agreement through joint problem-solving.

---

[337] Meerts Paul, Diplomatic Negotiation, Essence and Evolution. The Hague: Clingendael Institute, 2015, p. 26.

[338] Alfredson Tanya and Cungu Azeta, Negotiation Theory and Practice. A Review of the Literature, FAO Policy Learning Program, EASYPol Module 179, 2008, p.8.

Successful negotiations are also built around knowing what the alternatives are to a negotiated agreement on a specific issue or a set of issues. *Alternatives* are options that negotiators resort to if settlement is not deemed to be satisfactory. A delegate who can choose from different alternatives has the power of choice, a strong **"best alternative to a negotiated agreement"** or **"best alternative to no agreement"** (BATNA). The alternatives are at the same time increasingly better and increasingly worse, but identifying BATNA helps negotiators set goals, identify what items need to be included on the agenda, draft proposals that are sound and that reflect their interests, and weigh the merits of the proposals of their counterparts. Far too often negotiators begin negotiating without alternatives (let alone a best alternative) and, as a consequence, they may agree to otherwise unacceptable terms of an agreement. An attractive alternative to a negotiated agreement is perhaps the delegate's single most important source of power in negotiation.[339]

It is crucial for negotiators to know, assess and develop their BATNA both before and throughout all stages of a negotiation. To do so, parties begin by making a list of the alternatives available if an agreement is not reached. Negotiators should also take the time to understand and anticipate the BATNAs of the other side, consider the options available given the two sets of BATNAs, develop a plan for implementing them and then choose the best of these developed alternatives. Negotiators who fail to evaluate (and re-evaluate) their alternatives to an agreement both before and during the process may therefore also be vulnerable of rushing to an agreement without having fully considered their or the other party's alternatives, leading one side to end up with a deal that should have been rejected.[340]

However, identifying alternatives and the best alternative is not always easy, and the number of alternatives that actually exists in a negotiation may sometimes be quite limited. Some negotiators may find themselves in a situation where they simply say: "I don't have an alternative". In multilateral negotiations, the number and complexity of the actors and issues, in addition to the forces driving conferences forwards (or backwards) can at times be overwhelming. In such a situation, an alternative may be time (i.e. moving to adjourn debate or even a negotiation session) or attempting to shift negotiations to another forum for

---

[339] United Nations Institute for Training and Research (UNITAR), Performing Effectively in Multilateral Conferences and Diplomacy - Negotiation and Decision-making, 2006, p. 16.

[340] Alfredson Tanya and Cungu Azeta, Negotiation Theory and Practice. A Review of the Literature, FAO Policy Learning Program, EASYPol Module 179, 2008, p.21.

discussion where delegate's power base may be stronger (e.g. moving from discussions in the Plenary or committee to a contact group, where you may find it easier to exercise your "soft power" of persuasion). For example, failure to come to agreement in the Doha Round of trade negotiations[341] has resulted in many WTO Members negotiating bilateral trade agreements.

As important as they are, *alternatives are not always used as productively as they should be*. Quite often, negotiators use their alternatives to engage in hard bargaining,[342] such as "you can take it or leave it" type behaviour. While this may be appropriate (in some circumstances) to save the fundamental interests, alternatives should rather be used to uphold the commitments to the negotiation process - even if it means accepting a long, dragging negotiation process that at times may appear unproductive and wasteful. A strong alternative to a negotiated agreement is one grounded in criteria that are widely seen to be legitimate, such as previously agreed norms or precedents of negotiated outcomes in other forums.[343]

There are also situations when *the alternatives are no longer present*. For example, in the case of the European Union, the classical Westphalian situation whereby sovereign actors negotiate on a voluntary basis is partly gone in an EU where a substantial part of sovereignty is pooled in the EU institutions. In other words, BATNAs are often absent: if matters are on the agenda, then the alternative of non-negotiation is no longer existing. The fact that the EU and its Member States share sovereignty in the core areas brushes the BATNA issue aside and enhances the possibility of assured outcomes, or better said, "unavoidable outcomes".[344]

---

[341] The Doha Round is the latest round of trade negotiations among the WTO membership. Its aim is to achieve major reform of the international trading system through the introduction of lower trade barriers and revised trade rules. The work program covers about 20 areas of trade. The Round is also known semi-officially as the Doha Development Agenda as a fundamental objective is to improve the trading prospects of developing countries. The Round was officially launched at the WTO's Fourth Ministerial Conference in Doha, Qatar, in November 2001. The Doha Ministerial Declaration provided the mandate for the negotiations, including on agriculture, services and an intellectual property topic, which began earlier.

[342] Bargaining occurs when players want to coordinate expectations. Bargaining is the process through which actors try to influence each other's expectations. That is, they want to convince each other that they will not offer more than they currently are offering. Agreement becomes possible only after the expectations of all participants converge sufficiently that they become quite sure that they cannot obtain better terms (see Slantchev Branislav L., Introduction to International Relations - Bargaining and Dynamic Commitment, University of California - San Diego, 2005).

[343] United Nations Institute for Training and Research (UNITAR), Performing Effectively in Multilateral Conferences and Diplomacy - Negotiation and Decision-making, 2006, p. 16.

[344] Meerts Paul (quoting Fisher, Ury and Patton), Diplomatic Negotiation, Essence and Evolution.

All **negotiating positions** ought to have a **hierarchy of elements**. First there are so-called "*essential elements*" to which the negotiators attach prime importance. They are "non-negotiable". In this case, the negotiators have the least amount of flexibility as regards to making concessions. At the next level there are "*less essential elements*", which are important for each party, but there may be some readiness for exchange and compensation. Negotiators are willing to sacrifice some of these elements if they make a substantial gain in an area they consider as more important. Finally there are so-called "*non-essential elements*", (or even elements which were only introduced in order to have something to trade). The delegations are ready to move on such points (date of entry-into-force, for example) in order to improve the overall negotiating climate.

There is always **value and worth in negotiation**. All negotiations involve time (and human and financial resources), and many multilateral negotiations take considerable time (and resources) to reach agreement. We underline the negotiations are goal-oriented, there is a purpose, and the outcome - agreement - whatever nature that agreement may take, it should bring about increased value (worth, gains, satisfaction) to the parties. Of course, value in an agreement is hardly ever equally divided and often, it may be difficult to qualify any value or gains, particularly immediately after the conclusion of the negotiations. Negotiators may say, for instance: "All things considered, I generally feel quite good about the agreement", or, "The agreement could have been better for me, but at least it is a building block for further discussion and cooperation".[345] An agreement that clearly lacks any value for a party, in terms of meeting its interests or objectives, is not likely to be successful. Although the concept of value may at first appear abstract, it is a driver of negotiation. Delegates negotiate because they want a better deal (to improve on the status quo) or because a given situation (relationships, events, etc.) is not to their liking. Sometimes, negotiators may be engaged in discussions that seek to optimize what is of value to them and only them ("individual gains" or "private gains"). At times, this can require a corresponding loss on the part of other delegation(s), which is known as a "win-lose" situation. "Win-lose" strategies are designed to secure the biggest slice possible of the proverbial pie for one side (also called "claiming value"), while leaving the other side with the smallest helping possible.[346] At other times,

---

The Hague: Clingendael Institute, 2015, p.250.

[345] United Nations Institute for Training and Research (UNITAR), Performing Effectively in Multilateral Conferences and Diplomacy - Negotiation and Decision-making, 2006, p. 18.

[346] Alfredson Tanya and Cungu Azeta, Negotiation Theory and Practice. A Review of the

negotiators may be engaged in discussions that seek "joint gains" and reflected by the "win-win" metaphor. "Win-win" solutions involve uncovering interests, generating options and searching for commonalities between parties. Negotiators may look for ways to create value, and develop shared principles as a basis for decision-making about how outputs should be claimed and who claims them.

Diplomatic negotiation is not a "zero-sum" game. On the contrary, it is an interdependent world, achieving own objectives depending on the others reaching theirs. In other words it is about finding the points on which the concerns and objectives of most (preferably all) participants converge. To accomplish that, negotiators use different strategies, tactics and techniques (see chapter 6.3) through all phases of negotiation.

5.3.2 Phases of diplomatic negotiation

Diplomatic negotiation means going through various phases such as preparation and diagnosis, initiations and design, exchange information and introducing proposals, crafting formulas and trade-offs, searching for formulations, drafting the details, concluding and implementation.[347] The factors influencing this process are so numerous and intertwined that a thorough presentation requires a conceptualization that recognizes the importance of negotiation across all the core phases.

1. General background

The process of negotiation covers everything helping the conference progresses beyond an exchange of views (however valuable that is) to decisions acceptable to the whole conference. Delegates talk about the conference "**reaching agreement**" or "**achieving consensus**". These words imply that **agreement** or **consensus** (see chapter 4.4) is what the whole conference strives for from the beginning and this is the aim of all delegates except those intending to disturb the mandate of the conference.

When the mandate of a conference includes decision-making, everything that happens at the conference is part of the negotiation process, including the making of individual decisions. Even with this narrower definition, <u>negotiation is universal to all conference processes</u>. Every conference is preceded by

---

Literature, FAO Policy Learning Program, EASYPol Module 179, 2008, p.7.

[347] Meerts Paul (quoting Dupont and Faure), Diplomatic Negotiation, Essence and Evolution. The Hague: Clingendael Institute, 2015, p.27.

preparatory exchanges which often involve negotiation on such matters as the mandate of the conference, its provisional agenda, who will be the chairman and many other such issues, regularly extending also to at least preliminary discussion, which willingly slides into negotiation of the procedural and substantive issues the conference is to address. In some cases, as a result of these pre-conference negotiations, there is prior agreement among at least some of the participants, before the conference assembles, as to at least some aspects of its outcome. Negotiation is often required in the allocation of work between committees, in determining the composition of the bureau, in finalizing the agenda, in resolving procedural issues as the conference progresses, etc., but most time and resources are devoted to negotiation of texts: texts which relate to procedural issues, texts of non-binding decisions, texts issued from different committees, conference reports, budgets, and, even more intensively, the texts of treaties. All these negotiations, if they are successful, conclude with the conference adopting the text, meaning changing the status and ownership of a proposal put forward by one or more delegates to a <u>text of the conference</u>, which engages all its members (except observers). Usually, the final text is extensively modified from whatever was initially proposed, through the process of textual negotiation.[348]

Negotiation is a **highly interactive process** driven by parties seeking to settle differences and achieve agreement over an issue or set of issues. The process can be divided into a number of stages or key moments, beginning with the diagnosis of a problem or the identification of a situation requiring a negotiated response, and ending with the implementation of the agreement, which may include important legal procedures such as ratification and compliance, as well as non-legal processes such as reporting, training and awareness-raising. Between the diagnostic of a situation and the implementation of an agreement, there is a chain of successive steps as the negotiation is initiated and designed, consultations undertaken, objectives and positions defined, proposals and counter-proposals exchanged, formulas crafted, trade-offs identified, details resolved, and agreement finally reached.[349] The context in which these dynamics unfold depends greatly on the type of negotiation at hand (trade, human rights, environmental, etc.) and may range from simple "one-on-one" discussions

---

[348] United Nations Institute for Training and Research (UNITAR), Performing Effectively in Multilateral Conferences and Diplomacy - Negotiation and Decision-making, 2006, p. 19.

[349] Zartman William I. and Berman Maureen R., The Practical Negotiator. New Haven: Yale University Press, 1982, p.66.

between negotiators sitting across the table to a complex web of interactions taking place in capitals and conference halls, and in a multitude of formal and informal settings.[350]

Negotiation is generally **forward moving and incremental** (although some may be linear), but are occasionally marked by backward, lateral and/or tangential movements. Although the process is largely forward moving, negotiations may stall and turn in cyclical motion, sometimes coming to a halt before moving forward again. Momentum drives negotiation processes, and forward-driven momentum depends on a large number of factors such as: the degree to which the objectives of different parties are complementary; the amount of knowledge and information available on the substance of the issues; mutual information; the nature and quality of inputs, like agendas, background documents and proposals; the procedures; the context in which negotiations take place; commitments, co-operation and meaningful participation from delegates; negotiation skill; and leadership and management from those chairing and providing secretarial duties. A lack of or deficiency in any of these or other features may decrease momentum or bring the forward-moving dynamics of the negotiations to a standstill - if not a complete reversal - as parties seek to clarify uncertainties, consult constituencies, generate additional information, or rethink strategies. At times the negotiation process proceeds at a steady rate; at others the progression takes the form of a succession of incremental steps.[351] In addition to **forward momentum**, some negotiations in multilateral conferences may also experience (simultaneously) lateral or parallel movement if the nature of the issues or the negotiation process leads to negotiations taking place on the periphery of the original negotiating structure or in other institutional contexts. For example, the negotiations on intellectual property issues (Trade-Related Aspects of Intellectual Property Rights - TRIPS) which arose from broader negotiations on trade liberalization within WTO, or the ongoing discussions and ultimately perhaps negotiations about multilateral investment agreements, where OECD, WTO, UNCTAD, the World Bank, UNEP, ILO and other organizations have a role to play.

---

[350] UN Non-Governmental Liaison Service (NGLS) with Gretchen Sidhu, Intergovernmental Negotiations and Decision Making at the United Nations: A Guide, 2nd Updated Edition, United Nations, 2007, pp. 20-21.

[351] Walker R.A., Multilateral Conferences: Purposeful International Negotiation. London: Palgrave Macmillan, 2004, p. 69.

To summarize, the negotiation process is one of progression towards the outcome of these negotiations. This is why the concept of **momentum** is relevant and an important consideration for negotiators who are aiming for an outcome. Conferences can **lose momentum**, become **bogged down** or even **stall**. Some negotiations actually go backwards for a while in that they return to points which were previously thought to have been settled and **reopen** them for renewed debate and/or negotiation. Thereafter the conference must **resume**[352] its progress if it is ultimately to reach an outcome.[353]

As negotiation processes and their progression are marked by different patterns, they reflect an inductive approach and a deductive method. The **inductive approach** is based on parties exchanging proposals and making and receiving concessions until convergence is reached on an issue or set of issues. The **deductive method** is based on negotiation starting with general agreement on a framework of principles from which specific points of agreement are then deduced till the final agreement is reached. While some negotiations are predominantly inductive and others are predominantly deductive, most negotiations combine elements from both patterns.

2. Opening negotiations: from trigger factors to initiation and design

The opening of negotiations includes a number of sub-phases, beginning with a **response to a trigger factor** and a **request to negotiate**, subsequently leading to the design of the negotiation process and mechanism, and the exchange of initial proposals. For opening negotiations, the trigger factor might be any event, insight or inspiration that prompts a response or a reaction by a government (or intergovernmental organization or, sometimes, a NGO) to wish to address an issue through multilateral conferences. Initiation of negotiations is done by governments usually through diplomatic channels which convey their governments' desire to other governments. In practice, this is done through a combination of formal and informal methods, including consultations, representations in capitals via diplomatic missions and sometimes, through official visits, possibly at a higher level (ministers, and Heads of Government and State). These methods may also be accompanied by issuing appeals to the

---

[352] For example, The WTO Doha Round trade negotiations—formally, the Doha Development Agenda—was launched in November 2001. Despite initial optimism, the negotiations stalled and resumes several times and currently they are still going-on.

[353] Walker R.A., Manual for UN Delegates - Conference Process, Procedure and Negotiation, UN Publication, 2011, p. 120.

international community, for example, in an intervention to the UN General Assembly or the Plenary sessions of governing bodies of the specialized agencies and other international organizations, or by preparing a draft resolution which calls for negotiation on an issue of global concern.[354]

The negotiations at the multilateral level may also open as the result of decisions taken by an international conference, such as the governing body of an international organization. For example: the current round of negotiations in WTO (Doha Round) were officially lunched at the WTO's Fourth Ministerial Conference held in Doha, Qatar, in November 2001; the negotiations on the Plan of Action and Declaration of Principles in the context of the World Summit on the Information Society (WSIS) were launched as a result of the International Telecommunication Union (ITU) Council resolution; the United Nations Framework Convention on Climate Change (UNFCCC) was launched as the result of the adoption of a General Assembly resolution; the negotiations on the Convention of Biological Diversity (CBD) and those on the Basel Convention were launched as the result of the Governing Council of the United Nations Environment Programme (UNEP) deciding to set up ad hoc working groups of scientific and technical experts.

The **opening phase of negotiations** also requires planning the process, setting the agenda and designing the structure of the negotiation machinery. In multilateral and bilateral negotiations alike, this phase can get into elaborated details and require considerable negotiation itself, such as determining the number, definition and sequence of agenda items, selecting the venue and agreeing on the seating arrangements of a conference. There is always more complexity in multilateral conferences due to the higher number of administrative and strategic matters that has to be addressed, such as deciding on rules of procedure, approving credentials, establishing committees and subcommittees, delegating work, and electing presiding and other conference officers. The time required to complete such tasks varies hugely and, like so many other sides of negotiation, it depends on a number of factors. Most of these preliminaries take place before the conference starts, but some, such as the formal decisions on the presiding officer, the agenda, credentials verification and approval, and the allocation of work to committees are among the first items on the conference's

---

[354] We mentioned that one of the key events leading to the launching of the Third United Nations Conference on the Law of the Sea (UNCLOS III) negotiations (to update the Law of the Sea) was the intervention of the Maltese Ambassador to the United Nations before the First Committee of the General Assembly (see chapter 2.3).

agenda. This is mainly a matter of the conference formalizing decisions that were extensively pre-negotiated and settled in informal consultations before the conference.[355]

3. Introducing and exchanging proposals

Once the negotiation process is designed and the apparatus is in place, the next sub-phase involves **exchanging proposals and counter-proposals** on the issues before the conference. In practice, there is often an overlap between this phase and the design and preparation of the process. In some intergovernmental negotiations the draft convention or text may even be prepared months in advance by the Secretariat and in parallel to other on-going preparations.[356] Moreover, several organizations and conferences have rules requiring governments to submit items for inclusion on the agenda and/or proposals for consideration by deadlines fixed well ahead of the conference schedule. For example, parties wishing to submit proposals to amend the Convention on International Trade in Endangered Species of Wild Flora and Fauna (CITES) appendices, must submit proposals 150 days prior to the opening of the Conference of the Parties, while in case of UNCTAD Ministerial Conferences, the agenda is adopted by the Trade and Development Board (TDB) at least 300 days before the conference assembles (for example, for the UNCTAD IV held in Nairobi between 17-21 July 2016, the agenda was adopted by the TDB organized between 14-25 September 2015[357]).

One of the challenging tasks for negotiators is **defining initial positions**, elaborating proposals and deciding how and when to convey them to their counterparts. Very often, negotiators begin by **"floating"**[358] ideas in rather vague terms, in written form (in a concept paper, non-paper or draft proposal) and/or verbally (through consultations) to test the reaction of other delegations before specifying details. Usually this is done informally prior to the opening of negotiations, but negotiators may also do this formally in their opening statements

---

[355] UN Non-Governmental Liaison Service (NGLS) with Gretchen Sidhu, Intergovernmental Negotiations and Decision Making at the United Nations: A Guide, 2nd Updated Edition, United Nations, 2007, pp. 22-23.

[356] This was the case with the first drafts of the hazardous wastes and the biodiversity conventions, which were both prepared and circulated by the Secretariat, UN Environment Program (UNEP), for consideration by the respective ad hoc working groups of experts at their first sessions.

[357] See document TD/501/Fourteenth Session UNCTAD/UN/3 June 2016.

[358] Walker R.A., Manual for UN Delegates - Conference Process, Procedure and Negotiation, UN Publication, 2011, p.44 (to float a proposal means to describe and discuss it and perhaps show a draft informally in an exploratory manner before deciding whether or not to make it a formal proposal).

during general debate or, frequently, in debates on specific agenda items. Occasionally, negotiators begin the process by tabling an initial proposal (and sometimes a far-reaching or even extreme proposal), process that is called **"anchoring"**. While this may be perceived as a potentially risky and dangerous tactic to pursue, it is helpful in terms of structuring subsequent debate around a specific point or position for future reference. When there is much information (and varying preferences) on the issue(s) at hand, such proposals often trigger counter-proposals or "counter anchoring" from other parties who do not necessarily share the same objectives. Anchoring is primarily used by delegates who wish to head off alternative proposals or at least to establish the mind set of other delegates from an early stage. Any extreme position is unlikely to be accepted by the conference as a whole, but the first textual proposal to be widely circulated tends to become the basis or a reference point for discussion and counter-proposals. Because it is seen as a fairly aggressive strategy, this approach is most effective when a good reason for proceeding in this manner is given, or sometimes when that reason is apparent to all (for example when many of the other counterparts have less (or insufficient) information about the issue and they are looking for a lead).[359]

A third approach combines the two possibilities discussed above (floating and anchoring) by **making a far reaching textual proposal** but at the same time indicating that some of the specifics are open to negotiation. One way in which this can be done is by putting **"square brackets"** around those parts of the draft wanted to be emphasized as negotiable. The "square brackets" indicate that certain portions of the text have not yet been agreed upon in drafting or negotiating groups. For example, according to WIPO practice,[360] wherever the basic proposal contains words within "square brackets", only the text that it is not within "square brackets" shall be regarded as part of the basic proposal, whereas words within "square brackets" shall be treated as a proposal for amendment or negotiations. On the other hand, there are conferences that omit "square brackets" as an indication that everything is still negotiable (for example the Third Session of the Law of the Sea conference (1973-1982), which made a repeated use of the "single negotiating text" methods - pulling together all the drafts as they exist at a

---

[359] United Nations Institute for Training and Research (UNITAR), Performing Effectively in Multilateral Conferences and Diplomacy - Negotiation and Decision-making, 2006, p. 24.

[360] WIPO Rules of procedure of the diplomatic conference, document CRNR/DC/2, August 30, 1996.

certain point in time, drafts produced by each negotiating or drafting subgroups of a conference, did not make use of the square brackets).[361]

Any initial proposal by a delegate is examined by the other parties to the negotiation, who either accept it or suggest instead either whole alternative texts or changes to some aspects of the original proposal. Such alternative texts and suggested changes are called **counter-proposals**.

4. Crafting formulas and trade-offs

Once the initial proposals and counter-proposals have been exposed, the process of negotiation sometimes consists of simple **"give and take bargaining"** (such as: "I will accept this element of your proposal if you accept this other element of mine"). At other times, a delegate's insistence on his or her own proposal may ultimately lead the others to concede.

There is also a research phase in negotiation for finding ways for solving the differences and elaborating texts that all parties can agree upon. This is mainly a matter of **crafting texts** or sections of texts (known to delegates as *formulas* or *language*) that respond to the divergent positions. It requires negotiators to package information creatively and to explore different options through some sort of "trial-and-error" process. The **process of crafting formulas** is often accompanied by negotiators identifying and engaging in trade-offs on issues which have different importance to each party. We emphasize that issues in negotiation can be added, or removed from the agenda, treated individually or globally. The success of negotiation depends extensively on the ability of negotiators to manipulate issues in a creative fashion and respond to each other's objectives and concerns. A collaborative approach in this phase is known to yield optimum results for both the conference and each participant.

---

[361] Kaufmann Johan, Conference Diplomacy: An Introductory Analysis, 2nd revised edition, Martinus Nijhoff Publishers, UNITAR, 1988, p. 168.

5. Concluding negotiations

With agreement approaching, the final moments of a negotiation are often marked by renewed bargaining and **"horse-trading"**[362] as negotiators engage to ensure that the elements of most interest to them are included in the final agreement. A renewed toughness in behaviour towards the end of a negotiation may also be in response to domestic stakeholders or constituencies doubts about the expected terms of settlement.

There is no rule as to the appropriate or adequate duration of a negotiation. The negotiations might continue until the goal set at the beginning is attained (the Uruguay Round of trade negotiations, for example, was intended to last four years and ended up lasting nearly eight: 1986-1994); at times, when the goal appears unattainable, negotiators simply break-off or, in diplomatic terms, they **suspend negotiations** *sine die*, meaning without settling a date for resuming the talks. For example, in 2000 the negotiations on the biosafety Protocol under the Convention on Biological Diversity (CBD) broke down and they resumed several months later in Vienna, before agreement was reached and the protocol adopted in Montreal in December 2000. Similarly, following the breakdown in 2008 of negotiations on the WTO Doha Round of trade negotiations (Doha Development Agenda - DDA), several attempts were made to restart the talks. Stalemate was reached in 2011, leading ministers to admit (at a Ministerial Conference in Geneva in December 2011) that the Doha Round was in an impasse. Ministers nevertheless agreed to pursue negotiations in areas where progress could be achieved, and talks continued on trade facilitation and on development issues, as well as on agriculture and export competition, leading up to the agreement at Bali.[363] **Suspending a negotiation** is considered reasonable whenever prospective outcomes or external circumstances radically change during a negotiation and delegation-leaders need new instructions from their capitals in order to cope with the new situation - the new instructions have to be agreed upon by the relevant ministries. Thus, coordination and collaboration within a delegation remains of utmost importance, especially when new guidelines for negotiations to be resumed have to be approved by the headquarters authorities.[364]

---

[362] Horse trading: hard bargaining to obtain equal concessions by both sides in a dispute (see Collins English Dictionary – Complete and Unabridged, HarperCollins Publishers, 12th Edition 2014).

[363] 9th WTO Ministerial Conference which took place in December 2013 in Bali, Indonesia.

[364] United Nations Institute for Training and Research (UNITAR), Performing Effectively in Multilateral Conferences and Diplomacy - Negotiation and Decision-making, 2006, p. 27.

Eventually, the negotiations (or resumed negotiations) conclude, as the available time for negotiation expires and delegates are sufficiently satisfied with the outcome. At this point it is extremely important that the conference formally and collectively adopt the agreed text (often as well as a report of its proceedings) for not leaving any doubt about its status.

6. Implementation

The results achieved through negotiations have to be put in practice, meaning implemented and applied. In the case of treaties[365] (formal agreements between states) certain subsequent steps are required. This consist of **signature** of the treaty by a plenipotentiary[366] followed by **ratification** - the official way through which the supreme authority of a state formally expresses its **consent to be bound** (by lodging an **instrument of ratification** with the designated **depositary**: the Secretary General in case of the UN, the Director General in case of the WTO, the Government of Italy in case of the EU). Different countries have different requirements for ratification (for example, in the USA it requires the advice and consent of the Senate; in Switzerland, the Federal Assembly (both chambers of Parliament) approves the ratification of treaties, with the exception of those which the Federal Council is allowed, by virtue of a law or a treaty, to sign and ratify alone; in the EU, the Article 218 of the Treaty on the Functioning of the European Union (TFEU) lays down the procedures and powers of the EU institutions regarding the negotiation and adoption of agreements between the EU and non-EU countries or international organisations[367]). The entry-into-force of

---

[365] See The Vienna Convention on the Law of Treaties (VCLT). VCLT is a treaty concerning the international law on treaties between states. It was adopted on 22 May 1969 and opened for signature on 23 May 1969. The Convention entered into force on 27 January 1980.

[366] Plenipotentiary: a minister or a delegate who has been given **full powers** to engage his State. See notes 73 and 75.

[367] Article 218 TFEU — EU adoption procedures for international agreements. The article sets out the respective powers of the Council, the European Commission or the High Representative of the EU for Foreign Affairs and Security Policy, the European Parliament and the Court of Justice of the EU in the process. In general, the Council has the power to open negotiations, adopt negotiating directives and sign and conclude agreements. The European Commission (or the High Representative of the Union for Foreign Affairs and Security Policy for common foreign and security policy matters) submits recommendations to the Council to open negotiations for an agreement. The consent of the European Parliament is required before the Council can conclude certain types of agreements, including: association agreements; agreements on EU accession to the European Convention on Human Rights (ECHR); agreements with important budgetary implications for the EU; agreements establishing a specific institutional framework (e.g. when the agreements create a joint committee with decision-making powers); agreements covering fields to which either the ordinary procedure or the special legislative procedure, where consent by the European Parliament is required, applies. In all other types of agreements, the European

the treaty usually is linked to a certain minimum number of instruments having been deposited. Most treaties are published in the official journal of each contracting party, especially if their implementation requires that their exact terms are widely known by the administration, the judicial authorities and even the general public. The lapse of time between the adoption of the text by a conference and the ratification can sometimes be years and in extreme cases require renewed negotiations to secure the number of ratifications. All treaties have to be registered with the United Nations,[368] as required by the Charter.

In the case of WTO, any new agreement needs to be included into the Annex 1 of the WTO Agreement. Thus, if negotiations on a new agreement are concluded,[369] the WTO Members adopt a Protocol of Amendment in order to insert this new Agreement into Annex 1A of the Marrakesh Agreement Establishing the World Trade Organization (WTO Agreement). The new agreement will enter into force (in the terms established in Article X.3 of the WTO Agreement) once two-thirds of the WTO Members have ratified and notified acceptance of the Agreement to the WTO Secretariat. To achieve this, WTO Members shall first complete the following three main stages: 1) Ratification stage: At the domestic level, each Member shall undertake ratification procedures, which vary from Member to Member; 2) Acceptance stage: At the multilateral level, WTO Members having completed their domestic ratification procedures should notify their acceptance of the Protocol Amending the WTO Agreement to other WTO Members; 3) Entry into force stage: The Protocol will take effect upon acceptance by two-thirds of the WTO Members.

These legal processes (when needed, as they apply only to treaties, not to other texts the conferences adopt) represent the beginning of implementation. The

---

Parliament is required to be consulted. At the request of an EU country, the Council, the Commission or the Parliament, the Court of Justice may provide an opinion on whether an envisaged agreement is compatible with the EU treaties. The Council may act on the basis of a qualified majority of its members except in areas where unanimity is normally required including, for example, for agreements regarding the accession of the EU to the ECHR.

[368] The Secretary-General of the United Nations is the depositary of more than 560 multilateral treaties which cover a broad range of subject matters such as human rights, disarmament and protection of the environment (see treaties.un.org).

[369] At the Ninth Ministerial Conference in December 2013, Members of the WTO concluded the negotiations of the Agreement on Trade Facilitation (TFA). Subsequently, on 27 November 2014, WTO Members adopted the Protocol of Amendment in order to insert this new Agreement into Annex 1A of the Marrakesh Agreement Establishing the World Trade Organization (WTO Agreement). The TFA enters into force (in the terms established in Article X.3 of the WTO Agreement) once two- thirds of the WTO Members, i.e. 108 Members as of July 2016, have ratified and notified acceptance of the Agreement to the WTO Secretariat.

treaty commitments have to be reflected in domestic legislation, that have to be applied by countries and found in Governments' practice. To end up with such a result, a successful outcome of all negotiation phases is needed, and for this preparation is vital.

5.4 Preparations for diplomatic negotiations

Preparation is the most important and strategic phase of negotiation of a multilateral conference. If governments and delegates want to be successful in diplomatic negotiations, they have to prepare thoroughly before conferences, at least for those with a major stake. Probably, scrupulous preparation is not possible in every case, but general principles and a benchmark for planning need to be applied depending on the resources and time available and the priority which the governments and delegates attach to diplomatic negotiations and to any particular conference. Negotiation is difficult and, like other difficult activities, preparation is essential.[370]

5.4.1 General background

Preparation is everything that an individual delegate, a delegation leader and those responsible for assembling and sending the delegation to the conference need to do before it starts. Preparation maximizes the prospects of the delegate(s) performing to the best of his, her or their ability and achieving his, her or their government's objectives. Preparation requires knowing the mandate of the conference and what outcome(s), if any, the conference is expected to produce. It also requires understanding as best as possible the history of the conference, the issues or agenda items to be discussed and debated, and the underlying interests and objectives that likely drive conferences and negotiations forward. To summarize, delegates need to know what the conference is all about, all about the government's interests, objectives in relation to the conference, and as much as possible about the interests, objectives and intentions of other governments and actors participating in the conference.

Operating successfully in diplomatic negotiations is very challenging. The environment in which delegates work and the processes open to them for achieving their objectives require special knowledge and skills, in addition to a

---

[370] Walker R.A., Manual for UN Delegates - Conference Process, Procedure and Negotiation, UN Publication, 2011, p.116.

careful preparation ahead of time. This preparation is more stringent when conferences are called to take specific actions and governments do not necessarily share common views or objectives. Deployment of effort and resources is justified by the practical consequences of the outcome of multilateral conferences, notably in the UN System and WTO context, as their impact on the real world is important. Conferences provide an information flow which has a strong impact on policy-making in most governments, they reinforce existing standards, both political and technical and constantly develop new ones, which are then expressed in the behaviour of government agencies and international organizations. Undoubtedly, the preparation stage is of tremendous importance for the success or failure of a multilateral conference. Taking into account the fast peace in which conferences operate, the informational and strategic groundwork for the conference must be positioned in the preparation period if the delegates and their governments wish to influence the outcome of the conference.[371]

Still, inadequate preparation for multilateral conferences is quite common and constraints of time and resources (financial, human, technological, etc.) weigh heavily on those concerned. Thus, delegates should be clear-sighted as to what, ideally, should and needs to be done, prioritize carefully and do the best they can in the encountered circumstances. Nevertheless, it is difficult to assess the consequences for unprepared or inadequately prepared delegations, however:

- more effort might be deployed and more time might be needed than would have been necessary had the preparations been adequate;

- their objectives might not be attained, despite the conference achieving an outcome;

- opportunities to achieve benefits for their country might be missed;

- some delegations might fail to achieve their objectives because of lack of or inadequate preparations of others, and thereby resentment might be earned; and

- their government's international reputation and its relations with other governments might be deteriorated.

---

[371] Rittberger Volker, International Conference Diplomacy: A Conspectus, in M.A. Boisard and E.M. Chossudovsky, Multilateral Diplomacy: The United Nations System at Geneva, A Working Guide. The Hague: Kluwer Law International, 1998, p. 23.

5.4.2 Preparation at the national level

Well-prepared conferences can strengthen the state's image in international arena, increase government's chances to reach its objectives, build new relationships, and generate referrals for good standing. For delegates, it gives the opportunity to connect personally with other delegates, and build mutual awareness. All these start with the preparation at the national level.

Preparation within the responsible authority

Governments operating effectively have units focusing on international relations and multilateral conferences in each department, ministry or government agency, units in charge with that body's field of responsibility (trade, health, environment, etc.). These units keep up-to-date with the schedule of conferences, the on-going international debate on the topics addressed by these conferences as well as the evolution of their own national policies and programs that could benefit or otherwise be affected by decisions taken at future conferences. They maintain a **standing brief**, which all relevant officials can consult at any time, and which defines the government's objectives and priorities in that field of policy, report the recent history of the international debate, especially as regards matters of particular interest to the government, predict forthcoming conferences and other relevant events as well as any plans the government may have to use these conferences to advance its objectives. It is very important to update this standing brief whenever new information is received. Sometimes, in developed countries, and for matters of high importance to the governments, this standing brief is maintained on a secure website with access, from anywhere in the world and at any time, for relevant officials. More commonly, the standing brief is on paper and on file and it is reproduced and distributed for the use of interested officials. However, in most cases the standing brief exists only in the mind of one or more officials who can draw upon it to brief others, including delegations to the relevant conferences.[372]

Generally, Ministry of Foreign Affairs maintains such standing briefs on a large number of different topics, due to its areas of responsibility that is affected by multilateral conferences in many fields. Ministry of Foreign Affairs can alert all relevant officials, to the extent that they have access to such a standing brief, about any opportunities for advancing the government's objectives at forthcoming

---

[372] United Nations Institute for Training and Research (UNITAR), Performing Effectively in Multilateral Conferences and Diplomacy - Preparing for an International Conference, 2006, p. 9.

conferences or about any undesirable developments which they would wish to anticipate and forefend. If these relevant officials have the necessary policy authority, they can develop and implement plans to that effect. All such officials need to be sensitive to the fact that their own particular area of responsibility is unlikely to cover the totality of their government's possible interests in any particular conference. It is very important that before developing and acting on any ideas, they make sure to take due account of the relevant concerns of other departments of their own governmental authority or ministry. A thorough standing brief contains clear indications of which other parts of governmental authorities have a possible interest in the topic or the conference. Many governmental authorities have **standing committees** to coordinate the activity of the different bodies and make sure to support and do not hinder each other, and that any differences of perspective are reconciled at an early stage.[373]

Inter-governmental coordination and consultation

Considerable efforts are needed to ensure that the activities of all the various departments of any government authority are fully coherent and well-coordinated, but it is more demanding to make sure that different bodies of the same government do not pursue mutually incompatible policies or activities. The ideal is that all governmental bodies, departments, agencies, ministries etc. and all levels of government work are mutually supportive. In all governments, Ministry of Foreign Affairs has responsibility for international political issues and for many multilateral conferences. In some governments, it has prime duty for all multilateral conferences, while in others the Ministry of Health is in charge with country's participation in conferences of the World Health Organisation (WHO), the Ministry of Transport is responsible for participation in conferences of the International Civil Aviation Organization (ICAO), the Ministry of Trade leads in WTO multilateral trade negotiations, the Ministry of Finance leads on financial negotiations and so on with each **line ministry**[374] leading on conferences in its own specific field. Whichever ministry has prime responsibility, it has to be aware of the fact that other authorities of the same government (and sometimes

---

[373] Walker R.A., Manual for UN Delegates - Conference Process, Procedure and Negotiation, UN Publication, 2011, p.20.

[374] Line ministry: This term is applied in some countries to government agencies which have specific areas of responsibility such as health or agriculture, to distinguish them from the ministries that are responsible for such topics as economic policy or international affairs, which cut across all fields of activity (see UNITAR, Performing Effectively in Multilateral Conferences and Diplomacy, 2006).

other levels of government, such as state or cantonal governments in federations) may also have responsibilities that interest them in any particular conference. In many instances, the lead governmental authority mandated to prepare for and take part in multilateral conferences and negotiations are different than those authorities mandated to implement outcomes of conferences and negotiations.[375] Whichever the authority overseeing the conference and the negotiations, a close cooperation between and among all governmental authorities and an inter-governmental coordination is essential for policy coherence and important for:[376]

- responding to the interconnected issues on policy-making agendas;

- addressing the increased importance of crosscutting issues (finance, education, training, etc.) affecting multiple ministries and governmental authorities;

- facilitating the identification the many interests and objectives that a country may have for a given conference or negotiation;

- facilitating the identification of issues or questions that a government may wish to put forward for consideration at a conference or in negotiation;

- helping to ensure a multidisciplinary perspective in exploring all dimensions of issues, thereby having a more complete pool of information; and

- requiring from delegates broad based substantive knowledge on the issues (technical, legal, scientific) to be successful in negotiations and perform effectively in conferences.

The level and amount of inter-governmental coordination and consultation for a particular conference depends on a number of factors, such as: the nature and number of agenda items, linkages (if any) with other conferences or institutions, the complexity of national decision-making processes, the importance allocated to the conference by the government, etc. The better these issues are prepared and organized prior to negotiation and conference, the easier the task of the delegation.[377] Generally, the more agenda items are linked and crosscutting, the more coordination and consultation across ministries and governmental authorities are required. In some countries and for some conferences, there are arrangements for inter-governmental connexion and inter-governmental meetings

---

[375] Walker R.A., Manual for UN Delegates - Conference Process, Procedure and Negotiation, UN Publication, 2011, p.20.

[376] United Nations Institute for Training and Research (UNITAR), Performing Effectively in Multilateral Conferences and Diplomacy - Preparing for an International Conference, 2006, p. 12.

[377] Winslow Anne, Benchmarks for Newcomers, in M.A. Boisard and E.M. Chossudovsky, Multilateral Diplomacy: The United Nations System at Geneva, A Working Guide. The Hague: Kluwer Law International, 1998, p.190.

to determine the position of "entire government" (for example, in preparations for the 2015 COP21 also known as 2015 Paris Climate Conference or the fourteenth UNCTAD Conference - 2016 UNCTAD XIV). Any government should try to improve its inter-governmental coordination in order to be successful in negotiations and participate more effectively in multilateral conferences, which means in the long-run better national policies and better performance by the government which is beneficial for the country.[378]

Dissemination of information about or gathered at multilateral conferences is another significant aspect of inter-governmental coordination. Many multilateral conferences provide a lot of information that is potentially useful (or necessary to follow-up on implementation requirements) to governmental authorities and sometimes to other stakeholders outside the government. The conferences produce also many standard-setting texts that can be of great value to national administrations. To benefit from this information, it has to be effectively distributed to those governmental authorities and relevant officials who can use it, avoiding duplication, and through appropriate structures and routines.[379]

Consultation with other stakeholders at the national level

Consultation with other stakeholders[380] including parliament, local governmental authorities, non-governmental organizations, businesses, universities and other stakeholders may be important and even essential depending on the negotiation and conference in question. For example, in multilateral trade negotiations, a lot of consultation takes place with businesses and industries representatives; in preparation for the 2015 UN Sustainable Development Summit, considerable consultation took place in many countries with NGOs and other major groups;[381] and in federated states, consultation regularly takes place with local governmental authorities.

---

[378] Walker R.A., Manual for UN Delegates - Conference Process, Procedure and Negotiation, UN Publication, 2011, p.20.

[379] United Nations Institute for Training and Research (UNITAR), Performing Effectively in Multilateral Conferences and Diplomacy - Preparing for an International Conference, 2006, p. 12.

[380] Potential targets for national consultation: Other divisions/sections within the ministry/department/agency; Other ministries/departments/ agencies concerned with the topic of the conference and which could provide information; Ministries/departments/agencies likely to play a role in implementing or following-up on the outcome of the conference; Non-governmental organizations; Private sector or State-run enterprises; Universities/academia (see UNITAR, Performing Effectively in Multilateral Conferences and Diplomacy, 2006).

[381] Since the first United Nations Conference on Environment and Development in 1992 - known as

The importance of consultation with other stakeholders at the national level comes from the fact that the governmental authorities which lead and supervise the preparations for and participation in negotiations and multilateral conferences realize that, in some cases, the expertise and knowledge on a specific subject matter of a conference actually exist outside the government, and consultation with these "other stakeholders" is very useful and their assistance is pertinent. Leading governmental authorities also need to be as forward looking as possible, and acknowledge that the outcomes of negotiations and conferences require very often implementation into national policies and legislation, and application by the government in question. It is true that the government takes decisions and represents national interests, but in many cases, governmental authorities are different from those who effectively take part in negotiations and multilateral conferences, in addition to the fact that the implementation and application of negotiations' results and conference's outcome is eased with the implication of the stakeholders.[382]

Consultation at the international level

International consultations are another important aspect of pre-conference preparations at headquarters. Long before a conference is held, effective governments want forewarning of the topics to be addressed, any initiatives planned by other governments or international agency secretariats and all relevant background. They therefore **instruct** their embassies to speak to other governments and to the secretariats of relevant international organizations[383],

---

the Earth Summit, it was recognized that achieving sustainable development would require the active participation of all sectors of society and all types of people. Agenda 21, adopted at the Earth Summit, drew upon this sentiment and formalized nine sectors of society as the main channels through which broad participation would be facilitated in UN activities related to sustainable development. These are officially called **"Major Groups"** and include the following sectors: women, children and youth, indigenous peoples, NGOs, local authorities, workers and trade unions, business and industry, scientific and technological community, and farmers. Two decades after the Earth Summit, the importance of effectively engaging these nine sectors of society was reaffirmed by the Rio+20 Conference. Its outcome document "The Future We Want" highlights the role that Major Groups can play in pursuing sustainable societies for future generations. In addition, governments invited other stakeholders, including local communities, volunteer groups and foundations, migrants and families, as well as older persons and persons with disabilities, to participate in UN processes related to sustainable development, which can be done through close collaboration with the Major Groups.

[382] United Nations Institute for Training and Research (UNITAR), Performing Effectively in Multilateral Conferences and Diplomacy - Preparing for an International Conference, 2006, p. 13.

[383] Potential targets for international consultation: Governments with which the government has close ties and share common concerns; Governments from which the government expect troubles; Regional and/or like-minded groups; Intergovernmental organizations; Conference secretariat;

seeking information on these matters.[384] Instructions to embassies to make enquiries or representations in relation to forthcoming negotiations and multilateral conferences need to take into account several considerations:[385]

-   The staff acting on these instructions in all likelihood is not expert on the topic - probably the staff knows little about the relevant institutions, the past history of negotiation, the current issues and the related government's policies. In most cases, this staff has busy schedule and no time to search the background to their instructions. The staff perform more effectively if as much background as needed is given on all matters, including the meaning of acronyms and other specific terms to the theme and institutions;

-   Accuracy in conveying the message and relaying it effectively (even using a text on a piece of paper) within the other governments or international organizations' administration. If circumstances allow, this can be in the form of an official communication from the government (an *aide memoire*[386] or a *note verbale*[387] or a *memorandum*[388]), but it is equally acceptable, and in many circumstances more appropriate and easier, to offer the message in the form of simple "speaking notes", more or less explanatory or exploratory;

-   Provide for guidance and instructions for the embassies, in case the officials they approach return the questions inquiring about the representing government's understanding of the issues, its attitudes and any initiatives it may be planning. The representatives should be equipped to answer such questions and the guidelines provided should also cover obvious points to the one asking instructions, taking into account that the staff acting on these instructions is probably not expert in the field, nor up to date on developments.

President / chairman (elect); International non-governmental organizations (see UNITAR, Performing Effectively in Multilateral Conferences and Diplomacy, 2006).

[384] Walker R.A., Manual for UN Delegates - Conference Process, Procedure and Negotiation, UN Publication, 2011, p.21.

[385] United Nations Institute for Training and Research (UNITAR), Performing Effectively in Multilateral Conferences and Diplomacy - Preparing for an International Conference, 2006, p. 14.

[386] *Aide-mémoire* (called also *pro memoria*) is the document used to registered diplomatic conversations (see Năstase Dan, Drept diplomatic şi consular, Editura Fundaţiei România de Mâine, Bucuresti, 2006).

[387] *Note verbale* is the document used to transmit administrative, political or juridical communications. It has special form, characteristics and language see Năstase Dan, Drept diplomatic şi consular, Editura Fundaţiei România de Mâine, Bucuresti, 2006).

[388] *Memorandum* (called also *memorium*) is the document used to register diplomatic conversations, similar to *aide-memoire*, but more detailed (see Năstase Dan, Drept diplomatic şi consular, Editura Fundaţiei România de Mâine, Bucuresti, 2006).

Through international consultations that embassies are instructed to conduct, governments are looking for information that might be of interests to future diplomatic negotiations,[389] such as:

* Interests and objectives of other governments taking part in the conference;

* Issues that other governments may want to place on the agenda;

* Positions that governments may have on those and other issues;

* Strategies and tactics that governments may employ prior to or during the conference or negotiation;

* Any information that other governments may have already obtained through their consultations;

* Other information from intergovernmental organizations (objectives, interests, technical knowledge).

If governments receive reports of initiatives planned by others, they may consider whether they wish to try to influence developments before the conference meets. They might, for example, wish to offer encouragement and support (and perhaps join a "like-minded group" or take part in the preparation of a joint statement), or conversely to try to dissuade another government from proceeding with its plans, or to try to secure some modification of the initiative to make it more supportive of their own objectives. If governments themselves are planning any initiatives, they also issue instructions to their embassies to speak to relevant officials. There are usually considerable benefits in giving other governments advance notice of projected initiatives, explaining the motives, seeking to influence other governments to support the project, hearing their objections or suggestions, if any, and perhaps modifying own plans in consequence.[390]

Very often, many aspects of a conference will be the subject of intensive consultations among interested governments, to plan such matters as the selection of the presiding officer and other conference officers, reach prior agreement on the agenda and general course of the conference, sometimes settle agreed limits to its mandate or, at times, begin preliminary exploration and even negotiation of

[389] United Nations Institute for Training and Research (UNITAR), Performing Effectively in Multilateral Conferences and Diplomacy - Preparing for an International Conference, 2006, p. 17.

[390] Walker R.A., Manual for UN Delegates - Conference Process, Procedure and Negotiation, UN Publication, 2011, p.22.

some of the issues on the agenda. A number of actors are involved in these tasks (see chapter 2), from Members, secretariats, host governments, intergovernmental organizations (and sometimes even NGOs).[391]

We underline that preparation through international consultations is not only an opportunity to obtain information from others, it is also an opportunity to contribute information (e.g. in the form of communications, working papers, non-papers, etc.). For all these purposes, governments make use of all the standard tools of bilateral diplomacy: consultations and representations between embassies and foreign ministries, government to government messages or even visits by special envoys, etc. At times groups of governments hold meetings to exchange information and views about the prospects for the negotiation positions and conference and/or to plan how to influence its outcome.[392]

We conclude that the pre-conference international consultations, as well as the preparatory and preliminary negotiations are as important in determining the outcome of negotiation or conference as all the processes commencing once the conference assembles and negotiation begins.

Briefing the delegation

Potentially, the most important aspect in preparing for diplomatic negotiations consists in the guidance given by headquarters to the delegation, to the people who actually attend the multilateral conference and conduct the diplomatic negotiations. This guidance is generally referred to as **briefing the delegation**.

Ideally, if the standing brief is well prepared and kept up-to-date, no additional work is needed to brief the delegation as all the delegation needs to do is to access the standing brief. The most convenient way to provide it is to keep the standing brief on a site or server to which the delegation and all other relevant officials have access via the internet or an intranet.[393] Until such technology is

---

[391] United Nations Institute for Training and Research (UNITAR), Performing Effectively in Multilateral Conferences and Diplomacy - Preparing for an International Conference, 2006, p. 15.

[392] Walker R.A., Manual for UN Delegates - Conference Process, Procedure and Negotiation, UN Publication, 2011, p.22.

[393] The well-resourced governments use this system, but they also usually use encryption to deny access to this information to outsiders, but if this is strictly necessary should be considered. At least a large portion of the brief is not sensitive information. It may be possible (and relatively cheap) to keep the bulk of the standing brief on an unrestricted web page, accessible with only a simple password. If necessary this can be supplemented by classified and encrypted messages to cover any sensitive elements.

universally available, most governments use other techniques, but the objective is the same: to transfer information and guidance that the delegates need from the standing brief. The common techniques, used either singly or in combination by all governments, are for the delegation to speak to (or receive messages from) the individuals who hold the standing brief in their heads, or for officials at headquarters to reproduce the standing brief (or at least much of it) as a document which is then given or sent to the delegation. In governmental authorities that, for whatever reason, have failed to maintain a standing brief, a much more time consuming, inefficient and imperfect process is needed: staff have to go through the files and other sources of information and compile a brief from scratch for each conference. Inevitably such a standing brief is likely to be less comprehensive than a well maintained one.[394]

The delegation needs to be sufficiently equipped to do the best it can as representative of a State, whether the standing brief is delivered as a verbal briefing, an electronic briefing is prepared or a comprehensive written brief is handed on. The easier the headquarters make it for delegation, the better the prospects to be successful. Any failure on government part to brief the delegation adequately is likely to have adverse consequences for the government.[395] In addition, the pressures of time and inadequate resources[396] play a significant role as they might impede over a proper guidance and a striving briefing.

To be fully equipped to handle diplomatic negotiations and multilateral conferences a delegation needs an **ideal (perfect) brief**, whose **contents**[397] should include:

a. The issues to be addressed at and by the conference;

b. The government's interests and objectives;

---

[394] United Nations Institute for Training and Research (UNITAR), Performing Effectively in Multilateral Conferences and Diplomacy - Preparing for an International Conference, 2006, p. 17.

[395] Walker R.A., Manual for UN Delegates - Conference Process, Procedure and Negotiation, UN Publication, 2011, p.22.

[396] Limited human and/or financial resources can restrict the ability of many governments to take part in pre-conference meetings and consultations, as well debriefing the delegation. While these constraints are sometimes difficult if not impossible to overcome, they should not be used as an excuse for failing to prepare for conferences and negotiations. Information from such meetings can often be accessed indirectly, from like-minded governments, governments belonging to the same regional group or otherwise willing to share information, secretariats, etc.

[397] Walker R.A., Manual for UN Delegates - Conference Process, Procedure and Negotiation, UN Publication, 2011, p.23.

c. The substantive background (for example, the legal, technical, economic or other issues that are the subject matter of the conference);

d. The international political background. This includes a description of the attitudes of other governments on the issues to be addressed, the negotiating history, the results of pre-conference consultations and negotiations, plans for coordination with other delegations during the conference, etc.

e. All available conference papers. These include the pre-session conference documents, such as the provisional agenda (and, if available, an annotated provisional agenda), background reports or pre-existing texts that have already been the subject of earlier negotiations as well as any initiatives foreshadowed by other delegations (non-papers, communications, draft proposals), etc. (see chapter 3 on pre-session conference documents).

f. Specific guidance as to what headquarters wants the delegation to do. This often includes points for, or even the full text of, a general debate statement. It is likely to include political guidance such as wish to associate with positions taken by a certain delegation(s)/group(s) or immediate report about any reactions from other delegations towards government's statements. This guidance may even include details of any initiatives the government wants the delegation to take and can include the text of a draft resolution which it wants introduced, possible alternative language, and perhaps even an established hierarchy of positions on specific agenda items, etc.

g. Guidance as to reporting. Headquarters should make very clear its reporting requirements and priorities: what information it wants, which conference documents or other texts that emerge at the conference it wants to see and when, etc. Thus, for example, it may ask for any draft resolution on a certain topic to be reported as soon as it emerges, or for the full text of general debate statements by certain delegations to be sent after the conference closes. It may ask for a full account of the attitudes taken by certain delegations or a simple short statement of the main points agreed by the conference, etc.

The (ideal) brief contains guidance but not instructions or directions[398] to the delegation, and there is an important difference between the two: guidance leaves the final judgements and decisions to the delegation.

---

[398] "Instructions" and "directions" are often used interchangeably, as is "guidance" at times, but strictly speaking: **Directions** or more emphatically **directives** mean that the delegation is told exactly what to do; **Guidance** means that the delegation is told of the government's objectives and sometimes suggestions as how to achieve them, but the decision as to what to do as the situation unfolds is left to the delegation; **Instructions** can be either guidance and directives (see Walker

Instructions or **directions** tell delegations what to do, involving making the judgements and decisions, in advance, from headquarters. Most successful governments in diplomatic negotiations and at multilateral conferences find that they get better results if they refrain from giving explicit directions to their delegations, as they believe that directions can tie a delegation's hands and it is more difficult for the delegation to react appropriately to situations which headquarters did not anticipated. Obviously, the headquarters is never aware of all the information held by its delegation at any given moment, nor of all the sensitivities of tactical situations as they arise. Moreover, if headquarters takes many of the decisions, the delegation is likely to become reliant on these instructions instead of remaining alert to better options that may emerge. Hence, instructions relieve sometimes a delegation from responsibility for getting the best achievable result. Nevertheless, for the government the way of achieving best results is almost always to give the delegation guidance as to what the government hopes to achieve (including prioritizing its different objectives), coupled with the freedom to do what the delegation judges to be the most effective way of pursuing those objectives, in the light of the situation as it develops in the conference. Of course, there are situations in which governments prefer to give explicit instructions to their delegations, at least on some agenda items. For example, they may place some limits or boundaries on the delegation's freedom of action, or give detailed directions. This can include specific wording for placing the government's position on the record, or for draft proposals or amendments. On sensitive issues, it is quite common for governments to not only identify their most preferred outcome, but also what would be generally acceptable or realistic given the interests and objectives of other delegations (e.g. perhaps alternative language which would be acceptable but less preferred). They also often specify the point at which further concessions on the proposal or movement away from the initial position is unacceptable. On highly sensitive issues, headquarters may require constant reporting and in particular insist on being consulted before any concessions are made by the delegation. Some delegates prefer to have clear instructions, precisely because they relieve them from responsibility and protect them against reproaches if headquarters is not happy with the conference outcome. This applies particularly in cases where there are big differences of perspective between various national governmental authorities.[399]

R.A., Manual for UN Delegates - Conference Process, Procedure and Negotiation, UN Publication, 2011).

In any situation, instructions to delegations are indispensable, even in practice there are considerable differences in the amount and nature of instructions which delegations receive. The absence of instructions indicates either a certain lack of interest of the government concerned, or a full confidence in the experience, knowledge and good sense of its delegation. The instructions could be classified[400] as:

a. *everything dealt with the detail*: instructions for questions of paramount importance to the instructing government, for example, a political conflict in which it is involved, or an international treaty to be negotiated to which it attaches great importance. If the delegation wants to deviate from the prescribed line, it must ask for specific authorization;

b. *general position outlined*: instructions where certain limits within which the delegation can operate are outlined, while technical and other details are left to the delegation itself. In this category fall the so-called "position papers" which are the preferred method for writing instructions (for each agenda item or issue) of some countries;

c. *position related to that of other countries*: the delegation of a country is instructed to align itself with the position either of a group to which it belongs or to that of specifically named countries. If the delegation feels that such alignment leads to positions incompatible with general or specific policies of its government, it will ask for modified instructions. Similarly, a delegation does generally not like an isolated position, and in that case also ask for new instructions.

The **format of the brief** is very important, too. The people for whom the brief is written have a busy schedule both when the brief arrives and when it is most important that they have to refer to it during the negotiations or in the conference. For making their task easier, the brief should be as "user friendly" as possible. This means to be written very clearly and organized in such a way that it is easily read and quickly skimmed. It is possible the reader to be familiar with at least some of the background and is looking at the brief mainly to see the developments and the news. In preparing the briefing, aspect like lay-out, the headings, paragraphing and the use of bullets are carefully thought about. All texts the delegation needs to refer to is attached as annexes, which are carefully

[399] United Nations Institute for Training and Research (UNITAR), Performing Effectively in Multilateral Conferences and Diplomacy - Preparing for an International Conference, 2006, pp. 20-21.

[400] Kaufmann Johan, Some Practical Aspects of United Nations Decision-Making, in M.A. Boisard and E.M. Chossudovsky, Multilateral Diplomacy: The United Nations System at Geneva, A Working Guide. The Hague: Kluwer Law International, 1998, pp.237,238.

indexed so that they are easily found. If the brief is in hard copy, separator pages with tabs and/or colour coding are used, so that the delegates find immediately the relevant guidance. Color-coding is also used and helps in briefs issued in electronic forms.[401]

There is no "one size fits all" format of the brief that is easily applied for all negotiations and conferences,[402] but the brief might be organized as follows:

1. Conference overview: background information, mandate of conference, expected outcome, key players, etc.;

2. List of issues to be discussed at and by the conference: Issues / agenda items explained, supported with an annotated agenda from the secretariat;

3. The government's interests and objectives: What are the major substantive interests and objectives? Are there any other interests and objectives important to the government?

4. Detailed discussion of issues: Discussion on the issues emerged on policy-making agenda, links between and among issues, and other conferences discussing issues or related ones;

5. International political background: Results of pre-conference consultations, describing the interests and objectives of other governments, groups, international organizations, etc.;

6. Guidance and instructions: From general guidance to very specific instructions on positions to be taken on agenda items, dealings with other delegations, etc.;

7. Reporting requirements: What to cover in reporting, which documents to be sent to headquarters, and the frequency and timing of reports;

8. Annexes: Key pre-session documents, including provisional agenda, draft texts, non-papers, reports, key policy statements by the government, prepared texts of statements to be made by the delegation, etc.;

9. Contacts: Contact details and travel schedule of delegation members, other important delegations, contacts of secretariat, etc.

In all situations, a delegation is not looking only at the "letter of its instructions". It must understand the spirit in which they are written and do the

---

[401] Walker R.A., Manual for UN Delegates - Conference Process, Procedure and Negotiation, UN Publication, 2011, p.24.

[402] United Nations Institute for Training and Research (UNITAR), Performing Effectively in Multilateral Conferences and Diplomacy - Preparing for an International Conference, 2006, p. 22.

best it can in achieving its and government's objectives, asking for additional instructions if necessary.

5.4.3 Preparation at individual and delegation level

The delegates who personally participate in the conference and conduct the diplomatic negotiations also prepare themselves at headquarters before the conference convenes. Similarly, if there are more delegates from a country, it is important for the delegation to meet and prepare as soon as possible.

Individual preparation

Ideally, at least one member of the delegation was involved in the preparation of the brief and in the internal and intra-governmental consultations, but usually the delegates have little time to focus on a forthcoming negotiation and conference. Even in such situations and under time pressure, the delegates have to prepare themselves for the tasks ahead. The more thoroughly they prepare, the better they perform in negotiations and at the conference.

Thus, the **self-briefing** is crucial as in practice delegates often find themselves entering into negotiations or going to a conference without an optimal or adequate brief. And even when the headquarters provides the delegation with a comprehensive and well-designed brief, the delegate is the person who has to use it. Hence, the delegates have to study and master it and also to ensure that it is as useful as it can be.[403] Even the brief is comprehensive, the delegates check it against any shortcomings and gaps in order to fill them by asking advice from headquarters and/or other colleagues, seeking additional information from the relevant secretariats and/or contacts in other delegations and, if possible, drawing on their own pre-existing knowledge, the files of the Permanent Mission and publicly available resources.

The most important thing the delegate decides before the negotiation and conference is **clarity of purpose**. The delegate's aims need to be known with precision, with the help from the headquarters, supervisors or colleagues. Once that is clear, the delegate proceeds to set priorities and plan the time allocation. The specifics vary from one conference to another, but they are likely to fall under one or more of the following rubrics.[404]

---

[403] Walker R.A., Manual for UN Delegates - Conference Process, Procedure and Negotiation, UN Publication, 2011, p.26.

[404] United Nations Institute for Training and Research (UNITAR), Performing Effectively in

1. Participation. The minimal objective of every delegation is to be present and to have its presence recorded. Thus, the delegation registers and occupies the seat bearing the country's nameplate, at least on the most important occasion: the formal opening. Depending on the government's objectives and the priority it attaches to a particular conference, this may be all that is required from a delegation (there are situations when concurrent meetings take place and a small delegation cannot cover them all in detail). In most cases, the delegate is also required to do at least some of the following.

2. Monitoring. The next objective of any delegation is to find out what is happening at the conference. If government's objectives and/or resources are limited, it is sufficient for the delegates to wait until the conference is over, collect its final document and other documents as record of its main decisions or other points of interest. Delegates look for assessments from secretariat and selected delegations, if a detailed monitoring is asked. If the level of interest warrants and their resources permit, delegations also keep abreast of what is happening at the conference as it progresses. For a small delegation this is very challenging, as it cannot be present in every committee and peripheral meeting, and cannot possibly track the state of work on every agenda item or the state of play on every issue engaged. Thus, the delegation is highly selective and focussed on what matters most to them and the government. Its effectiveness depends on the delegation's reliance on others, for example: counting on a caucus group with similar objectives at least for several issues, negotiating with others and deciding how to act or vote in relation to them, involving some well-informed sources that are better placed to consult widely and to gather and assess information about everything that is happening at the conference and able to give the delegate a condensed account.

3. Reporting. Each delegation has the fundamental task to report to headquarters. It needs deliberate planning and priorities setting, taking into account what is useful to their governments. For example, headquarters requires information about reaction to any development impacting on its interests (which may trigger new instructions to the delegation), about possible questions they may face (which may require the warning of political representatives), about briefing the media, etc. Depending on the conference, this reporting is constantly done, as events unfold. At a more technical level and not in an immediate time frame,

Multilateral Conferences and Diplomacy - Preparing for an International Conference, 2006, pp. 24-28.

headquarters prepares the brief for the next meeting and, especially in the case of treaties (but also for any other agreement), a record of the negotiating history. Headquarters needs to know any decisions or other outcomes that are likely to have important practical consequences to the government or to inform other governments about future discussions. To this list, delegates add any information that comes on their way during the conference (through conference documents, formal statements or private conversations). Moreover, delegates keep in mind that their government's interest is not confined to the issues on the formal agenda as they find useful information about relations between other governments, their changing expectations, future programmes of international organizations, etc. There is always much more that delegates should report than they physically are able to. Thus, the delegates and governments' priorities, the ways of maximizing delegate's efficiency as a reporter and the means of allocating time for reporting have to be clear from the beginning.

4. Extraneous objectives. At a conference, delegations achieve also other objectives, independently of any decisions taken by the conference or regardless of its outcome. They are common objectives such as: being seen to participate, placing a particular view on the record, nourishing relations with selected countries, gathering or disseminating information just about anything, projecting to national audiences an image of a government taking effective action to advance domestic interests and standing up bravely against outside forces, etc. Sometimes, these objectives are extremely important to the government, and they may even be worthy and constructive. For the delegate it is useful to keep in mind that they are, technically, extraneous to the work of the conference itself, which is no more than the venue in which delegate's activities take place. Therefore, delegates pursue them unburdened by the constraints applied to delegations trying to influence the conference outcome. In particular, they often do not require delegates to secure the cooperation of other delegations. This means that delegate's prospects of success are higher and the cost of attempting such objectives is relatively low. However, there are limits to this dispensation: these are approached when delegate's activities start to impede the efforts of other delegations to advance their objectives. The more peculiar delegate's objective, the more it irritates other delegations if it is pursued in ways damaging their endeavours. In the diplomatic negotiations and multilateral conferences, such irritation manifests itself as a reduced willingness to accommodate delegate's concerns, or extremely, in a determined effort to penalized the delegation, either personally or nationally.

5. Operational objectives.[405] Shaping the outcome of the conference itself or of some of its specific decisions is more difficult and more resources and determination demanding. For this reason, just few delegations make the effort and only when they have particular reasons to do so. Such operational objectives are, for example, the establishment of a new regime to help meeting a problem faced by the government, making an existing regime operate helpfully, (or negatively), ensuring that the efforts of other governments to address their problems through multilateral actions do not adversely affect own government.

Before multilateral conference start, the delegate thinks about a lot of issues, administrative, political, substantive, logistical, etc., and it is useful to write down the fundamental elements, so to have a **"check-list"**[406] of essentials, including but not limited to the followings: credentials, brief, pre-conference papers, provisional agenda, provisional rules of procedure, provisional list of participants, conference venue etc. *Delegate's credentials* are in the form of a letter from a minister or from the permanent representative. Sometimes the originals are delivered directly to the secretariat, but at times a photocopy is sent. The first task of the delegate is to register, meaning presenting his/her credentials and passport to the office set up by the conference secretariat at the conference venue. The delegate might also be asked to fill out a *registration form*. Once the delegate has registered, he/she receives a pass or *badge*, needed to access the conference hall. It is possible to register in the morning before the conference starts but experienced delegates usually register a day or two before that. This enables them to avoid queues and to devote their time on the first day to more productive activities. Delegates has also a quick look at the *conference venue*, preferably a day or two before the conference opens, for not wasting time finding the various meeting rooms, or conference copying documents centre, interpreters and record writers booths, cafeterias, etc. as activities take place and conference unfolds. The delegate's work is more difficult if, once the conference begins, he/she has not copies of *all pre-conference papers*, notably the *provisional agenda*, but these might have been included in the brief. There are three other very important documents (but these will not be available until the conference

---

[405] Operational objectives: What a delegation wants the conference to do. For example that it should draft a treaty with certain provisions or, conversely that it not take certain decisions (see Walker R.A., Multilateral Conferences: Purposeful International Negotiation. London: Palgrave Macmillan, 2004).

[406] United Nations Institute for Training and Research (UNITAR), Performing Effectively in Multilateral Conferences and Diplomacy - Preparing for an International Conference, 2006, pp. 29-30.

gets under way): the *programme of work*: which agenda items are covered by which committee, when meetings and other events are scheduled. This document is drawn up by the chairman, sometimes assisted by a steering committee, within the first days of the conference and distributed to all delegations by the secretariat; the *daily journal* (usually at large conferences), issued early each morning, with more details of the activities scheduled for that day (sometimes including regional group meetings) and where they take place; the *list of participants*. If a delegate wants to do anything with the conference, he/she needs to know who the participants are. Initially a provisional list, the secretariat needs few days to prepare a final one. Even before receiving the list of participants, the delegate plans and starts the *informal consultations* (principal activity of most delegates). Social activities provide additional opportunities to meet other delegates like receptions and lunches (some of them organized even before conference opens), sightseeing or various gatherings outside conference venue. As with reporting, there are more consulting that delegates should do than they have time to actually do. For this reason, delegates plan carefully in advance the best use of the available time.

Delegation preparation

If there are more delegates from a country, it is important for the delegation to meet, as early as practicable. The first delegation meeting is especially important and has several purposes. Perhaps the most important aspect is to weld the delegation as a team. Each delegate need to understand that whatever his/her relations with the other members of the delegation, once they represent a Government in a diplomatic negotiations and a multilateral conference they have to do their best to achieve their Government's objectives. This means that each delegation member must support each other and the **delegation leader**. It should be beyond dispute that the delegation leader is formally in charge and the success or the failure of the delegation and of each individual member depends of the success or failure of the delegation leader.[407] It is during this first meeting that the members of the delegation make sure they all have the same understanding of the brief and of what the delegation as a whole is trying to achieve. If not at this first meeting, very soon thereafter, and as part of the **team building**, the delegates need to discuss to ensure that they have a clear and fully shared understanding of

---

[407] Walker R.A., Manual for UN Delegates - Conference Process, Procedure and Negotiation, UN Publication, 2011, pp.24-26.

the delegation's aims for the conference, in the light of any (additional) briefing from headquarters or any other knowledge.

Since the delegation is not made of one delegate, and delegates are members of a delegation, that permits a division of work but also demands effective coordination. Both of these lead to a need for delegation meetings during the whole conference. The first meeting is also the occasion to allocate tasks,[408] usually several tasks to each delegation member. The following ones are an opportunity to take stocks of the activities and to apprehend the fulfilment of task by each member of delegation and to take adjusting measures if needed.

Respecting the conference rules and norms regarding interaction with other delegates is another important element to be discussed and followed up during these meetings. Any sign of lack of courtesy (or worse, hostility) towards any other delegation, not only worsen the relations with that government, but also lower own and government's esteem in the eyes of other delegations and entire conference.

All delegation leaders have to make sure that delegations' meetings are held both before the conference starts and as often as necessary during its course. At large conferences, when the work is intense, many find they need to meet every morning, before the conference and the many informal meetings that surround it. These meetings have three main purposes: to pool information as to what is happening at the conference, to apportion work among the various members of the delegation and to make sure that they are all working to a common plan. It is very disruptive if other delegations do not get a consistent attitude or intention from members of the same delegation and very inefficient if a delegate missed an opportunity to support his team-mate.

It is noteworthy that the relation of the delegation leader with the source of instruction is highly important:[409] if the delegation leader is very close to these

---

[408] Tasks for a delegation member might include: 1. Each morning before the delegations meeting collect several copies of the daily journal and bring them to the meeting for you colleagues; 2. Cover everything that happens in Committee I and follow those agenda items in Plenary; 3. Consult regularly with the Group of Latin American and Caribbean Countries (GRULAC) and its most active members; 4. Draft reports on the agenda items covered by Committee I. 5. Brief other delegations, the media, NGOs, etc. on developments. Although this is another task which may be assigned from the outset, the delegation leader does not have to do all this personally, but he or she has to be satisfied that it will be done correctly (see UNITAR, Performing Effectively in Multilateral Conferences and Diplomacy, 2006).

[409] Kaufmann Johan, Some Practical Aspects of United Nations Decision-Making, in M.A. Boisard and E.M. Chossudovsky, Multilateral Diplomacy: The United Nations System at Geneva, A

sources and has their full confidence, his or her instructions will tend to be somewhat more widely formulated than if the delegate is not personally known to those who draw up the instructions. This is not relevant for the numerous more or less routine items which fill conference agendas, but it can make a difference for example, when the country is directly involved in an important question, or where the country is not directly involved, yet is able and eager to play a mediation role in a dispute.

5.4.4 Preparing to report

Finally, the delegation needs to prepare to report. If there is one delegate alone at a conference, he or she also needs to think from the start about this task and how to do it efficiently. The situation is similar for a delegation of several members, however there are team and coordination efforts.

In any case, the responsibilities need to be allocated, both for the preparation and sending of reports, with the additional requirements: access to communications, couriers, etc. Information gathering and reporting efficiency is enhanced when using templates. This helps to standardize the record keeping and highlight the priority issues. Monitoring should cover more than can be actually be reported using the resources available and especially the time. Therefore, tight prioritization is a must.

We conclude by saying that states, organizations and individuals, as actors in diplomatic negotiations enter into complex and interdependent relationships. No diplomatic negotiation happens without interactions between parties at the state, delegation and individual levels. Diplomatic negotiation employs specific forms of interaction, using a distinct language, protocol, symbols, ceremonies, and rituals. By successfully preparing and managing all aspects, negotiating parties advance the process and effectiveness of diplomatic negotiation.

Working Guide. The Hague: Kluwer Law International, 1998, pp.238-239.

Chapter 6 – Diplomatic negotiations in multilateral conferences

Multilateral conferences were introduced in the nineteenth century as a method to regulate the international power structure, thereby facilitating positive outcomes. Choosing the negotiation fora and acknowledging the parties' common interests are two important aspects for reaching agreement. Diplomatic negotiations occur only when the involved states are interested in solving their problems in a peaceful manner and finding common grounds. Approaches and processes are relevant to start any diplomatic negotiation and create an outcome, taking into account the multitude of factors influencing its course and thereby its closure.

6.1 Approaches to diplomatic negotiations

Considering diplomatic negotiations in multilateral conferences, the importance of the approaches through coalition-building, leadership and the role of structuring elements such as procedures, are highlighted.[410] There are four approaches to diplomatic negotiation: as puzzle solving, as bargaining game, as organizational management and as diplomatic politics, typology crafted around the dimensions of symmetry-asymmetry and prescription-description. Practitioners analyse five core approaches: structural, the strategic, the processual, the behavioural and the integrative approaches.[411]

6.1.1 Structural approach

In short, the **structural approach** uses power as the means to explain outcomes of negotiation processes, asserting that the strongest wins.[412] At length, the structural approaches to negotiations consider negotiated outcomes to be a function of the characteristics or structural features that define each particular negotiation. These characteristics may include features such as the number of

---

[410] Meerts Paul (quoting Zartman), Diplomatic Negotiation, Essence and Evolution. The Hague: Clingendael Institute, 2015, p. 34.

[411] Alfredson Tanya and Cungu Azeta (quoting Druckman, Raiffa and Zartman), Negotiation Theory and Practice. A Review of the Literature, FAO Policy Learning Program, EASYPol Module 179, 2008, p. 9.

[412] Meerts Paul, Diplomatic Negotiation, Essence and Evolution. The Hague: Clingendael Institute, 2015, p. 41.

parties and issues involved in the negotiation and the composition or relative power of the competing parties.[413] The relative power of each party affects their ability to secure their individual goals through negotiations.

The perspective that power serves as a central structural feature of every negotiation has its intellectual roots in traditions of political theory and military strategy, the central idea of this approach being that the strong will prevail. The conception of power as underpinning the basic structure of negotiation originates in the "structuralist" tradition, which proposes that negotiation begins with a certain distribution of power among the parties. This initial distribution is said to accompany the entire negotiation process and determines the eventual outcome. Based on how much power each party possesses, the structural approach to negotiation is also seen as one of power symmetry or asymmetry, power asymmetry being the most common structural setting for diplomatic negotiations.[414] For example, trade relations between the global North and South are generally considered as asymmetrical given the North's superior economic power.

Nevertheless, the structural approach has its limitations. It is considered too narrow as it analyses negotiation only from a symmetry-asymmetry point of view and too emphatic on static conditions for negotiation, as:

- The "structuralists" debate as to which power structure, symmetric or asymmetric, is more favourable to effective negotiation but even in conflicts that quarry the strong against the weak, the range of outcomes is wide. History provides examples about the power of the weak and the feebleness of the strong (such as the USA and Vietnam, the Soviet Union and Afghanistan, the United Kingdom and Iceland) that shows that smaller states, despite inferior structural power, do not necessarily submit to the will of the stronger ones.[415] Thus, it is inaccurate to assume that in negotiation the "stronger" state will prevail, even the structural approach recognizes that the symmetry-asymmetry perspective, is too narrow. In order to understand this phenomenon, the comparative power needs to be analysed, meaning the power structures around the issues being negotiated, or the power that is relevant in a particular situation, and additional properties need to be looked at such as the availability of

[413] Alfredson Tanya and Cungu Azeta (quoting Raiffa, Bacharach and Lawler), Negotiation Theory and Practice. A Review of the Literature, FAO Policy Learning Program, EASYPol Module 179, 2008, p. 10.

[414] Yan Ki Bonnie Cheng, Power and trust in negotiation and decision-making: a critical evaluation, Harvard Negotiation Law Review, 2009 (available at hnlr.org).

[415] Meerts Paul, Diplomatic Negotiation, Essence and Evolution. The Hague: Clingendael Institute, 2015, p. 28.

alternatives or the role of tactics, in order to try to understand why success in negotiations does not always go to the ostensibly more powerful. For example, most non-governmental organizations (NGOs) are less resourceful than the World Bank. Yet, the World Bank can enhance the legitimacy of its programs by including NGOs and over time, participating NGOs could influence the World Bank's agendas to some extent. Thus viewed, parties with asymmetric resources may well share a mutually dependent relationship;

- The "structuralists" emphasize on the static, structural conditions for negotiation but this can be altered with willingness and through skilful manoeuvres, involving all the power factors available to a country in relation to that of other nations. Weaker states actively attempt to ensure fairness and change the perception of stronger opponents to their advantage by highlighting their strengths in specific fields and associating themselves with bigger and/or more powerful states. While structural power could be an important edge, the party yielding superior power may not be vigilant about the strategies of the weaker party or motivated to obtain accurate information about the negotiation. Likewise, the power-based approach can be costly and risky. It may give rise to short-term gains but undesirable long-term consequences. This is because humans tend to reciprocate power and engage in contests when confronted by a hostile opponent. Such confrontation causes resentment and even acts of retaliation, which hinders effective negotiation, damages the parties' relationship and forestalls future opportunities for collaboration. Negotiators should be aware that a blind attachment to "winning" all they can from a negotiation regardless of the resulting satisfaction of other parties, can be a poor strategy if it means that the other side loses its will, or ability to maintain its side of the negotiated agreement. Nevertheless, a power-based approach is not detrimental under all circumstances. For example, power tactics are necessary or even desirable when facing an impasse, or when the parties' interests are fundamentally opposed.

Due to the specific sources and forms of power, the common tactics under a power-based approach include coercion, intimidation, and using one's status and resources to overpower opponents, for example:

- the power of authority, which is often a kind of structural power. For instance, in negotiation on environmental treaties, the scientific community commands some influence due to its authority;

- the "best alternative to a negotiated agreement" or "best alternative to no agreement" - BATNA (see chapter 5.3.1) as a source of power in negotiation. A BATNA can form part of the given structure of negotiation, but it can also be subject to strategic manipulation. In negotiation, not only can a party improve its own BATNA, but it may also alter the objective/perceived value of the other side's BATNA;

- the threat. To be effective, it has to aim at the target's underlying interests, such as a country's security concerns. It also needs to be perceived as credible - the target must believe the issuer has the ability to carry out the threat. While the target may submit to the issuer (like other tactics under a power-based approach) the use of threats can potentially backfire, risking escalation and relationship breakdown.

- pressure, lies, unfairness. These are contrary to the principle of cooperation and as a result, they are considered only to the extent that negotiator is forced to face them and overcome them to enable further negotiation and building understanding.[416]

We conclude that power is a complex phenomenon that can derive from different sources and take multiple forms in negotiation. When deployed as strategy, its strengths and limitations are highly dependent on the negotiation's context and the parties' dynamics.

6.1.2 Strategic approach

Strategic approaches to negotiation have roots in mathematics, decision theory and rational choice theory, and also benefit from major contributions from the area of economics, biology, and conflict analysis. Whereas the structural approach focuses on the role of means (such as power) in negotiations, the emphasis in strategic models of negotiation is on the role of ends (goals) in determining outcomes. Strategic models are also models of rational choice. Negotiators are viewed as rational decision makers with known alternatives and making choices guided by their calculation of which option will maximize their ends or "gains", frequently described as "payoffs". Actors choose from a "choice set" of possible actions in order to try and achieve desired outcomes. Each actor has a unique "incentive structure" that is comprised of a set of costs associated with different actions combined with a set of probabilities that reflect the likelihoods of different actions leading to desired outcomes. The strategic approach uses game theory[417] (which is essentially a prisoner's dilemma) and

---

[416] Năstase Dan, Drept diplomatic și consular, Editura Fundației România de Mâine, Bucuresti, 2006, p. 329.

[417] Game theory uses formal mathematical models to describe, recommend or predict the actions parties take in order to maximize their own gains when the consequences of any action they choose will depend on the decisions made by another actor. It is concerned with "games of strategy" in which the best course of action for each participant depends on what he expects the

critical risk theory[418] to explain the connection between process and result, as the "strategists" consider that there is one best solution to every negotiation problem.[419]

In game theory "The Negotiator's Dilemma" [420] can be summarized as follows:

-   If both parties cooperate, they both have good outcomes;

-   If one cooperates and the other competes, the one who cooperate gets a terrible outcome and the competitor gets a great outcome;

-   If both compete, they both have mediocre outcomes;

-   In the face of uncertainty about what strategy the other party will adopt, each party's best choice is to compete;

-   However, if they both compete, both parties end up worse off.

In real diplomatic negotiations, parties can communicate and commit themselves to a cooperative approach. They can also adopt norms of fair and cooperative behaviour and focus on their future relationship. This fosters a cooperative approach between both parties and helps them find mutual gains. In long-term interactions, the outcome of negotiations - the choice of parties to either cooperate or defect - can depend heavily on the amount of trust that is established between the two sides.[421]

In multilateral conferences, strategic approach plays a significant role, as it implies discussion on competitive and interactive situations (i.e. bargaining), cooperation and coordination, exogenous geopolitical shifts, changes in conflict dynamics, the way to negotiate for cooperation, the strategic interests involved and their legitimacy, and achievement of coordination.[422] Strategic approach is of

---

other participants to do.

[418] Critical risk theory uses cardinal utility numbers to explain decision-making behavior but introduces the notion that parties use probability estimates when making rational calculations of whether or not to concede, or to stand firm in a crisis negotiation. These probabilities are derived from each player's calculus of their own critical risk, or the maximum risk of a breakdown in negotiations that the player is willing to tolerate in order to stand firm, combined with each player's estimation of the level of their opponent's inherent resolve to stand firm.

[419] Alfredson Tanya and Cungu Azeta (quoting Raiffa, Bacharach and Lawler), Negotiation Theory and Practice. A Review of the Literature, FAO Policy Learning Program, EASYPol Module 179, 2008, pp. 10-11.

[420] Lax David and Sebenius James K., The Manager as Negotiator: Bargaining for Cooperation and Competitive Gain, New York: The Free Press, 1986, p. 29.

[421] Alfredson Tanya and Cungu Azeta (quoting Raiffa, Bacharach and Lawler), Negotiation Theory and Practice. A Review of the Literature, FAO Policy Learning Program, EASYPol Module 179, 2008, p. 13.

paramount importance in the EU negotiating process, as EU Member States are not only negotiating on their needs, but also on their common and opposing values. Coordinating is also important in the EU context. The role of the member states might be less prominent than non-EU negotiators often assume. As EU negotiators are aware, there are only limited possibilities for influencing EU negotiations, and states have to operate within strict legal limits in these areas. This brings up the point of qualified majority voting (see chapter 4.4.3), a decision rule that has increasingly been applied as a tool for advancing EU negotiations. Without this instrument, the European Union would not have been as successful in decision-making as it is today. However, the fact that countries can be out-voted puts a great deal of pressure on their negotiators. Coalition-building is one of the answers in this context, as is a change in attitude. Negotiators will have to show an increased willingness to accept compromises, something that is not too common among the actors entering the EU negotiation scene after a new round of enlargement.[423]

We conclude that strategic approach and the effective use of tactics are therefore important in pushing for the needs and values that negotiators want to fulfil. Coalition-building and cooperation are some of the major options, but might, in turn, dilute the individual delegation's position. From the perspective of the common interest, this is a wonderful instrument for forcing counterparts into a given frame, but for those that want to uphold the priorities set by their governments, this dynamic is problematic.

6.1.3 Concession exchange / Procedural approach

Concession exchange/Procedural approach uses the economic approach, whereby a range of concessions is analysed. At a certain moment the costs become too high and the margins disappear, but just before this happens the optimal outcome will be reached, as determined by the balance of costs and benefits.

Concession exchange/Procedural approach is applied to distributive or "competitive" negotiation. It assumes a relatively fixed pie, and the parties "compete" to distribute that pie among themselves. It is a "zero-sum exchange" in

---

[422] Vukovic S., Analysis of Multiparty Mediation Processes. Doctoral dissertation, University of Leiden, 2013, p. 57.

[423] Meerts Paul, Diplomatic Negotiation, Essence and Evolution. The Hague: Clingendael Institute, 2015, p. 252.

that the parties assume that whatever one side gains, the other loses. It is inherently "position" focused, and the parties move from one proposed resolution to another. Positions are changed and agreement is sought through a series of concessions or compromises. Agreement is typically reached at about the mid-point between to the first "reasonable" proposals made by each side, i.e., proposals that are outside the zone of agreement but perceived as setting an acceptable bargaining parameter. One need to keep in mind that "reasonable" proposals are distinct from "credible" or "insulting" proposals both of which are viewed as "unreasonable" by the other side and does not set any bargaining parameters, though "insulting" proposals are often viewed as so unreasonable that they may cause one party to terminate negotiations. Concession exchange/Procedural approach (a distributive negotiation process) is often referred to as the "negotiation dance", and is generally predictable: each concession tends to be about half the size of the concession that preceded it, and takes about twice as long to be made.[424]

Concession exchange approach shares features of both the structural approach (power) and the strategic approach (outcomes). From this perspective negotiations consist of a series of concessions. The concessions mark stages in negotiations. They are used by delegations to both signal their own intentions and to encourage movement in their counterpart's position. The risk inherent in this approach is that delegations engaged in concession-trading may miss opportunities to find new, mutually beneficial solutions to their shared dilemma and end-up instead in a purely regressive process which leaves both sides with fewer gains than they could have had if they had pursued a more creative approach.[425] There are several tactics that delegations could envisage in order to avoid missing opportunities:[426]

- Discourage offensive opening proposals. Encourage realistic proposals in caucus, and emphasize the danger of an "insulting" proposal that could end up negotiations;

---

[424] Doto David M., Facilitating Distributive and Integrative Negotiation in Mediation, The Opening Statement, 2011 (available at theopeningstatement.wordpress.com).

[425] Alfredson Tanya and Cungu Azeta (quoting Zartman), Negotiation Theory and Practice. A Review of the Literature, FAO Policy Learning Program, EASYPol Module 179, 2008, p. 15.

[426] Doto David M., Facilitating Distributive and Integrative Negotiation in Mediation, The Opening Statement, 2011 (available at theopeningstatement.wordpress.com).

- "Normalize the dance". Learn about the "negotiation dance", and manage negative reactions to extreme positions and proposals by formulating them as need to express emotion;

- Extract concessions. Emphasize the need for concessions and compromise, while evaluate whether a proposed concession will accomplish its goal;

- Use signals such as concession size and timing;

- Maintain credibility and save face.[427] Develop proposals in a constructive manner. Saving face is often more important than the rational basis of a proposal;

- Keep the process moving. Negotiator proposes, and suggests hypothetical proposals and reveals acceptances thereof if all parties agree to do so.

Concession exchange approach tends to limit potential options for dispute resolution. Moreover, this type of negotiation tends to create aggressive strategies that often rely upon concealing information to preserve the "pie", and other tactics aimed at overpowering the counterpart(s). The delegations must be aware about the considerable risk of damaging the governments' relationship, and they must work together to prevent such consequences by using integrative or "cooperative" approaches to diplomatic negotiations.

6.1.4 Behavioural approach

Behavioural approaches emphasize the role negotiators' personalities or individual characteristics play in determining the course and outcome of negotiated agreements. Wherein this approach, personality types are the variable and outcomes are explained by the chemistry between the negotiators. Thus, "behaviourists" explain negotiations as interactions between personality "types" that often take the form of dichotomies, such as "hard-liners" and "soft-liners", where negotiators are portrayed either as ruthlessly battling for everybody and everything or diplomatically conceding to another party's demands for the sake of keeping the peace. Two categories are distinguished:[428] "dominating" behaviour: insisting on preconditions before negotiating, or insisting that certain items are non-negotiable, or attempting to fix the agenda unilaterally; "shaping" behaviour:

---

[427] Saving face is defined as a person's need to reconcile the stand he/she takes in a negotiation or an agreement with his/her principles and with his/her past words and deeds (see Fisher Roger, Ury William, and Paton Bruce, Getting to Yes: Negotiating Agreement Without Giving In, New York: Penguin, 1991).

[428] Kennedy Gavin, The Perfect Negotiation, Random House Business Book UK, 1999, p.178.

showing personal willingness to accommodate the other delegate' point of view, but making clear that others in our delegation may take a stricter view. The behavioural approach derives from psychological and experimental traditions but also from centuries-old diplomatic treaties. These traditions share the perspective that negotiations - whether between nations, employers and unions, or neighbours are ultimately about the individuals involved. While game theory relies on the assumption that players to a negotiation "game" are featureless, uniformly rational, pay-off maximizing entities, the behavioural approach highlights human tendencies, emotions and skills. It emphasizes the role played by "arts" of persuasion, attitudes, trust, perception (or misperception), individual motivation and personality in negotiated outcomes. The behavioural school highlights also factors such as relationships, culture, norms, skill, attitudes, expectations and trust.[429]

The "behaviourists" consider that to observe the behaviour of the counterpart is one of the tool that negotiators use to better understand the motivation and psychological needs of the other party. Non-verbal behaviour, especially non-verbal disclosures, unveils the real intentions of the negotiator. Behavioural analysis is not sufficient alone and has to be supplemented by the background knowledge of delegate's counterpart and the culture and political history of his or her country, while at the same time being aware of oneself own culture and experiences, and their impact on the behaviour. A delegate may combine both by making good use of the corridors. In the informal talks that take place, such as in plenary sessions, both verbal and non-verbal signals should be registered. However, informal talks may disclose more about the personality of the other negotiator, while in Plenary sessions delegations are probably limited to observations of more superficial signals. On one hand, to probe deeper in informal talks, it is often necessary to open oneself up to an extent that could be dangerous during the rest of the negotiations, as it could give to the counterpart "material" that could be used for intimidation purposes. On the other hand, trust can only be established by opening oneself up, at least to a degree. This is one of the more difficult dilemmas in negotiation processes in general, and in entrapment in particular. Openness can work both ways. There are many dreadful examples of negotiators doing things to cover up mistakes that, when discovered by the counterpart(s), trigger serious entrapment processes.[430]

---

[429] Alfredson Tanya and Cungu Azeta (also quoting Nicholson), Negotiation Theory and Practice. A Review of the Literature, FAO Policy Learning Program, EASYPol Module 179, 2008, p. 13-14.

6.1.5 Integrative approach

Integrative approach to negotiations involves a joint effort directed at finding a solution that will be perceived as beneficial to both parties. Typically, the collaborating parties search for ways to increase the total payoff, while expressing little concern for how much each party will receive. Integrative negotiations are referred to as "non-zero sum" games. Parties engaged in integrative negotiations share norms that value reasoned, analytic, and objective problem solving. They recognize that they have common interests, and they believe that they will all benefit from their common effort.[431] Integrative approaches are used to facilitate convergence towards mutually beneficial agreements. Seeking to draw adversaries into recognizing interests outside narrow nationally-bounded perceptions, integrative approaches are employed to bridge differences and construct new understandings of interests. If solutions are not possible within currently recognized structures and assumptions, then cognitive strategies are used to reframe the perceived options and expand the zones of possible agreement, where acceptable compromises may be forged.[432]

Integrative approaches (contrast to distributive approaches), frame negotiations as interactions with "win-win" potential. Whereas a "zero-sum" view sees the goal of negotiations as an effort to claim one's share over a "fixed amount of pie", integrative theories and strategies look for ways of creating value, or "expanding the pie", so that there is more to share between parties as a result of negotiation. Integrative approaches use objective criteria, look to create conditions of mutual gain, and emphasize the importance of exchanging information between parties and group problem-solving. Because integrative approaches emphasize problem solving, cooperation, joint decision-making and mutual gains, integrative strategies call for participants to work jointly to create "win-win" solutions. They involve uncovering interests, generating options and searching for commonalities between delegations. Negotiators may look for ways to create value, and develop shared principles as a basis for decision-making about how outputs should be claimed (and who claims them).[433]

---

[430] Meerts Paul, Diplomatic Negotiation, Essence and Evolution. The Hague: Clingendael Institute, 2015, p.102.

[431] Bigoness William J., Distributive versus integrative approaches to negotiation: experiential learning through a negotiation simulation, Developments in Business Simulation & Experiential Exercises, Volume 11/1984, p.64.

[432] Johnson Rebecca, Arms Control and Disarmament Diplomacy, The Oxford Handbook of Modern Diplomacy, Edited by Andrew F. Cooper, Jorge Heine, and Ramesh Thakur, 2013, p. 604.

Integrative approach require delegations to understand what is important to them, what their priorities are, and what trade-offs they are willing to make. The overall diplomatic negotiation can be disaggregated into individual issues than can be negotiated separately. In the best cases, there are issues that are critical to one delegation but less important to the others, and vice versa. That allows each delegation to give ground on issues less important to them in exchange for the issues they do value. To reach integrative, mutually beneficial outcomes, three aspects[434] are important:

- *Awareness*: To make the right trade-offs, each delegation must understand the interests at play and the relative importance of each interest to each delegation. A delegation has to be self-aware of its own priorities and understand the other delegations' primacies;

- *Trust*: To arrive at mutually beneficial trade-offs, delegations must be transparent about needs and priorities. If a delegation does not trust the others, it might not want to let on that a particular issue is less important to the delegation, fearing that the other delegations do not as much to concede it;

- *Cooperation*: Integrative negotiations are an exercise in collaborative problem solving. Individual issues and priorities are like puzzle pieces that delegations have to work together to assemble into a "win-win" outcome.

Collaboration or cooperation is the hallmark of integrative approach as it leads to a negotiation result whereby each side wins more than it loses. To facilitate integrative negotiation process, the following[435] might be considered:

- *Encourage collaboration*. Formulate positions and proposals in a positive manner, trying to create an environment that values and promotes dignity through delegate's own conduct and demeanour;

- *Explore delegation's interests*. This requires recognizing, acknowledging, identifying and respecting emotions, interests and needs. The negotiator must actively seek the reasons underlying positions, and ask questions that deliver such information. Active listening is imperative to gain understanding of what the delegations say and do not say. The negotiator has to look for mutual or compatible goals and interests.

---

[433] Alfredson Tanya and Cungu Azeta (quoting Lewicki), Negotiation Theory and Practice. A Review of the Literature, FAO Policy Learning Program, EASYPol Module 179, 2008, p. 15.

[434] McKinsey Business Concept 101, 2013 (available at businessconcepts101.blogspot.ch).

[435] Doto David M., Facilitating Distributive and Integrative Negotiation in Mediation, The Opening Statement, 2011 (available at theopeningstatement.wordpress.com).

- *Encourage creativity*. The negotiator has to understand how each delegation might be willing to meet the needs of the others. He or she should be aware that solutions that "expand the pie" and meet the concerns of delegations are more likely to be accepted than those that more narrowly meet the needs of only one delegation. Accordingly, the negotiator should gently emphasize and explore options that secure the most satisfaction for all delegations.

We acknowledge the negotiation is seen as an instrument to be used in situations where competition and cooperation are both immanent. If competition is dominant, distributive negotiation can be expected; where cooperation is the dominating mode, however, integrative negotiation can be implemented. If the cooperative mode is excluded, negotiation is not applicable. The delegations might use force, or freeze, or flight as instruments in dealing with the negotiation at hand. Where the competitive mode is absent, negotiation is needed. Delegations can discuss how to cooperate or not to cooperate, but a "give-and-take" process will not (or will hardly) be applied.[436]

Above all, **diplomatic negotiation is a process**. As such, planning for and negotiating over the process itself are as critical for the outcome of a negotiation as the negotiation over the substantial issues themselves. The delegations must take time to consider questions such as: Who will be negotiating? What issues will be discussed? How will these be discussed? What should the order and value of the issues be? And how will commitments be decided? Taking the time to negotiate the process before diving into talks is beneficial to all the parties involved.[437] Even finding answer to these questions, the reality in today's world, is that there is no "one size fits all" approach to all negotiations and all negotiation processes.

6.2 Negotiation processes in multilateral conferences

Multilateral conferences are the best place where successive phases of negotiation and their respective dynamics can be seen. The process starts with governments or the secretariats of international organizations identifying objectives they wish to achieve through negotiation at a multilateral conference. They then exert themselves to ensure that a conference is convened with an

---

[436] Meerts Paul, Diplomatic Negotiation, Essence and Evolution. The Hague: Clingendael Institute, 2015, p.42.

[437] Alfredson Tanya and Cungu Azeta, Negotiation Theory and Practice. A Review of the Literature, FAO Policy Learning Program, EASYPol Module 179, 2008, p. 16.

appropriate mandate and they engage in preliminary exchanges to prepare the way for the conference both making administrative arrangements and to gather support for their preferred outcome. When the conference ultimately convenes, the process of negotiation starts with delegates exposing their respective attitudes and intentions, in short, their general negotiating goals. Thereafter they begin the process of making and exchanging proposals for specific wording, finding formulas and trade-offs on which agreement can be reached, and ultimately the conference makes its decisions (see chapter 5.3.2).

6.2.1 Informal negotiation

A great amount of negotiation in conferences takes place very informally between delegates meeting in twosomes or in larger groups, mainly in the corridors and lobbies of the conference venue, but also in contact groups (see chapter 2 and 3), talking like friends who are trying to find common ground. The exchange can be very quick or continue for hours. Its outcome is likely to be a text which is then formally proposed to the conference by one or more delegates. Among the benefits of these informal negotiations[438] there are:

- helping restore confidence when formal negotiations get bogged down;

- promoting constructive dialogue among negotiators often in a depoliticized environment;

- contributing to identify new approaches or helping delegates reformulate issues or conflicts of interest;

- providing possibilities to incorporate drafts into texts to be considered in formal negotiations; and

- serving as a basis of agreement.

In some cases, governments form contact groups, or hold "**informal informals**", which are strictly off-limits to anyone except a core group of delegates. These meet outside the main negotiation rooms, generally at a time and place announced in the working group, and bring together only those

---

[438] Delegations have to keep in mind the "Slippery Slope": The purpose of informal negotiations – whether structured (e.g. in contact groups) or not – is to be able to step back and listen carefully (active listening and not passive listening) to what the counterparts have to say, understand their interests and try to forge consensus. Occasionally, discussions in informal working groups/contact groups degenerates and take on non-cooperative negotiating styles, where negotiators tend to position themselves (see Performing Effectively in Multilateral Conferences and Diplomacy, UNITAR, 2006).

governments with a strong interest in a particular issue that has caused disagreement. Contact groups seek to bring widely conflicting positions closer together, before presenting the results of the discussions to the meeting at large. They also save time by allowing concerned delegates to have a detailed discussion while the rest of the working group continues its deliberations.[439]

In any situation, some of the language in informal negotiation is sacrificed in a spirit of compromise. The process of informal negotiation has always been marked by the spirit of compromise which led to shifts in positions, ideas, norms of behaviour and formal practices that created new multilateral customs and conventions.

6.2.2 Formal negotiation

A very similar process takes place in the formal negotiations: a draft text is **introduced** by one or more delegates (known, in the case of a resolution, as the **sponsor** or **co-sponsors** - see chapter 4) or sometimes proposed by the chairman, a subsidiary body or the secretariat, usually in written form. Delegates seek the floor in turn to comment on the draft, expressing either support or reservations and sometimes proposing alternative or additional words. These discussions typically are conducted with politeness and a display of deference for each other's preferences. The possibility of giving offence is reduced by using diplomatic device such as **different** or **alternative language**. Likewise (see chapter 4), a great effort is made by most negotiators to avoid ever saying outright "no" or anything else which closes off discussion. All participants understand, however, that if a delegate proposes a different set of words it is because he or she has some objection to the original draft. Particularly in the early stages of negotiation, delegates give reasons for their preferences - sometimes in an apologetic tone. If so, this may be to soften the impact of their not accepting the original proposal; but it can also be for the purpose of, in effect, inviting others present to look for a way of accommodating these concerns. Delegates fully understand that to achieve their own objectives it is also necessary that the objectives of most (and preferably all) other delegations are also met, as far as possible.

Formal negotiation processes are, of course, vital and are a conference's daily reality, but progress is made in the corridors, before and after the meetings,

---

[439] UN Non-Governmental Liaison Service (NGLS) with Gretchen Sidhu, Intergovernmental Negotiations and Decision Making at the United Nations: A Guide, 2nd Updated Edition, United Nations, 2007, p. 24.

and in informal talks between the different formal and informal layers. For a successful outcome, both informal and formal negotiations should be effectively performed.

6.2.3 Elaborate textual negotiation

The text of a negotiated agreement can travel through many different versions and revisions in the course of a negotiating process. In general, the debate relies most heavily on two kinds of documents: those presented as the foundation for discussion towards an agreement, which are regularly revised and updated, and the various proposals, additions and corrections submitted during the course of the meeting. If the text is long with several aspects that need to be closely negotiated, the process becomes more elaborate. The process often used to negotiate treaties and other lengthy and solemn texts is similar to the followings.[440]

The creation of such a text starts with a debate in which delegates express their views about the proposed document, its purpose and general reach. At some stage in this debate, if there is sufficient degree of agreement about broad purposes, agreement is reached to mandate a committee or other subsidiary body or even a **negotiating group** to develop the text. When that body convenes, it too often starts with a general discussion about the broad reach of the future document. As the debate progresses, delegates are more specific in identifying points which they like to be covered by the document and ultimately in proposing a broad language of its main provisions and perhaps some ideas about structuring the text. After sometimes prolonged exchanges, a delegate or the chairman produces an initial set of **elements** for the document. These elements describe concepts rather than propose specific wording for the final document. This text, which in its earliest versions is called "non-paper" [441] or a similar title, emphasizing its tentative nature, reflects the debate which has taken place so far and expresses points which appear to be widely supported. These elements are debated afterwards, often leading to a series of successive versions, each (hopefully) closer to being generally accepted. It is not necessary to reach formal agreement on these elements before proceeding to the next stage, when delegates

---

[440] United Nations Institute for Training and Research (UNITAR), Performing Effectively in Multilateral Conferences and Diplomacy - Negotiation and Decision-making, 2006, pp.33-36.

[441] Non-papers are prepared primarily by government representatives to facilitate the negotiating process and contain proposals and amendments on the text under consideration. They often do not bear a document number, and are not considered part of the official record of the meeting (see chapter 3.1.2).

start proposing specific **language** (words) for the definitive text. These proposals are made verbally or in writing. In most cases they provoke reactions from other delegates, often in the form of expressions of support or counter-proposals. From this stage onwards, and often earlier, there is probably more activity in the corridors that in the conference room itself. When delegates come forward with textual suggestions, these were most probably already discussed with a number of other delegations and formulated with the intention of gaining their support.

Eventually, there are **a lot of proposals**, most of them being already subject of informal or formal debates, or perhaps inferentially (if other delegations introduce a competing proposal, this infers dissatisfaction with all other proposals already **on the table**). Chairman, most of the time, working with the help of the secretariat, produces a **"compilation text"**,[442] which puts all these proposals together in an orderly fashion, together with whatever other text is needed to make the total document coherent and complete. This compilation is an attempt to express all the common ground exposed in the debate, but if there are substantially different proposals for some sections of the text, these are also incorporated in a way which clearly shows that they are alternatives. This is done in different ways, the most common practices being: to place a slash (/) between the alternative proposals and square brackets around them (see chapter 5.3.2 on introducing and exchanging proposals).

If the negotiating body agrees, the **examination** of this text paragraph by paragraph or line by line, proceeds. Each paragraph without dissent is considered to be provisionally agreed. Delegates who wish to amend the text can make **suggestions, verbally or in writing**. If these are accepted they are incorporated into the text. Otherwise, usually after some discussion and sometimes revision of the original proposal, they are incorporated in square brackets (as parts of the text not agreed). Likewise, if any delegation objects to any part of the composite text it asks the section to be put in square brackets. At the end of this **first reading** of the whole text, some parts are provisionally agreed while others are in square brackets (as yet not agreed and/or with alternative wording). Thereafter, the negotiating body proceeds to a **second reading**, with the aim to **remove square brackets**, by looking at each square bracketed word or passage in order to find

---

[442] Periodically during the negotiations, the Secretariat will issue a compilation text that includes all agreed changes or additional proposals. This document then becomes the basis for continued discussions (see UN Non-Governmental Liaison Service (NGLS) with Gretchen Sidhu, Intergovernmental Negotiations and Decision Making at the United Nations: A Guide, 2nd Updated Edition, United Nations, 2007).

those on which the committee can agree. There is willingness to do so for two reasons: now delegates have a better idea about the whole document and some of their initial reservations are relieved; and solutions were found to the initial difficulty due to the informal discussion and negotiation. Throughout this second and subsequent readings there are frequent reiterations of two principles: "the text provisionally agreed should not be reopened" and "nothing is agreed until everything is agreed".[443] This last approach is modelled after the "single undertaking" approach of the WTO. In many cases, developing countries want to ensure there are certain provisions regarding means of implementation (finance, technology transfer and capacity building, for example) or the principle of common but differentiated responsibilities before they agree to the entire package. If, as it is often the case, several sections remain in square brackets, there is **a third and possibly subsequent readings** of the text until ultimately every single word of it is accepted. A text which is going through a succession of readings is known as a **rolling text**.

All these decisions are made by consensus (see chapter 4.4), there is no voting in this process. However, in some unusual cases, if one or a small number of delegations stick firmly to isolated positions, the majority sometimes find ways to circumvent this opposition.

Often the process of reaching agreement on a long and controversial text can be very time consuming and involve recourse to a number of established procedures. For example, the *chairman or another mediator* (often acting with the chairman), convenes informal meetings of the most interested delegations in a particular segment of the text and mediate their discussion or negotiation aiming to help them to reach agreement. Such meetings can be formally constituted as **negotiating committees**, or convened with varying degrees of informality and called **contact groups**, **Chairman's consultations**, or meetings of **Friends of the Chair**.[444] If during the process a facilitator was appointed to assist the negotiations, he or she listens to input from governments and then drafts a new or revised text, the **Facilitator's text**. This document may be accepted by

---

[443] Accordingly, all sides acknowledge that nothing either side has said, implied, or proposed is irrevocable until a full agreement is reached. This principle of "nothing is agreed until everything is agreed" can help overcome deadlock by allowing delegations to make concessions safely (see Malhotra Deepak, Negotiating the Impossible: How to Break Deadlocks and Resolve Ugly Conflicts, Berrett-Koehler Publishers Inc., 2016).

[444] The term "Friend of the Chair" is also sometimes used to designate a delegate who has been commissioned by the chair to act as mediator or facilitator and try to develop an agreed text on a particular point or section (see chapter 3.3.2).

delegations as expressing their areas of agreement or may become the basis for continuing line-by-line negotiations.

Sometimes, in the final stages, the chairman (or, less commonly, one or a group of delegations) produces a **compromise text** or **Chairman's text** in order to bridge differences on some of the more difficult issues and as an attempt to find a solution acceptable to all. Occasionally, this is called **composite text** by the chairmen, for the diplomatic purpose of down- playing their personal role in drafting it. On other occasions, chairmen present such text as their own making and offer it on a "take it or leave it" basis as the only alternative to the conference failing. It is not unusual of chairmen's texts to be drafted by an informal committee of the delegations most deeply engaged in the negotiation or sometimes drafted and privately given to the chairman by one or a small group of helpful delegations. Any such exchange potentially expose the chairman to criticism and accusations of partiality, but at times they are the means whereby a difficult conference ends successfully, including by lending political authority to persuade delegates to accept the text without much revision and move forward.

6.2.4 Group negotiation

Groups are the natural consequences of the various manifestations at different negotiation levels. At some conferences delegations form groups for a variety of purposes, which in turn become involved in negotiation. The group system has become the main feature in practically all international, global negotiating processes.[445]

One example is a **group of co-sponsors**: delegations which join in sponsoring a proposal, usually a draft resolution or a draft ministerial declaration. After consulting widely, one or more co-sponsors may appreciate that the draft should be modified, in order to accommodate the concerns of other delegations and to increase its prospects of being accepted by the conference. As they are no more than "**co-owners**" of the text, they cannot decide by themselves. Thus, a **meeting of cosponsors** is organized, the ideas are discussed and any changes to the text are collectively decided. Such decisions are always by consensus: meetings of co-sponsors groups do not vote, but sometimes negotiation among the co-sponsors are required. Next, the **lead sponsor**, acting on behalf of the group,

---

[445] Nyerges Janos, How to negotiate, in M.A. Boisard and E.M. Chossudovsky, Multilateral Diplomacy: The United Nations System at Geneva, A Working Guide. The Hague: Kluwer Law International, 1998, p.179.

enters into negotiation over the text with one or more other delegations. He or she may, during such negotiation, agree to further alter the text, but always subject to the concurrence of the other co-sponsors. Thus, the lead sponsor delegation is involved in two levels of negotiation: one with outsiders and one within the co-sponsors' group.

Another example are the **caucus or political groups**, which articulate common policy concerns (see chapters 3 and 4), such as the Group of 77, the European Union (a group with a strong determination and a legal obligation to promote common positions at multilateral conferences) and the African Group (a group of delegations which have both many common policy concerns and a general policy commitment to mutual solidarity). These three are permanent groups, but often there is a **group statement** made on behalf of a number of delegations which act as a "group" only for the purpose of that particular statement - just as the co-sponsors vary from one draft resolution or decision to another. Nevertheless, in every case, the elaboration of such statements involves some negotiation within the group, as national positions and preferences are rarely identical in every respect. In extension of this practice, at some conferences, negotiations (usually on a text, e.g. of a treaty or a declaration) take place not directly between all delegations acting individually but between representatives of groups of delegations (generally well established or permanent groups). Similarly, the distribution of electoral positions and other issues is subject of negotiation between representatives of electoral groups. As with a co-sponsors group, there is often a two layered negotiation: one between a representative of the group and outsiders, and a second layer within the group, to develop positions supported by all members of the group.[446]

All these groups are negotiating instruments, using the combination of the number of delegations and the unity of real political forces. Their main asset is their unity, their cohesion. The unity within the group is achieved by compromise solutions, but this is often tested during negotiation processes since the various level of interest within a group or even within a delegation are not automatically identical, and sometimes are even contradictory. If within a group there are different motivations or different level of interest, the situation is complicated, the unity is not easy to create and the multilateral negotiations become cumbersome, which might influence the conference outcome. Though, by applying the

---

[446] United Nations Institute for Training and Research (UNITAR), Performing Effectively in Multilateral Conferences and Diplomacy - Negotiation and Decision-making, 2006, p.39.

appropriate negotiation strategies, tactics and techniques the outcome is a successful one.

6.3 Diplomatic negotiation strategies, tactics and techniques

Participating in multilateral conference requires a clear picture about diplomatic negotiations and their aim to get the participating delegations to reach an agreement. On one hand, this is a matter of the processes and group dynamics (see chapter 3), on the other hand it is a matter of dealing with the individual delegates (see chapter 2) with factors such as: they usually carry instructions and always have responsibilities; they are accountable to the sending authorities and sometimes more widely, each has a distinctive viewpoint and/or come to the conference with certain expectations; and, they have personal traits and share the common features of all human beings.

These factors are determinant in what the delegates agree to. Negotiation strategies[447] "exploit" these elements in order to influence delegates' behaviour for achieving a successful outcome. Consequently, the *instructions* of delegates may be helpful or not to the delegations' objectives while *accountability* of delegates is often more helpful; the *point of view* of a delegate is readily influenced by providing him/her with new information, explaining the proposal and the reasoning of the position (Expectations of each delegate evolve as he/she is better informed and the situation develops); *personal characteristics* such as personality traits, worries, distractions, interests etc. are all responded to or played upon to influence the behaviour of delegates; the most important, *all human beings like to be treated with respect* and to satisfy their basic needs (eating, resting, etc.). In addition, the conference environment plays a role in securing a delegate's agreement to a preferred outcome.[448]

Negotiations strategies, tactics and techniques are all about anticipating and controlling the counterpart(s) reactions. In order to do this the delegates must be aware of the factors influencing the others' behaviour, must be able to assess and calculate them, without underestimating their impact. There is no general valid

---

[447] A **strategy** is "a careful plan or method, especially for achieving an end", whereas the use of **tactics** refers to "the skill of using available means" to reach that end (see Alfredson Tanya and Cungu Azeta, Negotiation Theory and Practice. A Review of the Literature, FAO Policy Learning Program, EASYPol Module 179, 2008).

[448] Walker R.A., Manual for UN Delegates - Conference Process, Procedure and Negotiation, UN Publication, 2011, p.129.

recipe as to the best strategy, but depending more or less on the mentioned factors, there are sixteen strategies for securing agreement, three "damage limitation" strategies and six strategies for frustrating agreement.[449] Also, negotiation strategies are generally categorized as being either distributive or integrative and these differing approaches to negotiation frequently lead to vastly different behavioural and attitudinal outcomes.[450] Besides, there are so-called **cooperative strategies and techniques** that pursue the maximization of mutual gains, seeking to increase the outcome satisfaction for all delegations. The cooperative, problem-solving strategies result in more effective and efficient agreements, even many negotiations do not begin in a collaborative way. Likewise, all negotiations are not always cooperative and, at times, there are moments when delegates have to find ways of **dealing with difficult negotiators.** Similarly, there are situations when negotiators are engaged in **hard bargaining**.

6.3.1 Cooperative strategies, tactics and techniques

A **cooperative or collaborative negotiation strategy**[451] supposes that issues are essentially problems, and that while negotiators' positions may be different, goals are not mutually exclusive. This style or orientation of negotiation is the basis of consensual decision-making, and it always produces a superior result, commonly known by the "win-win" outcome. Adopting a collaborative negotiating behaviour does not imply that parties to a negotiation do not have different positions or values to uphold. It means that negotiation positions are not the ends, but only the beginning of a *process designed to sustain trust, communicate and share information*, and uncover the interests that reflect the concerns, needs and desires of the parties. *The tactics and techniques used in this type of negotiating behaviour are distinctly different from a more competitive negotiation style.* The process is one of defining problems in such a way that is acceptable to all parties, seeking to integrate interests and searching for innovative solutions that may be entirely unknown at the outset. As a pre-condition, it requires open channels of communication, constant flows of

---

[449] Walker R.A., Multilateral Conferences: Purposeful International Negotiation. London: Palgrave Macmillan, 2004, pp. 187-194.

[450] Bigoness William J., Distributive versus integrative approaches to negotiation: experiential learning through a negotiation simulation, Developments in Business Simulation & Experiential Exercises, Volume 11/1984, p.67.

[451] United Nations Institute for Training and Research (UNITAR), Performing Effectively in Multilateral Conferences and Diplomacy - Negotiation and Decision-making, 2006, pp. 40-43.

information, redefining issues, willingness to explore other options that may meet one's interests and acceptance of related issues or making trade-offs.

Positive feelings towards the other delegations lead to cooperative (problem-solving, collaborative or accommodative) strategies:

1. Begin by asking politely. This is the most simple and elementary strategy. It is not usually sufficient to overcome a strongly held objection, but failure to ask politely for support can, of itself, become a reason why that support is withheld.

2. Reason and logic. Most delegates, most of the time, are strongly influenced by sound logical arguments which appeal to their own reason and that of their governments. These often meet delegates' concerns for accountability and provide them with good reasons to find some flexibility in their instructions or, if necessary, to look for revised instructions.

3. Appeal to solidarity. Many governments and delegations are responsive to appeals for solidarity with others with whom they identify or wish to be closely associated. Examples of this include members of several regional associations who, as a matter of policy, prefer to take common stances, applicant countries which wish to display their willingness to join such associations and, in the absence of such formalized relations, neighbouring or otherwise closely associated countries which place high value on their relations.

4. The pull of the crowd. Many governments and delegations show a tendency to join positions which are widely supported. There are many reasons for this, including a reluctance to impede international cooperation and predisposition to assume that if a proposal is widely supported it must have merit. Another powerful reason is the equivalent wish to avoid isolation. Most governments and even more delegates greatly dislike being isolated. Delegates can be rallied to support a proposal if they can be persuaded it has overwhelming support and especially if they can be persuaded that to oppose it would leave them isolated.

5. Expand the "pie". Contrary to looking at a negotiation as a "fixed pie" with a "fixed value" to be distributed, delegates look for ways of increasing value by adding issues that others may find attractive, unbundle issues that may be grouped together, and which later may be exchanged or connected. Expanding the scope of the negotiated matter and including issues not directly linked (e.g. during negotiation on trade facilitation in WTO, provisions for assistance to Members

were included to enable them to better implement the agreement) facilitate the inter-disciplinary *quid-pro-quo*[452] which satisfies all parties.

6. <u>Building creative packages</u>. If a solution pleasing all is not found, it is often possible to assemble a "package" of proposals which, taken together gather widespread support because each delegation finds more "likes" therein than "dislikes". The essential character of a package is that each delegation has to accept the whole package if it wants to get the elements it likes. In this way, the elements wanted by a delegation are included in the conference outcome, even if, on their own, they do not attract much support. The technique is powerful, because once a delegation finds the proposed package attractive, it has an incentive to persuade other delegations to accept it.

7. <u>Creative linkages and trades</u>. Building packages often requires negotiators to connect issues and make value trades creatively - not through distribution or redistribution (i.e. "horse-trading" without any consideration to what one and the other values). For creative deals, negotiators prioritize carefully which issues are important for them, and which issues are less important in order to meet their interests and objectives. Making concessions on issues of low importance, in exchange for receiving concessions of issues highly valued, is a common technique that leads to superior agreements.

8. <u>The wish for a solution</u>. Most governments support the mandate of conferences to which they send delegates: they wish that the conference succeeds. They are predisposed to support a proposal which appears capable of resolving problems before the conference.

9. <u>Leadership by the quality of ideas</u>. The most effective way to secure support in a conference is to put forward proposals which have very wide appeal, because they meet the objectives or concerns of most delegations. Developing such proposals rests on widespread consultation, so as to fully understand the concerns of other delegations and ingenuity to find formulations that suit the overwhelming majority - as well as own objectives.

10. <u>"Welcome solution"</u>. After a protracted period of negotiation it is sometimes possible for someone (often the chairman, sometimes one of the delegations) to produce a text which all accept. Such a text needs to take account of all the negotiations that have taken place previously and to be based on deep

---

[452] quid-pro-quo: something given or received for something else (see The Merriam-Webster Dictionary, 2016).

knowledge and understanding of all concerns. It must be so balanced that the overwhelming majority of delegations judge that it is about as good a result, for them, as they hope to achieve.

11. <u>Mediation</u>. Sometimes, if it is difficult to reach agreement, the best way of achieving the objectives is to invite or accept mediation. This is a process whereby a third party (sometimes the chairman or a delegate specially commissioned by the chairman for that purpose) intervenes to try to help negotiators to reach agreement. The mediator or facilitator's role varies from simply carrying messages from one party to another, to advising the parties separately and/or together of his or her assessment of their prospects, the zone of potential agreement (ZOPA) and perhaps the best strategy for reaching agreement, to, ultimately, himself or herself proposing solutions to the issues in contention.

12. <u>Positive relationships with other delegates</u>. At times, delegates agree to a proposal simply because they wish to please other delegates. This may be because of the relations between the governments, or personal good will towards a country or a delegate personally. The potential power of personal friendship should not be underestimated, nor that of a charming personality or personal charisma. Of course, such factors tend to be more powerful when they do not conflict with a delegate's instructions or sense of responsibility.

These negotiation strategies are seen more productive and more appropriate in dealing with issues in the multilateral conferences. As they start from the basic recognition that parties are interested in reaching an agreement and therefore are willing to make proposals that will likely be agreed upon. Through cooperative strategies negotiators create favourable condition that may lead to a "win-win" situation: all parties involved get more out of the process than they put into it. The more common ground the delegations share, the more cooperative behaviour is expected.

6.3.2 Competitive strategies, tactics and techniques

A **competitive negotiation strategy**[453] supposes a process where each delegation is concerned primarily with maximizing its own gains and minimizing its costs. This kind of behaviour readily generates a competitive or even

---

[453] United Nations Institute for Training and Research (UNITAR), Performing Effectively in Multilateral Conferences and Diplomacy - Negotiation and Decision-making, 2006, pp.43-47.

combative spirit and encourages negotiators to consider a loss by their counterparts as a gain for themselves. Thus, it is characterized by negotiators pursuing their goals and objectives and ignoring those of others. For many people, this is what seems to exemplify negotiation most: exerting power and employing a range of tactics so that own proposal prevails over the others without any consideration to their interests.

Negative feelings towards the other delegations lead to competitive (or avoidance) strategies, the tactics commonly associated with such behaviour include the following:

1. <u>Formulating unreasonable proposals</u>. Tabling a proposal that is far beyond or far short of what the counterpart(s) could accept is a tactic commonly pursued at the outset of negotiations. It is also referred to as "highball"/"lowball" tactic.[454] This strategy is risky as it discourages the counterpart(s) from responding or starting the process of finding a mutually acceptable middle ground. Thus, the delegation proposing it, may end up with no agreement at all. On the other hand, it helps the counterpart(s) to walk away with a perceived victory.

2. <u>Concealing or misrepresenting information (bluffing)</u>. Delegates to multilateral conferences are an elite group and difficult to trick. Moreover, if found out, a delegate who tried to mislead others incurs considerable resentment and long term mistrust, which makes it difficult for him/her to operate effectively in the future. Additionally, this damaging reputation is likely to carry over to other delegations from the same country. Everybody understands the need to present own position in the best light and avoid disseminating unhelpful information. But that is different from attempting to deceive, either actively or by omission. Deception is definitely not recommended as a strategy for delegates participating in multilateral conference.

3. <u>Refusing to make concessions or to discuss options or related issues</u>. Insisting on own proposal or position and not willing to listen to others or move from the initial position is generally a sign of inexperienced negotiators and is usually unproductive. The exception to this negative judgment is that of countries

---

[454] "Highball"/"lowball" is also called "Door-in-the-face Technique", a slang from the days of the door-to-door sales person. A salesperson would offer a price so high that a customer might literally slam the door in their face. They would knock again and offer a much lower price. For some negotiators this is still a common way to begin negotiations. By starting with an outrageous offer, one side help to make the other side to write their victory speech (see Mar Anna, 15 Diplomacy Strategies For Negotiations, Simplicable Business Guide, 2013).

whose bilateral relations are so strong, or whose participation in the project so essential, that they insist on their own wishes, regardless of the wishes of all others. Powerful countries that engage in such tactics may secure their immediate objectives in the conference, but at a considerable cost in the long-term. In particular, governments are not keen to implement agreements imposed in this manner.

4. <u>Insensitive perseverance</u>. This tactic consists of simply reiterating delegate's demands so often that ultimately resistance is worn down and others concede, merely to put an end to an unpleasant experience. This strategy pre-supposes a willingness to accept a considerable degree of unpopularity and is not recommended for delegations which hope to engage constructively on several issues. It can also be defeated by appropriate counter measures.

5. <u>Inducement</u>. In practice this strategy is very uncommon, particularly as inducement is regarded as external to the conference itself. One of the reasons is that once it is known that a certain delegation is offering inducements, many delegations line up and their support, previously free, comes now at a price. Another reason is practicality: most delegations lack the resources to offer adequate inducements, especially to overcome serious objections. More commonly encountered is an exchange of favours, on matters within the conference (see point 8 below, on bargaining). When inducements are offered to governments - or sometimes individuals - this is usually done in private and often in capitals, away from the conference venue.

6. <u>Attempted intimidation (threats or warnings) or making last-chance offers</u> (e.g. "take it or leave it"). This strategy is not often encountered in practice. Threats against individuals are difficult to be credible, while threats conveyed from one government to another are very serious matters, with heavy consequences for their bilateral relations. Most governments lack the resources to make effective threats. Another disadvantage of this strategy is that it locks delegations into inflexible positions, denying opportunities that might otherwise be open.

7. <u>Dominating other delegations</u>. It is often not necessary to make explicit threats or to offer specific incentives. Some delegations accept a degree of subservience to certain other delegations, for reasons that can derive from the relations between their governments or simply from the force of character of individuals (or lack thereof on the part of others). This strategy, however, does not pass the test of accountability: it is difficult for a delegate to report to his

headquarters that his/her delegation agreed to the proposal because the delegation leader was intimidated by another delegate.

8. Bargaining or "horse-trading". This involves in effect saying: "I will agree to this if you will agree to that" or "Neither of us can have everything we want, let us accept something in between". While this latter technique appears "fair" it is in many cases inefficient (i.e. "We could have done better"). This is a technique that has been used in market places around the world for millennia. For diplomatic negotiations, a potential problem with the bargaining strategy is that it gets very confrontational, as individuals are carried away by their combative spirit and the sense of "winning" or "losing". This leaves an unhelpful atmosphere for most other strategies and most other conference work which thrive on harmonious cooperation. Nevertheless, bargaining is a common feature of multilateral conferences. It is also common in relation to elections: "I support your candidate for position X in exchange for your support of my candidature for Y".

9. Blackmail. The most confrontational form of bargaining is to say: "unless you agree to what I want, I will insist on A". Occasionally, this tactic is successful, even it should not be effective since it carries a clear inference that "A" is just a bargaining chip.

10. Destructive strategies. Sometimes, delegates that strongly oppose an emerging text resort to more drastic measures, underestimating, perhaps, the damage which this can do to their personal and national reputation. Examples include:

- *Walking out*. It is the sovereign right of a government to withdraw its representative from a conference and thereby not be part to its decisions. Apart from the adverse effect on relations with other countries, a delegation that walks out thereby renounces to have any influence on the course and decisions of the conference.

- *Saying No*. Although the institutionalized veto in the UN Security Council is often quoted as an extreme, all delegations at most conferences have powers very similar to veto rights. They do not normally use this power, because that involves frustrating the will of the vast majority of the conference. It is often therefore seen as the wrong strategy and gives rise to lasting resentment and mistrust.

- *Brinkmanship*. Short of actually walking out or saying No, it is possible to threaten to do so, if one does not get one's way. This carries the same risks as other forms of blackmail mentioned above, with the added risk that others may "call the bluff".[455] In most cases the delegates do not want to walk out or block consensus.

- *Attempt to side track the meeting.* This strategy is used at times to prevent a conference from reaching an unwelcome decision by sabotaging the conference, by getting it to waste time and other such tactics. As most delegations are supportive of the conference mandate and/or have other objectives which depend on the conference reaching agreement, they see such an attempt as inimical to their interests, do all they can to defeat it and carry a lasting resentment towards the perpetrator.

11. <u>Defensive strategies</u>. Delegates who do not like an emerging solution have a number of strategies for making it less problematic, from their point of view. For example, they seek to "soften" the text by making it less sharp, less explicit, less categorical, or perhaps introduce explicit "escape clauses" (e.g. exceptions, conditionalities or delays in implementation). Ultimately, they try to make the text less clear or even ambiguous, so that different governments place differing meanings on it. Other delegations are often willing to concede something in this direction (although it is not ideal for their own objectives) for the sake of securing consensus.

The more diverging the interests, the more competitive the delegations are. Competitive or aggressive negotiating behaviour in multilateral conferences is harmful to delegations' relations and thus to the process of give and take and to the prospects of cooperation and mutual tolerance. This strategy as a consequence of the veto threat comes to closure by the lowest common denominator: deadlock or non-decision. Competitive behaviour, even though it occurs quite often, is almost always counter-productive and costly. Nevertheless, delegates may respond to such behaviour in various manners.

6.3.3 Dealing with difficult negotiators

One of the delicate aspects of diplomatic negotiation is figuring out how to deal with delegation or delegates who cannot be convinced of the benefits of reaching agreement. Thus, frequently, discussions and debate stall, and, sometimes, they stall to the point where negotiations or a conference are on the brink of collapse. When faced with a particularly difficult and competitive negotiator, delegates instinctively position themselves defensively by trying to

---

[455] Walker R.A., Multilateral Conferences: Purposeful International Negotiation. London: Palgrave Macmillan, 2004, p. 191.

respond in a similar manner. Thus giving in or breaking off the negotiation is imminent, unless negotiators use strategies[456] which help unblock the situation. Once delegates start thinking on these aspects, other strategies may emerge.

1. Analyse the situation and be able to identify and assess what motives[457] the difficult behaviour of the counterpart(s).

2. Do a "reality check" for finding out who and what provoke this behaviour: too high expectations, the context in which the proposal was tabled, the discussion of the proposal in an informal group or insufficient consultation, communication problems, proper interpretation of the proposal, etc.

3. Assess the emotional and human environment. It is important to assess if oneself and the counterpart(s) are in full control of the emotions, thinking clearly and free from anger or competitive spirit; to realize if either party is exhausted, hungry, hot or otherwise uncomfortable, even ill (as it is often the case); to ask for a break, a coffee or a snack even having a rest.

4. Discuss possible response strategies by consulting with likeminded delegations and perhaps with the chairman, who shares your interest in getting out of the deadlock.

5. Have informal consultations or create a contact group, if debate in the committee has stalled. Moving from formal committee to an informal contact group changes both the delegations and social context of the negotiations.

6. Modify the "issue" context of the negotiations. For example, add items or unbundle items into sub-items where priorities can be fixed and/or where some progress can be made. Often what is needed is a new start, which can be done by: going back to the beginning of the text; conversely laying the current issue aside and going on to a later one that may be more readily soluble; or coming up with the process of "reframing"[458] (new "angle of attack") or a new proposal.

---

[456] United Nations Institute for Training and Research (UNITAR), Performing Effectively in Multilateral Conferences and Diplomacy - Negotiation and Decision-making, 2006, pp.48-51.

[457] Reasons of competitive tactics: there is insufficient information or time available; parties assign a high value or priority to a given issue or question; as a result of a negotiator or party having a very attractive alternative; as a response strategy; as a result of one's culture ("I like heated debates" behavior); internal political motivations; focusing too much on substantive interests and not enough on relationship interests (or vice versa) – see UNITAR, Performing Effectively in Multilateral Conferences and Diplomacy, 2006.

[458] "Framing" refers to the way a conflict is described or a proposal is worded. "Reframing is" the process of changing the way a thought is presented so that it maintains its fundamental meaning but is more likely to support resolution efforts. Parties can engage in reframing on their own, but it

"Reframing" is the process of changing the way a proposal or position is presented so that it maintains its fundamental meaning but is more likely to be supported. In general, longer processes are needed to overcome complex difficult situations. Interests have to be reframed, and negotiators' mind-sets will have to be turned over. It takes energy, time, and resources to deal with difficult negotiators in an effective way.

Sometimes, delegates cannot find the way of breaking the impasse and they share that challenge with their counterparts, thereby reminding them of common interest in finding a solution on which all can agree.

7. Look for assistance from third parties or facilitators who can mediate or act as a "go-between". The parties and the mediator must agree as to what his or her role is and what are its limits.

8. Unblock the situation by the Chairman or one of the negotiators by drawing attention to the negative consequences of not reaching an agreement or insisting on the positive opportunities or benefits that parties can derive from agreement. They remind delegations that they are all engaged in a common effort, aiming for everybody's joint interest.

9. A development of this approach is to remind to the counterparts of what they have already achieved in the negotiation and give them a new indication of the willingness to go at part of the way towards meeting at least some of their objectives. Thus, a delegate gives them an incentive to resume negotiations more constructively.

---

can be extremely helpful to have a third party (mediator or facilitator) to guide the process. It becomes the mediator's or third party's job to restate what each party has said in a way that causes less resistance or hostility. In other words, the mediator helps disputants communicate and redefine the way they think about the dispute, in the hopes of enabling cooperation between opposing sides. The ultimate goal of reframing is to create a common definition of the problem acceptable to both parties and increase the potential for more collaborative and integrative solutions (see "win-win" situation). The process of "reframing" can occur quickly if parties are receptive to it, or it may take more time if they are not. In many cases, parties are not aware of the true nature of the conflict. They know they are angry, that they have been wronged, and that they want retribution. However, they may not be able to identify the problem clearly. With the assistance of a mediator and the passing of time, the parties are given the chance to explore the nature of the conflict. Through this process they will hopefully begin to understand the underlying causes of the conflict. Once parties begin to truly understand each other's point of view, it makes it easier for them to think about solutions that will work for both sides (see Spangler Brad, Reframing, in Beyond Intractability. Ed. Guy Burgess and Heidi Burgess. Conflict Research Consortium, University of Colorado, Boulder, Colorado, USA, 2003).

10. Use conciliatory language and stress overarching goals by discerning interests from positions, reframing issues and questions, giving fair consideration to different options and writing proposals in language that can facilitate reaching agreement.

11. Place the proposal in the context of previously agreed principles. It is important to maintain momentum by returning to the principles previously agreed, notably when negotiations are bogged down or stalled.

12. Take a break from the negotiations to regroup, rethink, etc. This gives delegates a chance to talk privately with delegation's members, to conduct research about the issues that came up during the negotiation, to rethink the strategy and approach, especially when new information has surfaced that the delegation needs to review and strategize.

It is easy for delegates to get heavily involved in their work and in matters whose importance is largely confined to multilateral conferences (e.g. who prevails in negotiations over a small detail or who gets elected to a prestigious position), and they run the risk of forgetting the real-world consequences of a certain strategy and what need to be done during difficult negotiations. Many conferences address the woes of mankind: poverty, disease, underdevelopment, environmental degradation, oppression, insecurity, etc. Delegates must keep in mind the larger picture and the enormous potential of negotiation, formulating standards, effective international programmes and wise strategies to mitigate these problems.

6.4 Evolving elements in diplomatic negotiations

The purpose of diplomatic negotiations, throughout the ages and at different levels of societal evolution, whether at inter-personal, inter-communal, or eventually at international level, has always been to find a solution to an identified problem which is common to the parties engaged. That endeavour has led to the steady development of international relations and multilateral conferences aimed at avoiding wars, stimulating trade, fostering understanding and promoting acceptance by reaching successful outcomes.

An important difference between diplomatic negotiation processes of the past and present is the question of the relevance of the bargaining process in conflict management. If warfare and negotiation are seen as alternatives - if both are politics by other means - warfare was the priority tool in inter-state conflict until the twentieth century. This is an interesting paradox, as no other era has seen such massive warfare as the last century. On the other hand, no other period in European history has witnessed such substantial periods of stable peace as the nineteenth century.[459]

Throughout the centuries, negotiation became a more relevant tool and nowadays most multilateral negotiations are part of a long-term ongoing negotiation process, often in the framework of an intergovernmental organisation such as the UN or WTO. Structured and with a history of precedents as well as a perspective of the future, these conferences form relatively stable structures that allow for more or less successful outcomes by protecting the processes.[460] In addition, diplomatic negotiations gained strength due to several evolving elements, the four most noticeable and with greater impact on development and outcomes of multilateral conferences being: technology and telecommunication, regime creation, building trust and power distribution.

These factors have a huge and more evident impact on multilateral conferences (compared with the bilateral ones) and diplomatic negotiations because they are more complex and this complexity has positive and negative

---

[459] Mertees Paul (quoting Kissinger), Diplomatic Negotiation, Essence and Evolution. The Hague: Clingendael Institute, 2015, p. 55.

[460] The example of the EU as an intergovernmental and supranational organisation shows how important this is for effective negotiations and decision-making (see Mertees Paul, Diplomatic Negotiation, Essence and Evolution. The Hague: Clingendael Institute, 2015).

effects on the process of give and take between the representatives of the parties involved.

6.4.1 Technology and telecommunication

One hundred years ago the question of the future of diplomacy was raised as a result of technological progress - the invention of the radio and telegraph and the intervention of public into the domain of foreign policy. The first factor brought the apprehension that diplomats would become "honorary mailmen" and the second raised the issue of open diplomacy. However, the role of diplomatic negotiations in the twentieth century has not been restricted by these two factors,[461] but the consequences of technological and telecommunication development for the diplomatic services is significant. Of particular relevance to the diplomatic negotiations and multilateral conferences are two technological developments - satellite broadcasting and digital networks including the Internet.

The widespread use of the Internet and social media has profoundly impacted the conduct of negotiations. In essence, these technological advances have sped up and intensified exchanges between all those involved in the negotiations, making the submission and exchange of proposals and ideas infinitely easier. During negotiations in the early 1990s, most proposals from delegations were submitted to the secretariat in hard copy and had to be re-typed before they could be published in an official compilation document.[462] Now, the negotiating text is often projected onto big screens in the front of the room. As each delegation makes a textual proposal, a member of the Secretariat puts the proposal, often with attribution, onto the screen, in an attempt to provide transparency. As a result, all delegations know whether or not their proposals have been incorporated into the draft and feel honour-bound to defend their precise formulation. Each time a country's name is removed from the screen it is seen as a concession. This also reduces the Chairmen' manoeuvring marge, in the privacy of their own offices, to "twist" submitted proposals in the interest of producing a more consensual draft text. Furthermore, the ease of submitting proposals - verbally, by email or by text message - has discouraged restraint among delegates, resulting in an ever-greater volume of proposed texts reaching

---

[461] Petrovsky Vladimir, Diplomacy as an instrument of good governance, Modern Diplomacy. Ed by J. Kurbalija, 1998 (available at diplomacy.edu).

[462] Chasek Pamela, Wagner Lynn and Zartman William I. (quoting Depledge and Chasek), Six ways to make climate negotiations more effective, Policy Brief, Fixing Climate Governance Series No. 3/June 2015, p. 3 (available at cigionline.org).

secretariats and chairs.[463] Still, on-screen negotiations became difficult and politically charged. While the screen gives the illusion of transparency to the negotiations, it also leads the parties to defend their own proposals rather than strive for an agreement. In the end, it is often the Chairman (representative of the host country) that has to take over the negotiations and present delegates with a "take it or change it" text that includes all of the text negotiators had agreed upon to that point as well as the (eventual) Chairman's proposed text.[464] This is the reason why many conferences are unable to reach an agreement using this technology and has to resort to the usual end-game with a small group of self-selected delegations meeting behind closed doors and emerging in the last moment with a "take it or leave it" text. While this process does usually result in an agreement, it is not always viewed as legitimate or democratic, different methods being proposed.[465]

Also the technological and telecommunication developments impacted the role of the mission, delegates and negotiators. For example, one of the functions of the diplomatic missions accredited to UN or WTO is to collect UN documents and send them to their Ministries of Foreign Affairs or other governmental authorities. UN and WTO introduced an electronic system of document distribution. It is no longer necessary for the missions' staff to collect documents from the conference headquarters - they can obtain them via computer connection without leaving their offices. Similarly, the documents database is connected to the Internet. Accordingly, the Ministries of Foreign Affairs are able to retrieve the documents they need, directly bypassing the missions. Likewise, the senior managers at the UN are being provided with video-conferencing equipment. Thus, the cabinet meetings of the UN Secretary General are held with the participation of Geneva, Vienna and Nairobi senior managers through video-conferencing.[466] Another feature of technological development is the

---

[463] op.cit., p.3.

[464] op.cit., p.3.

[465] This was the case at the Cancun Climate Conference in 2010, where Bolivia dubbed the meeting a betrayal of the democratic principles and core values of the United Nations. Bolivia and many non-governmental organizations accused the meeting of setting aside "open and participatory methods normal in the UN", and claimed that senior negotiators' work was "overtaken" by ministerial-level guidance. The use of "open and participatory" on-screen negotiations led to closed and non-transparent negotiations both before and since Cancun (see Chasek Pamela, Wagner Lynn and Zartman William I. (quoting Khor and Vihma), Six ways to make climate negotiations more effective, Policy Brief, Fixing Climate Governance Series No. 3/June 2015).

[466] Vladimir Petrovsky, Diplomacy as an instrument of good governance, Modern Diplomacy. Ed by J. Kurbalija, 1998 (available at diplomacy.edu).

extraordinary ease of traveling in today's world. Whereas, before First World War, participation in multilateral conferences or bilateral negotiations was limited by the lack of affordable and speedy transport, at present, the venue of negotiations no longer matters. The transport revolution combined with the communications revolution has definitely changed the rules of the game of diplomatic negotiations and multilateral conferences, making the local diplomatic representative no longer irreplaceable.

The conduct of negotiations is profoundly changed and some functions of the diplomatic mission are diminished but the ambassador of a Member to the UN or WTO continues to assume a negotiating function. The instructions he or she receives from the capital leave ample room for manoeuvre. The dynamics of negotiations in multilateral conferences are such that the capital is rarely in a position to allow the Ministry of Foreign Affairs to restrain the diplomatic staff of the mission concerned. Equally, in the case of the EU, the Permanent Representative of a Member State and his/her diplomatic staff are constantly involved in the "negotiation machine" of the EU. The EU Treaty confers upon Permanent Representatives the important role in the negotiating process of representing their countries in the "Coreper" (Committee of Permanent Representatives) which, in its different formations, prepares the decisions of the Council of Ministers. In the field of the common and foreign policy of the EU, the representatives of Member States in the Political and Security Committee are also involved on a daily basis in negotiations. The agenda of the Council is "precooked" to a large extent by Coreper, in which the chiefs of mission are the main actors. Therefore, it is fair to say that in the EU context, the diplomatic function with regard to the negotiations has by no means diminished.[467]

However, the diplomat no longer enjoys a position of monopoly. Whereas, in previous centuries, the diplomatic representative of a sovereign used to be the only official negotiator, in the modern world, there is a multitude of actors, each influencing the negotiating process in one way or another. In the past, it was generally agreed that the emissary of a sovereign, duly endowed with full powers, had the exclusive authority to negotiate with the authorities of another state. That is no longer the case. Given the complexity of many international negotiations, it is the role of experts that often becomes decisive. Due to technology and

---

[467] Cede Franz, Changes in the Diplomatic Function and Their Impact on International Negotiations, PIN Points Network Newsletter 26/2006, p.2.

telecommunication developments, their advice are obtained directly and from anywhere in the world using the Internet and social media tools.

If anything characterizes human history, it is the change in technological and telecommunication devices. It is obvious that technology evolved in a positive way, that it reached a higher standard than in classical times, medieval times, or the Renaissance. Technology influenced warfare in the sense that it created more destructive weaponry than ever. At the same time, technology gave diplomacy the sophisticated tools needed to forge organizations channelling negotiation processes. It contributed to the availability and speed of information, facilitating effective negotiation. While technology made warfare an often too dangerous sword to wield, it made negotiation a more effective tool to bridge the gap.[468]

6.4.2 Regime creation

Regimes are frameworks of rules, expectations and prescriptions that states and other actors may agree on in specific policy fields, based on commonly perceived needs.[469] Regimes meet the demand for institutionalized multilateral consultations as a derivative of international agreements and institutionalism, and are created because of the lack of an international framework with enforcement capability. Another reason for their existence is the high transaction costs for successive multilateral agreements.[470] Moreover, supporters of the regime theory state that these types of permanent, multilateral consultation structures (regimes) are not only useful, keeping in mind international agreements, but that they also focus on implicit or explicit principles, values and codes of conduct.[471] Thus, when confronted with regimes, diplomatic negotiations and multilateral conferences might be called to change the "rules of the game", the principles, norms and rules of international relations.

Regimes are also seen as being capable of compensating for the lack of trust by imposing control, through international agreements stipulating rules of conduct and regulations and, at best, allowing for sanctions against those parties

---

[468] Meerts Paul, Diplomatic Negotiation, Essence and Evolution. The Hague: Clingendael Institute, 2015, p. 55.

[469] Reinalda Bob, Routledge History of International Organizations From 1815 to the present day, by Routledge 2 Park Square, Milton Park, Abingdon, Oxon OX14 4RN, 2009, p.6.

[470] Meerts Paul (quoting Keohane), Diplomatic Negotiation, Essence and Evolution. The Hague: Clingendael Institute, 2015, p. 81.

[471] Op.cit. (quoting Krasner), p.81.

that do not comply with the understandings that have been made. They provide information about the parties' behaviour and monitor their activities. Regimes can go a step further by establishing international organizations, in order to have a more durable and ongoing surveillance of the (mis)behaviour of states. Not having any regimes to supervise behaviour, stabilize negotiation processes and secure the outcome contributed to the idea that bargaining could be, at most, a sideshow in conflicts. Trust has always been a foremost problem in negotiation. Governments have proven to be reluctant to rely solely on negotiation as an alternative to conflict for lack of guarantee that the other parties stick to agreements.

Negotiators tried to deal with this problem in different ways. From swearing oaths and asking gods to bless the forged treaties, through strengthening relationships or exchanging hostages, to asking guarantors (like France and Sweden in the Peace of Westphalia in 1648) to help implement the treaty. In the eighteenth century, the number of conferences multiplied in an attempt to stop the wars in Europe and to make bargaining the dominant mode in conflict management. During the nineteenth century, multilateral conferences proved an appropriate way to reach international agreements and to monitor their implementation. Starting with the multilateral Vienna Conference (1814 - 1815), the meetings between heads of states and diplomats became a systemic feature, but ongoing organizational structures were still lacking. This changed in the twentieth century after the First World War (with the Paris Conference and the Peace of Versailles in 1919) and then the Second World War (Conference of San Francisco in 1945), by creating regimes of ever-better quality and strength, not only on a regional, but also on a global level. The conferences lend themselves to discussing and establishing relations among states, to correcting violations of agreements and to the further specification of those agreements. They agreed on several means, such as norms, rules for behaviour and procedures. The essential international norms of the Concert of Europe (see chapter 1.1) were self-restraint, consultation in crisis times, willingness to act together, refusal to act unilaterally and constant assurances of the pacific intent and commitment to the maintenance of stability. The essential rules of behaviour alongside these norms were the use of conference diplomacy to deal with crisis, the approval of territorial changes by the great powers, the protection of the essential Members of the system and the absence of challenges to the interests and honour of the great powers. Among the common procedures were the mutual consultation and collective decision making, the creation of buffer states, the establishment of neutral states and demilitarized zones, the localization of regional conflicts, the limitation of resources in third areas, the delineation of interests and areas of involvement, the intervention by multilateral action, the peaceful settlement of disputes and the communication and provision of advance notification.[472]

International organizations have tried to temper the Thucydides' dictum that "the strong do what they can and the weak suffer what they must". Multilateral conferences differ from traditional interstate diplomacy in several respects. Guided by the UN Charter principles, WTO Agreements' provisions and other similar standards, they offset somewhat, albeit not totally, the unfavourable position of the weaker party. They aim to establish a just peace as well as a stable balance of power, taking into account the interests of Members as well as the parties in dispute, thereby broadening the support base for any solutions reached.[473] International organizations can help states to solve collective problems by considering a long-term perspective rather than taking into account short-term interests. International regimes and institutions enable states to attain their goals more efficiently. In an interdependent world, in which states and economies depend on each other, regimes and institutions facilitate cooperation through the functions they perform for states, such as providing information about other Members and thus reducing uncertainty. They enable governments to enter into mutually beneficial agreements. The States profit from cooperation, making them more efficient than when acting on their own.[474]

By transforming negotiation into increasingly rationalized tools and promoting long-lasting cooperation, regimes addressed the problem of trust in an effective manner.

6.4.3 Building trust

The development of trust is the third remarkable trend in the evolution of diplomatic negotiation. Secrecy was a major issue in early European diplomacy, much more than today. Ambassadors had to be versed in publicly representing

---

[472] Reinalda Bob (quoting Richardson), Routledge History of International Organizations From 1815 to the present day, by Routledge 2 Park Square, Milton Park, Abingdon, Oxon OX14 4RN, 2009, p. 25.

[473] Cooper Andrew F., Heine Jorge, and Thakur Ramesh (quoting Thucydides, Javier Pérez de Cuéllar and Ramesh Thakur), Introduction: The Challenges of 21st-Century Diplomacy, The Oxford Handbook of Modern Diplomacy, 2013, p. 10.

[474] Reinalda Bob, Routledge History of International Organizations From 1815 to the present day, by Routledge 2 Park Square, Milton Park, Abingdon, Oxon OX14 4RN, 2009, p. 15.

their monarchs as well as dealing with issues under conditions of complete secrecy. Being able to keep secrets, to be specialized in treason, maintaining a "poker-face" and the like were the qualities of the effective ambassador-negotiator. *Distances, time-lags, transportation problems and communication distortions all helped secrecy.* Nowadays there are still secrets in diplomatic negotiation and there are pleas for openness and transparency as a means to further the effectiveness and speed of negotiation processes, although it remains unwise for delegations to show "publicly" their decisive assets. So-called "corridor work" (outside the conference room) and "huddling" (small groups of negotiators talking informally in the conference room during a break in the formal session) are still an essential part of bargaining, also for cultural reasons. Open concession-making can lead to losing face, as negotiators might refuse to give in openly, only in informal sessions.[475]

The chain of command constitutes another feature that distinguishes secrecy in diplomatic negotiations in the past from those in the present. In previous times, designated negotiators did not really have to take into account extraneous factors. What counted was quite simply the will of their political masters, to whom they had direct and often exclusive access. In a modern democratic system, negotiations cannot be conducted in an aura of secrecy dominated by exclusive interaction between the sovereign and his/her diplomatic emissary. In today's context diplomatic negotiations involve a multitude of actors, who make the process more complex and sometimes unpredictable. Although the subordination of the diplomat to his/her superiors still determines the setup of negotiations, other factors come into play in ways unthought-of in the past. For instance, the role of parliaments, the media, or nongovernmental organizations in certain issues are just a few examples of the multifaceted nature of current negotiations. It is obvious that, in such a negotiating environment, diplomats no longer enjoy the privileged position of their colleagues in previous centuries, when foreign affairs were usually considered as the *domaine réservé* of the sovereign, who could act outside any democratic control.[476]

Nowadays this democratic control requires negotiators to disclose (at least some elements of) their positions and multilateral conferences to publicly inform about the results of their debates. While some negotiations historically are done in

---

[475] Meerts P. (quoting Colson and Berridge), Diplomatic Negotiation, Essence and Evolution. The Hague: Clingendael Institute, 2015, p. 55.

[476] Cede Franz, Changes in the Diplomatic Function and Their Impact on International Negotiations, PIN Points Network Newsletter 26/2006.

secret to ensure the possibility of states putting forward their best proposals (for example trade negotiations in WTO), the extraordinary secrecy around several negotiations has led many to question the integrity of any potential outcome and to call for greater openness.[477]

In any case, trust is important to effective negotiation. But is it a precondition for negotiation? In certain situations, the presence of trust is indispensable for parties to negotiate at all. In traditional Chinese business circles, for example, personal trust is so important that business people invest heavily to cultivate it. However, the significance of trust is cultural and context-specific and it may stem from the intrinsic value of trust in human relationships. It may be an overstatement to claim that trust is necessary for all kinds of negotiation as trust-building *per se* can be an objective of negotiation. There are suggestions that a "win-win" negotiated outcome allows negotiators to maximize whatever utilities they care about, and trust can legitimately be one of them. Trust also enables parties to develop and preserve their relationship. For example, a primary goal of the 1985 Geneva summit between the USA President Ronald Reagan and the one of the Soviet Union Mikhail Gorbachev was to cultivate certain mutual trust amidst the Cold War climate of suspicion and hostility.[478] In long-term interactions, the outcome of negotiations - the choice of parties to either cooperate or defect - can depend heavily on the amount of trust that is established between the parties.

Negotiators should never underestimate the importance of trust in negotiations. It is critical and the perception negotiators have of each other is a crucial factor influencing the fluidity of negotiations. Being trustworthy and maintaining one's credibility is essential to creating positive personal relationships and preventing negative emotions that can result in recourse to some undesirable negotiations tactics. This is sometimes easier said than done as trust in multilateral conferences is slow to build and easy to destroy. Honouring commitments is one way that parties build trust, and thus serves as another essential element of negotiations.[479]

---

[477] Aaronson Ariel Susan, 5 Ways the U.S. Can Increase Trust, Responsiveness, and Transparency in Trade Negotiations, Institute for International Economic Policy, 2015 (available at internationaleconpolicy.com).

[478] Yan Ki Bonnie Cheng, Power and trust in negotiation and decision-making: a critical evaluation, Harvard Negotiation Law Review, 2009 (available at hnlr.org).

[479] Alfredson Tanya and Cungu Azeta, Negotiation Theory and Practice. A Review of the Literature, FAO Policy Learning Program, EASYPol Module 179, 2008, p.20.

However, trust-based strategies are not universally appropriate, as the use of power tactics is not necessarily harmful. By committing to a trust-based relationship, the right to seek competitive advantage may be lost even when the benefits outweigh the costs. Also, as one is likely to act in favour of a trusted counterpart, one's interests could be jeopardized if trust turns out to be misplaced. The concept of trust intertwines at some point with that of power.[480]

6.4.4 Power distribution

States are the basic and enduring entity in international relations and they are critical actors because they have power, which is the ability not only to influence others but to control outcomes so as to produce results that would not have occurred naturally. States number has grown manifold in the last hundred years, producing an exponential jump in the number of diplomatic interactions between them. One of the historic phenomena of the last century was the emergence of large swathes of humanity from colonial rule to independence. The first great wave of the retreat of European colonialism from Asia and Africa (1950s–1960s) and the South Pacific (1970s) was followed by the collapse of the large land-based Soviet empire and a fresh burst of newly independent countries in Eastern Europe and Central Asia (1990s). The number of independent state actors has quadrupled since 1945. And there is a great diversity among states, ranging from one superpower, two billion-strong, and nine nuclear-armed states to numerous mini-states, microstates, and failing states in a system of sovereign states that has famously been described as "organized hypocrisy".[481]

However, over the years, dramatic changes took place in global power structures. The velvet revolutions of 1989 in Central and Eastern Europe, followed by the collapse of the Soviet Union in 1991, created a new world system in which the United States played an absolutely dominant role in terms of political, economic and military power. The effects of this on international regimes and the channelled flow of negotiations were clearly visible. The international trade regime was enforced by shaping the General Agreement on Tariffs and Trade (GATT) into the World Trade Organization (WTO) in 1995, in order to provide it with a mechanism for settling trade disputes. The International

---

[480] Yan Ki Bonnie Cheng, Power and trust in negotiation and decision-making: a critical evaluation, Harvard Negotiation Law Review, 2009 (available at hnlr.org).

[481] Cooper Andrew F., Heine Jorge, and Thakur Ramesh (quoting Stephen D. Krasner), Introduction: The Challenges of 21st-Century Diplomacy, The Oxford Handbook of Modern Diplomacy, 2013, p.7.

Monetary Fund (IMF) and the World Bank threw themselves into liberalizing the planned economies of the former Eastern Bloc countries and raised the Western views on democracy and the economy as absolute norms.[482]

China, India and Brazil emerged as powerful modern economies, important global powers creating political waves across Europe and the USA. In particular, China and India, which have spectacularly risen over the past two decades and are gradually assuming leading positions at the global and regional levels. The rapid ascent of India and China announces an era of profound change in international relations, as it gives a new facet to existent power equations.

These developments placed the distribution of power under scrutiny. The rise of multilateralism has been real and important, but so is the need for consensus among the world's most powerful states on the core norms of international relations. Such a consensus can no longer be taken for granted. Power shifting toward emerging states complicates the task of reaching consensus because it multiplies the number of influential actors who must agree. There is no guarantee that new powers will subscribe to previous ideas about how, and to what ends, international relations should be organized. Some scholars argue that such rising states as China, India, Turkey, and Brazil already hold different views about the foundations of political legitimacy, the rules of international trade, and the relationship between the state and society.[483] Others are arguing that the overarching trend in the preference of China, India, and Brazil on existing regimes has been one of convergence on the *status quo*.[484] This debate will be resolved in time, by learning whether emerging powers accept, seek to revise, or attempt to overthrow existing international arrangements. At present, however, increased competition in global world seems all but inevitable, which in turn raises questions about the future of international regimes and multilateralism.[485]

---

[482] Meerts Paul (quoting Cohen and Meerts and Van Staden), Diplomatic Negotiation, Essence and Evolution. The Hague: Clingendael Institute, 2015, p. 82.

[483] Kupchan C., No One's World: The West, the Rising Rest, and the Coming Global Turn, New York: Oxford University Press, 2012, p. 7.

[484] Kahler Miles, Rising Powers and Global Governance: Negotiating Change in a Resilient Status Quo, International Affairs 89, no. 3/2013, p. 718.

[485] Paris Roland, Global Governance and Power Politics: Back to Basics Roland Paris, Ethics and International Affairs Carnegie Council, December 11, 2015 (available at ethicsandinternationalaffairs.org).

Navigating our era of global power transition is a challenge that requires enlightened leadership with an understanding of how power, norms and international organizations can interact to produce a stable power structure.

Chapter 7 – Diplomatic negotiations viewed from the top

All negotiations in international organizations and all multilateral conferences are led by Member's representatives or supranational officials who have mandates to manage the agenda, structure the deliberations, and reach agreements. The person who leads the diplomatic negotiations and presides over a multilateral conference is the Chairman. The person occupying this function must exploit its full potential to achieve agreement.

7.1 Negotiators and Chairman interaction

The smooth conduct of diplomatic negotiations in multilateral conferences requires the appointment of a Chairman to exercise, initially, procedural control over the negotiations. The roles were extended to cover agenda management, debate facilitation, and conference leading and become critical in defining the negotiation space, affecting the negotiation direction and influencing the outcome.

The Chairman[486] directs the conference and ensures it runs smoothly and efficiently. He/she is the facilitator of the conference and in many ways its quintessence. The Chairperson does more than make sure the debate is orderly and that the conference takes all necessary decisions. At many multilateral conferences there are several chairmen operating concurrently: the "Chairman" or "President" of the whole conference whose duties include presiding over the plenary; the chairmen of subsidiary bodies (committees, working groups, etc.); the chairmen of several geographical groups, who usually also act as spokesmen for their groups; lead sponsors, who act as convenors and spokesmen for a group of co-sponsors; the convenor(s) or Chairs of contact groups; etc.

On one hand, the <u>Chairman's task can be divided into two distinct aspects:</u> 1) the formal or procedural role which is indicated by rules of procedure; and 2) a more demanding role, not mentioned in the rules, in relation to the substantive outcome of the conference.[487] <u>Four elements of effective chairing can be</u>

---

[486] He/she may also be referred to as: Presiding officer, President, Chairman, Chair. The person who calls together and leads the work of an informal group or a group of co-sponsors is often referred to as convenor, but his/her role is also that of a chairman (see UNITAR, Performing Effectively in Multilateral Conferences and Diplomacy, 2006).

[487] Walker Roland A., Manual for UN Delegates - Conference Process, Procedure and Negotiation,

distinguished, and chairpersons operate at each of these levels, which run in parallel during the whole process of negotiation: managing substance; procedure; process; and behaviour. Although all four dimensions have to be managed at any one time, there is a certain shift in intensity as the negotiation evolves. Procedure is a main issue at the beginning of the meeting (rules and regulations) and at the end (decision by unanimity, consensus, or simple or qualified majority). Managing the process pops up at regular intervals, especially if the negotiation becomes tense, for example, if a deadlock is imminent. While the management of procedure and process is mainly done in and around the plenary sessions, people management is very much a question of lobbying. Chairmen have to be available to negotiators throughout the negotiation process. Issue management has to be done at all times, of course.[488] Moreover, the delegates should support the Chairman's efforts if they want the conference to succeed. Hence, a successful conference needs strong and able chairmen and chairmen, to be effective, need supportive and cooperative delegates.

The process and outcome of a multilateral conference, apart from the involvement of participants, depend on how well it is managed and led. A **poor chairmanship** can have disastrous consequences, resulting in a conference that: takes more time than necessary; follows a more laborious and contentious way to its final outcome; produces an outcome that is less satisfactory to many of the participants than they expected; reaches agreement, but one with which governments are later dissatisfied or find difficult or impossible to implement; fails to fulfil its mandate; fails entirely to agree on anything; or, worse, collapses altogether.

Some conferences are "condemned" to an unsatisfactory outcome from the beginning because of unrealistic mandates, sharp differences between the objectives of different delegations, unproductive negotiation behaviour, organization of an unnecessary conference with discussion of trivial issues (wasting Members' valuable time), the presence of wrong people (preventing the conference proceeding effectively as those present have to refer back to headquarters and are therefore unable to comment effectively), personality clashes and other problems conferences face, to the point that even the most outstanding chairmen could not do anything to save them.

UN Publication, 2011, p.149.

[488] Meerts Paul, Diplomatic Negotiation, Essence and Evolution. The Hague: Clingendael Institute, 2015, p. 278.

But in general, **effective chairmanship** overcomes or moderates many of these aspects, and inspired chairmanship sometimes rescues a conference that is close to failure. For this reason, becoming a chairman is a great responsibility. There <u>are modalities by which one can become chairman</u>:

- *Automatically by rotation*. In some bodies, such as the Security Council, the Conference on Disarmament and the Governing Council of the Economic and Social Commission for Western Asia (ESCWA), the chairmanship rotates on a monthly (or other regular) basis and in the alphabetical order of the names of the participating Members. Then the leader of the delegation whose turn it is automatically becomes chairman for the next month (or other period). For the European Union, the presidency of the Council of the EU rotates every 6 months.

- *By appointment*. In some other cases, the chairman of a working group or other subsidiary conference is appointed, often by the chairman of the parent body.

- *By election*. In most cases, however, and notably for the UN General Assembly (UNGA) and its committees, chairmen are elected by the conference. Such elections are in most cases uncontested and consequently decided without a vote. This implies that there is prior agreement, in the informal or formal preparatory process, on the selection of the individual concerned. Although typically this person is a delegation leader (or for lower level conferences and subsidiary bodies, another member of a delegation), at times it is an individual with no such affiliation. For example, Mr. Harald Neple who chaired the WTO General Council in 2016, was at that time Ambassador of Norway to the UN and WTO in Geneva. Also by tradition, many conferences and particularly ad hoc conferences elect a representative of the government convening it or a nominee from the host country: President Thabo Mbeki of South Africa presided the 2002 World Summit on Sustainable Development and the Kenyan Cabinet Secretary for Foreign Affairs and Trade Amina Mohamed chaired the 10th WTO Ministerial Conference in December 2015, etc.

The **criteria**[489] **for selecting a Chairman** for appointment or election are a combination of nationality and personal qualities. <u>The nationality considerations</u> are: preoccupation for geographic balance; in most UN bodies, it is traditional not to elect as Chairman representatives of the five Permanent Members of the Security Council (P5) ;[490] the Chairman, if an official, should come from a

---

[489] United Nations Institute for Training and Research (UNITAR), Performing Effectively in Multilateral Conferences and Diplomacy - Chairing International Conferences, 2006, pp.11-12.

government which is generally believed to support the collective purpose of the conference, (i.e. its mandate) and trusted not try to use the chairmanship as a means of advancing its own national objectives at the expense of those of the other delegations. The personal qualities sought in a chairman are those which will help him/her discharge the duties successfully. They include managerial and diplomatic abilities, experience, stature, and understanding of the policy issues involved in the conference, as well, ideally, has an established reputation for conducting meetings efficiently and impartially. A Chairman must at all times: treat all delegates equally; be seen to behave impartially; not appear to favour any party; not appear to favour any side of a contentious issue. A Chairman must make sure that: all the items on the agenda are discussed, everyone's views are heard, clear decisions are reached and the meeting starts and finishes on time. **An efficient Chairman** will also: always be thinking about the conference overall, not just the topic under discussion, always aim to draw a balance between hearing everyone's views and getting through the items on the agenda; and never use their position as chairpersons as an opportunity to put forward their views to the exclusion of others, or to dominate the meeting.[491]

No matter how the chairmen are nominated, their role is very challenging, they have responsibilities and tasks to be fulfilled, as well as constraints and defies that accompany them. This degree of challenge or difficulty experienced by a Chairman depends largely on the type or characteristics of a conference (see chapter 7.4, on UN, WTO and EU).

7.1.1 Chairman's responsibilities

The roles and responsibilities of the Chairman ensure that the works and activities of the multilateral conference are conducted in an orderly and efficient manner and in accordance with the rules of procedure (see chapter 3.2). In many rules of procedure, the functions empowering the presiding officers are listed under a distinct heading, although additional functions and powers are also often found elsewhere in the rules. The usual functions[492] of a Chairman include: declare the opening and closing of each plenary meeting of the session, direct the discussions in plenary meeting, ensure observance of these rules, accord the right

---

[490] China, France, Russia, the United Kingdom, and the United States of America.

[491] Resource Centre, Chairing a meeting, 2007 (available at resourcecentre.org.uk).

[492] See Rule 35 of the Rules of Procedure of the UN General Assembly and Document WT/L/161/25 July 1996 - Rules of procedure for sessions of the Ministerial Conference and meetings of the General Council in WTO.

to speak, put questions and announce decisions, rule on points of order, complete control of the proceedings at any meeting and over the maintenance of order thereat, propose to the conference the limitation of the time to be allowed to speakers, the limitation of the number of times each representative may speak, the closure of the list of speakers or the closure of the debate, propose the suspension or the adjournment of the meeting or the adjournment of the debate on the item under discussion, etc.

As conference unfolds, it is the Chairman's responsibility to ensure that it continues to flow smoothly by involving all Members and by not permitting any delegations to dominate the debate. During the conference, the Chairman can summarise by: indicating progress or lack of; refocusing discussion that has wandered off the point; concluding one point and leading into the next; highlighting important points; assisting the secretary if necessary; clarifying any misunderstanding. The Chairman paces the meeting, ensuring it runs to time. There is no problem in succeeding this if the planning was properly executed. At the end of the conference, the Chairman reminds Members their achievements and thanks them for their contributions. Finally, the time and date of the next meeting is settled. Fulfilment of these responsibilities make effective meetings, but successful outcomes are attained in different ways with different strategies for different purposes, adapted as appropriate to specific situations.[493]

Apart from these functions, in practice, the role, responsibilities and powers of the Chairman are even broader. Thus, for example, the Chairman represents the conference, thanks the host country, congratulates individuals, expresses condolences, etc. on behalf of the conference. He or she may also give a press conference or otherwise communicate with audiences outside the conference on behalf of the conference. More substantively, the Chairman also has a key role in the conference's decision-making process. Typical rules of procedure require the Chairman to put questions and announce all decisions. When he or she says the conference has made a decision, he or she speaks on behalf of the conference. Unless the statement is immediately overruled by the conference, then that decision has been made by the conference. Indeed, the chairman has a structural role in the conference: not only is the seating arranged so that all delegates face the Chairman, but all statements intended to be heard by the whole conference must be addressed to the Chairman. Thus, the Chairman represents the embodiment of the conference.[494]

---

[493] Adapted from Conducting a meeting, 2016 (available at skillsyouneed.com).

The ways in which the Chairman represents and acts on behalf of the conference point to the central responsibility and constraint of which the chairman is subject: he or she is called upon to behave not in an individual or national role but as an embodiment of the whole conference. In short, the Chairman acts for the conference and only with its consent. The Chairman needs to understand what needs to be done and to take appropriate initiatives, as required, to make sure it is done. He or she acts for the good of the conference and in the belief that his or her actions help produce the results the conference wants.

As a general rule, with few exceptions, the Chairman represents the whole conference and thus, he/she cannot simultaneously represent one of the participating delegations. This important element in Chairman's responsibilities is called **"denationalization"**.[495] Most rules of procedure specify that the Chairman does not vote but logic and tradition are far more constraining. The Chairman is expected to cease operating as a member of his/her national delegation, as long as he or she is in the Chairman position or otherwise acting as Chairman. If, as is often the case, he or she is a delegation leader, another member of that delegation takes over the role of speaking and voting on behalf of the delegation. The Chairman speaks and acts impartially on behalf of the whole conference, and does not seek to promote any national or personal views which deviate from the mandate and the general will of the conference.

This denationalization applies to most large UN conferences and their committees. It does not necessarily apply to working groups, expert groups, etc., or informal meetings not subject to the rules of procedure, such as contact groups, co-sponsors' meetings, regional groups, etc. Likewise, it does not apply at summits and the Security Council is another exception. In such meetings a delegate often combines the two roles of national delegate and Chairman (or a role equivalent to that of Chairman but without that title). In informal meetings without the support of explicit rules of procedure there are nonetheless minimal unwritten rules of procedure or mutual expectations, providing for example that participants still speak one at a time and generally maintain decorum, and the person acting as Chairman acts to keep the debate orderly and to record any

---

[494] Walker Roland A., Manual for UN Delegates - Conference Process, Procedure and Negotiation, UN Publication, 2011, p.149.

[495] United Nations Institute for Training and Research (UNITAR), Performing Effectively in Multilateral Conferences and Diplomacy - Chairing International Conferences, 2006, p.16.

decisions. Usually, all delegations understand when that delegate is speaking for the conference or for his/her delegation alone.

7.1.2 Chairman's tasks

The key tasks of the Chairman during the conference are: getting through the business on time, involving everyone in the debate, reaching decisions and dealing with difficult people to the best of him/her abilities.

An essential function of the chairman is <u>to provide information</u>, to help delegations at all times to understand what is happening and where their attention should be focused. This task is perform by providing guidance from the Chairman as the meeting proceeds, such as: announcing each phase of conference activity; reminding delegates of the recent past; explaining procedural situations, especially as regards voting; informing about future events and meetings; confirming decisions.[496]

Another essential role of the chairman is <u>to guide the work of the conference</u>, to ensure that the conference goes about its business in the manner he or she considers appropriate, in the light of the rules of procedure and his or her understanding of the mandate and the wishes of the conference. To this end, a chairman can use four different techniques (or combinations thereof) for performing multilateral conference's activities like: granting permission; enabling things to happen; indirectly causing them to happen, and/or doing them himself/herself.[497]

By <u>allowing things to happen</u> the Chairman keeps order by selectively permitting some activities and by disallowing others, at least until such time as he or she considers appropriate. Thus: the conference can undertake no formal activity if the Chairman (or an acting Chairman) is not chairing; the conference is not in session until the chairman says it is; no delegate may speak (formally) without permission from the Chairman, and the Chairman can withdraw permission; the conference cannot act (e.g. start discussion on an agenda item) unless the Chairman permits it; the conference has not made a decision until the Chairman confirms it; and the conference is in session until the Chairman declares it closed. But <u>just as keeping a gate shut blocks activity</u>, opening it

---

[496] United Nations Institute for Training and Research (UNITAR), Performing Effectively in Multilateral Conferences and Diplomacy - Chairing International Conferences, 2006, p.18.

[497] Walker Roland A., Manual for UN Delegates - Conference Process, Procedure and Negotiation, UN Publication, 2011, p.151.

permits the same activity. Thus, for example, the Chairman: opens the conference and each meeting, hence enabling the conference to start work; initiates each action or decision (e.g. closure of discussion on one agenda item and proceeding to the next).[498]

For facilitating the work of the conference, the Chairman uses many techniques, such as: allowing adequate time for debate and informal consultations; resolving any issues over procedure, thus enabling the conference to continue its work in the appropriate manner; suspending the meeting for informal consultations.

The Chairman indirectly causes things to happen by: inviting a delegate to make a statement; suggesting that informal consultations take place; appointing a "Friend of the Chair" or facilitator to conduct consultations or to try to find consensus on a particular issue; asking the Secretariat to provide a particular service (e.g. interpreter service for a night session). In terms of personal initiatives by the Chair, the chairman can take a very "hands on" role, for example: personally convenes a contact group and chair it; acts as intermediary, facilitator or "broker" to resolve disagreements among delegates; proposes a procedural step, such as setting an issue aside, referring it to another body etc.; or presents formulations or whole draft texts to the conference in his/her own name.[499]

In case of the Chairman as organizer, the Chairman accepts responsibility for seeing that the conference performs and completes its work. Thus he or she plans, oversees and leads: the development of a programme of work, including: the allocation of work to committees and other subsidiary bodies, the allocation of time for each task (e.g. for the discussion of an agenda item); and the execution of the work programme by: initiating debate on each agenda item, ensuring that the debate is orderly, "harvesting" elements of the conference outcome as they emerge, initiating decision-making, and ensuring that results are recorded.[500]

All these accountabilities are assumed during the diplomatic negotiations and multilateral conferences within which chairmen take responsibilities and accomplish their task, taking into account the four elements of effective chairing which encompasses the four roles of the Chairman: substantive, procedural, processual and behavioural.

---

[498] Op.cit., p.151.

[499] Op.cit., p.152.

[500] Walker Roland A., Manual for UN Delegates - Conference Process, Procedure and Negotiation, UN Publication, 2011, p.152.

7.2 Roles of the Chairman

Chairman roles are an essential part of diplomatic negotiations. They help to reach an agreement and to achieve the successful outcomes the multilateral conferences are aiming at.

7.2.1 Substantive role of the Chairman (managing substance)

Managing substance is the aim of the negotiation process - the negotiations are conducted in order to achieve an outcome. For the Chairman, it is essential to have a thorough knowledge of the negotiation and conference with which he or she is dealing. The history of the issues has to be understood by the presiding officer, who has to be capable of explaining the background to those negotiators who are new to the process. To acquire such a thorough knowledge, the Chairman have to work closely with the Secretariat of the conference and/or working group that he or she is managing.

Planning is of the utmost importance. Effective planning is done only if the Chairman is aware of the priorities of the delegations involved and the possible concessions that they are willing to make. Without understanding the rank and order, the Chairman will not be able to set a relevant agenda. As the negotiation process moves on, the Chairman divides the substance into comprehensive parts - to put together various issues into acceptable packages - and eliminates certain sentences appearing not to be negotiable.

Understanding the problems and possibilities regarding substance gives the Chairman a chance to do "preventive" guidance. He/she tries to remove unnecessary obstacles if possible, preventing any loss of face on the part of the delegations on the substantive issues relevant to them. One of the major issues is the need to have a thorough understanding of the position and interests of the Chairman's country. Sometimes chairmen have to coordinate their own delegation but should not identify with its needs. Chairmen have to be fair, but their complete neutrality is not always expected. After all, the Chairman's own delegation should not be defenceless, but the delegation should also be aware that it cannot take a very outspoken position without undermining the legitimacy of its compatriot who is chairing the meeting.

It is understood, however, that it is much easier for chairmen to be impartial if the interests of their delegation are close to the common ground of the negotiation. This is why chairmen from powerful countries are often not as effective as those from smaller countries that have less conflict of interests.[501] It is difficult to appreciate the "distance" that a Chairman should take from the position of his/her own government: too far out weakens a Chairman's position, making it impossible for the Chairman to fall back on its own national delegation, but a relationship too close provokes interventions by the Chairman's government, leading to interference from the headquarters that might hamper the negotiation process.

In any situation, a multilateral conference is a meeting between representatives of States (and at times other entities). It has a collective purpose, set out in its mandate, while the governments of each State have their own purposes, as do the individual delegates. The Chairman's task is to give effect to the collective purpose. His/her responsibility therefore is not only to manage the conference so that it operates smoothly and to fulfil a ceremonial role but also to take responsibility for seeing that the conference fulfils the mandate, and produces a result that is comprehensive, coherent and technically sound, legally sound, politically sustainable and immediately acceptable to all, or at least an overwhelming majority. In every matter, the Chairman acts as a representative of the conference and his/her actions must be acceptable to the conference. The chairman receives all the support in managing the substance of the conference, as long as he/she acts in accordance with the conference mandate and has a good understanding of the wishes of delegations.

In his substantive role, the Chairman has several **key tasks,**[502] as the Chairman's necessity to be impartial does not imply that he/she is uninterested in the substantive outcome of the conference or he/she abdicates the responsibilities of leadership.

Planning and agenda setting. He/she must have in mind a concept of the possible and desirable outcome and a plan as to how it is to be achieved. Both of these have to be subject to constant monitoring and possible revision as the conference unfolds. Their evolution is strongly affected by the Chairman's monitoring of the debate and negotiations and what he or she hears in extensive and continuing consultations with delegates. But the desirable outcome is more than the sum of the wishes of all delegates: it is also an outcome that is coherent,

---

[501] Meerts Paul (quoting Tallberg), Diplomatic Negotiation, Essence and Evolution. The Hague: Clingendael Institute, 2015, p. 279.

[502] United Nations Institute for Training and Research (UNITAR), Performing Effectively in Multilateral Conferences and Diplomacy - Chairing International Conferences, 2006, pp.33-35.

legally and technically correct, and ideally one that will prove sustainable both politically and realistically in terms of implementation.

Implementation. As long as the conference is proceeding in accordance with this (flexible and evolving) plan, the Chairman's responsibility is to facilitate its course. If, however, the conference shows signs of stalling or delaying, the Chairman's responsibility for the outcome requires him/her to take a more active role, for example, by encouraging delegations to act in a manner helpful to the conference resuming its progress. In the final resort it may require the Chairman to act more directly, e.g. by convening a consultative group, drawing the conference's attention to options or making suggestions, based on his/her knowledge and understanding of the wishes of delegations and the technical, legal and other such considerations.

Harvesting results. As the conference progresses, the Chairman's procedural responsibilities (see chapter 7.2.2) requires him/her to note the points of agreement as they emerge and draw them to the attention of the conference so that he/she gradually builds up on agreed substance and words which, when completed, will constitute the agreed conference outcome. Similarly, the Chairman also takes account of the substance of what is being agreed to ensure that the outcome is also substantively sound (i.e. coherent, legally and technically correct, etc.).

In achieving these tasks, the chairman needs to manage and draw upon a range of **resources and tools**[503] available to him/her.

Rules of procedures. These support the "powers" of the Chairman.

Atmosphere. The atmosphere ("mood") of the conference is another factor to be used and managed by the Chairman. As long as it is positive and constructive it is helpful to the conference achieving its objective expediently. Sometimes, chairmen want to exert their managerial skills to keep it as close as possible to this ideal and to resist any tendency to slide into tiredness or animosity which are unfavourable for an agreement.

Time. The Chairman needs to manage the available time, not only with a view to its effect on procedure but also because of the possible impact on the substantive outcome. Thus he or she needs to provide more time for consultation, when this seems likely to broaden the extent of agreement on substance. The

---

[503] Walker Roland A., Manual for UN Delegates - Conference Process, Procedure and Negotiation, UN Publication, 2011, pp.156-157.

Chairman also at times makes arrangement to enable formal debate or negotiations (with interpretation) to continue in the evening. Conversely, he or she decides to restrict the time available for purposes which seem inimical to the desired substantive outcome, or to help "force" agreement.

Control of opportunities to speak. Without exposing him/herself to accusations of partiality, sometimes the Chairman creates opportunities for constructive interventions or conversely to limit the opportunities for destructive or otherwise unhelpful interventions. This is mainly achieved by keeping the debate focused on a search for areas of agreement and closing it off when it threatens to degrade into repetition or unproductive dispute.

Information. By following the debate attentively, consulting widely and due to his/her role in procedure, the Chairman ensures that he/she is very well informed at all times of the wishes and intentions of delegations. The Chairman assists the development of the desired result by ensuring that information is shared and he/she eliminates "threats" to the substantive outcome before they materialize.

Centrality to the aspirations of all delegations. All delegates understand that the achievement of their national objectives depends on the conference success, and usually a high proportion of delegates are committed to the achieving the conference-s collective objectives. This leads to a widespread disposition to help the Chairman as much as possible. Delegates are often inclined to defer to the Chairman's wishes, in the well-founded belief that he/she is uniquely well placed to assess what is possible and how best to proceed towards a satisfactory outcome.

Prestige. The Chairman is the acknowledged leader and representative of the conference, moreover, if he or she performs well, a person who has demonstrated a commitment and ability to bring it to a successful conclusion. Any of these is a source of prestige and cumulatively they are more compelling. As long as the Chairman retains the confidence of delegations, the prestige of his/her position has considerable potential influence.

Assistance. All delegations with constructive intentions are supportive of the Chairman and willing to assist with information, advice, tolerance and cooperation. The conference secretariat, likewise, wishes the Chairman to succeed and is able to assist him/her in many ways. For many large and important conferences the secretariat prepares a scenario, with suggested words for the

Chairman to use as he/she goes through the procedural steps. Often it is apparent when the Chairman is reading from such a text. Other times, the Secretariat draws the Chairman-s attention to a procedural requirement or document to be cited. However, the Chairman should not simply read whatever the secretariat gives him/her. It is the Chairman's responsibility to make sure that the text is correct and in some instances, secretariats have aims of their own which are not necessarily those of the Chairman.

Context. Because of his or her responsibility for organizing the work of the conference, the Chairman is well placed at the start of a conference to allocate issues or agenda items to the forum (e.g. plenary or a committee) in which he or she thinks they have the best prospects of constructive treatment. As the conference progresses, if problems develop, the Chairman can take the initiative to refer an issue to informal consultations (if necessary convening these him/herself) or perhaps to transfer an item, for example, from a committee to the Plenary (except in the case of the UN General Assembly).

To effectively fulfil his/her substantive role, the Chairman needs many things, among the **prerequisites for success**[504]: to prepare carefully for the conference and for each phase of it; to stay informed, notably by frequent and widespread consultations with delegations; to maintain support for emerging agreed outcome; to show respect for the concerns of all delegations; to support a positive atmosphere; to use allies effectively, his/her "normal" allies being all delegations that are seeking a constructive agreement; and/or to pay particular attention to his/her relations with the secretariat. *The Secretariat* is not only the provider of essential support services but an invaluable source of information and advice. All *delegates* except those who want the conference to fail have a strong incentive to support and assist the Chairman. Their prospects of achieving the desirable conference outcome depend on the Chairman being successful. Moreover, the better the Chairman understands what they are trying to do, the better the prospects that these objectives are reflected in the conference outcome. Consequently, delegates who have a stake in a successful outcome of the conference exert themselves to: support the authority of the Chairman; ensure that the Chairman is well informed of their own intentions and objectives, as well any developments in wider consultations and negotiations which may be useful to the Chairman; assist the Chairman by accepting his or her leadership, minimizing the

---

[504] Walker Roland A., Manual for UN Delegates - Conference Process, Procedure and Negotiation, UN Publication, 2011, pp.156-158.

demands they make on the time of the conference, helping to smooth over any difficulties which arise; advise the Chairman, should the occasion arise, as to possible procedures or compromises that might secure agreement. Provided such advice is genuinely helpful, it may contribute to a successful conference outcome. But delegates must also be ready to understand that the Chairman is conscious of a wider range of factors than the delegates are, so that they feel no offence if their advice is not followed. When delegates disagree with the Chairman, they speak as respectfully and constructively as possible, avoiding any suggestion that the Chairman is at fault.

The Chairman has various **methods**[505] available for meeting the challenges associated with his or her substantive role, such as:

- facilitating discussion and negotiation by providing time for that purpose. If a more active hand is needed to ensure this is happening, the Chairman can: suggest consultations; prompt delegations to form a contact group; appoint a Friend of the Chair to conduct consultations; hold series of separate consultations; convene an informal contact group; convene a contact group under his or her leadership ("Friends of the Chair");

- influencing the course of debate and thus the conference outcome by taking care to ensure that delegates fully understand the purpose, context and past history of the issues under discussions; influencing the outcome by making suggestions as to how delegates should approach their work;

- stepping into the role of intermediary or "broker of agreement" between delegations that are at odds, to help them find a satisfactory solution to their differences. This intermediary role can take many forms, sometimes concurrently, consisting of carrying messages between the protagonists, offering explanations for their respective positions, urging understanding and a willingness to compromise, making suggestions to both parties as to how they can act to advance their objectives and also as to what is realistically achievable;

- taking a more significant role in ensuring that constructive texts appear on time, culminating in producing and circulating a text in his/her own name. These can range from a compilation of agreed texts and square bracketed alternatives proposed by delegations to provide a starting point for negotiation, through a Chairman's "non-paper" to stimulate thinking, to a "Chairman's text" which is a proposal by the Chairman based on his/her assessment of what may be acceptable to the conference in the

---

[505] United Nations Institute for Training and Research (UNITAR), Performing Effectively in Multilateral Conferences and Diplomacy - Chairing International Conferences, 2006, pp. 39-43.

light of the foregoing debate and negotiation, supplemented by the Chairman's consultations (see chapter 3.3). Decisions as to whether to produce documents, and if so their timing, the extent of prior consultation or forewarning before doing so and the degree of assertiveness with which the Chairman advances his/her proposals are all matters for careful judgement. *Verbal decisions* by the conference are very often based on verbal proposals by the Chairman;

- taking on the role of a supportive spectator, instigator or, if necessary, principal actor in developing and implementing strategies to secure the final acceptance by the conference of an outcome in accordance with its mandate, the other responsibilities of the Chairman and the wishes of the conference.

In all these activities, the Chairman continues to act on behalf of the whole conference and with its consent. Thus, by a combination of frequent consultation, knowledge and understanding of the concerns of delegations and empathy, the Chairman has a very good sense of what the conference collectively wants and will approve or at least accept.

Ultimately, in extreme circumstances, chairmen who had a strong sense of the positions and desires of delegations and who enjoyed a very high level of confidence and deference from delegations have been known to draw fully on this capital and impose a compromise solution of their own devising. Obviously, chairmen can behave in this manner only if they have gained the full confidence of all relevant delegations that any solution they produce is the best they could hope to achieve in the negotiations and would contain no unacceptable element. It should be emphasized that we are talking here about highly exceptional situations, unlikely to be encountered by most delegates and that such extreme tactics are of course hostage to being accepted by the conference and are inherently high risk.

7.2.2 Procedural role of the Chairman (mastering procedure)

Mastering procedure means being very well aware of the rules and regulations of the organization and the conference over which the Chairman is presiding. The secretariat plays an important role here, its members having a thorough and continuous insight into the procedures and their effectiveness. The Chairman has to be firm, especially at the outset of the negotiation process, in implementing the procedures that have been decided upon, but remain flexible - assertive, but not unnecessarily bureaucratic. Culture has its influence in adherence to strict or loose procedures. The Chairman has to take into account that in some cultures procedure is not considered to be a very important facet of the negotiation process - it might even be seen as an obstacle to a smooth process. In other cultures, however, procedures are essential for saving the face of the Chairman and the negotiators. Rituals play a role in avoiding risk, which is especially important in collectivistic societies.[506]

The stronger the institution, the more outspoken its rules are. Though, paradoxically, the more integrated the organization, the less the need for strict rules. The continuity of the negotiating body, and the standards and values that it develops, create mutual understanding among negotiators, making it easier for the Chairman. Negotiators "automatically" adhere to the rules. There is no need for the Chairman to impose them. Trust also has an important role: the more trust, the fewer rules are needed to protect the negotiators and the negotiation process. On the other hand, the procedures are seen as a tool useful for the Chairman to compensate the lack of trust.[507]

Finally, there is the decision-making procedure, which is different from conference to conference, and which has a decisive impact on the outcome of the negotiation processes. If unanimity or consensus is the rule, it will be difficult for the Chairman to reach substantive outcomes. Nevertheless, if (qualified) majority voting is the decision-making procedure, the majority can outvote the minority, although the Chairman, most of the time, will conceal this by stating that he/she assumes that there is consensus. Those who are aware that they will be out-voted prefer not to show this to the public, leading to so-called the "shadow of the vote": when there seems to be consensus, but it has been forged by the threat of an overruling majority. The Chairman can hence more easily push for substantive outcomes.[508]

For his/her procedural role, the Chairman performs several **tasks**[509] which encompass:

Allocation of work and time. This is one of the first tasks of a conference - *allocating work to its various subsidiary bodies*. For example, the agenda is split

---

[506] Meerts Paul, Diplomatic Negotiation, Essence and Evolution. The Hague: Clingendael Institute, 2015, p. 279.

[507] Op.cit., p.279.

[508] Meerts Paul, Diplomatic Negotiation, Essence and Evolution. The Hague: Clingendael Institute, 2015, p. 279.

[509] United Nations Institute for Training and Research (UNITAR), Performing Effectively in Multilateral Conferences and Diplomacy - Chairing International Conferences, 2006, pp. 39-43

between several committees, working groups are tasked to address particular topics, etc. There should be enough subsidiary bodies for the full work programme to be completed on time. Another factor which may be relevant at certain particularly large conferences is the question of *geographical balance*. For example, the conference wishes to provide a position on the bureau or in a committee chairmanship for each of the principal political groups represented at the conference. Truly, the mandate or rules of procedure of some conferences stipulate such a requirement. In planning the allocation of the work the Chairman does not act alone. He/she receives advice from the secretariat and takes steps to get informed of the views and wishes of delegations. At large conferences, he/she is assisted in developing the work programme by a Steering Committee or "*General Committee*". The allocation of time is a challenging task and a constant preoccupation for the Chairman throughout the conference. The secretariat is likely to give helpful advice concerning the allocation of time but the responsibility remains with the Chairman. He/she needs a timetable or time-line within which the conference accomplishes each of its tasks. This implies a time budget which the Chairman monitors and manages as the conference unfolds - he/she wants to: allow time for delegates to settle in, get their bearings and develop their focus; allow time for formal debate and negotiation; allow time for delegates to consult (each other and their headquarters; before and during debate); use the time preciously, to build up a reserve; and make time available for constructive uses.

Opening the conference. The chairman arrives early before the scheduled start of each meeting of the conference. Apart from courtesy towards the conference and efficiency, this enables him/her to exchange information with conference secretary about any developments since they last met. From the appointed starting time and as soon as the Chairman considers there are enough delegates in the room, he/she "calls the meeting to order", greets the delegates and declares the meeting open. He or she announces the purpose of the meeting, recalls the procedural situation and gives a brief introduction to the work at hand.

Announcing each phase of conference activity. As the conference unfolds, the Chairman announces each procedural move: e.g. "we now resume debate on agenda item 4" and he/she explains any procedural matter that might not be clear. Similarly, the Chairman closes each phase of debate, and explains what has been done and what is to follow.

Keeping the debate orderly. Maintaining order involves controlling the level of noise in the debating chamber, giving speakers the floor as they request it or in accordance with the list of speakers, if necessary proposing and enforcing time limits on interventions or closure of the list, etc. Sometimes, it is required that the Chairman takes a more obvious leadership role in getting the conference to work in an orderly and efficient manner. Therefore, the Chairman uses not only his/her voice but also the gavel as a means of communicating with the delegates. Another responsibility of the Chair is to rule on "points of order" - questions raised by delegates about the way the proceedings are being conducted. There is no debate on points of order and the chairman is required to rule immediately. Should a delegate appeal against a ruling by the chairman, his/her challenge is immediately put to the vote: "*that the Chairman's ruling stands*" (see chapter 3.2.2). Such appeals and especially successful ones are extremely rare, but the fact that they are possible is a significant limitation on a Chairman's freedom of action.

Time management. A constant preoccupation of every Chairman, even those moderating the easiest conference, is to manage the time available to the conference. He/she does this in two ways. When drawing up the work programme, he/she establishes a time line (this task will be finished by such and such a date, x hours will be devoted to that agenda item, etc.). As the conference unfolds, the Chairman constantly checks that the time line is being adhered to and, if it is not, take remedial action. Concurrently, the Chairman manages a time budget, constantly pressing delegates to complete each phase of the conference as quickly as possible, constantly vigilant against any anything which threatens to use up time unproductively, so as to build up a reserve of time in hand. Then the Chairman carefully makes time available for constructive purposes.

Harvesting the results of debate. As the debate develops, the Chairman is alert to emerging areas of agreement, draws them to the attention of the conference and makes sure they are gathered for inclusion in the conference's report or decisions. He can do this verbally or make a written compilation, which can be distributed as a "conference room paper" or "Chairman's compilation" at the appropriate moment.

Decision-making. This is a particularly sensitive phase of conference activity, to which the Chairman pays particular attention. Sometimes, the Chairman himself/herself may orally propose the terms of a draft decision by the conference and declare it adopted if the conference indicates its willingness. In the case of written draft proposals submitted by other delegates, the Chairman explains the procedural situation to make sure that all delegations fully understand it. He/she ensures that the decision-making process is fully transparent and that the wishes of delegations are accurately reflected. The most common mode of decision-making is for the Chairman to declare that it was made by consensus. This requires the Chairman having a very good sense of the delegations' wishes, since, like all other decisions by the Chairman, it is subject to conference's acceptance. The rules of procedure of some conferences place restrictions on the Chairman's ability to declare consensus. An important part of the Chairman's responsibilities is to ensure that all requisite decisions are taken and duly recorded.

Overnight. Each evening, after closing the meeting, the Chairman takes steps to ensure he/she is informed of what has happened in the consultations and other meetings at which he or she was not present and of likely developments in coming days. He/she plans the next day's work. As appropriate, the Chairman prepares the interventions he or she makes the next day and/or arrange to alert delegations to coming developments.

Closing the conference. Finally, it is also the Chairman's role to declare the conference closed. Before doing so he/she usually thanks the delegates, the Secretariat and the interpreters. He or she also makes some observations on the conduct and outcome of the conference and perhaps future procedural arrangements (like the next meeting of the conference or its report being considered by another conference).

7.2.3 Processual role of the Chairman (managing the process)

Managing the process is itself one of the best tools that chairmen have at their disposal for reaching assured outcomes. If the chairmen dos not manage well the process, successful outcomes are hard to reach, so they have to be conscious of the most effective sequence of the process. If certain issues are decided upon too early in the process, more effective "package deals" might be blocked resulting in less optimal outcomes. Therefore, the chairmen have to allow for a stage of exploration, process influenced by the culture of negotiators. In some cultures (such as Japan), the "give-and-take" is seen as a dangerous part of the process. Thus, the Chairman has a special task to save the face of the negotiators, to be aware of so-called "salami tactics"[510] and the development of an entrapment situation. They also have to ensure that the process is even-handed.

Similarly, the chairmen have to take into account the two different orientations to time that exist across the world: *monochronic*[511] and *polychronic*,[512] as these might influence the management of the process. Negotiators from *monochronic* cultures: prefer prompt beginnings and endings, schedule breaks, deal with one agenda item at a time, rely on specific, detailed, and explicit communication, prefer to talk in sequence, view lateness as devaluing or evidence of lack of respect. Negotiators from *polychronic* cultures: start and end meetings at flexible times, take breaks when it seems appropriate, be comfortable with a high flow of information, expect to read each other's thoughts and minds, sometimes overlap talk, view start times as flexible and not take lateness personally.[513] The Chairman has to understand that the delegations may be seeing things very differently, thus being less likely to make negative judgments and more likely to make progress in negotiations.

Managing the "end-game" might be the most difficult task facing the chairmen. They have to use insight, knowledge and intuition to assess if the time is favourable for making a decision, if the negotiations are going to mutual agreed deadlock or towards a mutually attractive agreement. It is essential for the Chairman to observe the context of the negotiation process. Even it is a matter of timing, political developments may also influence the progress of the process in the sense of either moving forward or going backwards. In this case also, the

---

[510] Salami tactics: prolonging a negotiation to a painstakingly slow pace, only giving a very small concession to the other side when it can no longer be avoided in order to placate the other side for a little while longer (see Alfredson Tanya and Cungu Azeta (quoting Saner), Negotiation Theory and Practice. A Review of the Literature, FAO Policy Learning Program, EASYPol Module 179, 2008).

[511] Monochronic approaches to time are linear, sequential and involve focusing on one thing at a time. These approaches are most common in the European-influenced cultures of the United States, Germany, Switzerland, and Scandinavia. Japanese people also tend toward this end of the time continuum (see LeBaron Michelle, Culture-Based Negotiation Styles, Beyond Intractability. Eds. Guy Burgess and Heidi Burgess. Conflict Information Consortium, University of Colorado, Boulder, 2003).

[512] Polychronic orientations to time involve simultaneous occurrences of many things and the involvement of many people. The time it takes to complete an interaction is elastic, and more important than any schedule. This orientation is most common in Mediterranean and Latin cultures including France, Italy, Greece, and Mexico, as well as some Eastern and African cultures (see LeBaron Michelle, Culture-Based Negotiation Styles, Beyond Intractability. Eds. Guy Burgess and Heidi Burgess. Conflict Information Consortium, University of Colorado, Boulder, 2003).

[513] LeBaron Michelle, Culture-Based Negotiation Styles, Beyond Intractability. Eds. Guy Burgess and Heidi Burgess. Conflict Information Consortium, University of Colorado, Boulder, 2003 (available at beyondintractability.org).

availability of the Chairman is essential, both inside and outside the actual process of negotiation.[514]

7.2.4 Behavioural role of the Chairman (managing behaviour)

Managing behaviour assumes that the Chairman has some psychological competence and therefore diplomatic skills. The style of the chairperson is very important as it can more or less influence the outcome of the conference depending if he/she: has an action-oriented style, or process-oriented, or people-oriented, or idea-oriented; adapts the overall style to the situation in which they find him/herself. The situation is similar regarding the leadership style of chairmen, as they might have a chairing style: dominant, avoidant, accommodative, compromising, collaborative, etc. Also, the most important aspect is if the chairman adapts his or her leadership style to the circumstances. The chairmen have to develop formal and, especially, informal relationships with negotiators and also with their own delegation and the governmental authorities at the headquarters. The atmosphere of the negotiations is influenced by the Chairman in a way that it enhances the chances of a successful process. Being emotional is counterproductive, but not being empathetic does not make a favourable climate in the negotiations either. The behaviour of the Chairman is characterized by the different roles that he or she performs. The roles of a Chairman are distinguished as representing the negotiation group, an "agenda-seller", and a "broker/mediator".[515] The chairmen have to be fully committed to the task, but over-commitment can be a burden for the conference. Correspondingly, a balance has to be struck.

The Chairman has to keep in mind that he/she has to deal with more or less "difficult" people, such as: delegates who talks non-stop, negotiators who "know it all", or delegations who are just focussed on one particular issue. The role of the Chairman is not easy, but the general way he/she conducts the meeting makes a difference, such as to: remind delegates of the rule of procedures, and that everyone has agreed to these; be firm and consistent - do not allow difficult delegate to get away with things and then come down hard on easier people; summarise the points of a heated debate, then move the focus away from the

---

[514] Meerts Paul, Diplomatic Negotiation, Essence and Evolution. The Hague: Clingendael Institute, 2015, p. 280.

[515] Meerts Paul (quoting Tallberg), Diplomatic Negotiation, Essence and Evolution. The Hague: Clingendael Institute, 2015, p. 280.

individuals by asking what other delegations think about the issues; (when someone keeps repeating the same point), assure them that their point has been heard, and then turn the discussion back to the group; (if someone is continually criticising) try to turn the question round to them, asking, for example, what are their suggestions in order to solve or improve the issue raised. Rarely, the Chairman has to deal with delegates who are really disruptive in the conference, and do not listen to any of helpful suggestions. In situations like these, the Chairman may ask the conference for support by demanding if the other delegations want to spend more time on that discussion or move on to the next topic. This approach makes clear to the disruptive delegate/negotiator that everyone, not just the Chairman, wants to move on the other agenda items.[516]

Likewise, the behaviour of the chairmen is characterized by their ability to apply the most effective techniques. As a positive example, there is the use of the technique of writing a Chairman's draft of his/her own as an informal alternative to the official text, with thousands of brackets, text that is subject to change only after the consensus is reached - which finally is leading to the replacement by the negotiators of the official text with the Chairman's informal draft as a final document. A less effective technique is the preparation of a final draft in consultation with only some of the negotiators. This raises suspicions among those who are left out, thereby lowering trust in the Chairman.[517]

Finally, towards the end of complicated negotiations, when the time pressure is great, delegates may huddle, either in or across the negotiating groups, on the negotiating floor itself to hammer out last minute details. Truly sticky issues often end up being tackled by measures such as the use of a facilitator, an extended Bureau, or "Friends of the Chair". The Chairman, working with a handful of governments on a particularly contentious subject, may have to use all his or her powers of persuasion or creative suggestions on new language in order to bring about consensus and reach agreement.[518]

A Chairman has always to remember that the conference is supporting his/her efforts as the whole conference is looking for a successful outcome.

---

[516] Resource Centre, Chairing a meeting, 2007 (available at resourcecentre.org.uk).

[517] Meerts Paul (quoting Hauck), Diplomatic Negotiation, Essence and Evolution. The Hague: Clingendael Institute, 2015 p. 280.

[518] UN Non-Governmental Liaison Service (NGLS) with Gretchen Sidhu, Intergovernmental Negotiations and Decision Making at the United Nations: A Guide, 2nd Updated Edition, United Nations, 2007, p. 24.

7.3 Prepare for leading and chairing

Anyone who is trusted with the position of a Chairman of a multilateral conference needs to prepare carefully for this challenging and prestigious role. Preparations to chair a multilateral conference require four axes:[519] rallying the assets; drawing up a list of aspects to be studied before the conference starts ("checklist"); planning the outcome; planning strategies and tactics.

7.3.1 Rally the assets

The first and essential asset of every Chairman is his/her own personal resources: clarity of purpose, commitment and problem-solving. Future chairmen need to honestly assess their personal capabilities for the task ahead and consider possible sources of assistance to make up for any shortfall. Similar approach is done towards the networks which they are reliant on.

The *headquarters* is one important potential resource: it should be able to supply the Chairman with relevant information, with access to relevant people and, if the chairmanship is likely to be especially demanding, may also be able to provide some support staff or services, without compromising Chairman's "denationalization" (see chapter 7.1.1). Useful staff for a Chairman include: a personal assistant to help manage the papers, appointments etc.; a middle-rank diplomat to perform liaison and gather information; and a senior diplomat, with extensive experience of conferences, who can advise the Chairman on tactics, procedure, political sensitivities, etc.

If the headquarters does not provide such support, *a member of the national delegation* can possibly be assigned, perhaps part time, to this task. Sometimes another delegation may be able to give some assistance. Actually, it happens quite often that large delegations offer their help either to the Chairman or to the small delegations "deprived" of one of their members acting like a Chairperson. And sometimes the conference secretariat is able to help with administrative support.

The *conference secretariat* is an obvious asset which the Chairman uses, not only for support services to the Chairman but also as a source of knowledge of the issues to be addressed, a wide network of contacts, extensive conference

---

[519] United Nations Institute for Training and Research (UNITAR), Performing Effectively in Multilateral Conferences and Diplomacy - Chairing International Conferences, 2006, pp. 48-55.

experience, knowledge of personalities and, above all, a shared commitment to a positive conference outcome.

A chairman can also be helped by a strong relationship with the *other conference officers* and, as with the secretariat, the assistance they can provide can be assessed in advance and prepared, for example, by making personal contact well ahead of the conference. It is also prudent for the Chairman to plan and arrange from the start to maintain communications during the conference.

Similarly, the prospects of success for the Chairman are greatly assisted by good communications and understanding with those delegations most able and willing to advance the goals of the negotiations and conference. For some major conferences, the future Chairman spends weeks travelling to selected capitals to develop these relations and to start the process of shaping positions and expectations, long before the conference. For less elaborate conferences it is useful for the Chairman to meet key delegations as soon as they gather at the conference venue.

These potential resources also need to be inventoried and assessed, in order to identify the supportive delegations with wide influence, the persuasive speakers, the skilled peace-makers, the empathetic and creative thinkers that can find solutions to apparent impasses. The Chairman should not hesitate to ask for this kind of assistance that is often forthcoming because the success of all delegations depends on that of the Chairman. The community of purpose between the Chairman and all constructively minded delegations is so strong that the Chairman often profits by bringing them into the process of planning the course of the conference.

Yet, other assets can be used by the Chairman as "outside" resources, notably the mass-media and NGOs. These play a very constructive role in shaping expectations, disseminating information and ideas and in influencing government attitudes. However, in this area chairmen must exert the greatest caution. Delegates (those whose consent is needed at every phase and process) prefer to be dealt with directly.

7.3.2 Aspects to be studied before the conference starts ("checklist" of elements)

The Chairman needs to gather information about several important aspects before the start of the conference he/she is going to preside (to do the "checklist" of the elements he/she needs to be informed about), such as:

Venue. One of the items on the Chairman's checklist is the venue, the place where the conference is to be held. An incoming Chairman is well advised to visit the venue or at least enquire about it as he/she needs to know: where the meeting takes place, if there is a Chairman's office, what is a good place for informal consultations, how far is any refreshment area (for knowing the time needed to get to the conference room), if there are break-out rooms available for meetings of cosponsors, caucus groups, contact groups, etc., what are the factors likely to affect the comfort of delegates (crowding, aeration, access to food and drink etc.), if the signage is adequately helpful to the participants, etc.

Papers. The incoming Chairman needs to familiarize himself/herself with the papers that have been circulated in advance for the conference by the secretariat and in some cases by some delegations. The Chairman also wishes to know what other such papers are in preparation or otherwise expected. Yet, the most important papers that the Chairman has to know are those the conference is expected to approve or produce. Among the items the Chairman would want to be informed about before the conference starts: mandate of the conference, underlying issue(s), history of negotiations to date, purpose(s) of main participants, tactics they have used, own government's objectives and concerns, prominent personalities, rules of procedure, other applicable traditions and expectations, legal aspects, secretariat support, personal staff, setting the scene for discussions, provisional agenda, other documents, social calendar and any relevant events.

7.3.3 Planning the outcome

A Chairman is unlikely to be effective unless he or she has a fairly clear concept, before the conference even begins, as to its desired outcome. Actually, the chairmen should visualize the best possible outcome achievable in the light of the known ambitions and wishes of delegates, the resources at their disposal (e.g. time and information) and any limitations imposed by the system or circumstances. The Chairman has to be ready to adjust this concept in the light of the views expressed by delegates, developments during the conference and any unexpected events that might happen.

The Chairman should envisage the possible scenarios which the conference could follow, paying particular attention to those which lead to harmful outcomes and those which lead to the best achievable outcome. In predicting these scenarios, the Chairman has to keep in mind that the conference outcome is likely to have two dimensions: the texts it produces and its political impact or legacy.

7.3.4 Planning strategies and tactics

The Chairman needs to keep an overview of the conference and helps it to reach decisions. This is one of the most difficult task of chairing, but with confidence and proper strategies and tactics it can be achieved.

Planning the strategy. Once the Chairman has a clear view of his/her objectives, the next step is to plan how each of them is to be achieved, how support for this process is to be mobilized and sustained, and how to avoid or overcome possible obstacles. Two additional essential considerations are to plan the implications in terms of time management and, if the tasks looks excessive, what matters the Chairman can afford to neglect.

Planning, implementation and tactics. The elementary management principles need to be adapted to the specificities of multilateral conferences in order to be implemented properly. Thus, from the moment the Chairman has a plan, he/she should consider sharing it with own government or delegation (so they are not taken by surprise), the conference secretariat and selected key delegations. This can focus their attention in the direction the Chairman desires, influence their expectations and start gaining their support. It may also give to the Chairman better information on potential obstacles. Ideally, the conference goes in accordance with the chairman's wishes, without having him/her interfere in any way. The Chairman's role will then be mainly to monitor the unfolding of the preferred scenario, with possible mid-course corrections. Obviously, if the Chairman sees the need, he/she has to be ready to take appropriate action towards developing a favourable outcome.

Consultations are a vital part of the Chairman's activities throughout the conference. The Chairman should give thought before the conference starts and in its early days for the Chairman to know how to judiciously allocate time for consultation. Ideally he/she would meet privately with all delegations in turn, but as the conference unfolds time pressures will impose selectivity. It is, of course, particularly important to stay in close touch with the delegations which play a leading role in the conference (including those whose objectives are unhelpful to those of the Chairman), but the Chairman should also allocate time to those delegations which are most supportive of his/her objectives and strategy (if only to sustain that support) and to newcomers to the conference, to evaluate them, flatter by his/her attention and help (as the Chairman is well placed to do so) out of common courtesy and in the hope of gaining their support. At some stage the Chairman is likely to feel a need to prompt the formation of a contact group or to convene one him/herself. The composition of that group, its mandate (if any) and reporting tasks are all matters that a Chairman needs to plan in advance.

Another important element is planning the text submitted to the conference for approval. Preferably, a good text is tabled before all delegations, in the event a damaging text is tabled first, a more constructive competing text has to be tabled with no delay. The Chairman needs to plan in advance who will elaborate and table the text, if the delegate(s) will act spontaneously or the Chairman needs prompt their action.

Daily planning. As the conference unfolds, the need for preparation does not relent until the very last moment. At the end of each day the Chairman must take stock of the situation and plan for the next day, anticipating problems and opportunities and making contingency plans to handle whatever may arise (for example, to reserve a room in case the Chairman decides to convene a contact group.)

We conclude that a Chairman's role can be highly demanding and, even when there appear to be no problems, the responsibilities are considerable. But the role is a prestigious and rewarding one and the ability to perform in this role is one of the skills expected of a fully effective delegate (conference diplomat), so that opportunities to acquire them should not be missed. In any situation, to be an effective Chairman, he/she has to prepare for this task with preliminary reflections and considerable consultation, keeping in mind the differences and particularities of each specific diplomatic negotiations and multilateral conference.

7.4 Negotiating in the United Nations, WTO and the European Union

The membership in international and regional organizations has greatly expanded, including nowadays developed and developing countries, states with a tradition of democracy and authoritarian countries, post conflict societies that barely function and nations ruled by religious decree. Nevertheless, all these states are part of the system of multilateral cooperation that rests in the pretext that everyone must work inside the system. Within this framework there must inevitably be concessions, but these should be acceptable as they are for the greater benefit of the group.[520] Still, the membership represents diverse interests and objectives and has complicated the methods of reaching agreement.

In general, the United Nations, the WTO, and the EU are given as examples of fairly successful cooperation among states. However, negotiations in these fora encounter serious challenges, that make it harder to reach a deal that satisfies the current 193 UN Members, 164 WTO Members and even the 28 EU Member States (see chapter 7.4.3 on "Brexit"), representing a highly heterogeneous membership, some of which being previously outsiders or inactive players in diplomatic negotiations.

7.4.1 Diplomatic negotiations in the United Nations

The continued expansion of the international community after 1945 has been one of the major factors shaping diplomatic negotiations. The expansion in membership had four main effects: on diplomatic style; on the entry into force of conventions; and on the operating agendas and procedures of multilateral fora. A fourth effect is the emergence of a variety of UN conference management styles, lobbying, "corridor work", and the institutionalisation of the Group of 77 (see chapter 3.3.3), which significantly affected the way in which diplomatic negotiations are conducted within the United Nations.[521]

At the start of any negotiation process, delegates propose, individually or collectively, that a particular issue be raised in the appropriate forum, such as the UN General Assembly, ECOSOC or through a global conference. The delegations discuss the issue and negotiate the written language of a draft agreement, the decision being adopted in one of a variety of formats. The vast majority of UN

---

[520] Cockburn Andrew Mark, The Unique Challenges Presented by Multilateral Diplomacy, May 10, 2012, p. 3. (available at SSRN: ssrn.com or dx.doi.org).

[521] Barston R.P., Modern diplomacy, fourth edition, Routledge, 2014, p. 6.

decisions appear as resolutions (see chapter 4.3.3), other outcomes include declarations, programmes of action, and complex and legally binding conventions and treaties. Delegations also make decisions on organizational issues, meant to guide the structure and administration of the negotiation process. These can include the election of officers for a meeting, the adoption of the agenda and the determination of who may attend negotiations aside from Members.

To summarize,[522] whatever format a decision takes, it starts as a draft text that is prepared by one of several sources, generally based on advance inputs from governments. Those responsible for drafting work in close consultations with delegates before the formally scheduled negotiations begin. The draft text then becomes the focus of discussion and reaction among delegates. They go through the text from beginning to end, agree on minor adjustments, identify those passages that they cannot easily accept and offer amendments that could be deletions or additions. Sometimes delegates agree to language *ad referendum*, which means they must check with their capital or ministry for final approval. As negotiations approach their final stages and conclusion, there may be some "give-and-take" as delegates consider the balance of elements in the "package", and whether they can renounce of some elements in order to retain others. When all delegations finally reach agreement on the exact wording of all parts of the text, they adopt it officially, using various methods (see chapter 4.4).

Negotiating at the UN usually take place in two daily sessions one in the morning and one in the afternoon. If the debate becomes protracted, extra evening sessions may be scheduled. It is not uncommon for the final sessions to be extended, possibly throughout the night, to complete the negotiations. Sessions take place in two formats: open or closed. Formal or **open sessions**, which are part of the official record, can be attended by everyone with proper accreditation, including NGOs and the media. These usually include plenary sessions, where Members make their individual policy statements. They are also the forums where formal decisions are made, including the final adoption of an agreed text, by consensus or a vote, or the noting of reservations (see chapter 4.4). When governments reach the point in a negotiation process where they need to hammer out agreement on particularly contentious topics, they may break into informal sessions, **closed sessions** or the so-called working groups. These can be closed to

---

[522] UN Non-Governmental Liaison Service (NGLS) with Gretchen Sidhu, Intergovernmental Negotiations and Decision Making at the United Nations: A Guide, 2nd Updated Edition, United Nations, 2007, pp. 20-22.

everyone except delegates and Secretariat staff, although NGOs may also be allowed to attend as observers, depending to some extent on past practice in a given process and the discretion of the Chairman. A negotiation process working on a long document may ask delegations to break into a number of informal working groups, with each taking a specific issue or section of the text. *In theory only two working groups can meet at any given time, in order to accommodate smaller delegations.*[523]

The negotiation system at the UN functions in large part through negotiating blocs, or groups of countries speaking with a common voice (see chapter 3.3.3). Most negotiation processes are overseen by a Bureau (see chapter 2.4) and the various institutional structure of the UN support all multilateral negotiations and decisions.

A special attention in the negotiation process needs to be given to the **Security Council** (SC) to whom the UN Members gave primary responsibility for the maintenance of international peace. The Security Council has 15 Members, five permanent - China, France, the Russian Federation, the United States of America and the United Kingdom, and ten elected by the General Assembly for two-year terms. Each SC Member has one vote. Decisions on procedural matters require at least nine affirmative votes. Decisions on substantive matters require at least nine affirmative votes including those of all the permanent Members. A negative vote by any one of the permanent Members vetoes the decision. If a SC permanent Member does not support a resolution but does not want to block it, it may abstain.

Although every sovereign state is a member of the UN General Assembly (UNGA), it is the Security Council that makes the most important decisions. In the UNGA, every Member gets a vote and all votes are weighed equally. The difference is that each of the permanent Members of the Security Council has veto power.[524] This rule is also known as the "great Power unanimity", but is

---

[523] Op.cit., pp. 20-22.

[524] States and non-state actors have put forth a number of proposals concerning potential reform of the size, composition and work of the Security Council. Concerning size and composition, the General Assembly adopted resolution 48/26 in 1993 that established an open-ended working group to consider all aspects of the question of increase in the membership of the Security Council. In 1965 the non-permanent membership of the Security Council was enlarged from six to its present ten. However, any changes in the membership of the Security Council will require an amendment of the Charter, which can only take place with the consent of all the permanent members (see UN Non-Governmental Liaison Service (NGLS) with Gretchen Sidhu, Intergovernmental Negotiations and Decision Making at the United Nations: A Guide, 2nd

more commonly known as "the veto power". Despite the fact that SC can formally take decisions without resorting to unanimity, lately seeking consensus became the norm. As a result, fewer votes are being cast nowadays, since an item does not usually enter the public phase of SC meetings unless the necessary support has been ensured through informal consultations. In any situation, the sensitivity of the SC's agenda requires extensive negotiating in advance to avoid grievances aired during an open formal SC meeting.[525]

The Security Council makes decisions in the form of resolutions and Presidential statements. When a resolution is adopted, it is binding for all the UN Members. The Presidential Statement is issued by the President of the SC to give the opinion or position of the SC on an issue. A Presidential Statement, unlike a resolution, is not legally binding, but it requires unanimous approval by the SC. When a Presidential Statement is issued instead of a resolution or as a complement to a resolution, it generally reflects the mood of the Security Council on a given issue and outlines the SC's future intentions and course of action.[526] The SC President's mandate is rather narrow and specific, reflecting the limited formal role envisaged for the SC President by the UN's founders.[527] He or she has limited capacity to intervene in formal and informal SC deliberation procedures, there are constraints on presidential activities imposed by the veto potential of the SC Permanent Members, and his/her ability to manoeuvre is curtailed by the SC's decision-making system.

7.4.2 Diplomatic negotiations in the World Trade Organization

The need for successful trade negotiations in WTO is widely recognized. Still, the negotiations in the WTO pose a serious challenge, namely to reach consensus among its 164 current Members, the vast majority of which are developing countries. In addition, since the creation of WTO in 1995, the trading

Updated Edition, United Nations, 2007).

[525] Blavoukos Spyros and Bourantonis Dimitris, The Chair in the UN Context: Assessing Functions and Performance, Discussion Paper. Netherlands Institute of International Relations Clingendael, 2005, p.6 and Blavoukos Spyros, Bourantonis Dimitris and Tsakonas Panayotis, Parameters of the Chairmanship's Effectiveness: The Case of the UN Security Council. The Hague Journal of Diplomacy I, Koninklijke Brill NV, Leiden, 2006, p. 163.

[526] NMUN-Europe conference, Security Council, Background Guide, National Collegiate Conference Association, 2012 (available at nmun.org).

[527] Blavoukos Spyros, Bourantonis Dimitris and Tsakonas Panayotis, Parameters of the Chairmanship's Effectiveness: The Case of the UN Security Council. The Hague Journal of Diplomacy I, Koninklijke Brill NV, Leiden, 2006, p. 167.

system, which was once bi-polar, driven by the USA and the EU, has considerably changed to become multi-polar, with the large emerging economies, such as China, India and Brazil, becoming major economic powers in their own right. The existing impasse in the Doha Round is largely due to the great transformation in international relations taking place in the world today, but also as a result of the characteristics of WTO negotiations and the impossibility to build consensus among all WTO Members.

One characteristic of WTO negotiations is that they are **complex and uncertain**. Complexity is created by the number of WTO Members negotiating and by the various issues on the debating table, whereas uncertainty is generated by the difficulties of communicating preferences and exchanging information among a large number of participants that impede the possibility of identifying potential agreements and therefore demanding more active conciliation for reaching consensus. Another characteristic of WTO negotiations is that they take place on at least **three levels**: firstly, there is the local level of negotiations within the governmental structures of Members together with affected interest groups; secondly, there are negotiations among governments that often form a group of countries that have equal minded interests (intra-group negotiations); and finally, there are inter-group negotiations. The greatest "fight" usually occurs at on the inter-group level inside WTO. Negotiators tend to be insensitive to problems of their negotiating partners as they have enough trouble worrying about how they will get proposals accepted by their own governments to appreciate fully their adversaries' political difficulties.[528] Consequently, unrealistic proposals and positions are tabled, and a Chairman would be best placed to communicate this to the parties concerned.[529]

Yet, the WTO Members tend to delegate their interests to a consensus builder on behalf of a particular group or of the whole meeting/conference. Generally, the task of a Chairman within WTO negotiations is that of a facilitator, mediator and communicator, the choice of WTO Members going towards persons reflecting the capacity and the availability to undertake the special responsibilities required.

---

[528] Pfetsch Frank R., Chairing Negotiations in the World Trade Organization, Négociations 1/2009 (n° 11), p. 126 (available at cairn.info).

[529] Winham Gilbert, The Mediation of Multilateral Negotiations. Journal of World Trade Law 13, no. f:, 1979, p. 197.

Since the WTO is a Member-driven organization, Members have only given a limited role to the chairmen of their negotiating bodies to build consensuses and progress from deadlocks. There are few rules for chairing at WTO. Chairpersons, according to the WTO, are supposed to continue the GATT tradition of being impartial and objective, ensuring transparency and inclusiveness in decision-making and consultative processes, aiming to facilitate consensuses. What is remarkable with regards to the WTO is that it provides its Members with chairmen to run ministerial proceedings, but does little to specify the Chairman's mandate and his/her interaction with other Members. Therefore, few codes of practice have evolved, which chairmen could rely on.[530] This is so unusual as chairing WTO negotiations is a crucial part of the process of negotiation that itself shapes the outcomes. The way the chairmen operate have a significant effect on the likelihood of agreements, the distribution of gains and losses, and the WTO's legitimacy in general.

The most noticeable tactics of WTO chairmen consist of observation, diagnosis, and communication.[531] In these cases, the Chairman is supposed to communicate and develops an ability to listen, to become aware of the emotions and psychological concerns and to communicate clearly and effectively.[532] He or she has the task of collecting information and of providing an accurate record of the discussions. Being a chair as a communicator, therefore, is a rather passive exercise. The basic functions of a Chairman also include presiding the sessions. In this role, the Chairman enjoys considerable leeway to set the agenda and decide on the frequency as well as on the invitations to formal meetings. He or she can also force issues on the agenda. In this sense a WTO Chairman works as a policy promoter by selecting proposals and placing them on the ministers' agenda.[533] Yet, a WTO Chairman's main role is that of moderator between WTO Members, mediating between conflicting views and thus assisting a conference towards a conciliatory solution of existing problems.[534] In complex trade negotiations such

---

[530] There are rules regarding the appointment of directors-general (WT/L/509), and rules for those named officers to standing WTO bodies (WT/L/510) – see Pfetsch Frank R., Chairing Negotiations in the World Trade Organization, Négociations 1/2009 (n° 11).

[531] Odell John, Chairing a WTO Negotiation, Journal of International Economic Law 8(2), 2005, p. 431.

[532] Fisher R. and Ury W., Getting to Yes – Negotiating agreement without giving in, Harmondsworth, The Penguin books, 1981, p. 130.

[533] Pfetsch Frank R., Chairing Negotiations in the World Trade Organization, Négociations 1/2009 (n° 11), p. 131 (available at cairn.info).

[534] Kaufmann Johan, Conference Diplomacy. An Introductory Analysis, Dordrecht, Martinus Nijhoff, 1988, p.95.

role requires a high degree of professional skills and access to the necessary technical expertise and information that a Chairman usually possesses.[535] Conversely, many trade ministers and WTO delegates know very little of the technical and economic issues they are negotiating. WTO negotiations, therefore, entail a substantial amount of analytical groundwork, without assuming that these efforts will generally produce an exhaustive and accurate list of successful possibilities, since, more likely, each party is concerned primarily with its own payoff.[536]

A WTO Chairman has to bring parties together and negotiations to an achievement. Thus, a *single negotiating text* is essential for large multilateral negotiations such as in WTO, as it is meant to help a large group to move towards an agreement. This move can help to reduce many issues to a few, excluding proposals that are not generating support, without taking a position. More than 160 countries cannot constructively discuss 160 proposals, nor can the Chairman make concessions contingent upon mutual concession by everybody else. He or she needs a means to simplify the process of decision making and the one-text procedure serves that purpose.[537] Negotiations are likely to succeed if a Chairman introduces a single negotiating text in his or her own name. It is a formulation tactic often used by WTO chairmen. Once there is a written text, parties have incentives to initiate compromises among themselves and it becomes easier to get a consensus. Similar to UN System, the Chairman is not alone in introducing a text, he/she is also helped by the "Friends of the Chair" or facilitators appointed to organize discussions in identified areas. Even it is not always the case, the single text has to be balanced. Finding a mutually agreed deal provides incentives for other negotiators to accept it. Thus, the Chairman's role is to sum up the different positions, which have to be reflected in the reference papers. Unfortunately, the organization has a penchant for improvisation and, besides the fact that there are little rules for chairing at WTO, chairmen tend to act on their own, without the backing of the organization. In addition, another WTO Chairman's dilemma is the different weight of the WTO Members. The Chairman needs to find a balance between unequal members with extremely unequal powers - even though, at the

---

[535] Sojsdedt Gunnar, Negotiating the Uruguay Round of the general Agreement on Tariffs and Trade, in Zartman William ed., International Multilateral Negotiation. Approaches to the Management of Complexity, San Francisco, Jossey Bass, 1994, p. 45.

[536] Pfetsch Frank R., Chairing Negotiations in the World Trade Organization, Négociations 1/2009 (n° 11), p. 131 (available at cairn.info).

[537] Fisher Roger, Beyond Machiavelli, Tools of Coping with Conflict, Cambridge/Mass, Harvard UP, 1994, p. 148.

WTO, each country has a vote and it follows the rule of the legal equality. It is sometimes difficult for a Chairman to decide which proposal to include in his/her text, but shares of the world trade are taken into account when deciding what elements to add or to exclude from a package.[538] Proposals might be left aside if they are coming from weak powers and, to the contrary, always included if coming from the USA or the EU.

In any situation, chairing WTO negotiations requires imagination, skills, technical knowledge and logical ability. The WTO chairmen must be endowed with vision and intellectual guidance, they must assess the situation and take appropriate decisions. Even skilful chairmen often cannot compromise diverting interests of powerful nations, chairing is an essential part of the WTO negotiations. It helps to reach an agreement and to achieve the trade liberalization the WTO is devoted to.

---

[538] Odell John, Chairing a WTO Negotiation, Journal of International Economic Law. 8(2), 2005, p.441.

7.4.3 Diplomatic negotiations in the European Union

Negotiations are a vital instrument in integrating Europe. Negotiations are central to the functioning and dynamic development of the European Union. Negotiation is seen as the predominant policy mode and the main source of the EU's successful functioning.[539] The negotiation process in the European Union is a multilateral process of an international nature with supranational elements. The process is sandwiched between national and international negotiation. There is more control than in international negotiation processes, but less than in national processes.[540]

Based on the distinction between supervised delegation and coordination models of the EU's presence in multilateral conferences (see chapter 4.3.1), there are two different negotiation style, reactive and proactive.

EU trade policy has been long time characterized as promoting a reactive negotiation style.[541] Subsequently, externalization processes elevated the EU from a reactive to a proactive player that is capable of making international initiatives and even of turning initiatives into agreements. Thus, the European Community[542] was a reactive player for years, during most of the GATT's existence, a period that was characterized by American initiatives and European responses. With the creation of the WTO, this reactive style changed profoundly. Whereas the use of the supervised delegation model has remained a constant, the EU in the first place contributed[543] to the institutional design of the WTO, of which the European Community is a member in its own right, represented by the European Commission. The EU became a perfect match for the other trade superpower: the United States. Furthermore, the EU has become proactive in trying to set the

---

[539] Lodge J.E. and Pfetsch, F.R., Negotiating the European Union: Introduction, in International Negotiation. 3.3., 1998, p. 293.

[540] Meerts Paul (quoting Putnam), Diplomatic Negotiation, Essence and Evolution. The Hague: Clingendael Institute, 2015 p. 248.

[541] Cerchez Octavia, Politica comerciala comuna a Uniunii Europene, Editura Logos, Bucuresti, 2009, p. 127.

[542] The Maastricht Treaty, signed on 7th February 1992 and entered into force on 1st November 1993, creates the European Union, which consists of three pillars: the European Communities (European Community, the European Coal and Steel Community (ECSC) and Euratom), common foreign and security policy and police and judicial cooperation in criminal matters (see eur-lex.europa.eu).

[543] In 1990, Canada and the European Community began to moot their ideas for a "world" or, as the Europeans would prefer, a "multilateral" trade organization (see VanGrasstek Craig, The History and Future of the World Trade Organization, WTO Publications, 2013).

agenda, as the Doha Round enterprise is largely based on EU policy templates for world trade.[544]

Also, reactive diplomacy that is based on a coordination model of governance characterizes EU negotiation styles in relations with International Monetary Fund. To the degree that EU Members States coordinate their positions, this coordination is effectively blocked by the IMF's governance structure, according to which EU Member States belong to several different constituencies where they are sometimes in a minority position.[545]

From the proactive style that is based on coordination, negotiation in the UN General Assembly (UNGA) organs displays some dynamics. In many ways the degree of prior coordination is impressive in its effectiveness and degree of consistency if we take into account the high percentage of consensus voting by EU Member States.[546]

Whatever the negotiation style of the EU, when engaging in multilateral negotiations, the EU is marked by its dual nature: an international organization in its own right - acting unitary as an actor within the international system; and as coordinator of the EU Member States' positions - counting in diplomatic negotiation as a multi-member international organization.

Consequently, internally, EU Member States operating in the EU Council of Ministers have different approaches to the process of EU negotiation, not only because of differences of interest, but also because of differences in structure. The larger EU Member States share their potential for dealing with the whole range of EU issues in a balanced way, while the smaller Member States - because of the relative smallness of their governmental apparatus - are forced to follow more of a single-issue strategy.[547] Most of the EU internal negotiations focussed on the interaction and cooperation (see chapter 3.3.3, on coalitions within EU) between the EU Member States, directed at reaching an agreed outcome (or the close approximation to an agreed outcome due to the voting system by qualified majority). Under the EU Council's current qualified majority voting system, both

---

[544] Jorgensen Knud Erik, The European Union in Multilateral Diplomacy, The Hague Journal of Diplomacy, August 2009, p. 201 (available at researchgate.net).

[545] Op.cit.,p. 201.

[546] Jorgensen Knud Erik, The European Union in Multilateral Diplomacy, The Hague Journal of Diplomacy, August 2009, p. 203 (available at researchgate.net).

[547] Meerts Paul (quoting Bal), Diplomatic Negotiation, Essence and Evolution. The Hague: Clingendael Institute, 2015 p. 253.

the Southern protectionist bloc (including France, Italy, Spain, Greece, Portugal and Cyprus) and the Northern liberal bloc (including the UK, Germany, Sweden, Denmark, the Netherlands, Finland and the Baltics) hold a blocking minority. Without the UK (following the UK referendum on EU membership that took place on 23rd June 2016, so-called "Brexit"), the collective weight of the liberal bloc would decline, whereas the protectionist bloc would strengthen. Assuming no changes in EU Member States' positions, this raises the possibility that an EU without the UK could become less open.[548]

A major difference between EU internal negotiation and non-EU negotiations is the common understanding of EU negotiators that: EU decision-making is a "non-zero-sum" process; that the European Commission is the agenda setter - with the European Council as the major body for strategic decisions - and will therefore enhance the possibility of coordinated solutions. An additional factor is the long-standing influence of understandings on the negotiation process and, as a consequence, on the development of an EU negotiation culture with characteristics that cannot be found elsewhere. This evolution of cooperation creates an integrative bargaining process in which non-cooperation is very rare. As negotiators meet each other on a day-to-day basis, EU negotiations are more personalized than other international negotiations. This, in turn, creates a chemistry that furthers integrative bargaining, just as the collective gathering of information shapes a common referential frame. The enormous number of issues in the EU negotiation processes provides negotiators, in principle, with numerous possibilities for "package deals", thereby facilitating integrative outcomes. However, "package deals" sometimes work within one and the same dossier area if the deadline is approaching. "Package-dealing" between dossiers is not really feasible, with the exception of trade-offs at the highest political level.[549]

An important element in all these EU negotiation processes is the Chairman, who is called to manage the agenda, negotiate deals, and represent the negotiation party to outside groups. In the EU, the chairmen of the working groups rely heavily on the Council Secretariat's support. The role, functions and responsibilities of a Chairman in the EU context are similar with the ones in the UN and other international organizations. Conversely, the Chairman of an EU Council Working Group does not need to cumulate both individual and collective

---

[548] Oliver Patel and Christine Reh, Brexit: The Consequences for the EU's Political System, UCL Constitution Unit Briefing Paper, 2016, p.4. (available at ucl.ac.uk).

[549] Meerts Paul (including quoting Bal), Diplomatic Negotiation, Essence and Evolution. The Hague: Clingendael Institute, 2015 p. 254.

interests, as a second government representative will take the floor to express the Chairman's country position. The leadership and success of an EU Presidency rely heavily on its ability to ensure momentum and achieve results. The Presidency has to deliver results within complex procedures, intricate dynamics and long negotiation, as well cross-cultural boundaries.

These elements show that chairing EU Member States has an important role to play. To be effective, planning is essential. Most countries prepare seriously for their term in the rotating Presidency of the Council of the EU, and broad levels of the bureaucracy are trained in understanding the issues at hand and in dealing with them in an effective way. "Pathfinders" are sent out to gather information in EU capitals in order to obtain a thorough insight into the perceptions of the other EU member states concerning the issues that will be dealt with in the next half year. During its term in office, the chairing country must keep in mind that technical chairing is just not enough. Maintaining order will not - by itself - lead to progress in the negotiation process. So-called "corridor work", informal talks, mediation initiatives between opponents, performing well with the other institutions of the European Union, as well as pleasing public opinion in member states, are all activities that can help the chair to be seen as effective.[550]

---

[550] Meerts Paul, Diplomatic Negotiation, Essence and Evolution. The Hague: Clingendael Institute, 2015 p. 256.

Chapter 8 – Challenges in the current globalized context

States developed international relations and decided to engage in multilateral fora with other countries through diplomatic negotiations. Since the end of the Second World War multilateral approaches have exponentially increased and new factors emerged subsequently. Globalized developments in technology, communications, finance and trade gave rise to a world in which citizens, governments and organizations engage in trans-national interactions on a daily basis. National frontiers are becoming less relevant in determining the flow of ideas, information, goods, services, capital, labour, and know-how. The current global context witnesses new dynamics for both multilateral conferences and diplomatic negotiations.

8.1 Globalization

The creation of the nation-state is a key moment in the development of globalization, marking the beginning of a multilateral conduct of diplomacy. The ever-increasing number of actors, the power of modern media and communication technology shape the development of globalization with further consequences on the multilateral conferences and diplomatic negotiations. Due to these significant developments and thanks to the globalisation that affects all the countries around the world, the very concept of state representation is being gradually transformed and the traditional role, which was previously assigned to diplomatic envoys, as sole representatives of the interests of a sending state in a receiving state or in a multilateral conference, is being eroded.[551]

It is considered that there are fivefold noticeable aspects of globalization, with impact on development of multilateral conferences and outcomes of diplomatic negotiations:[552]

- expansion of the number and type of actors, from governments to national private sector firms, multinational corporations (MNCs), non-governmental organizations (NGOs), and regional and intergovernmental organizations (IGOs);

---

[551] Kumi N. B, Ghana's challenges in a new diplomatic environment. GREAT Insights, Volume 3, Issue 3. March 2014. (available at ecdpm.org).

[552] Cooper Andrew F., Heine Jorge, and Thakur Ramesh, Introduction: The Challenges of 21st-Century Diplomacy, The Oxford Handbook of Modern Diplomacy, 2013, p.6.

- development of a vast range of new issues, due to the expansion of domains and scope of the subject matter or content towards a very broad array of the different sectors of public policy and government;

- continued fusion of domestic and foreign policy reduction the separation between the different layers at which diplomatic activity take place, from the local through the domestic-national to the bilateral, regional, and global levels;

- changes in the functioning of international relations, multilateral conferences and diplomatic negotiations;

- changes in the ways, forms, and techniques of conducting diplomatic negotiations and multilateral conferences.

8.1.1 Expansion of the number and type of actors

Since the seventeenth century, the state has developed into a stronger actor in diplomatic inter-state negotiation processes. Still today, the states are the basic and enduring entity in international relations and their number has grown manifold in the last hundred years, producing an exponential increase in the number of diplomatic interactions between them. The number of independent state actors has quadrupled since 1945, the new states facing triple challenges: national integration, state-building, and economic development. In addition to the number of state actors having grown, there is a military, financial, political, and moral rebalancing underway in the global world's structure.[553]

Within the aftermath of the Cold War, the conduct of multilateral negotiations is influenced by inclusion of non-state actors (from local to international) which represented a multi-centric world instead of a state-centric predominance.[554] As a consequence, diplomatic negotiations ramified into a multilateral conduct in which state actors would negotiate equally with non-states acknowledging their capacity[555] and using them to leverage scarce resources and improve their ability to address transnational issues. Nevertheless, multilateral diplomacy still proves to be unable of representing a solid alternative to the traditional state to state, and is rather perceived as a mere subcontracting of state practice.[556]

---

[553] Cooper Andrew F., Heine Jorge, and Thakur Ramesh, Introduction: The Challenges of 21st-Century Diplomacy, The Oxford Handbook of Modern Diplomacy, 2013, p.7.

[554] Puntigliano A. R., Going Global: An Organizational Study of Brazilian Foreign Policy, Review International Brazilian Politics, Vol. 51, No. 1, 2008, p. 29.

[555] Talbott S., Globalization and Diplomacy: A practitioner's Perspective, Foreign Policy, No. 108, 1997, p. 79.

Globalization questioned the relevance of traditional actors like the state to the extent that it erodes spatial sovereignty and tends to promote pressure "from both above and below" that threatens the dominance of the state in the conduct of diplomacy. From above, international institutions, international law, transnational nongovernmental organizations and of course multinational corporations put intense pressures on even the most powerful of states and therefore easily shape its diplomacy. From below, civil society, labour movements, public opinion, mass-media, students' associations and the common tensions between and among these social formations tend to undermine the dominance of the state in the arena of diplomatic negotiations.[557] For example, the involvement of NGOs embraces almost every level of organization, from the village community to global summits, and almost every sector of public life, from the provision of micro-credit and the delivery of paramedical assistance, to environmental and human rights norm promotion and activism. Their main contributions with respect to multilateralism are related to advocating multilateral solutions to global problems, cultivating popular constituencies for multilateralism, and connecting local and national struggles to global norms and international institutions.[558] Nevertheless, the NGOs face many challenges to their legitimacy as they are often seen as unelected, unaccountable, unrepresentative, self-serving, and irresponsible.[559] Conversely, multinational corporations (MNCs) are considered to have a role and influence in modern diplomatic negotiations, as several MNCs employ agents to liaise and negotiate directly with foreign governments to obtain concessions, modify laws or taxes, permit repatriation of profits or duty-free entry of necessary parts and inputs, provide facilities or subsidies, relax labour and environmental standards and regulations, etc.

Although traditional state to state diplomatic negotiations remains stronger, power is to be shared with non-state actors, as their influence increase. The number of actors in world affairs has grown enormously, the types of actors have changed very substantially, the interactions between them have grown denser, and

---

[556] Constantinou C., The Transformation of Foreign Policy and Diplomacy, European Consortium for Political Research - Antwerp 2012, Workshop Summary, 2011, p. 3.

[557] Akin Iwilade, The Impact of Globalization on Diplomacy, the World Press, 2010 (available at akiniwilade.wordpress.com).

[558] Smith Jackie, Social Movements and Multilateralism, in Edward Newman, Ramesh Thakur, and John Tirman (eds), Multilateralism under Challenge: Power, International Order, and Structural Change, Tokyo: UN University Press, 2006, p.32.

[559] Cooper Andrew F., Heine Jorge, and Thakur Ramesh, Introduction: The Challenges of 21st-Century Diplomacy, The Oxford Handbook of Modern Diplomacy, 2013, p.7.

the agenda of international public policy has been altered in line with the changing circumstances. Consequently, all actors engaged in the world of diplomacy have to adjust their goals and actions to the reality of the globalized changing world.

The central goal of diplomatic relations still remains the advancement of national interest. Thus, states remain the domain of negotiation and they are enhancing their capacity for diplomatic negotiation, due to growing economic interdependency, diplomatic institutionalization and the progress in international public law.[560] The State is the main actor in diplomatic negotiations and multilateral conferences and this continues into the globalization era and in spite of the growing challenge to state authority by non-state actors. Even the role of the state has changed in response to the rapidly changing international environment and the involvement of new actors, as a result, diplomatic negotiations and multilateral conferences have changed with it, the State interest remains central to the conduct of diplomacy.

8.1.2 Development of a vast range of new issues

Considering the rapid development of events in the circumstances of globalization, diplomatic negotiations have to handle now a vast range of new issues which present different types of challenges from those that faced the world in 1918 or in 1945. The growth of post-war multilateral regulatory diplomacy has led to the involvement in external relations of a wider range of ministries, such as industry, aviation, environment, shipping, customs, health, education and sport. Linked to this development is the widening content of diplomacy, particularly through the internationalising of issues relating to terrorism, immigration, political refugees and other population issues, leading to international coordination by interior, justice and intelligence ministries. With the new realities and challenges have come corresponding new expectations for action and new standards of conduct in national and international affairs. For example, the environment issues, population, terrorism, transnational crime, drugs, and sustainable development would overrun the old order.[561]

---

[560] Meerts Paul, Diplomatic Negotiation, Essence and Evolution. The Hague: Clingendael Institute, 2015, p. 322.

[561] Didzis Klavins, Understanding the Essence of Modern Diplomacy, The ICD Annual Academic Conference on Cultural Diplomacy 2011: Cultural Diplomacy and International Relations; New Actors; New Initiatives; New Targets, Berlin, December 15th-18th, 2011, p. 4.

The impact of globalization has also greatly enhanced the cross border relevance of many domains in international politics. Among those, climate change is considered crucial. Globalization also heightened the relevance of issue linkages. Therefore, policy related to climate change has human rights implications, regional security policy has implications for democracy, good governance has implications for peace and stability. The new issues brought up by globalization include but are not limited to, climate change, spread of disease (HIV/AIDS, bird flu, etc.), increased linkages in the international political economy, refugee crisis, terrorism and resistance, instantaneous international communication and travel, regionalism and integration. In addition, the movement of people in large numbers, whether seeking fresh opportunities in new lands through migration or escaping cycles of violence, famine, persecution, natural disasters, or poverty, has been a major political problem domestically in many countries and a major diplomatic challenge internationally.[562]

The pressures brought to bear on the conduct of diplomatic negotiations by a growing population of knowledgeable and actively interested public is also a critical new issue that modern diplomats have to contend with.[563]

Unfortunately, the size and number of issues calling for attention did not find response in multilateral outcomes, seeing that the successful multilateral rule making is now a rare occurrence. Globalization, population growth, urbanization, technology and interconnection have produced a regrettably long list of real problems, many of which seem inherently to lie beyond the power of any one State to resolve because they involve the movement of persons, arms, pollution, diseases, capital, products or ideas across multiple borders.[564] Actually, the enumeration of potentially suitable subjects for diplomatic negotiations suggests that the size of the capacity for multilateral conferences' response is varying in inverse proportion to the size of the problems.

---

[562] Cooper Andrew F., Heine Jorge, and Thakur Ramesh, Introduction: The Challenges of 21st-Century Diplomacy, The Oxford Handbook of Modern Diplomacy, 2013, p.14.

[563] Akin Iwilade, The Impact of Globalization on Diplomacy, the World Press, 2010 (available at akiniwilade.wordpress.com).

[564] Gurry Francis, Challenges for International Organizations and Multilateralism, Lakshman Kadirgamar Memorial Oration 2013, November 13, 2013 (available at wipo.int).

8.1.3 Continued fusion of domestic and foreign policy

A striking impact of globalization on the diplomatic process is the continued fusion of domestic and foreign policy. The reasons for this are primarily the internationalisation of previously domestic issues, the erosion of the concept of domestic jurisdiction, transnational boundary-crossing transactions and, of course, the globalisation of economies. Further special sets of factors are found in regions in which there is substantial population cross-movement or non-observance of borders in integrative organisations (such as the European Union). The main effect of the increasing fusion of domestic and foreign policy is to alter the nature of diplomatic activity, bringing it into some policy areas and issues considered as "domestic". Some examples of these would include economic and financial policy; promotion of medical and pharmaceutical products and trade regulatory requirements; the international diplomacy of agriculture; land acquisition and oil licensing, in federal or transition states. In the political category, the diplomatic agenda would include issues of: governance; corruption; "foreign" economic policy; international banking oversight (standards); sovereignty and moral hazard decisions (e.g. whether to support a failed state; participate in a banking "rescue"; or agree to a "sunset" clause[565] ending preferential assistance to heavily indebted poor countries). To these would be added traditional political concerns such as human rights and rule of law issues. The extension of the agenda finds its expression in the international role of ministries that have traditionally been considered as essentially "domestic". In other words, external policy is no longer necessarily the preserve of the Ministry of Foreign Affairs. The increasing complexity of foreign policy, too, has been accompanied, especially in larger states, not only by a proliferation of ministries but also by tendency for fragmentation of responsibility. Ministries or agencies acquire foreign policy interests, stakes and perspectives which are promoted and defended.[566]

Another important aspect of the fusion of domestic and foreign policy is the growing involvement in the international interactions of local or provincial authorities. For example, it is not uncommon for the heads of a local government to visit a UN agency because they wish to participate in its programmes directly rather than through the national government. A few years ago this was difficult to

---

[565] "Sunset" clause or provision: A statutory provision providing that a particular agency, benefit, or law will expire on a particular date, unless it is reauthorized by the legislature (see West's Encyclopedia of American Law, edition 2, 2008, The Gale Group, Inc.).

[566] Barston R.P., Modern diplomacy, fourth edition, Routledge, 2014, pp. 10,14.

imagine. During the conference of the mayors of the Mediterranean cities in Barcelona, many recognised that they often have more close economic or cultural ties with their partners across the sea than with their national capitals. Many big cities and provinces have enough resources not just to influence the national governments but also to actually maintain their own "diplomatic" agencies. The immediate implication of this development for the diplomatic practitioners is that now, in addition to their colleagues representing formally recognised states, they also have to deal with numerous other non-state counterparts who conduct their own "foreign policy".[567] These developments show that sometimes, the effective action frequently lies with the central (or local) governments, consequently collaboration must extend beyond governments and political elites towards local authorities, even civil society and business. Being able to identify and work with domestic constituencies is a reference in the direction of reducing the separation between the different levels at which diplomatic activity took place, from the local through the domestic-national to the bilateral, regional, and global levels.

The breakdown of the distinction between domestic and international affairs means that the national interests of a country now involve the "whole of government" and, therefore, the importance of coordination between government agencies. Ministry of Foreign Affairs should see itself as part of this "national diplomatic system" and consider their changing role in this light. The increasing demands of regulatory diplomatic agendas will imply increasing involvement of financial and other ministries in international policy.[568]

Modern diplomacy is characterized by the fact that dynamics of international relations are no longer dominated by concerns with balance, sovereignty and the separation of "the foreign" and "the domestic", overseen by a highly centralized state with claims to total control.[569] Rather, modern international relations are driven by the logic of interference with domestic affairs, pursuing commonalities through transparency and transparency through interdependence. The most developed example is the European Union. While it has a clear standing in the context of global affairs the modern diplomacy calls for a continuing recourse to national sovereignty and local authorities.

---

[567] Petrovsky Vladimir, Diplomacy as an instrument of good governance, Modern Diplomacy. Ed by J. Kurbalija, 1998 (available at diplomacy.edu).

[568] Hocking Brian, Melissen Jan, Riordan Shaun, Sharp Paul, Futures for diplomacy - Integrative Diplomacy in the 21st Century, Netherlands Institute of International Relations Clingendael, 2012, p.19.

[569] Op.cit., p. 5.

8.1.4 Changes in the functioning of international relations

We acknowledged that international relations as we know them today are based on the Westphalian model of sovereign states. The Congress of Vienna in 1815 conferred upon the state the role of the primary practitioner of diplomacy, a fact enshrined in the UN Charter of 1945. Firstly, the League of Nations and the UN were seen as a multilateral response in attempt to regulate international relations and as an effort to prevent a repeat of conflict similar to the two world wars. The League of Nations and the United Nations are unique in history as they provided for universal membership to a forum grounded in the ways of traditional diplomacy.[570]

The UN Charter was drawn up in 1945, yet the world has changed greatly afterwards. These changes significantly reduced the East-West and North-South dimensions of the international relations. From G77 and United Nations Conference on Trade and Development (UNCTAD), the developing country development agenda moved uneasily into the World Trade Organization (WTO) Doha Round of trade negotiations, scattered through the UN System or attached to EU policies. Moreover, several bilateral agreements and treaties related to trade were negotiated and entered into force. In short, from 1945 till now, among other things, the Cold War come and finished, the cooperative relations with Russia opened, the creation and enlargement of the European Union took place, new blocs, groupings and international institutions appeared and changed, new major world powers like China, India, and Brazil emerged and joined in the governance of globalization symbolized by the G20. Current system of international relations is characterised by the fluidity in international relations, without clear cooperation; the international system is not multipolar, but rather distinguished by the absence of polarity; norms and core concepts are contested, in the key pillars of international order (security, trade and international financial and economic relations); the high level of regional organisation and bilateral diplomatic activity.[571]

The speed at which the geopolitical and human society changes presents a challenge of adaptation for the international relations. There is a growing disconnection between economic reality and political architecture of international organizations. The political architecture of the multilateral system, in terms of the institutionalized distribution of power, political groupings, or development, is

---

[570] Cockburn Andrew Mark, The Unique Challenges Presented by Multilateral Diplomacy, May 10, 2012, p. 2. (available at SSRN: ssrn.com or dx.doi.org).

[571] Barston R.P., Modern diplomacy, fourth edition, Routledge, 2014, pp. 9-10.

based on the economic reality of the world at the end of Second World War. Change is working its way through the system, but it has not yet found its full institutional expression.[572]

Views of the current state of world affairs demand international relations theories and changes focusing on both growing gaps and interdependencies, conflicts and cooperation, economic and social issues.

8.1.5 Changes in the ways, forms, and techniques of diplomatic negotiations and multilateral conferences

Traditional diplomacy cannot handle all the new ways, forms and techniques at the disposal of diplomatic negotiations and multilateral conferences in present globalized context.

Middle Ages diplomacy once the exclusive domain of kings and princes is now replaced by a myriad of diplomatic summits with a resulting convergence between foreign policy-makers and the practice of diplomacy. Even some summits offer little beyond symbolism, some can make genuine progress on shared global challenges and problems. In any case they are inevitable forms in contemporary diplomatic context.[573]

International cooperation now takes place in a world of multiple speeds and layers (national, bilateral, plurilateral and multilateral), multiple dimensions (public, private and a range of mixtures of both) and multiple power balances (economic, financial, political, people, information, idea, diplomatic and military). The one-dimensional world of a single balance of political power is a thing of the past. But this complexity is not necessary a bad thing, as it led to the practice of international relations on two tracks: the standard form of diplomatic relations involving negotiations between officials of two or more countries, and (which lately grew in intensity and influence) that involving unofficial and generally informal interaction between non-governmental actors including celebrities, NGOs, scholars, humanitarian organizations, and former government officials.[574]

---

[572] Gurry Francis, Challenges for International Organizations and Multilateralism, Lakshman Kadirgamar Memorial Oration 20131, November 13, 2013 (available at wipo.int).

[573] Cooper Andrew F., Heine Jorge, and Thakur Ramesh, Introduction: The Challenges of 21st-Century Diplomacy, The Oxford Handbook of Modern Diplomacy, 2013, p.18.

[574] Op.cit., p.18

Multilateral conferences also introduces in international relations new forms of diplomatic negotiations like public debates, extensive committee work, parliamentary procedures that back in the home country are the provenance of politicians, diplomatic caucusing akin to political caucusing in national parliaments, and forging coalitions and alliances.

New digital environment has a multiplicity of implications and consequences[575] for ways, forms, and techniques of diplomatic negotiations and multilateral conferences:

- it has empowered a range of actors to participate in diplomatic negotiations by putting them on an equal information footing with Members and by linking them throughout the world. The Internet has busted the state's monopoly on information and has facilitated the creation of networks of all conceivable varieties - social, political, economic, cultural, scientific and technological. It created a shift in access to information and knowledge and in the capacity to use knowledge for all sorts of purposes;

- the Internet and social media have changed the way in which people communicate and consequently the actors of international relations and delegates should engage in a radical change of communication methods;

- the digital environment is also producing the phenomenon of big data, meaning the vast amount of data that is being generated from all the electronic devices, connections and terminals that it is increasingly use to transact the daily social and economic existence, together with the new techniques that have been developed to process and to analyse those data. Big data has an enormous potential in social, economic, development and humanitarian policy, but it involves an entirely different methodology from the classical multilateral diplomatic processes of identifying problems and developing solutions through discussion in meetings held at six-monthly intervals to enable national consultations with interested parties between meetings.

These elements affecting the ways, forms, and techniques of diplomatic negotiations and multilateral conferences show a picture of great complexity. This involves an understanding of changing patterns of diplomatic communication, which is called "integrative diplomacy".[576] Through "integrative diplomacy", the governmental authorities responsible with international relations must devise

---

[575] Gurry Francis, Challenges for International Organizations and Multilateralism, Lakshman Kadirgamar Memorial Oration 20131, November 13, 2013 (available at wipo.int).

[576] Hocking Brian, Melissen Jan, Riordan Shaun, Sharp Paul, Futures for diplomacy - Integrative Diplomacy in the 21st Century, Netherlands Institute of International Relations Clingendael, 2012, p.10.

effective public diplomacy strategies integrated fully into the policy-making machinery, task that requires a sophisticated understanding of stakeholders and audiences.

The speed of modern communications makes borders increasingly permeable, while the volume of cross-border flows threatens to overwhelm the capacity of states to manage them. Far from diminishing, complex interdependence and globalization have increased the scope and volume of diplomatic negotiations, especially in multilateral conferences. The growth in the number of participants taking part in the negotiations, the number of issues that are now the subject of international negotiations, the diversity of negotiating styles of officials coming from vastly different political cultures and levels of development, and the technical complexity of the matters make the process of negotiation more elaborate, highly technical, and more prolonged.

8.2 Negotiation and decision making

The difficulty and speed of negotiations, and the outcome of negotiation processes are affected by many factors. And in a multilateral context these problems are multiplied by a further subset of factors such as culture and the values of the various participants.[577] The dynamics of multilateral negotiations is influenced by numerous challenges triggered by the issues on debate, the seriousness of the dispute and availability of common ground for agreement, the complexity and shape of political alignments, the personalities involved and the interplay between them, the impact of external (related and unrelated) events, skills and political weight of the negotiators, national policy positions and negotiating strategies.[578]

The two basic challenges confronting international relations today are those of decision-making, and of implementation of said decisions,[579] as it is very difficult to assess how a diverse group of actors with varying levels of interest in a subject votes on it, if only those with a stake in the matter should be allowed to

---

[577] Cockburn Andrew Mark, The Unique Challenges Presented by Multilateral Diplomacy, May 10, 2012, p. 6. (available at SSRN: ssrn.com or dx.doi.org).

[578] Buzan B., Negotiating by consensus: developments in technique at the UN Conference on the Law of the Sea, American Journal of International Law, 75(2), 1981, p.330.

[579] Newman E., Thakur R., Tirman J., Multilateralism Under Challenge? The performance and effectiveness of multilateralism are under scrutiny according to 21st-century standards of legitimacy and democracy, United Nations University Research Brief Number 1/2006, p.4.

vote or the voting form should be based on majority, weighted, consensus based or in another form. Each of these methods has strengths and weaknesses, and some forms will suit some parties better than others.[580] But it is not just the decision-making process itself that poses a challenge to multilateral diplomacy.

In the same time diplomatic negotiations need to be functional in size and the participants need to feel they are part of the process for it to be legitimate and stand any chance of success.[581] The size and scale of the negotiations is an important aspect related to workable discussions and successful negotiations. For example, weighted voting always ends up alienating minorities, who in turn can simply ignore decisions reached without their consent, thus a challenge presented by multilateral diplomacy as that of states with no interest in an area casting equal votes with those who have much invested in the subject (for example, the case of the UN Conference on the Law of the Sea - UNCLOS).[582]

On one hand, a voting system would have been out of the question in the seventeenth, eighteenth and nineteenth centuries. It only became feasible in the twentieth century with the League of Nations. At the Congress of Vienna it was completely out of the question to limit sovereignty in any way, as this would undermine the system of formally independent states and the legitimacy of their rulers. Such a precedent would not only touch upon the small powers, which did not want to be vassals (although many of them were) but would also affect the Great Powers. Nowadays that voting power, economic size and domestic constraints create the context in which negotiators have to operate. Negotiators look for opportunities to form coalitions to strengthen their power, they lean on the institutional power that they have rely on skilled and well informed experts, working on as many levels and with as much frequency and reciprocity as possible in order to create optimal effectiveness and defend the interests of their country or organization.[583]

Thus, the substitution of voting for simple consensus procedures runs the risk of talks with no end, which go on and on, and even then maybe the outcome

---

[580] Cockburn Andrew Mark, The Unique Challenges Presented by Multilateral Diplomacy, May 10, 2012, p. 6. (available at SSRN: ssrn.com or dx.doi.org).

[581] Kahler M., Multilateralism with small and large numbers, International Organization, 46(3), 1992, p. 695.

[582] Buzan B., Negotiating by consensus: developments in technique at the UN Conference on the Law of the Sea, American Journal of International Law, 75(2), 1981, p.326.

[583] Meerts Paul (including quoting Bailer), Diplomatic Negotiation, Essence and Evolution. The Hague: Clingendael Institute, 2015, Mertees pp.199, 264.

being no decision at all.[584] Also, the idea that consensus provides for equality among Members is flawed in that it wrongly assumes that any Member is equally able to sustain a veto.[585] Where a Member is alone in opposing a decision, it can find itself in quite some isolation and exposed to quite some pressure which arguably only big powerful Members can sustain for an extended period of time. Accordingly, it seems unavoidable that the proposed texts that emerge in a negotiation process reflect the views of different Members to very different degrees. These texts arguably give more weight to the positions of Members who are less likely to give up their veto than to the views of Members with weaker consensus resistance capacity. This capacity tends to be linked to their size and importance (in international trade, in case of WTO). In a way, consensus is a partial substitute for weighted voting. It has been said that the negotiation process which is overshadowed by the danger of any Member's veto tends to be less transparent because negotiations take place in informal mode and are often not recorded. Yet, it would seem that this is not inherent in this type of negotiations and can equally be the case where a formal majority vote marks the end of the procedure.[586] Likewise, the moves away from majority voting to active consensus voting weakens the power held by smaller Members who have tended to vote in blocks so as to increase their voice. So although large Members end up less likely to be excluded, this is done at a cost to the smaller and weaker nations.[587]

A distinction between negotiations and treaty-making should be made. The process of multilateral negotiations consists of two stages: exploratory, as the initial stage, and treaty-making as the highest stage. The latter could be subdivided into the definition of parameters of a future agreement and the working out of it. By keeping in mind this structure, the negotiations process can be built in such a way that the result is achieved quickly and minimal resources are used. Unfortunately in some multilateral conferences, the participants confuse the different stages and the whole process goes into disorder, with such negotiations lasting for years and consisting of endless positional statements.[588]

---

[584] Buzan B., Negotiating by consensus: developments in technique at the UN Conference on the Law of the Sea, American Journal of International Law, 75(2), 1981, p.329.

[585] Cottier Thomas and Satoko Takenoshita, The Balance of Power in WTO Decision-Making: Towards Weighted Voting in Legislative Response, Aussenwirtschaft, 2003, p. 171, 176.

[586] Ehlermann Claus-Dieter (quoting Cottier and Satoko, and Jackson), Decision Making in the World Trade Organization: Is the Consensus Practice of the World Trade Organization Adequate for Making, Revising and Implementing Rules on International Trade?, WilmerHale, 2005, p.9.

[587] Cockburn Andrew Mark (quoting Newman), The Unique Challenges Presented by Multilateral Diplomacy, May 10, 2012, p.7. (available at SSRN: ssrn.com or dx.doi.org).

These assessments show that there is not, for the moment, one system that can satisfy the demands of all, displaying yet another challenge of multilateral negotiations. Therefore traditional decision making process of the UN has been increasingly seen as being inadequate for international decision making. The problems of getting large numbers of nations with diverse interests and demands to come to a consensus on subjects that will result in lasting and binding agreements are surely unique to multilateral diplomacy.[589]

This aspect is linked to another dynamics of diplomatic negotiations - the art of making concession, to compromise. Compromise requires "constructive parallelism" in all areas of negotiation, which presupposes that progress in one area creates the opportunity for advancement in other directions. Compromise is neither a capitulation nor a sign of weakness. The art of compromise is a concession in secondary matters, not in principles. However, not everything depends on the negotiators, without a political will even the best negotiator cannot do much.[590] The absence of political will to find compromise solutions is one of the causes of paucity in successful outcomes at multilateral level, even the need for compromise and compensation is evident in any diplomatic negotiation.

Creative negotiators can try to bridge the gap by exploring alternative options and acceptable halfway solutions. They might even have to forge package deals if trade-offs are the only way to create an artificial zone of overlap. Without these attempts, the negotiations might stall and the process goes nowhere. To complicate matters, several processes might develop at the same time. The multilateral context of this basically bilateral process will generate problems, but also options. It adds to the complexity of the negotiation process, where actors are striving for practical solutions. The slow flow of the negotiation process might frustrate them and have an impact on the climate of the negotiation. Processes therefore have to be taken seriously, as they are the means that we have to materialize what we want. Too much focus on the end-game and not enough feeling for the process itself might be a source of ineffectiveness and failure.[591]

---

[588] Petrovsky Vladimir, Diplomacy as an instrument of good governance, Modern Diplomacy. Ed by J. Kurbalija, 1998. (available at diplomacy.edu).

[589] Cockburn Andrew Mark (quoting Newman), The Unique Challenges Presented by Multilateral Diplomacy, May 10, 2012, p.7. (available at SSRN: ssrn.com or dx.doi.org).

[590] Petrovsky Vladimir, Diplomacy as an instrument of good governance, Modern Diplomacy. Ed by J. Kurbalija, 1998. (available at diplomacy.edu).

[591] Meerts Paul, Diplomatic Negotiation, Essence and Evolution. The Hague: Clingendael Institute, 2015, p. 285.

8.3 Bureaucracy

International organizations are the fora that channel negotiation processes in the direction of outcomes. They compensate for insecurity, which is one of the greatest threats to effective negotiation processes. While stabilizing the processes, they also hamper their flow as a consequence of bureaucracy and concentration of resources hence power.[592] Thus, international organizations are seen as international bureaucracies which are autonomous actors in a broader process of global governance and whose actions are oftentimes removed from the intentions and control of their creators. They affect other actors and engage in subject matters not formerly within their reach but their factual impact remains underestimated. Little consolation can be found in the contention that international bureaucracies merely seek the effective implementation of global goals.[593]

International bureaucracies are established to assist governments and other stakeholders in institutionalized multilateral negotiations about international norms and in their application. In addition to conducting administrative functions, international bureaucracies increasingly influence politics by initiating and implementing international affairs. The effectiveness of bureaucracies relies heavily on their ability to take autonomous action, i.e. the capabilities to act in accordance with own aspirations and ambitions without being halted or vetoed by mandating authorities. It becomes increasingly evident that the actions and outcomes of international bureaucracies may dissent from the intentions of their creators.[594]

In 1815, the Congress of Vienna had a multitude of parties represented on a scale unheard of, but the days when a few nobles were sitting around a table discussing the fate of nations to whom they did not belong are far away. Since 1945, the Congress's institutionalised successor, the United Nations demonstrated an un-precedent capacity to set up bureaucratic committees, sub committees and groupings by geographical and economical relation, that are currently too numerous to list. Consequently, one of the most common accusations and critics levelled at multilateral bodies such as the UN is that of being all talk and no

---

[592] Op.cit., p.313.

[593] Venzke Ingo, International Bureaucracies from a Political Science Perspective - Agency, Authority and International Institutional Law, German Law Journal, Vol. 9, 2008, pp. 1401.

[594] Kühn Nadja Sophia B., Autonomy of International Bureaucracies: On the Actor-Level Autonomy in the WTO Secretariat, Universitetet i Agder, høst 2014, p.1.

action, of the bureaucracy being so vast with permanent secretariats, assemblies, councils, committees, working groups and such like, that in case of emergency, decision making can be slow and can fail to react in time to a fast developing situation.[595]

Likewise, since the Uruguay Round, the World Trade Organization (WTO) has become an increasingly controversial institution. Some authors[596] argue that, when the WTO was created in 1995, it was intended as a high-profile bureaucracy which was to decide how to hold a ministerial conference, constitute a general council and set up a secretariat to run the organization and implement the agreements; the intention was that the WTO bureaucracy should have sufficient power to pressure nations to change their domestic laws and prevent a decision being finalized in favour of the developing countries as far as possible. Other authors[597] consider that WTO has been assailed for having gone too far - critics, typically reflecting the concerns of many developing countries, claim that by making all of its members adopt agreements such as those relating to Trade Related Intellectual Property and Investment Measures (TRIPs and TRIMs), the WTO has strayed beyond its basic trade mission and forced many of its Members to accept obligations that are (a) not in their interest; (b) intrusive of their sovereignty; and (c) beyond their implementation capacities.

Similarly, the European Union, whose humble origins date back to the creation of the European Coal and Steel Community[598] in 1951 and the signature of the Treaty of Rome,[599] in 1957, by the six original EU Member States (Belgium, France, the Netherlands, Italy, Luxembourg, and Germany) became an amalgamation of 28 distinct cultures, polities, economies, and histories had

---

[595] Cockburn Andrew Mark (quoting Newman), The Unique Challenges Presented by Multilateral Diplomacy, May 10, 2012, p.8. (available at SSRN: ssrn.com or dx.doi.org).

[596] DAWN, How WTO bureaucracy subverts the process, December 2004 (available at dawn.com).

[597] Lawrence Robert Z., Toward a More Effective WTO: The Role of Variable Geometry, East Asian Bureau of Economic Research, June 1, 2008 (available at piie.com).

[598] Treaty establishing the European Coal and Steel Community, the ECSC Treaty was signed in Paris in 1951 and brought France, Germany, Italy and the Benelux countries together in a Community with the aim of organising free movement of coal and steel and free access to sources of production. In addition to this, a common High Authority supervised the market, respect for competition rules and price transparency. This treaty is the origin of the EU institutions as we know them today (see eur-lex.europa.eu).

[599] Treaty establishing the European Economic Community, EEC Treaty, signed in Rome in 1957, brings together France, Germany, Italy and the Benelux countries in a community whose aim is to achieve integration via trade with a view to economic expansion. After the Treaty of Maastricht the EEC became the European Community, reflecting the determination of the Member States to expand the Community's powers to non-economic domains (see eur-lex.europa.eu).

proceeded apace in spite of a growing resentment among the European peoples and voices arguing for reforms. The real problem for those who wish to see EU reforms is that the EU establishment has a strong incentive to centralize decision-making in Brussels rather than decentralize, as EU bureaucrats believe the centralization of power is in their interest because it increases their power and resources.[600]

But these international organisations have their own needs as well, and they will push for them even if this is not always in line with the interests of their Members. The European Union is an example of the struggle between the whole and the constituent parts. In order to have successful diplomatic conferences and to cover the main negotiation issues, organisations are growing and thereby their bureaucracy. While negotiations will have to be embedded in order to be successful, this structuring will also reduce effectiveness as a consequence of loss of flexibility. Diplomats try to fight the negative rigidity by negotiating away from the table as much as possible, in "corridor work", huddles and informal bilateral reunions, etc. Nevertheless, structures and procedures are necessary instruments to direct the processes into closure. While informality is needed, it might create unnecessary fuzziness and ambiguity, as negotiators will lose oversight and the ability to control the processes.[601]

That is why international regimes have an important function in channelling bargaining processes in such a way that their efficiency and effectiveness will be optimized. Without these organizational boundaries, there can be no effective processes, but they have limitations as well, which might have negative effects, such as inflexibility through over-bureaucracy. Political reality, however, cannot be overlooked. Powerful nations cannot easily be constrained within the limits of international regimes. It could not be done in 2003-2004 when the French and Germans violated the three per cent budget limit prescribed by the European Monetary Union. Neither did it work when the United Nations Security Council could not reach agreement to use military force to defeat rulers in Iraq or in Syria.[602]

---

[600] Tupy Marian L., The European Union: A Critical Assessment, CATO Institute, Economic Development Bulletin no. 26/2016 (available at cato.org).

[601] Meerts Paul (quoting Kaufman and Walker), Challenges to Diplomatic Negotiation, PIN Policy Brief, The Hague: Clingendael Institute, 2015, p. 4.

[602] Meerts P. (quoting Spector and Zartman), Diplomatic Negotiation, Essence and Evolution. The Hague: Clingendael Institute, 2015, p.74.

The bureaucratic politics approach argues that policy outcomes result from a game of bargaining among a small, highly placed group of actors. These actors come to the game with varying preferences, abilities, and positions of power. Participants choose strategies and policy goals based on different ideas of what outcomes will best serve their organizational and personal interests. Bargaining then proceeds through a pluralist process of give-and-take that reflects the prevailing rules of the game as well as power relations among the participants. Because this process is neither dominated by one individual nor likely to privilege expert or rational decisions, it may result in suboptimal outcomes that fail to fulfil the objectives of any of the individual participants.[603] The diplomats working within this system are often caught in between serving their national interests and those of the greater community. How can, for example, an ambassador, who is a representative of his state/government (and thus bound to dutifully work towards the greater good of his state/government) operate in a transnational system when they are by definition state bound themselves. And when states are in need of increasing control over internal and external negotiation processes, they need more and more bureaucracy to exert control. Bureaucracy and control tend to enhance inflexibility, which in turn hampers the negotiation process and thereby its effectiveness as an instrument. Bureaucratic barriers slow down the negotiation process.[604]

The challenge presented by the UN multilateral diplomacy is that it is too wrapped up in bureaucracy to deal with many of today's problems, the proceedings are too slow and caught up in bureaucracy. Nevertheless, amongst all the layers of bureaucracy, the UN is fixed in shape and purpose. It was designed in a way that overwhelmingly favoured the major powers of the day, and still reflects this, even though times have changed, and various states have different standing now on the international scene, yet the concerned parties will not give up their privileged position.[605] This has made it appear clumsy and unwieldy in the face of many of today's problems. Unfortunately, the substantive and substantial reform has proved virtually impossible.[606] The fundamental structure of this multilateral forum is resistant to change and the bureaucratic make-up means it

---

[603] Encyclopedia Britannica, Bureaucratic politics approach (available at britannica.com).

[604] Meerts P. Diplomatic Negotiation, Essence and Evolution. The Hague: Clingendael Institute, 2015, p.327.

[605] Weiss T.G., The Illusion of UN Security Council Reform, The Washington Quarterly, Volume 26, Number 4, Autumn 2003, p. 151.

[606] Op.cit., p. 147.

will most probably stay this way. And this presents a great challenge to the UN as a multilateral forum for diplomacy, while its structure and functioning is seen as being set and rigid, many of the problems facing it today, like preserving international peace, while being never-ending, are ever changing in complexity.[607]

Without structural and procedural reforms, the international bureaucracies will accumulate more bureaucracy and performance deficits and there will be an intensifying crisis of confidence in the world's system of organized multilateralism centred on the United Nations.

8.4 Corollary

The United Nations (UN) and its broad family of specialized agencies and other affiliates is dedicated to promoting peace and security of all countries, prosperity, environmental sustainability and general well-being for all people, as well as their enjoyment of a rule-based international order, international interaction and cooperation and basic human rights. The World Trade Organization (WTO) is an inter-governmental organization for progressively liberalizing trade - the main approach adopted by Members to promote economic growth and development. The WTO negotiates global trade agreements, operates a system of trade rules that apply to all its Members and it is a place to settle their trade disputes. The European Union (EU), international organization comprising 28 European countries and governing common economic policies.

But the good of all countries is also the good of each country and it is only natural that most of delegates think primarily of their own country and government. Subordinating one's own interests for the common good is a great help to the purposes of those international organizations. Nevertheless, approaching multilateral conferences from a less idealistic perspective, with the national objectives at the forefront of delegation's motivation is also possible and productive. The reasons being the interdependence of the global world. What is good for a country, in most cases, brings indirect benefits to many others. Equally, the processes of multilateral conferences and diplomatic negotiations reward collaborative problem-solving attitudes.

---

[607] Cockburn Andrew Mark (quoting Weiss), The Unique Challenges Presented by Multilateral Diplomacy, May 10, 2012, pp.8,9. (available at SSRN: ssrn.com or dx.doi.org).

Objectives that are seen as detrimental by other governments have very reduced chances to be advanced through multilateral conferences. Thus, it is not beneficial to try to advance such objectives through diplomatic negotiations, as it might be counterproductive. Collaborative problem-solving is the means governments and delegates focus on to advance those national objectives that have reasonable prospects of being achieved.

It is important to keep in mind that multilateral conferences are not only the context in which delegates interact, but also an opportunity for governments to demonstrate their commitment to particular objectives or courses of action.

Thus, it is inevitable, and also legitimate that: the delegates use the general debate to communicate with domestic audiences and with other audiences beyond the conference room; all participants at all times are conscious of the image they wish to project of the states and organizations they represent; and the delegates do not neglect the opportunities for networking and discussing various matters not found on the conference agenda.

Multilateral conferences are also assemblies of delegates, who, with considerable (human and financial) efforts of their respective governments or organizations, were sent to participate in the event in order to perform certain tasks, in which considerable time and hard work has already been invested. Those delegates do not respond well, nor readily forget, if any delegate pursues public relations or their national or bilateral agendas at too great extent and on the expense of the collective and individual purposes for which all other delegates are present. (This is valid for the use of conference time that does not belong to any individual delegate. It also applies to something less concrete, but equally valuable that is the prospects for reaching agreement to which the longest period of conference time should be allocated.) With such conduct, they are acting in an un-friendly way to the common purpose of the conference and also to the individual purposes of most other delegations, thus inviting a hostile response from the majority of the participants.

The most important element during the multilateral conference is the interaction between delegates, directed at reaching agreement (or the closest approximation to an agreement that is a decision by a large majority). The conference agreement can only be reached by interaction between and among the delegates. If a delegate intends to work collaboratively with other delegations, he/she has to get to know them and their concerns, as well as to communicate with them frequently and in a constructive manner. Those informal exchanges, known as consultations, are vital both before and during the conference, and delegates have to also keep in mind the importance of the human interaction and make sure that they give it a central place in the planning and during the conference.

Another important part of the planning to interact frequently and intensively with other delegates is to consider how the delegate behaves towards them, with a view to maximizing the prospects of achieving the state/government's objectives for the conference. Naturally this means that the approach to them should be friendly and positive, with the emphasis on the importance of being open towards all other delegates. The openness refers to both hearing their views and arguments, and opening up to them. With this goal, the delegates need to meet up other delegates to make sure that they understand each other's concerns and aims. The reason is that the most effective way to achieve positive results is to develop proposals which others will willingly support, or at least accept, because they find them attractive. Likewise, the most effective way of overcoming resistance to a potential conference decision that meet the government's objectives is to understand the concerns that give rise to that resistance and to try to find ways of allaying those concerns. As this is likely to be the negotiations strategy pursued by the most effective delegations, it is in the delegate's interests to help them fully understand what is likely to win his/her delegation support and also the concerns that could cause a resistance to the agreement, giving them an incentive to try to diminish those concerns. Therefore, constructive problem-solving involves not only an active search for widely acceptable solutions, but also helping those who seek to give to the delegation an incentive to support their position. Even this may seem like an indirect way of achieving own objectives it is a very efficient one.

The delegates need also to keep in mind that not all conferences and diplomatic negotiation proceed according to their will and not all delegates will follow the strategies that own governments advocate. There is a high likelihood that delegates find themselves in some conferences or negotiation processes where other delegates, instead of engaging in collaborative approach and constructive problem-solving, choose (or simply, unprepared or unknowingly slide into), methods of unproductive arguing and dispute, insisting on their own positions, political posturing and other totally fruitless approaches. Mostly, this takes place when governments are uninterested in the outcome of the conference and negotiation (or too interested in promoting "their outcome") and unwilling to act on the issues that the conference addresses. In such cases, the instructions and guidance these governments give to their delegates is unlikely to be helpful to the conference resulting in an outcome beneficial to the country and the people the delegate represents, meaning a renunciation of governmental responsibility. Inevitably, such circumstances place delegates in difficult situations, without contradicting that collaborative approaches and cooperative problem-solving produces the best results, nor invalidating the various negotiation strategies, tactics and techniques successfully used for breaking out of impasses in the negotiations.

Even leading diplomatic negotiations and chairing multilateral conferences are highly demanding and the responsibilities are considerable, the role is prestigious and rewarding and the ability to perform in this role is one of the skills expected of a fully effective delegate, therefore opportunities to acquire them should not be missed.

The complexity and dynamics of the multilateral conferences and diplomatic negotiations should be kept in mind by participants in these international events, as these features have a number of inherent risks that need to be mastered by efficient delegates: risk of incoherence due to vast and details rules and procedure or useless instructions, risk of exclusion owed to inappropriate behaviour or lack of preparation and risk of representation of an uninterested and unaccountable government.

The delegates need to remember that the best outcome of a conference often results from lengthy and, sometimes, difficult negotiations. Yet, the best outcome is only achieved if all are committed to the process.

Annex 1 - Details[608] in drafting UN Resolutions

1. References to previous resolutions must be followed by their date, but only the first time the resolution is cited;

2. The names of organs, organizations and offices must be given in full, and this is different from what is seen in other UN documents. In the case of a resolution, the name has to be put in full. If the reference is to UNESCO, it has to be written each time "United Nations Educational, Scientific and Cultural Organization";

3. Some abbreviations of full titles are nonetheless customary. For example, references to the principal organs of the United Nations do not need full detailed titles. A reference to "the Secretariat General" or "the Secretariat" in a resolution of the UN General Assembly is understood to refer to the Secretary-General or the Secretariat of the United Nations. Similarly, if the full title of an organization has been mentioned once either in the preamble or in the operative part of a resolution (e.g. "the United Nations University") any subsequent references in either of those parts of the same resolution can be abbreviated ("the University") because by then the institution has been duly identified. The same applies to reference texts such as the Charter of the United Nations (subsequent references would be simply to "the Charter") and to individuals (e.g. the United Nations High Commissioner for Refugees, having been clearly identified once, would thereafter in the same resolution be referred to as "the High Commissioner"). In a small number of exceptional cases, acronyms are permissible. Thus, for example second and subsequent references to the United Nations Assistance Mission for Rwanda can be to "UNAMIR";

4. The verb or other key word(s) at the beginning of each preambular and operative paragraph is written in italics to give it prominence. Sometimes there is more than one word in italics, for instance "taking note" or "notes with appreciation". If in italics is just "notes" and not "with appreciation", the essence of the wanted satisfaction to express is lost. If the several times consecutively repetition of the same verb is not wanted (e.g. not to have a paragraph beginning with "decides" followed by another paragraph also beginning with "decides" followed by yet another "decides"), "decides" can be written the first time, the second time, "also

---

[608] United Nations Institute for Training and Research (UNITAR), Performing Effectively in Multilateral Conferences and Diplomacy - Interventions, Documents and Resolutions, 2006, pp. 35-37.

decides" and the third time "further decides". But "also" and "further" are not used unless the paragraphs starting with "decides" are consecutive;

5. The words "Member States" (of an organization) and "Parties" (to a treaty) are always capitalized. Likewise, any reference to a specific article in a treaty requires a capital A (e.g. "recalling Article 57 of the Charter of the United Nations"). References to sessions should spelled out (e.g. if the reference is to a report to be submitted to the General Assembly at its sixty-first session, it should not be written "61st", but spell it out in letters). Also, it has to be written "requests the Secretary General to submit a report to the General Assembly at its sixty-first session" and not "to the sixty-first session of the General Assembly" (because "sixty-first session of the GA" relates to time, not to the organ to which the Secretary General has to report);

6. In numbering the paragraphs and subparagraphs, operative paragraphs are identified by Arabic numerals. Within one of those operative paragraphs, beginning with an Arabic numeral, it is possible to have subdivisions. In those cases, the next subdivision will be a small letter "a" surrounded by two parentheses, (a). If there is a subdivision of the subdivision, this is indicated by a small roman number surrounded by two parentheses, e.g. (i). It should be noted that in French and Spanish, small letters and roman numerals are not preceded by a parenthesis, for example, a), b), i), ii);

7. References to paragraphs of resolutions have some delicate aspects. If the reference is to the preamble, since these paragraphs are not numbered, the reference should not be numbered. If the reference is to the preamble's third paragraph, it has to be written "recalling the third paragraph of the preamble to resolution ...". In the case of operative paragraphs, it should be written "recalling paragraph 7 of resolution ...". Because it is said "paragraph 7" it means that it is about the operative paragraph so there is no need and it is wrong to write "recalling operative paragraph 7 of resolution...";

8. One word which is used and which is considered better than another is the word "present". If the Secretary General is asked to report on the implementation of "this resolution" to the General Assembly, it is not said "this"; it is considered more elegant to write "present" as in "to report on the implementation of the present resolution to the General Assembly";

9. The usage of numbers in resolutions is different from that in UN documents. In other documents of the UN, letters are used up to 9 and this is true in English, French and Spanish, from 1 to 9, they are spelled out and then beginning with 10, figures are used. In the case of resolutions, figures are not used at all; all numbers are spelled out. If the resolution calls for the appointment of a committee of 25 members, the

"twenty five" has to be spelled out. However, in addition to references to paragraphs as indicated above, there are three cases in which the use of numbers must be retain: amounts of money, dates and percentages, e.g. "11 per cent".

Annex 2 - Details in drafting WTO Ministerial Declarations

The WTO Ministerial Declarations are organized in three parts, with the Preamble starting with "We, the Ministers...". Each preambular paragraph start with verb in the present tense (e.g. "we note", "we reaffirm", "we acknowledge", "we pledge", "we recognize", etc.). The paragraphs are numbered, with Arabic numbers, and each paragraph ends with a full stop. Part II continues by making reference to the Decisions and Declarations adopted at the present Ministerial Conference. Part III refers to the way forward in the negotiations. Similar to the Preamble, the paragraphs are numbered, with Arabic numbers, and each paragraph ends with a full stop. In terms of words used, in addition to verbs in the present tense (e.g. "we reaffirm", "we commit", "we recognize"), other adjectives are employed ("nevertheless", "while", "mindful of", etc.).

In the Ministerial Declarations references to previous declarations and decisions must be followed by their date and number; the names of WTO agreements, councils, committees, etc. must be given in full with the abbreviations in the brackets; the words "Members" (of WTO) and "Parties" (to GATT) are always capitalized. The usage of symbols and numbers in Ministerial Declarations follows the WTO patters (see chapter 3.1.2).

Bibliography

Aaronson Ariel Susan, 5 Ways the U.S. Can Increase Trust, Responsiveness, and Transparency in Trade Negotiations, Institute for International Economic Policy, 2015 (available at internationaleconpolicy.com).

Akin Iwilade, The Impact of Globalization on Diplomacy, the World Press, 2010 (available at akiniwilade.wordpress.com).

Alfredson Tanya and Cungu Azeta, Negotiation Theory and Practice. A Review of the Literature, FAO Policy Learning Program, EASYPol Module 179, 2008.

Anghel I. M., Răspunderea în dreptul internaţional, Editura Lumina Lex, Bucureşti, 1998.

Aper Alex, The diplomat in a changing world: reassessing contemporary dynamics in diplomatic relations, 2016 (available at: academia.edu).

Barnett Michael and Finnemore Martha, Rules for the World: International Organizations in Global Politics, Cornell University Press Ithaca 2004.

Barston R.P., Modern diplomacy, fourth edition, Routledge, 2014.

Benham Awni, The Group System, in M.A. Boisard and E.M. Chossudovsky, Multilateral Diplomacy: The United Nations System at Geneva, A Working Guide. The Hague: Kluwer Law International, 1998.

Bernstein Steven and Hannah Erin, The WTO and Institutional (In)Coherence and (Un)Accountability in Global Economic Governance, International Studies Association Conference, Montreal, March 16-19, 2011.

Berridge G.R., Diplomacy. London: Prentice-Hall, 1995.

Bigoness William J., Distributive versus integrative approaches to negotiation: experiential learning through a negotiation simulation, Developments in Business Simulation & Experiential Exercises, Volume 11/1984.

Brown Philip Marshall, The Theory of the Independence and Equality of States, The American Journal of International Law Vol. 9, No. 2 (Apr., 1915), pp. 305-

335, Published by: American Society of International Law DOI: 10.2307/2187161 (available at jstor.org).

Blavoukos Spyros and Bourantonis Dimitris, The Chair in the UN Context: Assessing Functions and Performance, Discussion Paper. Netherlands Institute of International Relations Clingendael, 2005.

Blavoukos Spyros, Bourantonis Dimitris and Tsakonas Panayotis, Parameters of the Chairmanship's Effectiveness: The Case of the UN Security Council. The Hague Journal of Diplomacy I, Koninklijke Brill NV, Leiden, 2006.

Buzan B., Negotiating by consensus: developments in technique at the UN Conference on the Law of the Sea, American Journal of International Law, 75(2), 1981.

Carter Peers, From the Interpreters' Booth, in M.A. Boisard and E.M.Chossudovsky, Multilateral Diplomacy: The United Nations System at Geneva, A Working Guide. The Hague: Kluwer Law International, 1998.

Cede Franz, Changes in the Diplomatic Function and Their Impact on International Negotiations, PIN Points Network Newsletter 26/2006.

Cerchez Octavia, Politica comerciala comuna a Uniunii Europene, Editura Logos, Bucuresti, 2009.

Chasek Pamela, Wagner Lynn and Zartman William I., Six ways to make climate negotiations more effective, Policy Brief, Fixing Climate Governance Series No. 3/June 2015. (available at cigionline.org).

Chrisspeels Erik, Procedures of Multilateral Conference Diplomacy, in M.A. Boisard and E.M. Chossudovsky, Multilateral Diplomacy: The United Nations System at Geneva, A Working Guide. The Hague: Kluwer Law International, 1998.

Cockburn Andrew Mark, The Unique Challenges Presented by Multilateral Diplomacy, May 10, 2012. (available at SSRN: ssrn.com or dx.doi.org).

Constantinou C., The Transformation of Foreign Policy and Diplomacy, European Consortium for Political Research - Antwerp 2012, Workshop Summary, 2011.

Cooper Andrew F., Heine Jorge, and Thakur Ramesh, Introduction: The Challenges of 21st-Century Diplomacy, The Oxford Handbook of Modern Diplomacy, 2013.

Cottier Thomas and Satoko Takenoshita, The Balance of Power in WTO Decision-Making: Towards Weighted Voting in Legislative Response, Aussenwirtschaft, 2003.

DAWN, How WTO bureaucracy subverts the process, December 2004 (available at dawn.com).

Diaconu Ion, Tratat de drept internațional public, volumul II, Bucuresti, 2003.

Didzis Klavins, Understanding the Essence of Modern Diplomacy, The ICD Annual Academic Conference on Cultural Diplomacy 2011: Cultural Diplomacy and International Relations; New Actors; New Initiatives; New Targets, Berlin, December 15th-18th, 2011.

Doto David M., Facilitating Distributive and Integrative Negotiation in Mediation, The Opening Statement, 2011 (available at theopeningstatement.wordpress.com).

Draz-Wolstencraft Susan and Garnier Alain, Further Working Suggestions by Interpreters, in M.A. Boisard and E.M. Chossudovsky, Multilateral Diplomacy: The United Nations System at Geneva, A Working Guide. The Hague: Kluwer Law International, 1998.

Ehlermann Claus-Dieter, Decision Making in the World Trade Organization: Is the Consensus Practice of the World Trade Organization Adequate for Making, Revising and Implementing Rules on International Trade?, WilmerHale, 2005.

Eckman C., Documentation and publication of the GATT and WTO-GATT Digital Library, StanfordEdu, 1981.

Fisher Roger and Ury William, Getting to Yes – Negotiating agreement without giving in, Harmondsworth, The Penguin books, 1981.

Fisher Roger, Beyond Machiavelli, Tools of Coping with Conflict, Cambridge/Mass, Harvard UP, 1994.

Gazarian Jean, UN documentation and document symbols, UNITAR, 2006.

Gurry Francis, Challenges for International Organizations and Multilateralism, Lakshman Kadirgamar Memorial Oration 2013, November 13, 2013 (available at wipo.int).

Goldstein Erik, Developments in protocol, Modern Diplomacy. Edited by J. Kurbalija, 1998. (available at diplomacy.edu).

Heath Elizabeth, Encyclopedia of Africa, Edited by Henry Louis Gates, Jr. and Kwame Anthony Appiah, Oxford University Press, 2010.

Hocking Brian, Melissen Jan, Riordan Shaun, Sharp Paul, Futures for diplomacy - Integrative Diplomacy in the 21st Century, Netherlands Institute of International Relations Clingendael, 2012.

Hywel D. Davies, From the Translators' Workshop, in M.A. Boisard and E.M. Chossudovsky, Multilateral Diplomacy: The United Nations System at Geneva, A Working Guide. The Hague: Kluwer Law International, 1998.

Iklé Fred Charles, How Nations Negotiate. London: Harper and Row, 1987, p.2.

Jacobson H.K., Networks of interdependence. International organizations and the global political system. New York, Alfred A. Knopf, 1979.

James Katie, Marmo Elena, Zona Michael and Bolton Matthew, Model United Nations Program, Diplomatic Language, Conduct and Decorum, Pace University New York City, 2013 (available at pacenycmun.org).

Johnson Rebecca, Arms Control and Disarmament Diplomacy, The Oxford Handbook of Modern Diplomacy, Edited by Andrew F. Cooper, Jorge Heine, and Ramesh Thakur, 2013, p. 604.

Jorgensen Knud Erik, The European Union in Multilateral Diplomacy, The Hague Journal of Diplomacy, August 2009, (available at researchgate.net).

Kahler Miles, Rising Powers and Global Governance: Negotiating Change in a Resilient Status Quo, International Affairs 89, no. 3/2013.

Kahler M., Multilateralism with small and large numbers, International Organization, 46(3), 1992.

Kaufmann Johan, Conference Diplomacy: An Introductory Analysis, 2nd revised edition, Martinus Nijhoff Publishers, UNITAR, 1988.

Kaufmann, Johan. Conference Diplomacy: An Introductory Analysis. Third Revised Version. London: Macmillian Press, 1996.

Kaufmann Johan, Some Practical Aspects of United Nations Decision-Making, in M.A. Boisard and E.M. Chossudovsky, Multilateral Diplomacy: The United Nations System at Geneva, A Working Guide. The Hague: Kluwer Law International, 1998.

Kennedy Gavin, The Perfect Negotiation, Random House Business Book UK, 1999.

Keohane, Robert O., Nye Joseph S., and Hoffmann Stanley, The End of the Cold War in Europe. Introduction. After the Cold War / International Institutions and State Strategies in Europe, 1989-1991. Cambridge, MA: Harvard UP, 1993.

Koh Tommy Thong-Bee, UNCED Leadership: A Personal Perspective, in Bertram I. Spector, Gunnar Sjéstedt and I. William Zartman, eds. Negotiating International Regimes: Lessons Learned from the United Nations Conference on Environment and Development (UNCED). Laxenburg: International Institute for Applied Systems Analysis, 1994.

Kühn Nadja Sophia B., Autonomy of International Bureaucracies: On the Actor-Level Autonomy in the WTO Secretariat, Universitetet i Agder, høst 2014.

Kumi N. B, Ghana's challenges in a new diplomatic environment. GREAT Insights, Volume 3, Issue 3. March 2014. (available at ecdpm.org).

Kupchan Charles, No One's World: The West, the Rising Rest, and the Coming Global Turn, New York: Oxford University Press, 2012.

Lawrence Robert Z., Toward a More Effective WTO: The Role of Variable Geometry, East Asian Bureau of Economic Research, June 1, 2008 (available at piie.com).

Lax David and Sebenius James K., The Manager as Negotiator: Bargaining for Cooperation and Competitive Gain, New York: The Free Press, 1986.

LeBaron Michelle, Culture-Based Negotiation Styles, Beyond Intractability. Eds. Guy Burgess and Heidi Burgess. Conflict Information Consortium, University of Colorado, Boulder, 2003 (available at beyondintractability.org).

Lee Donna Lee and& Hocking Brian Hocking, Diplomacy, published in Bertrand Bardie, Dirk-Berg Schlosser & Leonardo Morlino (eds.), International Encyclopaedia of Political Science, Sage, 2011.

Lemoine Jacques, The United Nations System: A Geneva Perspective, in M.A. Boisard and E.M. Chossudovsky, Multilateral Diplomacy: The United Nations System at Geneva, A Working Guide. The Hague: Kluwer Law International, 1998.

Lewicki R.J., Saunders D.M. and Barry B., Negotiation: Readings, Exercises, and Cases, New York, NY: McGraw-Hill, 2006.

Lodge J.E., and Pfetsch F.R., Negotiating the European Union: Introduction, in International Negotiation. 3.3, 1998.

Lloyd Peter, The Variable Geometry Approach to International Economic Integration, International Journal of Business and Development Studies, Volume 1, Issue 1, Autumn 2009.

Lydon Anthony F., The Making of a United Nations Meeting, in M.A. Boisard and E.M. Chossudovsky, Multilateral Diplomacy: The United Nations System at Geneva, A Working Guide. The Hague: Kluwer Law International, 1998.

Mahbubani Kishore, Multilateral Diplomacy, The Oxford Handbook of Modern Diplomacy, Edited by Andrew F. Cooper, Jorge Heine, and Ramesh Thakur, 2013.

Malhotra Deepak, Negotiating the Impossible: How to Break Deadlocks and Resolve Ugly Conflicts, Berrett-Koehler Publishers Inc., 2016.

Mar Anna, 15 Diplomacy Strategies For Negotiations, Simplicable Business Guide, 2013.

Marshall Brown Philip, The Theory of the Independence and Equality of States, The American Journal of International Law Vol. 9, No. 2/April 1915, pp. 305-335, Published by: American Society of International Law DOI: 10.2307/2187161, p. 305. (available at jstor.org).

McNeilly Mark R., Sun Tzu and the Art of Modern Warfare, Oxford University Press, 2001.

McKinsey Business Concept 101, 2013 (available at businessconcepts101.blogspot.ch).

Meerts Paul, Diplomatic Negotiation, Essence and Evolution. The Hague: Clingendael Institute, 2015.

Meerts Paul, Challenges to Diplomatic Negotiation, PIN Policy Brief, The Hague: Clingendael Institute, 2015.

Melissen Jan, Summit Diplomacy Coming of Age, Discussion Papers in Diplomacy, Netherlands Institute of International Relations Clingendael, Editor: Spencer Mawby, University of Nottingham, 1999.

Merlini Cesare, The Impact of Changing Societies on the Future of International Relations, US - Europe Working Paper, January 2016.

Mingst Karen A. and Karns Margaret P., The United Nations in the Twenty-first Century, 3rd ed., Boulder: Westview, 2006.

Năstase Dan, Drept diplomatic şi consular, Editura Fundaţiei România de Mâine, Bucuresti, 2006.

Newman E., Thakur R., Tirman J., Multilateralism Under Challenge? The performance and effectiveness of multilateralism are under scrutiny according to 21st-century standards of legitimacy and democracy. United Nations University Research Brief Number 1/2006.

NMUN-Europe conference, Security Council, Background Guide, National Collegiate Conference Association, 2012 (available at nmun.org).

Nyerges Janos, How to negotiate, in M.A. Boisard and E.M. Chossudovsky, Multilateral Diplomacy: The United Nations System at Geneva, A Working Guide. The Hague: Kluwer Law International, 1998.

Odell John, Chairing a WTO Negotiation, Journal of International Economic Law 8(2), 2005.

Odell John, Mediating Multilateral Trade Negotiation, Paper prepared for presentation at the annual meeting of the International Studies Association, Montreal, March 2004.

Paris Roland, Global Governance and Power Politics: Back to Basics Roland Paris, Ethics and international Affairs Carnegie Council, December 11, 2015 (available at ethicsandinternationalaffairs.org).

Patel Oliver and Reh Christine, Brexit: The Consequences for the EU's Political System, UCL Constitution Unit Briefing Paper, 2016, p.4. (available at ucl.ac.uk).

Petrovsky Vladimir, Diplomacy as an instrument of good governance, Modern Diplomacy. Edited by J. Kurbalija, 1998. (available at diplomacy.edu).

Petrovsky Vladimir, The United Nations Office at Geneva, in M.A. Boisard and E.M. Chossudovsky, Multilateral Diplomacy: The United Nations System at Geneva, A Working Guide. The Hague: Kluwer Law International, 1998.

Pfetsch Frank R., Chairing Negotiations in the World Trade Organization, Négociations 1/2009 (n° 11, available at cairn.info).

Puntigliano A. R., Going Global: An Organizational Study of Brazilian Foreign Policy, Review International Brazilian Politics, Vol. 51, No. 1, 2008.

Putnam Robert, Diplomacy and domestic Politics: The logic of two-level games, International Organization, Vol. 42, No. 3 (Summer, 1988), pp. 427-460, The MIT Press, 1988.

Raiffa H., The Art and Science of Negotiation. Cambridge, MA and London: Belknap Press of Harvard University Press, 1982.

Reinalda Bob, Routledge History of International Organizations From 1815 to the present day, by Routledge 2 Park Square, Milton Park, Abingdon, Oxon OX14 4RN, 2009.

Rittberger Volker, International Conference Diplomacy: A Conspectus, in M.A. Boisard and E.M. Chossudovsky, Multilateral Diplomacy: The United Nations System at Geneva, A Working Guide. The Hague: Kluwer Law International, 1998.

Sabel Robbie, Procedure at International Conferences: A Study of the Rules of Procedure of International, Inter-governmental Conferences. Cambridge: Cambridge University Press, 1997.

Slantchev Branislav L., Introduction to International Relations - Bargaining and Dynamic Commitment, University of California - San Diego, 2005.

Slaughter Anne-Marie, International Relations, Principal Theories, Wolfrum R. (Ed.) Max Planck Encyclopedia of Public International Law, Oxford University Press, 2011 (available at princeton.edu).

Smith Jackie, Social Movements and Multilateralism, in Edward Newman, Ramesh Thakur, and John Tirman (eds), Multilateralism under Challenge: Power, International Order, and Structural Change, Tokyo: UN University Press, 2006.

Sojsdedt Gunnar, Negotiating the Uruguay Round of the general Agreement on Tariffs and Trade, in Zartman William ed., International Multilateral Negotiation. Approaches to the Management of Complexity, San Francisco, Jossey Bass, 1994.

Spangler Brad, Reframing, in Beyond Intractability. Ed. Guy Burgess and Heidi Burgess. Conflict Research Consortium, University of Colorado, Boulder, Colorado, USA, 2003.

Talbott S., Globalization and Diplomacy: A practitioner's Perspective, Foreign Policy, No. 108, 1997.

Tupy Marian L., The European Union: A Critical Assessment, CATO Institute, Economic Development Bulletin no. 26/2016 (available at cato.org).

United Nations Institute for Training and Research (UNITAR), A Glossary of Terms for UN Delegates, 2005.

United Nations Institute for Training and Research (UNITAR), Performing Effectively in Multilateral Conferences and Diplomacy, 2006.

United Nations Non-Governmental Liaison Service (NGLS) with Gretchen Sidhu, Intergovernmental Negotiations and Decision Making at the United Nations: A Guide, 2nd Updated Edition, United Nations, 2007.

Venzke Ingo, International Bureaucracies from a Political Science Perspective - Agency, Authority and International Institutional Law, German Law Journal, Vol. 9, 2008.

Vukovic S., Analysis of Multiparty Mediation Processes. Doctoral dissertation, University of Leiden, 2013.

Walker Ronald A., Multilateral Conferences: Purposeful International Negotiation. London: Palgrave Macmillan, 2004.

Walker R.A., Manual for UN Delegates - Conference Process, Procedure and Negotiation, UN Publication, 2011.

Watson Adam, Diplomacy: The Dialogue between States, London: Methuen, 1982.

Weiss T.G., The Illusion of UN Security Council Reform, The Washington Quarterly, Volume 26, Number 4, Autumn 2003.

Winham Gilbert, The Mediation of Multilateral Negotiations. Journal of World Trade Law 13, no. f:, 1979.

Winslow Anne, Benchmarks for Newcomers, in M.A. Boisard and E.M. Chossudovsky, Multilateral Diplomacy: The United Nations System at Geneva, A Working Guide. The Hague: Kluwer Law International, 1998.

Wright T., Bilateral and Multilateral Diplomacy in Normal Times and in Crises, in P Kerr & G Wiseman (eds.), Diplomacy in a Globalizing World: Theories & Practices, Oxford University Press, New York, 2013.

Yan Ki Bonnie Cheng, Power and trust in negotiation and decision-making: a critical evaluation, Harvard Negotiation Law Review, 2009 (available at hnlr.org).

Zartman William I. and Berman Maureen R., The Practical Negotiator. New Haven: Yale University Press, 1982.

Printed in Great Britain
by Amazon